*Ending the Terror* makes accessible for the first time to an English-speaking readership a major revisionist assessment of a crucial moment in the history of the French Revolution. The months that followed the fall of Robespierre in July 1794 mark not only a turning point in the history of the Revolution: 'Thermidor' is also a symbolic moment which came to haunt the subsequent revolutions of the nineteenth and twentieth centuries. By this date the Terror as a system of power was discredited, and the engineers of the Terror were confronting the problem of how to dismantle it without repudiating the aims of the Revolution itself and its work. Professor Baczko analyses the Terror in detail through the political history of the French National Assembly, and looks at the broader issues of the political culture of Revolutionary France. He also uses the problem of the ending of the Terror to highlight contemporary problems in the break-up of the communist system.

Ending the Terror

# Ending the Terror

## The French Revolution after Robespierre

Bronislaw Baczko

*Translated by Michel Petheram*

**CAMBRIDGE**
UNIVERSITY PRESS

Editions de la Maison des Sciences de l'Homme

Published by the Press Syndicate of the University of Cambridge
The Pitt Building, Trumpington Street, Cambridge CB2 1RP
40 West 20th Street, New York, NY 10011-4211, USA
10 Stamford Road, Oakleigh, Melbourne 3166, Australia
and Editions de la Maison des Sciences de l'Homme
54 Boulevard Raspail, 75270 Paris Cedex 06

Originally published in French as *Comment sortir de la terreur*
by Bronislaw Baczko 1989
and © Editions Gallimard
First published in English by Editions de la Maison des Sciences de l'Homme
and Cambridge University Press 1994 as *Ending the Terror: the French
Revolution after Robespierre*
English translation © Maison des Sciences de l'Homme and Cambridge
University Press 1994

Printed in Great Britain at the University Press, Cambridge

*A catalogue record for this book is available from the British Library*

*Library of Congress cataloguing-in-publication data*

Baczko, Bronislaw.
[Comment sortir de la Terreur. English]
Ending the Terror: the French Revolution after Robespierre/
Bronislaw Baczko: translated by Michel Petheram.
    p.   cm.
Includes index.
ISBN 0 521 44105 6 (hardback)
1. France – History – Revolution, 1789–1799 – Atrocities.
2. Robespierre, Maximilien, 1758–1794 – Death and burial.
3. Vandalism – France – History – 18th century. I. Title.
DC183.5.B2513   1994
944.04 – dc20   93-30389 CIP

ISBN 0 521 441056 hardback
ISBN 2 7351 0593 8 hardback (France only)

SE

A la mémoire de
Rela
ma femme, mon amie, mon amour

# Contents

# Preface

This essay was born of surprise and amazement. I was reading, a little by accident, the diary kept during the Revolution by a certain Célestin Guittard de Floriban, a Parisian bourgeois, when I came across the page where the author mentions that during the night of 9 to 10 Thermidor a rumour ran through Paris, according to which Robespierre wished to proclaim himself king and even harboured intentions towards Louis XVI's daughter, who was imprisoned in the Temple. Having examined the evidence, I concluded that this absurd rumour had nevertheless found quite a large audience and influenced the course of events. How was that possible? What was the political and psychological context of this rumour and its at first glance paradoxical success? From this I became interested in the events of 9 Thermidor and, more widely, in the whole troubled and troubling Thermidorean period.

On 10 Thermidor no one yet knew – nor considered – where the fall of 'the last tyrant' might lead the Revolution. The importance of the Thermidorean period lies not in an initial political or ideological programme, but in the problems with which the political protagonists were confronted and which they had to resolve. While their responses were often hesitant and contradictory, worked out as they went along, the problems themselves still present today, in their connections, a quite remarkable coherence. What was to be done with the overpopulated jails? Who was to be freed from them and when? What form should justice take, now that it was 'the order of the day'? What freedom should be given to the press? How were the political, cultural and psychological consequences of the Terror to be remedied? How to permanently dismantle the Terror? Who bore responsibility for it and did this call for punishment?

These partial questions complement each other and all raise a single problem: *how to bring the Terror to an end?* By what choices and by what routes? What political arena should be created for after the Terror? How to prevent for ever any return of the Terror? And, similarly, how to end the Revolution and ensure a new start for the Republic? My investigation, therefore, bears upon the *Thermidorean political experience* which provides this period of fifteeen months with its unity and originality, and integrates it into the overall experience of the Revolution.

I quickly perceived that this investigation is indissolubly linked with another. How could revolutionary symbolism and imagery, victorious in Year II, disintegrate in such a short time, in the space of only a few months? What is the anti-terrorist and anti-Jacobin imagery, produced and repressed during the Terror, which, from the moment that fear starts to retreat, rises brutally to the surface, leaving the mark of its obsessions on collective memory for a long time? For the retreat of fear and the advance of freedom of expression led the political protagonists to formulate painful questions. 'How did *that* happen to *us*?' How could the Revolution, starting from the principles of '89, arrive at the terrorist practices of Year II? Could its principles be reconciled with its history? In other words, what light does the Thermidorean strategy throw on the winding paths already traversed, on the experiences and the workings of the Revolution, on its political institutions and their psychological environment?

The French Revolution quickly became a model, a kind of paradigm, for the revolutions which followed. Accordingly one sees revolutionaries identify themselves in turn with the Girondins, with the Jacobins, with the *sans-culottes* . . . They would dream of their 14 July and their 10 August. Yet they never identified themselves with the *Thermidoreans* and the idea of having *their own Thermidor* haunted them like a nightmare.

That is undoubtedly a lot of questions for one book, and certainly too many. They are connected, however, by the force of circumstances and this book is only an essay: it invites the reader to reflect and does not put forward definitive replies.

The plan of this book was first sketched out in the course of several lectures within the framework of the seminar of my friends François Furet and Mona Ozouf, at the Ecole des Hautes Etudes en Sciences Sociales. Our constant dialogue, which was particularly intense in the course of the discussions on 'The French Revolution and modern political culture', did much to enrich and stimulate me. For all that they brought me, let them be, once more, very cordially thanked.

I cannot tell how much this research owes to Jean-Claude Favez, infallible friend, privileged reader and partner in discussion, to his intellectual rigour, as well as his critical sense of history.

This book is dedicated to my wife; while she was alive, her presence and help supported me every day and allowed me to overcome the great difficulties that accumulated in the course of composing this work; after her death, her memory encouraged me to complete the writing of this text, despite everything.

# 1    Robespierre-the-king . . .

Today, Monday afternoon, Robespierre and twenty-one fellow-conspira-
tors are brought before the revolutionary Tribunal to have their condemnation confirmed since, being outside the law, their trial is over. It is
decreed that they shall be put to death in the Place Louis XV, now the
Place de la Révolution. They were taken there and passed along the Rue
Saint-Honoré and everywhere they were insulted by the people, angry at
seeing how they had been deceived. And they had their heads cut off at
seven o'clock in the evening. Within twenty-four hours it was all over; they
hardly expected to die so soon, these men who wanted to massacre 60,000
people in Paris. Behold how God allows the wicked, at the moment of
carrying out their plans, to perish.
  Robespierre was the moving spirit of the conspiracy with another
villain, Couthon, who backed him. It is said that he wanted to have himself
acknowledged as king in Lyon and in other *départements* and marry
Capet's daughter . . . How could a private individual get such an idea in his
head? Ambitious scoundrel, that is where your pride has led you. With him
dying as head of the conspiracy, everything falls with him.

Célestin Guittard de Floriban, who summed up the events of 9 and 10
Thermidor in these words, is an invaluable witness.[1] He set down in his
diary the small details of his life as a *rentier* – closer and closer to ruin – in
revolutionary Paris. Tireless, he hurried through the streets in search of the
latest news, reading posters and papers, joining discussions in the 'groups'
in the Place du Carrousel. He was all the more greedy for rumours because
he believed them, and with such credulity that one sometimes wonders if it
was real or feigned. He rejoiced at the arrest of Hébert who 'produces the
Père Duchesne paper': 'What good luck this plot has been detected; we
must hope that all its leaders will be discovered.' Three weeks later, on 16
Germinal, Year II, the revelation of another conspiracy delighted him.
'There was an infinite number of people in the square' when 'fifteen well-
known conspirators' had their heads cut off and it was Danton 'who was

---

[1] *Journal de Célestin Guittard de Floriban, bourgeois de Paris, sous la révolution*, edited with a
commentary by R. Aubert, Paris, 1974, pp. 437–8. Please see the appendix for a
chronology. It is not intended to provide an exhaustive chronology of the Revolution, but
to list the main events mentioned in the text.

1

head of the conspiracy'. Another frustrated plot: Chaumette, 'a young man of thirty-one, with a good education and intelligent ... put himself at the head of a conspiracy to slaughter the National Assembly. He received, along with his accomplices, all that they deserved: death, to which they submitted today. Into what disorder would they have put our country?' On 4 Prairial Guittard went with his *section*[2] to the Convention to 'congratulate Collot d'Herbois, deputy, and Robespierre' for having escaped 'the assassin Amiral' and Cécile Renault, 'also possessed by the devil'; very fortunately 'both have been arrested'.[3] He was not very surprised, two months later, to see this same Robespierre executed and to learn that he wanted to proclaim himself king.

Guittard, credulous though he was, was not the only one to believe this astounding news. Georges Duval, a young clerk working for a notary in Thermidor, Year II who was to become, some months later, one of the leaders of the '*jeunesse dorée*', maintains in his memoirs that after the punishment of Robespierre

there was a rumour, and all who lived then can remember it, that he really had dared to aspire to the hand of the little orphan in the Temple; and some confidential communications lead one to think that this rumour was not completely without foundation. Now, if it is the case that he had conceived such an insolent plan, he no doubt hoped that Mme Elisabeth, being indebted to him for her life, would use her favourable influence with her royal niece. Robespierre, the assassin of Louis XVI, husband of the daughter of Louis XVI! and, no doubt, his successor on the throne.[4]

Georges Duval was a shameless scandalmonger; he presented as true all the rumours which stirred up revolutionary Paris. His evidence is therefore admissible since he is reporting tales and rumours. In a case like this, he is a completely trustworthy liar.

### The history of a tale

The rumour according to which Robespierre wished to succeed to Louis XVI has not escaped historians of the Revolution, especially those who have studied 9 Thermidor. Most have dismissed it swiftly and scornfully: it is too implausible and, moreover, a complete fabrication. However, it seems a rumour that deserves to be taken seriously. Not in order to examine

---

[2] *sections.* The forty-eight divisions of Paris. All citizens with voting rights formed the assembly of each *section.*

[3] *Journal de Célestin Guittard de Floriban*, pp. 326, 334, 337–8.

[4] G. Duval, *Souvenirs Thermidoriens*, Paris, 1844, vol. 1, p. 146. Duval maintains that 'Robespierre lost his temper with the English only in order to impress the people and to cover under a thicker veil the secret relations he was carrying on with them, so that one day, with their assistance, he could seat himself upon the throne of Louis XVI, which he had done so much to make vacant on 21 January, 1793': *ibid.,* pp. 201–2.

its validity; on the contrary, it is because it is so obviously false that it holds our attention. It is a commonplace, too often forgotten, that a false rumour is a real social fact; in that it conceals a portion of historical truth – not about the news that it spreads, but about the conditions that make its emergence and circulation possible, about the state of mind, the *mentalités* and imagination of those who accepted it as true. Also, the more a public rumour is false, implausible and fantastic, the more its history promises to be rich in lessons. Now, the tale of Robespierre-the-king in actual fact circulated in the confused Paris of 9 and 10 Thermidor; it was taken to be the revelation of a truth hidden until that moment, at least by certain actors in these events. Therefore, it is not solely evidence of its own existence. If, on 9 Thermidor, the tale managed to insinuate itself into the social imagination, then the right thing to do is to ask oneself about this imagination and about the event with which the rumour was so closely linked that it influenced the outcome, false though it was.

As for the history of this tale, we can reconstruct it only very incompletely. There are two reasons for this: the tale has left only fleeting traces and the evidence referring to it is often confused. The rumour was spread by print and by word of mouth. This distinction is, it must be added, quite relative. The newspapers, placards and pamphlets which reported the news were distributed by street-hawkers who wore out their lungs to capture the attention of the public. In the streets and the squares, groups would form and the text would often be read out loud, discussed on the spot. The mass of written texts bequeathed by the revolutionary period should not hide the fact that the culture of the epoch remained largely oral and that political information in particular circulated among the popular masses mostly by oral means. This was especially the case during the 'revolutionary *journées*' in Paris when tens of thousands of people came into direct contact with each other in the street. The oral progress of a rumour therefore leaves few traces and these, when they exist, are often unreliable. Accordingly, for the night of 9 and 10 Thermidor, when our tale arose, there is abundant documentation: the reports of the debates of the Convention; the hearings of the revolutionary committees and the assemblies of the *sections*; the reports that these committees, as well as the commanders of the armed forces of the *sections*, sent, hour by hour, to the Committees of Public Safety and General Security; the hearings of the Commune, the countless testimonies, etc. But this mass of documentation is just as much, not to say above all, evidence for the confusion that reigned among the actors that night. This superabundance fails to fill certain gaps and even adds contradictions to the confusion that marks accounts of the events. Furthermore, the tale of Robespierre-the-king is, like all public rumours, protean. It has several variations, from the most rudimentary to the highly elaborate, with many ramifications. Its history can be begun only by drawing up an inventory, as an anthropologist would, which will still remain very incomplete.

On 9 Thermidor in the morning, at the time of the session of the Convention which was to culminate in the arrest of Robespierre, Couthon, Saint-Just and the others, our rumour was not in circulation. The *tyrant*: this is the word, both indictment and insult, that Billaud-Varenne hurled at Robespierre. The members of the Convention would take it up, crying *Down with the tyrant!*, exorcising their fear with uproar and preventing Robespierre, by their repeated shouts, from speaking. Tallien was to add other insults: *the new Cromwell, the new Catiline.* Among the accusations against Robespierre, as many as they were varied, no one claimed that he wanted to re-establish the monarchy, let alone that he aspired to be king. During this debate, an allusion to the 'throne' appeared but once, in a rhetorical flight by Fréron against Couthon: 'Couthon is a tiger corrupted by the blood of national representation. He has dared, for a royal pastime, to speak at the Jacobin Club of five or six leaders of the Convention. That was only the beginning, and he wanted to make our corpses so many steps to climb to the throne.' A cruel and ridiculous remark; Couthon was content to reply, as he displayed his paralysed feet, 'I wanted to reach the throne, yes ...' During the stormy debate no one went to the trouble of being precise as to what form of government the 'new tyrant' wanted to adopt. Elie Lacoste spoke vaguely of a triumvirate composed of Robespierre, Saint-Just and Couthon. Barère mentioned the threat of a military dictatorship, and denounced the collusion of the 'conspirators' with aristocrats and foreigners. He referred to an anonymous 'enemy officer', captured in Belgium, who had confessed: 'All your successes are worthless; we still expect to negotiate for peace with one party, whichever it is, with a fraction of the Convention and soon change the government.' He raged against 'the aristocracy, joyful at present events ... this aristocracy, which all our efforts seem unable to extinguish, and which hides in the mud when it is not in blood, the aristocracy [that] has seethed since yesterday with an activity that looks like nothing else but a counter-revolutionary movement'. The *Proclamation de la Convention nationale au peuple français*, voted through at the end of this session but drawn up in advance, a few hours earlier, by Barère, paraded all the dangers run by the Revolution.

The revolutionary government, object of the hate of the enemies of France, is attacked in our midst; the forms of republican power come close to ruin; the aristocracy appears to triumph, and the royalists are ready to reappear. Citizens, do you wish to lose in one day six years of revolution, of sacrifices and of courage? Do you wish to return to the yoke which you have broken? ... If you do not rally to the National Convention ... our victories will become a curse; and the French people will be exposed to all the furies of internal division and all the vengeance of tyrants.

Hear the voice of the *patrie*, instead of joining your cries to those of the men of ill-will, the aristocrats and the enemies of the people, and our *patrie* will be once more saved.

The transformation of 'conspirators' into royalists was sketched out, then, through hints and allusions to their common objective, namely the destruction of the Republic; but of Robespierre-the-king there was as yet no mention. This step would be taken on the evening of 9 Thermidor, in the panic that gripped the Convention. Having recommenced its session about seven o'clock in the evening, it received, hour by hour, more and more alarming news: the rebellion of the Commune which called on the *sections* to 'rise'; the movements of the armed force of the *sections*, about whose attitudes contradictory information came in; the arrival of the gunners in front of the Convention, in the Place de la Réunion (formerly Place du Carrousel), who had freed Hanriot (confined in the afternoon at the Committee of General Security, he now rode through the streets on his horse, haranguing the gunners and the companies of the *sections*); the freeing of Robespierre and of other deputies put under arrest. Yet it is not in the debates of the Convention that the first traces of the rumour are to be found. Neither the decrees outlawing Robespierre, the other arrested deputies and the rebel Commune, nor the stormy and disorganised discussion which followed their adoption make any mention of Robespierre's 'royalist designs'. The rumour spread in the street, particularly in the Place de Grève, and in the *sections*. The committees of the *sections* were at that time in permanent contact with the Committees of Public Safety and General Security; moreover, they exchanged information among themselves. The rumour was certainly being spread abroad at the time that the *huissiers*, surrounded by torches, were proclaiming in the streets the decrees outlawing Robespierre and the others. It was also spread by at least some of the twelve members of the Convention who were helping Barras, appointed general in command of the National Guard. Wearing tricolour sashes, sabres at their sides, plumed hats, they launched into the assault of the town, in order to mobilise the battalions of the National Guard, the gunners, the Committees and the assemblies of the *sections* – in a word, the whole population – around the Convention and against the conspirators. Information on all this feverish activity is incomplete. Léonard Bourdon, one of the twelve members of the Convention helping Barras, violently denounced Robespierre at the Gravilliers *section*, which was to play an important role in the course of events; but there is no information on the arguments that he used to support his accusation. Other representatives, to convince the hesitant *sections* of the faubourg Saint-Antoine, spoke of the fleur-de-lis seal found in Robespierre's house (we shall have to return to this seal); Barère, who described this episode in his report of 10 Thermidor, did not however give the names of the members of the Convention. We can guess, with more or less certainty, that during the night of 9 and 10 Thermidor the rumour spread through at least fifteen or so *sections* (or their battalions) – including those of the faubourgs Saint-Antoine and Saint-Marcel, as well as certain *sections* of the town centre.

But there is nothing to justify confining the circulation of this rumour only to those *sections* about which we have information. Once set going, the rumour flew from one *section* to another, found many new hawkers, was vigorously discussed wherever people, in the unrest and uncertainty, were greedy for news of the events unfolding in confusion. It was in this way that the meeting of the Indivisibility *section*, which hesitated for a moment between the Commune and the Convention, received a warning from the Lombards *section* to the effect that its revolutionary committee had arrested 'five villains', evidently accomplices of the Commune, who 'desiring to profit from circumstances that they considered favourable to their designs, proclaimed the son of Capet'. This news, which revealed the real purposes of the 'most appalling conspiracy', is not to be found in the archives of any other *sections*. However, the Lombards *section*, devoted from the outset to the Convention's cause, had 'fraternised' with a score of other *sections*, by sending them their delegates. One can therefore reasonably suppose that these messengers did not fail to report this overwhelming news everywhere they went. Like the Lombards *section*, most of the *sections* faithful to the Convention communicated between themselves and sought to convince the *sections* who were hesitating, thus forming a compact network for the circulation of news, rumours and hearsay.

What was the story? The stupefying news came in several versions, as if it were distorted as it spread (but it is not certain that all the first rumour-mongers related it in the same way). The constant element was, more or less, this: Robespierre was a royalist; he had at last been unmasked; this explained both the aims of his conspiracy and the measures for public safety taken by the Convention. To this outline were added improvisations, embellishments, corroborations. It is possible to arrange the versions of the rumour in order from the simplest to the most elaborate: a fleur-de-lis seal was found in Robespierre's house (and/or at the Commune, with the police administrators); two individuals had tried to liberate 'young Capet' from the Temple; five 'villains' were already planning to proclaim him king; Robespierre wished to marry Capet's daughter and the marriage contract had already been signed.

The same night there ran a rumour of collusion between the Committees of the Convention and the 'royalists', even the 'foreign party'. Robespierre the younger, just released from La Force prison, delivered a speech at the Maison Commune, violently accusing the faction who 'wished to enslave the people, slaughter the patriots, open the Temple and remove young Capet'. The executive Committee of the Commune decided, late in the night, to order the arrest of some fifteen deputies who 'were oppressing' the Convention. And it promised a civic crown to 'the generous citizens who arrest these enemies of the people ... who have more audacity than Louis XVI himself, since they have put under arrest the best citizens'. It is to be noted that to present the Convention as 'oppressed' by 'a handful of villains', 'enemies of the people', was to make short work of the very delicate problem of the legitimacy of the insurrection. The Commune and the 'best patriots' would represent, on this account, 'the risen people' which recovered its sovereignty but did not rise up against the Convention, the nation's representatives. The Commune was acting only to 'deliver the Convention from the oppression' under which the 'conspirators are keeping it'. Another effort of the Commune, the most desperate, perhaps, for which the rough draft of a proclamation of its executive Committee is evidence, is quoted by Courtois: 'The people is warned that a patrol sent by the foreign party which dominates the Committee of Public Safety presented itself at the Temple, in order to free the vile offspring of Capet; the patrol was arrested and the Council has had the Capets immolated.' Is this a distorted echo of the rumours which were exciting the street, as the Committees had in fact sent an armed force to protect the Temple? Or a sign of the panic breaking out in the last hours of the Commune, when, after midnight, the Place de Grève became increasingly empty, and the last companies of artillery began to leave? Whatever was the case with these proclamations and their actual circulation, they could only contribute to the general confusion. The rumours joined and became all merged together in a single rumour according to which the royalists were stirring and wished to liberate the 'vile offspring'.

The rumour was at full force on 10 Thermidor, in the early morning, when, after the capture of the Maison Commune, Robespierre and the other deputies 'declared traitors to the *patrie*' were transferred to the chamber of the Committee of Public Safety, adjoining the one where the Convention was in permanent session. It could be said that we are present at the return of the wave: the rumour, now swollen, comes back to its point of departure. The Convention at last possessed material proof of the royal plot hatched at the Maison Commune: someone brought along 'the registers of the Commune and the seal of the conspirators on which has been engraved just recently a fleur-de-lis and this seal was on the desk of the Commune'. Let us remember that the different versions of the report of the session diverge on one precise point: who brought along this 'infamous seal'? 'Citizens from the Gravilliers *section*'? 'The magistrate from the Gravilliers *section*'? 'A deputation of commissioners from the *sections*'? 'A magistrate appointed by the representatives to search the Maison Commune'? Whoever it was, several deputies shouted out that they had in fact seen this fleur-de-lis seal. Having obtained this corroboration, the commentaries set off at a good pace. Among the deputies and, certainly, in the galleries, the story was told that 'Robespierre had thoughts of marriage with the daughter of Louis XVI, that he wanted to re-establish Capet's son on the throne' and this gossip 'was on everybody's mind' (according to Barras who reports it in his *Mémoires*, but adds, nevertheless, that 'personally he gave no credence to these allegations'; we shall have to return to his testimony). Entirely absorbed in savouring the victory, they let themselves go; insults were now added to the rumours which circulated all night long. Someone announced to the Convention that 'the cowardly Robespierre is here' and asked if they wished to see him. The response was indignant.

To bring into the heart of the Convention the body of a man covered with every crime, would be to remove from this beautiful day all the glory it deserves. The body of a tyrant can bring nothing but pestilence; the place marked out for him and his accomplices is the Place de la Révolution. The two Committees must take the measures necessary for the sword of the law to strike them without delay.

Thuriot, who raged in this manner, would not fail to produce full particulars of these 'crimes'. His opportunity was to come some hours later through Fouquier-Tinville who, pedantic legalist that he was, raised a thorny problem at the Convention. Before proceeding to the execution of the outlawed rebels, it was necessary to establish their identity before municipal officers of their commune; now, it turns out that these officers were themselves outside the law ... Thuriot, who was presiding over the meeting, disdainfully removed the difficulty:

The Convention has demanded the swiftest death for the plotters. It is too long to wait, for the Committees to make their report and the traitors to mount the scaffold. We are so fully informed of the wickedness of our enemies, *that we know that Robespierre was in a position to have himself proclaimed king in Lyon and in other communes of the Republic.*

The most significant evidence of the spread of the tale, and certainly the most dramatic, does not, however, come from the chamber of the Convention, but from the Committee of Public Safety where Robespierre was stretched out on a table. A full retinue had accompanied his transfer; a crowd pressed to see him. Someone lifted his arm in order to examine his blood-stained face; the insults never ceased. Among these insults the rumour kept recurring, like a refrain. *Isn't he a handsome king?; Sire, your majesty suffers; I have to tell you the truth: 'you properly deceived me, you scoundrel'; stand back so that these men* [Saint-Just, Dumas, Payan who had just been brought in] *may see their king asleep on a table just like a man'*. To staunch the blood which filled his mouth, Robespierre made use of a little white leather bag, on which were the words 'At the Grand Monarque, Lecourt, sword-smith to the King and his armies, Rue Saint-Honoré'. Was he given this pistol bag by chance or from derision? Difficult to know, but the sign of the vendor provoked insults on 'the outcome his ambition had chosen'. Before his transfer to the Conciergerie, a surgeon, while dressing the broken jaw, placed a bandage over Robespierre's head; at this moment the sarcastic comments recommenced: *Look, his majesty receives a diadem* ...[5]

So Guittard's text, with which we opened this dossier, brings together several variants of the tale which were circulating on the day after 9 Thermidor. Taken up again and embellished, the tale was to be reused to consolidate the victory: first of all on the symbolic level, by the stage management of the execution of Robespierre and his accomplices. The Convention enthusiastically decided to move the guillotine from the Place du Trône Renversé (by the Vincennes gate) to the Place de la Révolution, the symbolic site of the death of the 'last tyrant'. The carts, setting out from the Conciergerie, had to cross the centre of the town. Moreover there were rumours that the remains of those executed had been thrown into the grave where the bodies of Louis XVI and Marie-Antoinette had been buried, and which had been specially reopened on this exceptional occasion. Barras claimed the honour of this initiative. To be sure, his memoirs, written under the Restoration, abound with boasting and tall stories. Let us recall, however, just for the interest of this tale, a macabre anecdote that he relates in his usual manner, putting himself forward and adding lugubriousness to its picturesque quality. 'Citizen Sanson, the executioner himself', had approached him 'respectfully, his hat removed and very humble: "Where shall we put the bodies, citizen representative?" "Let them be thrown into Capet's grave", I replied irritably. "Louis XVI was worth more than they. It

---

[5] The documents and works most useful for following the versions and the progress of the tale on 9 and 10 Thermidor are these: *Archives parlementaires*, Paris, 1982, vol. 93 (remarkable edition of Françoise Brunel, who includes the different versions of the accounts of the sessions of the Convention); C. Duval, *Projet du procès-verbal des séances des 9, 10 et 11 thermidor*, Paris, Year II (text not approved by the Convention); hearings of the *sections* in: E.B. Courtois, *Rapport fait au nom des Comités de salut public et de la sûreté générale sur les événements du 9 thermidor, an II*, Paris, Year III; G. Walter, *La Conjuration du neuf thermidor*, Paris, 1974; Ph. Buonarotti, *Conspiration pour l'égalité dite de Babeuf*, Paris, 1830, vol. 1; A. Mathiez, 'La Politique de Robespierre et le 9 thermidor expliqués par Buonarotti', *Annales révolutionnaires*, 1910; Guyot, *Relation sur le 9 thermidor*, AN F[7] 4432; *Faits recueillis aux derniers instants de Robespierre et de sa faction dans la nuit du 9 et 10 thermidor*, Paris, Year II, BN Lb[41] 1149; *Courrier républicain*, issues of 12 to 30 Thermidor; Barras, *Mémoires*, Paris, 1895, vol. 1; A. Mathiez, *Autour de Robespierre*, Paris, 1957; P. Sainte-Claire Deville, *La Commune de l'an II*, Paris, 1946.

will be more royalty for Robespierre, since it appears that he had a taste for it.'' '[6]

Barère, in his report presented on 10 Thermidor in the name of the two Committees, provided the official version of events. The rumours of the day before are found there as so many confirmed facts: the fleur-de-lis seal seized at the Commune; the mysterious individuals who turned up at the Temple. He also announced new revelations, which would not be slow in coming, about the plans of the conspirators. Hence the energetic security measures taken by the Committees: 'The Temple is guarded with care, as well as the Conciergerie; the same interest calls the people to guard them.' He did not go so far however as to take responsibility for the tale of the marriage, either planned or carried out, between Robespierre and the daughter of Louis XVI. The space granted in the report to the 'royalist aims' of Robespierre was in fact quite limited. The tone was, above all, one of reassurance and the emphasis was placed on the happy outcome of events, on the excellent state of the *sections* and public morale, and on the devotion of the entire people to the Convention.

The event that is the reference-point is not 21 January, but 31 May: 'On 31 May, the people carried out its revolution; *on 9 Thermidor, the Convention carried out its own*; liberty has applauded both equally.' What brings together and unites all 'tyrants', old and new, is loathing of both liberty and the people. 'May this dreadful era, with its new tyrants, more dangerous than those crowned by fanaticism and servitude, be the last storm of the revolution.'[7]

It was Collot d'Herbois and Billaud-Varenne who took it upon themselves to produce new revelations 'about the plan of the conspirators, who were led by Robespierre'. They did so at the Jacobin Club. On the night of 9 to 10 Thermidor, the Jacobins held a session even more inflamed than usual, and sent unanimous messages of solidarity to the Commune. Their assembly was broken up by members of the National Guard faithful to the Convention. Reassembling two days later, the Jacobins, again unanimously, affirmed their solidarity with the Convention and their outrage against the 'conspirators', the 'oppressors of the people' who had deceived them. With amazement they learned 'a few details relating to the conspiracy' delivered in turns by Collot and Billaud. 'The result is that this monster [Robespierre] in concert with Saint-Just and Couthon would share the empire between themselves. *Antony* Couthon would rule the Midi, *Lepidus*

---

[6] Barras, *Mémoires*, vol. 1, pp. 199–200.
[7] *Moniteur*, reprinted Paris, 1858–63, vol. 21, pp. 346–7. Henceforth we refer to this edition, by volume number.

Saint-Just the North and *Catiline* Robespierre the Centre. A letter from an English member of parliament has just informed the Committees of this.' Then again, the statement of a deserter related that 'foreign powers were in league with Robespierre and would negotiate only with him'. From all these revelations Billaud drew a moral and political lesson: 'Let this example teach you to have no more idols . . . Rally to the Convention which, in these stormy moments, has shown the strongest character.' The same day he was to announce at the Convention 'a prompt report of the Committees, which, documents in hand, will prove that the conspirators yesterday were to have 60,000 citizens slaughtered.'[8] The Convention was, however, to be left in the air; the promise would not be kept and the damning 'evidence' would never be produced.

In the days that followed the 'happy revolution', the papers and the pamphlets were active, in their turn, in revealing 'the countless threads of the plot which was to put liberty to death and erase the memory of Saint Bartholomew's Day'. The information provided by the reports of the Committees and the debates of the Convention was especially embroidered, with an increase in epithets and scenes of horror. 'The bloodstained throne of Charles IX would have been rebuilt here and now in Paris on piles of bodies. A tyrant, no less abhorrent, would with his own hand have assassinated and delivered up to the executioners, whom he directed, any energetic republicans who refused to become his subjects.' The rumour of the marriage project with 'the Capet girl', which was not taken up by the official documents, sprang up again vigorously. *New and interesting details on the horrifying conspiracy of Robespierre and his accomplices. Evidence found under the seals of the villains. Complicity of Hanriot in supporting their infamous plans to assassinate the national Convention and marry the daughter of Capet to Robespierre in order to reign together and put to death eighty thousand citizens.* The anonymous author of the pamphlet which opens with this alluring title adds, among other things, this 'interesting detail' which spun out the rumours circulating in the night of 9 to 10 Thermidor: 'On the 8th, a municipal officer said to some citizens who were rejoicing at the success of the republic: 'You would be very surprised if tomorrow a new king was proclaimed.' On the 10th, the daughter of the tyrant Capet, contrary to custom, woke at dawn, and dressed herself up. On

---

[8] A. Aulard, *Société des Jacobins*, Paris, 1897, vol. 6, pp. 298–9; *Courrier républicain*, 12 Thermidor, Year II; *Moniteur*, vol. 21, p. 356. On 11 Thermidor, Barère would announce to the Convention: 'everything was to conspire to re-establish tyranny on the blood-stained throne . . . Saint-Just was the plenipotentiary of the North; Couthon and young Robespierre, the peacemaking congress of the Midi; the elder Robespierre was the ruler of Paris over piles of corpses': *Moniteur*, vol. 21, pp. 358–9.

the 12th, she put on mourning.'[9] Another pamphlet, published in Rouen, announced the news of the fall of Robespierre under this sensational title, also intended to be shouted in the streets: *Horrifying conspiracy to raise Robespierre to royal rank. Seal with a fleur-de-lis seized at the Commune at Robespierre's side.* Although there were no new details to enrich the version spread by the official texts, the conclusion left no doubt: 'The conspirators wished to re-establish royalty in France.' To this was added an account of the execution of the 'tyrant' and his accomplices. 'The crowd was immense, sounds of joy, applause, cries of *Down with the tyrant*, of *Long live the Republic*, curses of every kind resounded all along the route. This is how the people gained revenge for praise commanded by terror, or deference usurped by a long hypocrisy.'[10]

Ten days after this execution, the *Journal de Perlet* was not content to repeat the rumours, but carried a long discussion of their validity. 'The rumour has spread that, to give himself more splendour in the eyes of his crowned colleagues of the future, the tyrant meant to force the hand of the young Capet girl and marry her. Why, indeed, those efforts on the night of 9 to 10 Thermidor to take control of the Temple?' This 'combination of circumstances' can only astonish those who are unfamiliar with 'courts and men of ambition'. In fact, 'the marriage could be, in his eyes, a means of having himself recognised by foreign powers, if his satellites had had him proclaimed king here'. Had not the kings of Europe recognised Cromwell as Protector of England? Had they withheld any recognition from Catherine who took possession of the throne by assassinating 'the tsar her husband'? 'Tyrants today would have happily done the same. Provided that France had a master, what did it matter to them whether it was Robespierre or Capet?'[11] The 'interesting details' on the private life of the 'tyrant' shed a new light on his royalist ambitions. He professed to be 'incorruptible' and never stopped appealing to virtue. But, it was now known, he had taken possession 'of the charming house of the former Princess of Chimay' at Issy.

It is there that were hatched the plots which would destroy liberty; it is there that, with Hanriot, Saint-Just and many other accomplices, the ruin of the people was prepared, among the most uproarious orgies. It was the Trianon of the successor of the Capets; it is there that, after meals for which the whole neighbourhood was

[9] *Nouveaux et intéressants détails* ..., Paris, n.d., BNLb⁴¹ 3971. Other 'interesting details' can be found in this pamphlet: the number of 'citizens for slaughter' is increased to 80,000; the juries of the Revolutionary Tribunal had the list and the Commune had itself allocated in advance a quarry which could contain 80,000 bodies. The police agents in their reports noted the great interest raised by the pamphlets and papers: 'The papers are read out loud in public places. Many citizens gather round the reader and then discuss what they have heard' (report of 17 Thermidor): A. Aulard, *Paris pendant la réaction thermidorienne* ..., Paris, 1898, vol. 1, p. 16.    [10] *Horrible conspiration* ..., Rouen, n.d., BN Lb⁴¹ 3972.
[11] *Journal de Perlet*, 20 Thermidor, Year II.

requisitioned, the tyrant rolled on the grass, pretending to be shaken by convulsive movements; in the presence of the court which surrounded him, he pretended to be Illuminated, in the manner of Mahomet, so as to impress fools and ingratiate himself with knaves.

Besides, Robespierre had concubines 'in nearly all the communes' of the Ile de France, while Couthon and Saint-Just had palaces at their disposal too, also 'scenes of orgies'.[12]

The attacks on Robespierre-the-king have little place in the countless addresses of congratulations which flowed to the Convention on behalf of the *sections*, the administrations of the *départements*, the municipalities, the popular societies, the armies, etc. True, the fleur-de-lis seal was mentioned from time to time, and 'the allies who must have a king' were vilified. The Gravilliers *section*, which distinguished itself during 'the memorable night' and whose delegation was loudly applauded by the Assembly, even discovered an original formula when it denounced Robespierre and his accomplices as 'popular royalists'.[13] Most of the addresses – to which we shall return – vehemently condemn the 'new Cromwell', the 'new Catiline', the 'despot', the 'tyrant' but without mentioning his royalist ambitions. It is as if the rumour were gradually running out of breath, as if it were confined to a brief moment and were only a response to that moment's needs and constraints. The development of the political situation seems to relegate it to the middle ground. This does not mean, however, that it disappeared completely. The parallel between Robespierre and the 'last Capet' would be perpetuated on the symbolic plane, particularly during the civic festivals. So in Lyon, during the festival 'of Return and Concord' (which exhibited only revenge against the terrorists) organised on 30 Pluviôse, Year III to celebrate the lifting of penal provisions against the town, a 'cart of terrorism' passed through the whole town to the sound of jeers. It contained four dummies: 'Robespierre-the-king', 'the god Chalier', the false informer and the Jacobin of 9 Thermidor.

During the commemorative festivals, notably those of 21 January, of 10 August and of 9 Thermidor, two thrones were burned, one for Capet and one for the 'triumviral tyranny', or instead the dummy of a Jacobin bearing a crown. The Convention was even to consider the possibility of fusing into one the two festivals of 10 August and of 9 Thermidor, thus making a

[12] *Journal de Perlet*, 20 Thermidor Year II; *Nouveaux et intéressants détails* . . .; the rumours of the 'orgies' had already been reported at the Convention on 10 Thermidor. Barras likewise mentions the 'pleasure-grounds' that the conspirators, 'these sultans', 'these satyrs', possessed in nearly all the communes around Paris, and where they 'abandoned themselves to every excess': *Moniteur*, vol. 21, p. 497.

[13] Cf. for example *Moniteur*, vol. 21, p. 375 (the popular society of Tours); p. 376 (the district administration of Lille); p. 385 (deputation of the Gravilliers *section*); p. 396 (disabled officers of the Rhine army); p. 435 (popular society of Maubeuge).

simultaneous celebration of the triumph of the Republic over the 'two thrones'.[14] On the other hand, the tale of Robespierre-the-king was to haunt the historiography of 9 Thermidor; it was to find, and this from Year III onwards, fervent supporters and fierce detractors. In Year III, the line of division between the two parties was relatively clear; the rumour was defended only by Thermidoreans and was rejected only by Royalists (there were as yet no 'Robespierrists' to object to it ...). Let us give just two examples of these positions, Courtois and Montjoie.

Courtois, commissioned to report on the events of 9 Thermidor (he was to deliver his report only on 8 Thermidor, Year III, the 'eve of the anniversary of the fall of the tyrant') and who, consequently, became the official historiographer of these 'glorious days', took up the essence of the tale: the fleur-de-lis seal; the small bag with the inscription 'at the Grand Monarch'; the 'orgies' in Auteuil, Passy, Issy etc.; the suspicious plans for 'Capet's children'. He gave a new and singularly machiavellian interpretation of these plans by introducing, as if it were documentary proof, the proclamation of the Commune, which has already been mentioned. Robespierre and his accomplices had wanted to remove from the Temple the children, 'the innocent remains of a guilty family', in order, first of all, to cast upon the Convention 'the odious suspicion of having wanted to reinstate a king'. Then, having carried out their 'homicidal plans against the Convention', they would have sacrificed these children 'for fear of rivals'. Thus, the 'incorrigible royalists' who hoped, thanks to Robespierre, 'to see reappear on the throne the last living remnant of Capet', were cruelly mistaken: the fleur-de-lis in the hands of the conspirators was only a bait to 'attract the foreign powers'. Courtois even had engraved, at the end of his report, 'the imprint of this kind of royal stamp' and he announced, in his turn, more new revelations about this seal.[15] This was, altogether, a 'weak' version of Robespierre's 'royalism'. To carry out his vile and tyrannical plans, Robespierre undoubtedly made use of the royal seal and Capet's children, but basically, he was only a common scoundrel, who did not shrink from the assassination of children, and not a real pretender to the throne. Besides, Courtois devoted only a few pages of his voluminous report to all these allegations and was not too concerned about making them agree with his other explanations of the plans of the 'conspirators'.

---

[14] Cf. *Messager du soir*, 4 Pluviôse, Year III; Archives Départementales Allier 791 (information provided by Mona Ozouf); R. Fuoc, *La Réaction thermidorienne à Lyon (1795)*, Lyon, 1957, pp. 72–3; *Moniteur*, vol. 25, pp. 315, 354. The Convention itself drew a symbolic parallel between the 'two tyrants' in decreeing on 21 January 1795, after the celebration of the anniversary of the execution of Louis XVI, that there would henceforth be established a festival commemorating 9 Thermidor, day of the fall of the 'last tyrant'. Finally, let us note a distant echo of the tale: the *Orateur du peuple*, Fréron's newspaper, reported on 5 Vendémiaire that, according to news coming from Martinique, Robespierre had protected Capet's children with the intention of getting them across to London.

[15] Courtois, *Rapport*, pp. 24–7, 73–5.

This report had a poor reputation even among the 'Thermidoreans'. It was a matter of public knowledge that its author was a shameless liar. Everyone knew that he had purloined several documents from among the papers found at Robespierre's home, which had been entrusted to him and from which he had written a previous report. He had kept certain documents for himself (they could always be useful . . .) and he had handed over to certain members of the Convention concerned other documents, notably letters of allegiance to Robespierre (and there were many who came to look for them after 9 Thermidor . . .). Nevertheless, no one at the Convention found it advisable to contradict Courtois's report; people contented themselves, at the most, with talk in the lobbies.

Félix Montjoie, a confirmed and militant royalist, author of the first royalist history of 9 Thermidor, reviewed all the conjectures on the plans of the 'conspirators' and, in particular, of Robespierre: he had proposed to overthrow the Convention, all the authorities and to become 'dictator or tribune'; he would have left France with the name of a Republic but he planned to govern it 'despotically with Saint-Just and Couthon'. But there was also the story 'that he aimed at nothing less than to become king of the French, that he wanted to assume both title and power . . . There was in the end a later version. It is said that his plan was to place on the throne the remnant of the kings of France and to enjoy the brilliant fortune that such an important service would deserve.' Now, for Montjoie, 'these are all so many tales with which to amuse the public'. If a plot of this nature had existed, there would be traces of it in the papers of Robespierre, Saint-Just and Couthon. Yet the authorities who possessed these papers had published no proof. It had to be said frankly, although the truth was terrifying: 'This conspiracy had no other goal than robbery and assassination' and Robespierre was only the leader 'of all the bandits and all the assassins then in France, and God knows how many they were, those blood-drinkers'. No credit therefore could be given to this tale, nor to this other story told about Robespierre: 'Royalist writers, either because they wished to revenge themselves through abuse for the harm done to their party, or because they had really been led into error by people who were misinformed, have proclaimed that he was the nephew of Damiens . . . This belief, which easily gained currency, is today fairly widespread, but it is a tale that deserves no credence.'[16] These are refutations which are just as much evidence for the persistence, and this in royalist circles, of the two tales – Robespierre the

[16] F. Montjoie, *Histoire de la conjuration de Maximilien Robespierre*, Paris, n.d. (1795). The fortunes experienced by the rumour in historiography and among the legends of 9 Thermidor deserve a study of their own. The watershed between those who consider it simply a slander and those who give it at least a grain of truth would not be the same as in Year III. The tale of Robespierre-the-king overlaps at times with the legends, powerful in a different way, which surround the 'mystery of the child of the Temple'.

regicide, nephew of Damiens, and Robespierre the ambitious terrorist, aspiring to become king or to re-establish the son of Louis XVI on his legitimate throne.

### The fabrication of a rumour

Let us add the last item to our dossier.

The tale, for whose history we have provided some reference points, was *fabricated* out of nothing. It did not come 'from below', from a disorientated crowd or from *sections* having to obey simultaneous and contradictory orders, those of the Convention and the Commune. It was launched from 'above', by the Committees of Public Safety and General Security, to rally the *sections* and the military, to channel their emotions, and overcome their hesitations, real or imagined. So no doubt remains on the key element of the tale, namely the fleur-de-lis seal, the famous material proof of Robespierre's 'royalist designs'. This seal, let us recall, was seized at the Maison Commune, then placed on the table of the president of the Convention, recognised as authentic by several deputies, and reproduced a year later by Courtois in his report. But it is a fraud. Twenty years later, in Brussels, the exiled regicides lived with their memories, harking back to their grandeur along with their old quarrels, trying to understand the history they had made as well as the history they had endured. And it was publicly notorious among them that the famous seal had been found at the Maison Commune only after having been hidden there by agents of the Committee of General Security. Vadier, who had directed the operation, admitted it himself. 'Cambon said one day to Vadier, exiled like him in Brussels: How did you have the villainy to think up this seal and all the other documents by which you wanted to pass Robespierre off as a royalist agent? *Vadier replied that the danger of losing one's head made one imaginative.*'[17] Was Vadier all on his own in inventing the tale and

---

[17] Cf. the authors' note in P.-J.-B. Buchez and P.-C. Roux, *Histoire parlementaire de la Révolution française*, Paris, 1837, vol. 34, p. 59. M.-A. Baudot reports another version of Vadier's admission. 'Cambon had doubts about the fleurs-de-lis found in Robespierre's house, which Courtois mentions in his report. He wanted to know what had happened and had a sharp set-to one day with Vadier, in the presence of Charles Teste and myself. Vadier agreed that they had been taken from the Committee of General Security to Robespierre's house after his death': M.-A. Baudot, *Notes historiques sur la Convention nationale, l'Empire et l'exil des votants*, Paris, 1893, p. 74. (There is an obvious error of detail in this account: the fleur-de-lis seal was handed over to the president of the Convention *before* and not *after* Robespierre's execution.) As a matter of duty, let us report yet another version from Vadier; Buonarotti reports his conversations with Vadier when they were both imprisoned in Cherbourg, after being sentenced to deportation for taking part in Babeuf's conspiracy. Vadier, questioned about 9 Thermidor and the famous seal found on the desk of the Commune or in Robespierre's house, cried out: 'As for that, it's a slander invented by Barère!' (Cf. Buonarotti's notes, published by Mathiez, 'La Politique de Robespierie', p. 508.) There is no doubt that, with the testimony of Vadier, and also with that of other participants in the events of 9 Thermidor, we remain deep in confusion.

fabricating the evidence? Who also had a hand in this operation? Was only one version of the rumour set going and which was it, or were there rather several versions started simultaneously in the hope that one would take over from the other? We shall probably never know, just as many other episodes of this *journée* will never be cleared up. These details are, in the end, secondary; the important point lies elsewhere. The rumour was invented and launched by the Committees of the Convention, notably by the Committee of General Security, that is to say by the police, who also saw to its widest and most effective dissemination. It was a political diversion which gambled on the credulity of the entire population, but especially on that of the *sans-culotte* militants and the Convention itself. The inventors of the tale wanted to reach the greatest number: once let loose upon the public, then repeated and exaggerated, the rumour would, on the one hand, win over the undecided to the cause of the Convention, and, on the other, consolidate the resolution of those who were already won over. The objective was as clear as the calculation was simple. Barras has given a full explanation and commentary. This time too, he can be given credit: he was a master of the arts of slander and political intrigue. He did not believe a word, he states in his *Mémoires*, of the allegations which 'preoccupied people's minds' and were spread by certain members of the Convention – neither in the fleur-de-lis seal found at Robespierre's house, nor in Robespierre's plan for marriage with Capet's daughter. (And with good reason, for we can be almost certain that he, appointed by the Convention as 'general' of the Parisian troops, in permanent contact with the Committee of General Security, was 'in the know' although he breathes not a word of it in his *Mémoires*.) He believed, however, that all these tales 'were, although hardly credible, perhaps not useless when passed on to the people'. His explanation of the reasons for this 'usefulness' reads curiously like a first-hand account of the intentions and calculations of the inventors of the tale.

The people could not be persuaded that Robespierre was a tyrant, other than by associating him with ideas of former royalty, the only one that was, in their eyes, a graspable *corpus delicti*. Something obvious to the senses is needed to gain the people's understanding. Now, how would they see that the man who every day offered them admiration, who spoke to them of liberty, of equality, who called himself their defender, and who appeared at this moment as their martyr, that this same person, I say, should be the man we were now calling an enemy of freedom, an oppressor, a tyrant? This is a rather complicated matter which cannot be directly grasped by the imagination of the people, except by saying in the same breath that this tyrant was a traitor, that he had come to an understanding with the enemies of the Republic, with the former kings, or with members of the royal family, and that he was therefore an infamous tyrant. With the word treason added to villainy, all can be understood, all is explained, and one could hope to rally the people, and see them turn swiftly against the men who were pointed out to them as traitors and whom they recognised as such.

The frankness is admirable; the portrayal, which is apparent in the text, of a people manipulable and manipulated, but always for the benefit of the good cause which is its own, of a people whose limited 'comprehension' demands that it be addressed through the 'senses' and by the 'imagination', deserves a full commentary. Is it not curiously related to the portrayal of a people needing to be educated, which is to be found at the heart of revolutionary discussion of education? Contrary to his claims, Barras did not leave matters only to those around him who were peddling the tale. He had found the latter so 'useful' that he repeated it in his turn when he delivered, at the Convention, the final report on the glorious mission he had performed on 9 Thermidor, in a plumed hat and with drawn sword.[18]

What, however, were the real effects of the tale on the course of events? Did it really sway the balance on the side of the men who circulated it? Information on the spread of the tale is too patchy and the confusion which reigned on the night too general for certainty as to what took place. In retrospect, one might be tempted to believe that the Committees could have managed quite well without. Did they not overestimate the forces of Robespierre and the Commune and, especially, underestimate the factors which worked in their favour? After 31 May, when the Convention had

---

[18]   Barras, *Mémoires*, vol. 1, pp. 200–1; *Moniteur*, vol. 21, p. 497. Before leaving Barras and his memories, it is difficult to resist the temptation to mention another episode in the history of the tale which is associated with him. As has been said, Barras boasted of having given the order to throw the corpse of Robespierre into the grave where had been placed the remains of Louis XVI and Marie-Antoinette. Now, it is almost certain that those executed on 9 Thermidor were not buried in this grave, in the Madeleine cemetery, but in the cemetery of Errancis, close to the Place du Trône Renversé, now the usual place for executions. Two cart-loads would have been dug out to receive the bodies of those executed on 10 Thermidor; the heads had been placed separately in a large chest; a layer of quicklime had been spread 'over the remains of the tyrants to prevent them from being one day deified'. (Cf. the documents quoted by C.A. Dauban, *Paris, en 1794 et en 1795*, Paris, 1869, pp. 416–17.) The rumour nevertheless persisted that for Robespierre they had not only moved the guillotine to the Place de la Révolution, but also that the grave in the cemetery of the Madeleine had been reopened. Barras, as we have seen, carefully cultivated this rumour which added to the lustre of his Thermidorean glory; perhaps he really believed it. Whatever the truth of the matter, under the Restoration he started another rumour, a kind of morbid joke. The opportunity came his way when the remains of Louis XVI were transferred from the cemetery of the Madeleine to the royal tombs of Saint-Denis. He declared, to whoever wished to know, that since Robespierre and his companions had been the last to be thrown into this same grave, where all the bodies were eaten up by quicklime, Robespierre would have been, very probably, buried at Saint-Denis 'with some odd bones from Saint-Just, Couthon or Hanriot'. His evidence for this claim is that in order to identify the remains of the royal couple at the time of their exhumation, the man responsible relied on certain buckles found in the grave and which had escaped destruction. Now, Robespierre, as a matter of fact, wore buckles on his breeches and his shoes on the day of his execution, (Barras, *Mémoires*, vol. 4, pp. 315–16; 416–20). So, one rumour taking over from another, Robespierre-the-king apparently found his last resting-place in the royal tombs of Saint-Denis . . .

capitulated by surrendering the Girondin deputies, the organisers of this *journée* had learned the political lesson of their own success. Montagnard power, with Robespierre at its head, was perfectly well aware that the possibility of a new putsch, proclaimed in the name of the 'risen people', was not to be neglected. To guard against that danger, a complete apparatus had been set up. Following the decree on the organisation of revolutionary government the Commune had practically lost the autonomy of action it had previously enjoyed. It was not only placed under the authority of a national agent, it was also banned from calling assemblies of delegates from the *sections*; what is more, the revolutionary committees of these *sections* were obliged to maintain continuous and direct contact with the Committee of General Security, that is to say, without passing through the Commune as an intermediary. These measures proved themselves during the struggle against the Hébertists and the latter's débâcle contributed, in turn, to weakening the authority of the Commune as well as reinforcing the links between the *sections* and the Committees. Certainly, on 9 Thermidor, the national agent Payan, loyal to Robespierre, was found on the side of the Commune; nevertheless these measures, taken all together, were shown to be quite effective. From the moment that the Commune took action, it became illegal; placing it outside the law only demonstrated and penalised the act of rebellion. The direct contacts between the *sections* and the Committee of General Security acted strongly in the government's favour. Once the battle against Robespierre and his few faithful allies had been won in the Convention, its authority, presented as 'the rallying point of all republicans', seemed easily to get the better of the Commune as well as the popularity of Robespierre and the influence of the Jacobins. Both were revealed, in actual fact, to be much more limited than the 'Thermidoreans' had imagined. These latter had equally underestimated their own effectiveness, all the greater in that the action of the Commune depended on continuous improvisation, the opposite of what it had been during the *journée* of 31 May, when it was carefully prepared in advance. The confusion, which characterised the days of Thermidor, was all the more to the advantage of the Convention, asserting its authority as both legitimate and effective, because revolutionary spontaneity this time was singularly lacking, weary and worn out as it was by the whole experience of the Terror. The political stakes of the struggle between the Robespierrists and the Convention were, at the time, very confused (we shall have to return to this). They did nevertheless underlie the choice made by the majority of *sections*, and that from the beginning of events: *in favour of legal order*, as embodied in the Convention and revolutionary government, and *against new disturbances*, or even a rebellion which only claimed to come from 'the best patriots unjustly oppressed'. The image of the 'risen people' regaining its sovereignty had increasingly less power to mobilise. A larger and larger majority of members of the *sections* no longer perceived those who made up this 'risen people' as the symbol of the revolutionary cause, but saw them as they were in reality: a minority which was melting away hour by hour, led by radical militants, who were just so many members of the personnel of the *sections* and of the Commune. The proportion of forces was therefore from the beginning largely in favour of the Convention and the advantage kept increasing, as is confirmed by the official reports of the meetings of the *sections* and the revolutionary committees. But at the very moment that the tale of Robespierre-the-king was launched, it seemed to the actors in the events that the issue of the struggle hung by a thread.

'The danger of losing one's head makes one imaginative . . .' The genesis of the tale would then be explained solely by Vadier's act of panic at the moment that the gunners assembled in front of the Convention. It was a flight of fancy that was, however, strangely shared; not only by those who, besides Vadier, were the fabricators of the tale, but also by their adversaries. In fact, we have noted that the 'imagination' of those who assembled at the Maison Commune seemed to follow an almost analogous pattern. Did they not accuse the 'villains oppressing the Convention' of being 'accomplices of foreigners', of indulging in suspicious manoeuvres around the Temple, of trying to liberate 'Capet's offspring'? These were allegations which had no hold on people's minds, aborted rumours, unlike the tale launched by the Committees of the Convention, which succeeded in imposing itself as a rumour. Of course, not everyone lent an ear to this tale; nevertheless it circulated and, so to speak, circulated successfully, by spreading wider and wider, creating a greater and greater stir.

Slander is a political weapon as old as politics. Robespierre had been, throughout his political career, the victim of slander and he himself knew very well how to wield this weapon. The tale invented on 9 Thermidor was no more defamatory or insulting than the other slanders launched against the 'Incorruptible' and which he had been able to hurl back. But this time, it was no longer a matter of defamation, of the ever-increasing verbal violence inseparable from the rhetorical jousts at the Assembly or among the Jacobins. Through the extent of its circulation, the slanderous tale took on the dimensions of a real *public rumour*. It had been conceived and launched as an instrument for manipulation in the sphere of Paris, and indeed of the entire country. So its fabrication is revealing of the political mentality of those who put it into circulation and who considered the recipients of the tale as *manipulable*: the 'ordinary classes', 'the people', but also public opinion as a whole, including the political class. A flight of fancy, true; but disseminated by a complete technique and with wide experience behind it.

The tale itself was skilfully constructed, with a plot at once simple and firing the collective imagination (the conspiracy, the mystery of the Temple, the marriage with the king's daughter, the secret negotiations with abroad, etc.); a whole network, notably the police network, had been used for spreading it; fake evidence had been introduced at the Maison Commune, then this 'proof' exhibited at the Convention. Among its recipients, the tale effectively found enough of an audience to turn it into a public rumour and so bring about the operation's desired result.

But the success of this tale is also to be set in the context of the history of the revolutionary imagination and, in particular, the history of *revolutionary rumour*. Inseparable from this imagination, rumour is nourished by it and stirs it up in turn: a very wide context, all the more difficult in that revolutionary rumour still awaits its historian; a very complicated history because of the specific character of its subject. Rumour is protean, both ever-present and fleeting. It is, however, impossible to understand revolutionary events without taking into account the role taken by rumour in the behaviour of the protagonists and especially in the exacerbation of their emotions and passions. In fact, rumours reappear throughout the Revolution, mobilising people's minds, channelling their fervour, orientating their fears. Rumours of the intervention of troops and the imminent massacre of Parisians, on 14 July; rumours of brigands, aristocrats, foreign troops, English, Polish and even Hungarian, who menace the countryside, during the 'Great Fear'; rumours of the 'prison plot', the foreign agents who will massacre the women and children as soon as the men have left Paris to fight at the front, during the massacres of September; rumours of the 'knights of the dagger' who are conspiring to free the king from the Temple, who are hidden everywhere, ready to come out at night and attack patriots, during the trial of the king; rumours of the foreign agents and traitor-generals, which surface at every defeat; rumours of the 'starvers of the people', hiding corn or destroying it, which arise at each shortage of food; rumours of *assignats*[19] that will be devalued, withdrawn from circulation, cancelled, etc. These are only some of the rumours with which historians are most familiar. Each would need a detailed study in the manner of *The great fear* by Georges Lefebvre which remains an outstanding model. But it would be above all necessary to broaden the setting, to move from the study of one case to the serial analysis of revolutionary rumours. Even a simple inventory is always inadequate, not to speak of the absence of any study of their themes and structures, of their proportions and of their means of circulation, of their epicentres and progress, of their spatial and social

---

[19] *assignats*. A paper currency created during the Revolution, whose value was guaranteed by national lands.

localisations, of their hold on people's minds. While waiting for these studies, let us risk some general observations, as hypothetical as they are provisional.

A very swift overview allows the picking out of a repetitive theme, – the *plot* – inseparable from another – the *hidden enemy*. The rumour is bolstered by a rich and compact symbolism, of occult and menacing forces, of the shadows where the wicked weave their machinations. The precise goal of the plot varies according to the case and the circumstances. It is, however, striking that the great waves of popular rumours speak not only of a plot against the Nation, the Revolution, but point to a conspiracy menacing the vital substance of the People. The 'enemies' are attacking its health, its life even, its women and its children. In this way, the rumour which accompanies a rise in popular violence has the direct result that the carrying out of this violence is viewed as a legitimate act of defence or of revenge against the 'villains' who are plotting abominable crimes – if they have not already committed them. Rumours which graft themselves onto very real social and political conflicts, but which feed and over-excite the passions, the fears and the hatreds – these are the material out of which moments of crisis during a revolution are made. They are political rumours, certainly, since they are fed by conflicts and events which are *par excellence* political. Very often, these rumours are *politicised* by the Revolution but they do no more, however, than extend, in a new context, very old themes and fantasies. This is the case with the rumour of the 'famine plot', remarkably studied by Steve L. Kaplan, which recurred throughout the eighteenth century and which flared up several times during the Revolution – proof, if any were needed, that although the Revolution certainly invented a new political arena and, in particular, new political institutions, the *mental environment* remained the largely traditional one of the *ancien régime*. One can therefore understand resistance to the rationalising innovations of the Revolution, often very abstract and doctrinaire, as a mixture of modernity and archaism – and this mixture is a characteristic trait of political behaviour during the revolutionary period. The popular credulity which guarantees the circulation and effectiveness of rumour itself represents an age-old heritage. It is inseparable from a largely oral culture, in which information is passed from mouth to ear. The revolutionary period is certainly notable for an explosion of political writing. But we should not forget that the written is relayed by the oral; our tale is a good example of this: the newspapers are shouted through the streets and discussed orally, just as much as they are read.

In a typology of revolutionary rumour a separate place should be reserved for political rumour in the narrowest sense of the term, that is, for the politician's rumour. The new circles of power – in the first rank of which were the assemblies, consisting of several hundred deputies – and the patriotic clubs – among which were the Jacobins – were so many epicentres of the rumours that are inseparable from political struggles and intrigues. Rumour tormented the political class unceasingly – especially the deputies and the government bureaucracy, which was growing all the time – but also those who frequented the galleries. Between these two groups communication was easily and permanently established, as well as between the corridors of power and the urban spaces, the streets and the squares, where the 'groups' formed to discuss politics and comment on the news. There the recurring theme was the 'plot' and it became an obsession during the Terror. Let us give just one example of this politician's rumour, which is very revealing of the political climate in which 9 Thermidor emerged. The battle to be fought against Robespierre was carefully prepared, in particular through a rumour meant specifically for the members of the Convention. It was not the tale of Robespierre-the-king, invented, as we have seen, by a 'flight of fancy' and meant for the street, for the people, supposed, simple as they were, to be able to understand only a *graspable corpus delicti*. A just as graspable *corpus delicti* was invented for the deputies, but quite different in nature from a fleur-de-lis seal: they were told of lists of deputies to be proscribed, drawn up by the 'tyrant'; sometimes, it seems, they were even shown these lists. On the eve of 9 Thermidor these lists were becoming longer and longer; in the corridors of the Convention and especially in gatherings of friends, rumour increased the number by several dozens, even by more than a hundred new names, to be added to the seventy-three Girondin deputies arrested after 31 May. The deputies to whom the lists were presented evidently found their own names on the list, and in this way the rumour served the intrigue by putting into concrete form the vague and allusive threats issued by Robespierre and Couthon at the Jacobin Club. Without this undermining, which mobilised the fears and hatreds accumulated during the Terror, and which promptly made the survival of each person the immediate stake, would that unanimous cry of the Convention have been possible: *Down with the tyrant*?

The success of the tale of Robespierre-the-king thus forms an episode in the history of the revolutionary imagination and revolutionary rumour. But the characteristics of this tale evoke a more specific context, that of the Terror. In fact, it is easy to establish that the tale is connected with other slanders, all meant to become so many rumours, made up by the Montagnard power, with Robespierre at its head. Hadn't Hébert been accused of organising the famine, of having stopped at the gates the bread which the people lacked? Hadn't Danton been presented as leader of a plot, an accomplice of foreigners, a traitor to the *patrie*, a protector of émigrés? Like these other fictions, the tale of Robespierre-the-king is a *terrorist* invention. Terrorist, because fabricated by a whole political and police machinery of the Terror, but also in the sense that it appeals to the social imagination fashioned by the Terror. To follow Michelet in speaking of the advent of the Revolution, one might say that, with the Terror, no longer everything, but anything, seemed possible. In an atmosphere strained to extremes by successive purges, by the elevation of informing into a civic virtue, by the ever-increasing and boundless accusations, by the unending discoveries of new plots, it seemed that no one could any longer escape from suspicion at some time or another. The revolutionary heroes of yesterday, were they not today unveiled as so many enemies, whose zeal was only a mask behind which were hidden the darkest designs of tomorrow and complicity with aristocrats and royalists? When Robespierre himself accused Danton, had he not made the call not to bow down before any idol? And concerning this same Danton, had there not been a rumour run that he wished to become regent? Had not the Hébertists been accused by Saint-Just of hatching a conspiracy to overturn the revolutionary government and re-establish the monarchy? On this account the false and vile Hébert prepared his career as future regent through compromising the Assembly by scandal and by 'disgust for corrupt men'. No slander, however disgraceful, was excluded. The day before the trial of Marie-Antoinette, had not the warders of the Temple sounded the alarm at the Commune by telling it that the widow Capet was having incestuous relations with her son, was making him taste the forbidden fruits of solitary pleasure? All of this – who would have doubted it? – for counter-revolutionary ends ... With the health of the boy ruined in this way, the responsibility for his death would not fail to fall upon revolutionary power and to complete the ruin of its reputation in the eyes of foreign powers. The fantasies which engendered this fiction, maintained publicly by Hébert in the course of the queen's trial, speak volumes about the pathology of the terrorist imagination.

The Terror was nourished by this imagination and fed it in its turn; it invented plots which merged all enemies into the overall figure of the 'suspect' and fed on the fear and suspicion that it secreted. The social imagination created by the Terror was over-excited and unbalanced, but it was also, and for the same reasons, marked by a sort of fatigue and inertia. Was everything, even anything, now to be acceptable to the social imagination? The men who invented the tale of Robespierre-the-king were well aware of this combination of circumstances and expected to draw the greatest profit from it. Their flight of fancy was not so spontaneous as Vadier would have it believed. The panic which, on the night of 9 Thermidor, seized hold of the purveyors of the rumour was, without doubt, real. But the reply which they found to parry the immediate danger was informed by a full experience, acquired through the exercise of terrorist power, of the invention of false plots and false accusations. Confronted with rumour and the people's credulity, they acquired an attitude that was, in a way, *technical*: both could be manipulated, both could be used as so many instruments for attaining a political objective. Now, on 9 Thermidor the situation was such that all means were thought justified for success. But to make a success of what?

## An event in search of its significance

It is not yet time to leave this *journée*, glorified by some as a heroic rising against the 'tyrant', denounced by others as a tragic moment when the very mainspring of the Revolution was broken. It is well known that throughout its course the Revolution manifested a strong tendency to dramatise its acts and gestures, to present itself as a compelling spectacle, imposing roles and costumes on its actors. 9 Thermidor, from this point of view too, was no exception and the descriptions of this *journée* were often inspired by it. It is necessary however to be precise each time about the theatricality of this performance. One recalls the episodes, told so many times, that turn it into a drama, even a tragedy in the antique style: the deputies who rose up, crying *Down with the tyrant*; these same members of the Convention, threatened by the artillery, who decided to remain in the chamber and die for the Republic, in the manner of Roman senators; Robespierre, at the Commune, hesitating to appeal to the people against the Convention, which was the legitimate power of the Republic; the hall of the Committee of Public Safety where Robespierre, wounded, was laid out on a table, where Saint-Just, impassive, fixed his eyes on the Declaration of the Rights of Man and the Citizen, stuck to the wall, and spoke these words: 'And yet that is my work, and the revolutionary government too.' Simplistic images, it will be said, and many do not resist historical criticism. No one will be surprised that these clichés have entered historical memory, where the representations engendered by an event are often more important than the event itself. But do not let the imagery mask the mixture of genres: the tragic keeps turning into the grotesque. Tallien, at the tribune of the Convention, waved a dagger which he had scarcely any intention of using, neither against Robespierre nor against himself; Hanriot, head of the Parisian National Guard, in turn bound hand and foot by some gendarmes and freed by his followers; several hundred Jacobins, who never tired of acclaiming Robespierre nor of launching heroic appeals to combat the 'villains' but whose numbers kept melting away, whom ten(!) people are enough to disperse and whose chamber, 'the invincible bastion of the Revolution' was, quite simply, locked with a key, as if to mark the end of the play. Thousands of armed men, arranged in battalions, seemed to sur-render to a strange ballet: the same who, in the afternoon, set out to support the Commune found themselves, in the evening, on the side of the Convention. The gunners went on a return journey, between the Place de Grève and the Place du Carrousel, without firing a single cannon shot. As if to add to this grotesque aspect, the character upon whom it fell to play the particularly dramatic role of the night, the gendarme who fired on Robespierre, was called Merda. And this seemed so ridiculous that he was quickly rebaptised Meddat before being presented to the Convention, which greeted him triumphally. During this night, when passions were let loose, when people on both sides swore only of 'living in freedom or dying', just two pistol shots were heard: the one from the 'brave gendarme' Merda and one from Lebas, who committed suicide. The real killing began only on the day after the victory, in the Place de la Révolution: twenty-two guillotined on 10 Thermidor, sixty-six executed on 11 Thermidor, the largest 'batch' that Paris had seen since the beginning of the Terror. We shall never know what the numbers of the executed would have been if the opposite party, Robespierre and his followers, had won the day ...

The strange spectacle offered by Paris on 9 Thermidor reveals the bewilderment in the minds of the thousands of people who were taking part in a conflict which was likely to turn at any moment into a bloody confrontation, but where the stakes never emerged clearly out of the confusion. As we have shown, the tale of Robespierre-the-king could influence the outcome of the conflict only because of this confusion. Everything happened as if the event, which has remained in history under the name of 9 Thermidor, supplied, at the time, a precise meaning neither to its own episodes, which followed one another chaotically, nor to the actors who took part in it: as if the event was only in search of its political significance.

We know that no historic event exhausts its full meaning at the moment it takes place. This, or rather these meanings, when there are several of them and they are as usual contradictory, tend to overrun the event, as its consequences progressively emerge in history. At the time, the protagonists can be more or less aware of the stakes of the conflict in which they are engaged. In this respect, the *journée* of 9 Thermidor is clearly different from many other revolutionary *journées*, particularly those of 10 August and 31 May. Yet at its crucial moment, 9 Thermidor seemed to be simply a re-run of these *journées*. Because the Commune proclaimed that 'the people have risen' and mobilised the *sections* against the Assembly, everyone had the impression they were re-enacting a scenario already well rehearsed on 10 August and 31 May. The reference to these *journées* especially to 31 May, was in fact explicit in the proclamations of Robespierre's followers. This resemblance, however, only increased the confusion. Far from clarifying the situation, it muddled it even more because the arguments – meaning the accusations and insults hurled from both sides which took the place of argument – strangely resembled each other: both sides swore fidelity to the Revolution and the Republic; all denounced their adversaries' conspiracy and collusion with 'the enemy'. Did not the revolutionary government, against which the Commune called the people 'to rise' as it had done on 31 May, itself emerge from this key *journée*? Did it not proclaim its loyalty to the direction to which it then committed itself, did it not promise to fight 'energetically' against all indulgence? Neither of the political parties was capable of formulating its political aims. Paradoxically, the slanderous rumour provides some light in so far as it points, with hatred and violence, to Robespierre as the key character of the conflict. So the central and hidden political stake of the conflict comes into view: *How to bring the Terror to an end?* – the essential and yet unarticulated question. This is the implicit factor in the political discourse which, on both sides, surpasses itself in noble rhetoric and dishonourable insults.

In this summer bringing Year II to an end, two months after the law of Prairial, when the prisons were packed with suspects and the revolutionary Tribunal stopped work only on the *décadis*[20] (it was to make an exception only on 10 Thermidor, in order to initiate the identification of Robespierre and his allies . . .), no one dared to pose openly the problem of the way out of the Terror. (On 9 Thermidor, when the battle against Robespierre was raging at the Convention, the guillotine executed its daily task and no one thought of suspending it.) For the emergence from the Terror to be *mentioned*, for it to be part of the government's or the Convention's 'order of the day', it had to have already begun in reality. In fact, after the 'springtime of victories', and with the nation's territory liberated, the Terror lacked this support, and even lacked the legitimacy provided by the discourse on the war, on the necessity of defending the Republic against the external threat[21] (in fact rumours of the imminent peace persisted). After the liquidation of the 'factions', of the Dantonists and the Hébertists, all political debate, however timid, was stifled by the glorifying of the unanimous and indivisible People. The Terror took its foundation and justification only from the discourse it held about itself and which merged into one the denunciation of indulgence and the glorification of republican virtue. Did this virtue not call for permanent vigilance, did it not accompany the practices engendered by the Terror: executions, informing, paralysing fear? United with the exercise of power, the Terror occupied the

[20] *décade, décadis*. One *décade* lasted ten days and there were three in each month of the revolutionary calendar. The tenth day, the *décadis*, was a day of rest.
[21] On the relations between the war and the Terror in revolutionary discourse, Mona Ozouf introduces innovative and pertinent ideas in her work *L'Ecole de la France*, Paris, 1984, pp. 109–28.

entire political arena, and blocked off from the start, within the framework of this power, any debate on what policy to adopt. The differences in the heart of government, whatever their aims and causes might be, beginning with animosities and personal quarrels, were aggravated through mistrust and mutual suspicion. (It is not part of our study to examine these many causes of discord; it is, however, significant that arguments to do with the control of the police should be particularly envenomed.) Any conflict, even of limited significance, risked being caught up in the mesh of the Terror, being made short work of by the mechanisms that the Terror made available. And it favoured one particular instrument ... Unnamed and unnamable, the problem: *What is to be done with the Terror?* was at the same time repressed and obsessive. This problem of revolutionary power is pre-eminently political, and one where the stake became the very lives of those who exercised it. It is a problem inseparable from the person of Robespierre. In the system of power that had emerged from the project of 'radicalising the Revolution, making it consistent with its discourse', Robespierre occupied, the day after the Festival of the Supreme Being and the law of Prairial, the position of a hinge, where were joined, in the same finality, Virtue and Terror.[22] *What is to be done with the Terror? What is the way out?* The replies passed through Robespierre. They could only come from him or turn against him. They could only be expressed in terms that were indirect and were all the more confused because it was the duty of the terrorists themselves, the architects of the Terror, to find replies. And they could only bring these into play through terrorist means. Marc-Antoine Baudot, a Montagnard member of the Convention, both an alert observer and an actor in these events, put it this way: 'In the inextricable and bloody state that the Republic had reached before 9 Thermidor, the only way out of this horrifying situation was by the death or ostracism of Robespierre ... *so, in the struggle of 9 Thermidor, it was not a question of principles, but of killing.*'[23]

Robespierre's political plan between Prairial and Thermidor lends itself to many interpretations, as is shown by the debate it aroused and which has lasted for two centuries. Did he wish to initiate a way out of the Terror, even bring it to a complete halt, as is implied by certain passages of his speeches and, in particular, his censure of the most blood-thirsty 'terrorists', notably the representatives *en mission* who were conspicuous for their high-handed actions and their corruption? Or did he, on the contrary, wish to continue the Terror, to make it even bloodier, to increase his domination over the Convention, as is suggested by other passages of these same speeches and,

[22] Cf. the remarkable analyses of François Furet, in *Penser la Révolution française*, Paris, 1978, pp. 84 *et seq.*    [23] M.-A. Baudot, *Notes historiques*, pp. 125, 148.

especially, the vigilant watch that he kept on the activities of the revolutionary tribunal and on police repression? Did he have a political plan other than that of asserting his own political power even more strongly and settling scores with his adversaries in the Committees and the Convention? Might he have been struck by a sort of paralysis, hesitating between contradictory plans, which would have enclosed him in a situation with no way out? The debate has become all the more entangled in that it is encumbered by all the passions raised by the Terror as much as by the character of Robespierre. But does this debate not reveal, on another score, the ambiguities and the contradictions inherent in the combination of political circumstances at that moment? Wouldn't Robespierre's political plan lend itself to multiple readings from the fact that it was itself troubled by these hidden ambiguities? This plan was not incoherent; on the contrary, it was because of its own political logic, but confronted with the many problems of the Thermidorean situation, that Robespierre was engulfed in ambiguity. Everything happened as if he were pursuing the same plan that had carried him all through the Revolution, but which he strangely muddled as soon as he had to reply to the unprecedented question: what was to be done about the Terror, about this system of revolutionary power which was the fruit of this very same plan? Beneath the words and acts of Robespierre can be perceived the idea-image of a *Terror purged of its degradation* and, consequently, a plan of action which meant *both* more and less terror.

Robespierre recognised himself in the pure and virtuous Republic, just as it was portrayed in the images that the Revolution gave of itself – like the images that the Festival of the Supreme Being offered to the people but also to Robespierre, the author and principal actor of this Festival. Consequently the pure and virtuous Republic must necessarily be confused with the person of Robespierre, at the same time as he became fully identified with its noble cause. Robespierre's plan implied, in some way, that the Revolution remained the Revolution and that Robespierre remained Robespierre, the two making but one in the exercise of revolutionary power. But to remain pure and virtuous, faithful to its own image of itself, the Republic had of necessity to purify itself, to get rid of the 'impure', of traitors, intriguers, careerists, vile profiteers, elements unworthy of the Republic, not to say its worst enemies, hidden and dissembling. The Revolution therefore progressed, of necessity, by exclusion. This was its majestic way forward and Robespierre had made it his own. It guided his political programme in the face of his successive adversaries. Their faces were, to be sure, multifarious, but these were so many masks with which the enemy, like an actor, covered his face, but who remained in the end always the same. Robespierre applied this political vision, which had been shown to be politically effective all through his political career – and its result was the Terror – to the Terror itself, as he assessed it in the weeks preceding Thermidor. Now the Terror, to take up his last words at the Convention – he, Robespierre, who was 'made to combat crime, not to supervise it' – he found it soiled: not by the blood of his victims but by the degradation of those charged with setting it to work and, therefore, with watching over its purity. Robespierre was a man who was desk-bound. He had never seen the guillotine function. He had never gone *en mission*, there where the enflamed words of the terrorist became action, where the Terror was inseparable from the exercise of an unlimited power, where it became engulfed in local intrigues and conflicts, where it engendered corruption. In the political experience of Robespierre, the Terror consisted of speeches to the Jacobins and the Convention; of decisions to be taken at the Committee of Public Safety, on paper, even though this paper carried lists of prisoners to be brought before the revolutionary tribunal or the appointment of judges for this tribunal. Now, since the winter of Year II, the reports which flowed towards Robespierre – all denunciations – proved that the Terror hardly conformed to the representations which justified it (in fact he obtained these reports by sending out special emissaries, such as the young Julien). In Lyon and Marseille, in Bordeaux and Nantes, the Terror was 'soiled' by arbitrary actions, by thieves who profited from the occasion to enrich themselves, by 'orgies', by the settling of scores. Was it not the same at the Committee of General Security and the Committee of Public Safety, torn apart by personal ambition and intrigue?

It was a Terror, then, debased by its own personnel, betrayed, so to speak, by the terrorists. Bound to his desk, Robespierre was also a man of ideology. Personal animosities were comprehensible to him only through an ideological screen. In relation to the 'rogues' and 'assassins', men like Tallien, Fréron, Fouché, Vadier (where this list would stop, we shall never know), the Plain gained in purity. These people were at least honest, they had never become involved in anything shameful. The scheme of Robespierre seemed therefore to comprise both *less* of the Terror and *more* of the Terror. Less of the impure, arbitrary Terror, as exercised by the 'rogues'; more of the Terror, for the purging could be carried out only by terrorist means, by once more amputating the Convention which was supposed to surrender the guilty in its ranks. More of the Terror, for it was never 'pure' and could become so only in speeches and on paper. It could purge itself only by attacking its own personnel from whom it was nevertheless inseparable, by attacking those terrorists which it had itself created.

We shall always remain ignorant of what would have become of the Terror 'purified' according to Robespierre. Those at whom his discourse was aimed could not wait, nor follow his tortuous proceedings, nor uncover his ambiguities. For them, his message gained in blinding and menacing clarity what it lost in rhetorical subtlety: the 'less' and the 'more' of the Terror did not cancel each other out; they added to each other. The stakes strangely decreased: it was neither Virtue nor the Revolution, but simply, their own skins. To be sure, Couthon took it upon himself to make clear to the Jacobins that it was only a matter of purifying the Convention of a few scoundrels. But that implied *how many?* and, especially, *who?* The allusive language of Virtue was that of suspicion. It therefore rounded on its own master and picked him out from now on as the master of suspicion. Instead of gathering people around him, he opened a breach to a gathering against him of all those – Fouché, Tallien, Vadier, Collot – who *thought themselves* aimed at by this language. In the face of immaculate Virtue, there were, in fact, very few among the members of the Convention who were involved in the real Terror, and who could consider themselves above all suspicion. From the start, the plotters were to exploit the climate of suspicion all the more adroitly, precisely because they were *terrorists*. Not only in the political and moral senses of the word, but also in the *technical* sense which we have already mentioned. They knew this 'profession' well; they had gained experience of the Terror, its methods and workings. They had wielded its language themselves, could use it skilfully and decipher it. The 'purified' Terror was purely an untarnished guillotine, that is, a little more carefully cleaned and oiled. Whatever the vocabulary of the language of the Terror – whether it denounced the federalists, the factions or the knaves – it could not become new again for it always turned into a mixture and its result was always the same. Virtue therefore only added another term, singularly cutting and pointed. From being architects of the Terror, these terrorists saw themselves transformed into its victims. All their technical skill, acquired during the Terror and underpinned by a very real fear, was required to form a coalition and consolidate it around a single objective, *to defeat the tyrant.* Just like Robespierre, they discovered 'pure' people in the Plain, victims of a tyranny with whom they felt solidarity, although only the day before they were scorning them. The mysterious lists for proscription of the deputies, put into circulation, aimed a double blow: they made fast the links of solidarity with the Montagnards who discovered their names there; the large number of the proscribed, proposed by these lists, transformed what could have appeared as a settling of scores between the 'terrorists' into an affair affecting the Assembly as a whole. Amputated again, denouncing once more its own members, was not the Assembly surrendering itself to the mercy of a man who would thus establish himself as its absolute master? *Defeat the tyrant!* It was both a slogan and a precise objective which permitted taking the quickest and most effective means, while glossing over all the potential differences between those who did not know that they would soon be the 'Thermidoreans'. It was also a means of avoiding the *central political problem, that of how to end the Terror*, of leaving it unexpressed, and implicit in the unanimous clamour of the Convention as it proclaimed, in the course of its morning session of 9 Thermidor, the arrest of Robespierre and his acolytes. The sequence of events, and especially the improvised insurrection of the Commune, which had hardly any place in Robespierre's plan, shifted the stakes of this *journée* and so clarified them. In fact, the sequence of events demanded a choice between two forms of legitimacy: one which appealed to the 'risen people' to direct sovereignty, and one where the Convention embodied the representative system.[24] But even when clarified, the terms of this choice made victory no more likely. The issue of the struggle seemed to be, at this crucial moment, particularly uncertain. Technical skill, both in politics and policing, then came quickly to aid the victory. To make the choice easier for the good people, to explain to them where their true cause lay, to convince them not to 'rise', to simplify for them all this complicated affair of a 'tyrant' who, nevertheless, embodied, only yesterday, the Revolution and Virtue, a plot was invented, a rumour was started, fake evidence was hidden and then discovered. Whoever the direct authors of this diversion were, it was, as we have shown, the product of a collective political experience, and it summed up perfectly terrorist imagination and practice. Fear and panic added a touch of spontaneity to the cynicism of the manoeuvre.

Parrying the immediate danger, the tale of Robespierre-the-king gave meaning to the event only for a day. It provided no help at all with the central political problem of the Terror, and muddled it even more. On the day after the victory, with the execution of the outlawed deputies and members of the Commune, with the reform of the revolutionary Tribunal and the first release of 'suspects', matters progressively accelerated. The meaning of 9 Thermidor, this revolution carried out by the Convention and not by the people, to adopt Barère's formula, was therefore to go beyond the simple overthrow of a tyrant. In fact, does not the tale of Robespierre-the-king already hide more than is revealed by its immediate use? If one separates the terms which it brings together – the Terror and the king – it seems a crude sketch for the way out of the Terror that republican power would copy after 9 Thermidor. A narrow and perilous way, defined negatively: neither Robespierre, nor king, neither Terror, nor monarchy. But this, on the contrary, would not prevent Thermidorean power from again having recourse to this combination to combat its enemies. Taught as it was by experience, it would do so with much less panic and much more cynicism.

[24] F. Furet, *Penser la Révolution*, p. 84.

# 2    The end of Year II

On 24 Fructidor, Year II, forty-five days after 9 Thermidor and ten days before the end of Year II, during a stormy debate in which the divisions tearing the Convention apart were let loose, Merlin (from Thionville), having attacked the 'terrorists', those 'knights of the guillotine', formulated three essential problems for the Republic, problems to which the Convention should give unequivocal replies: *Where have we come from? Where are we? Where are we going?* These questions were of capital importance; at a deep level they ran through the entire political debate. The Committee of Public Safety took these questions up on its own account and gave its own response. On a symbolic date, the day of the fourth *sans-culottide*,[1] which closed Year II, Robert Lindet, in a long speech, presented, in the name of the Committee, a sort of report on the state of the nation. This report, accepted by the Convention, was not, however, to put an end to its divisions; Lindet's replies, supposed to constitute the 'rallying point' and to restore lost unity, turned out to be provisional; they would be very swiftly challenged and overtaken.

The dramatisation of these questions plainly marks the feeling of being at a turning point, where the past, the present and the future can no longer be clearly distinguished, as if the period of Revolution had lost that magnificent transparency, glorified throughout Year II. At the end of this year, even the past had become opaque. The Committee of Public Safety was expected to give a twin evaluation of the route taken since the 'revolution of 9 Thermidor' and also of the more distant past of 'the terror' and the 'tyranny' from which this 'happy revolution' had delivered the Republic. As for the present, this was even more confused. The questions put by Merlin revealed that 9 Thermidor constituted a point of no return, but that the problem of ending the Terror was far from settled. On 10 Thermidor, the Convention triumphantly announced the victory of its 'revolution'; with the fall of the 'tyrant' and his acolytes the Republic had been saved and

---

[1] *sans-culottide*. Since each of the twelve months of the revolutionary calendar lasted thirty days, five more days (six in a leap year) were required to make up the difference. These were named in honour of the *sans-culottes* and were observed as national festivals and holidays.

its oppression ended. At the end of Year II the established fact was clear: *ending the Terror* was not an *act* but a *process*, tense and with an uncertain issue. The Terror was not brought to an end by the fall of Robespierre; it was a road to be discovered and travelled.

The experience was unprecedented. It is well known that the political history of the Revolution possesses this particular interest of offering, within a relatively short period of time, the experiences of several regimes and political situations: a constitutional monarchy, the Terror, a republic founded on a representative and property-owning system, a dictatorship by plebiscite, etc.[2] It is the same for *the emergence from the Terror*, a particularly complex experience. Begun on 9 Thermidor, this experience had to be worked out within a framework – political and symbolic, institutional and social – that was born of the Terror and modelled by it. Also, a number of questions inevitably had to be faced. What was to be done with the heritage bequeathed by the period of the Terror? What should be kept, and according to what criteria, of this political heritage, which emerged from the Terror as well as from the Republic, and even from the Revolution? What was to be done with the many consequences of the Terror, beginning with the gaols which overflowed with 'suspects' awaiting trial? How to dismantle both the institutions and the political and adminis- trative personnel, who were products of the Terror, trained to serve it and ensure its functioning? How to define the political arena that would follow the Terror? These were complex questions since ending the Terror had been accomplished by a political power and by people who had been agents of the Terror, who had actively and vigorously put it in place. The 'revolution of 9 Thermidor' had therefore to be thought of at one and the same time as a *break* in the history of the Revolution and as the pledge of its *continuity*. Beyond the Terror, the Revolution would thus affirm its allegiance to itself and its founding principles. The connection between the break and the continuity was not to be placed only in the political and collective field; it was also lived in tension individually by each person.

To insist on the unprecedented and complex character of this particularly political experience is all the more necessary in that the details and originality of the Thermidorean period are too often neglected by historio- graphy. There is a 'Jacobin' tradition of revolutionary historiography according to which the heroic period of the Revolution, symbolised by Year II, the year of the *sans-culottes*, of the Jacobins, of the Mountain, of the pure and hard revolutionary *élan*, is on 9 Thermidor irremediably broken. Afterwards, everything else would be 'reaction' and, to put it briefly, the

---

[2]  Cf. F. Furet, *Marx et la Révolution française*, Paris, 1986, pp. 86 *et seq.*

vain and heroic combat of the last *sans-culottes* and the last Montagnards, defending the stirring heritage of Year II against the 'reactionaries'. As if the 'last Montagnards' and the 'last Jacobins' were not themselves 'Thermidoreans': not only did they approve of and praise the benefits of the 'revolution of 9 Thermidor', but they also took part, after their fashion, in the experience, along with the other 'reactionaries', of *emerging from the terror*.

For Year II, in the symbolic sense of the word, does not come to an end, in the manner of an ancient tragedy, on 10 Thermidor, in the Place de la Révolution, when the blade of the guillotine cut off the head of the Incorruptible. The social imagery engendered by Year II, and which gave it its symbolic sense, would experience a less heroic and theatrical end. Much more prosaically, the novel political experience of emerging from the Terror entailed the quite swift disintegration of this imagery. To obliterate this experience, its originality and complexity, was to conceal the political, social and moral consequences of the Terror and, as a repercussion, to enclose it in a heroic legend which could only justify it *a posteriori*. To obliterate the details of this experience is also to run the risk of another anachronism: reduced to a 'reaction', the Thermidorean period, if not the entire period of the Directory, becomes in some way simply a transition from 9 Thermidor to 18 Brumaire. Can the heroic legend of the Terror find a worthy end only in another collection of legends, that of Napoleon? For nothing is more false historically. To understand the problems raised in the Thermidorean period is to throw light on the relatively open character of the experience which began on 9 Thermidor of Year II. No logic of history has ever intended that 18 Brumaire was monstrously prompted by the fall of Robespierre. To consider the Thermidorean period is first of all to wonder about the political *problems* these political actors had to define and resolve; and it is to examine, next, the political conflicts and machinery through which was chosen, very empirically, some way of ending the Terror.

Only *fifty-six days* separate the fifth *sans-culottide* which closed Year II from 9 Thermidor of the same year. A very short period but one which was especially crowded, rich in new political events and phenomena. A political change was already under way but the die was far from being cast. The political actors occupied a largely open space. We have chosen the end of Year II precisely in order to conclude the chronology and to attempt an analysis of the road covered since 9 Thermidor. This choice is certainly arbitrary. The date is symbolic: Year II, according to the revolutionary calendar and not revolutionary legend, came to a painful end at the moment when the political actors themselves felt the need to reply to the questions:

*where are we coming from? where are we? where are we going?* It is therefore a suitable date for the historian to take up these same questions, concentrating particularly on the concepts and values, on the representations and symbols, in the field of experience and on the horizon of expectations, of a people, of its representatives, of the historic shock it received.

### 'Where are we coming from?'

On 9 Thermidor, the revolution brought about by the Convention was contested by no one. No one defended Robespierre, or the triumvirs, nor had any doubts about their crimes and their treacherous schemes. In this sense, all the popular societies, all the constituted authorities, all the armies, in a word, all of France awoke on 10 Thermidor anti-Robespierrist, even 'Thermidorean'. This unanimity has struck historians. Michelet refers to the days after 9 Thermidor as so many days of general joy and relief; this description of rediscovered unanimity seems to recapitulate the account of the *fête de la Fédération* of 1790, itself a symbol of unity and revolutionary hope.[3] But examined more closely, this admirable unanimity, which took over on the day after 9 Thermidor, is seen to be quite disturbing: it has difficulty in hiding an extremely complicated reality.

The unanimous approval of 9 Thermidor is expressed nowhere better than in more than seven hundred formal addresses of congratulations which, after the 'fall of the tyrant', flowed into the Convention from the entire country, from the constituted authorities, from the popular societies, from the armies. (During the sessions of the Assembly only a portion of these addresses were read; often they were merely summarised, by receiving an 'honourable mention', in the *Bulletin*.)[4] These texts were carefully calligraphed, most of the time on the good quality paper reserved for special occasions; reading them is particularly instructive, despite the monotony of their grandiloquence – or rather, *just because* of this monotony.

Take, by way of example, the address of the popular society of Granville-la-Victoire sent to the Convention on 15 Thermidor (the text was read at the bar of the Convention on the 22nd and received an honourable mention):

A new Cromwell desires to raise himself upon the debris of the national Convention; active vigilance sees through his schemes; prudence disconcerts them; a firmness worthy of the first Romans has the audacious conspirator arrested with his

[3] Cf. J. Michelet, *Histoire du dix-neuvième siècle*, in *Œuvres complètes*, edited by P. Viallaneix, vol. 21, Paris, 1982, pp. 80 *et seq.*; cf. also R. Levasseur, *Mémoires*, vol. 2, Paris, 1829, pp. 3–5.

[4] Archives Nationales (AN) C 314, C 325, C 316. Gabriel Monod was the first to draw attention to the interest of this series of documents. Cf. G. Monod, 'Adresses envoyées à la Convention après le 9 thermidor', *Revue historique*, 1887, vol. 33, p. 121.

cowardly accomplices; their heads, destined for infamy, fall ingloriously under the avenging sword of the law which strikes without remission all offenders; the Republic is saved. Thanks be to Thee, Supreme Being who watches over the destinies of France; and you, virtuous representatives of a sovereign and free people, whatever your difficult labours, may love of the *patrie* keep you at your posts where trust has placed you and which you fill so worthily.

These are the wishes of the popular Society of Granville, which also swears an oath of living free or dying, of combatting all tyrants and of denouncing all traitors. Long live the Republic! Long live the Convention!

The reconstituted popular society of *sans-culottes* of the commune of Montpellier sent its address on 16 Thermidor; it was to be presented to the Convention on the 26th:

Citizen-representatives! Ever since the people elected you and entrusted you with the sublime mandate that you have been able to fulfil, you have advanced steadily to the conquest of liberty and equality. You have shown yourselves to be great and worthy of the people in all the important events which have put the *patrie* in danger. But there have never been circumstances like these, about which we come to express our feelings; a new Catiline, an insolent dominator of the people and its representatives, having for a long time misled public opinion, which was deceived by his artful seductions, finally dared to cast aside the mask and give you the choice between submission to his will and death. You did not hesitate. Surrounded by the satellites of the tyrant you pronounced his condemnation, and when you were threatened by the personal dangers gathering over your heads, you responded with this sublime saying, this expression of unanimous devotion: we shall all die here for liberty. Thanks be to you!

The agricultural and revolutionary society made up of the *sans-culottes* of the twenty-two communes of the canton of Aurillac reported its emotions during the session of 17 Thermidor like this:

The great news brought yesterday by the mail gave rise to an extraordinary meeting. A member read it out; at the account of the despicable conspiracy of Robespierre, all members of the society were seized with horror and indignation; but then what joy, what consoling calm took hold of all our souls, when the news followed that the traitors had already suffered the fate that their crimes deserved; what admiration for the virtuous people of Paris, for the forty-eight *sections* who were able to resist the despicable seductions of these scoundrels.

The popular society of Inzières experienced similar feelings:

At the news that we received of the treacherous plots which the infamous Robespierre and his accomplices planned in order to establish his illusory reign, we shuddered with horror. But immediately, learning of the firmness and wisdom that the Convention employed and deployed at this moment so dangerous for itself and the state, we cried out: Long live the Republic and may all her enemies perish for ever! May their infamous memory be doomed to universal execration from all peoples of the earth!

To finish, let us quote the address of the popular society of Montauban which inclined towards the Jacobins (the address was read at the Society of Jacobins on 26 Thermidor):

Behold then Robespierre, this tiger corrupted by the taste of blood, above all by the blood which circulates for liberty, *Behold him vanished in the twinkling of an eye* from the place where the scoundrel came to gorge himself. He has vanished to bear his head under the avenging sword of the Republic. Republicans will no longer suffer the bitterness of hearing his machiavellian accents point out everywhere, in the most innocent groups of men, conspirators, intriguers, traitors. Ah! Thanks be unto those who did in fact conspire and intrigue against him and his guilty conspirators. They did not betray the Republic, those who had hatched the plot which unmasked and destroyed him; they ... have raised public recognition to its highest pitch.

Nearly all the addresses use the same clichés, combine the same rhetorical elements; they resemble each other so closely that they give the impression of being inspired by a common model. They outdo each other in the denunciation of Robespierre. 'New Catiline', 'modern Cromwell': these epithets keep returning throughout the hundreds of pages. At times, others are added: 'monster vomited up by the crime that desired a throne to dominate the Republic and put the French in irons' (popular society of Charolles); 'a monster, a double-dealer, hidden protector of the Republic's enemies' (municipality of Grave-Libre); 'the hypocrite, the infamous, the crafty' (popular society of Segonzac); 'offspring of the hermaphrodite race of new Cromwells' (*section* of the Panthéon); 'a monster unparalleled in the high points of history' (3rd battalion of the Nièvre); 'reckless pygmy' (the *sans-culottes* of Ernée, *département* of Mayence). One also finds, in fact quite sporadically, the echo of the rumour of Robespierre-the-king ('Robespierre, this scoundrel ... who had formed the appalling plan of re-establishing royalty in France in order to take possession of the throne', protested the popular society of Anse).

The addresses also outdo each other in glorification of the Convention and its admirable courage, worthy of the ancient Romans, in the face of the terrible dangers that threaten it: 'Citizen-representives! We end by admiring your energy, this courage, this masculine boldness which distinguish you among the most pressing dangers. Ever firm at your post, continue to brave the dagger of the seditious, the traitors, the ambitious' (popular society of Pont-sur-Rhône). 'Remain at your post! May the universe that gazes upon you learn that the French people owes you both its salvation and its happiness' (the popular society, the constituted authorities, and all the people of Charli-sur-Marne). 'To the National Convention sitting on top of the holy Mountain, glorious Mountain, divine Mountain, holy and sublime Mountain, keep watching over the liberty of the people and hurl avenging thunderbolts against its enemies, receive our congratulations and our enthusiasm. Yet once more your energy, your courage, your wisdom and your firmness have saved the *patrie'* (society of the defenders of the republican Constitution, Vic-la-Montagne).

Not a single doubt, not a single reservation appears to trouble the enthusiasm with which these addresses overflow and below which figure sometimes hundreds of signatures.

However, these congratulations from the provinces, especially from little communes, reached the Convention en masse between 16 and 20 Thermidor and kept flowing in throughout the month of Fructidor. This time-lag was not due to political hesitations; we have noted that several addresses stress that their sending was decided 'on the spur of the moment', as soon as the news from Paris arrived. But the news travelled slowly, at best at the speed of a horse; it was still necessary to call the meeting, agree on the text, have it written down and sent to Paris. The slow pace of communication also explains the fact that in the files where the secretaries of the Convention arranged the correspondence, one finds, between two addresses congratulating the 'fathers of the *patrie'* for having defeated 'the monster, the despicable tyrant', other congratulations:

Remain at your post, unyielding Montagnards! All your decrees, bearing the stamp of Justice, announce to the astonished universe that all the virtues which are the order of the day preside over your government. The hearts of the citizens feel themselves attacked by the blow struck at Collot d'Herbois, by the ventures of the *assassins employed by Pitt against the sacred person of Robespierre.* (popular society of Caudecoste, district of Valence).

If the society of Sollès [*département* of the Var] has not let you hear its voice again, or rather if it has not offered you the just tribute of homage that you more and more deserve, this is because, filled with horror and indignation at the assassination aimed at two of your number, Collot d'Herbois and Robespierre, it has lost its power of speech. Today, now that the sword of the law has fallen upon the heads of the assassins, now that Collot d'Herbois and Robespierre are revenged and these infamous parricides can no longer make us fear for our lives, our voice is more eager than ever to congratulate you on your unshakeable firmness.

These addresses, which arrived towards the end of Thermidor, had been carefully filed, but they were not presented to the Convention in order that it might grant them an honourable mention ... The assassination of the 'sacred person of Robespierre' to which they refer is not, of course, 10 Thermidor, but the confused story of Cécile Renault, a young girl of twenty, who was found carrying a small knife as she tried to approach Robespierre. Accused of having intended to make an attempt on his life, she was condemned to death and led to the scaffold, on 29 Prairial, dressed in the red shirt of parricides. The addresses, expressions of unanimous indignation and enthusiasm, reached Paris after too long a delay; but the clichés employed were largely reusable for condemnation of the 'new Catiline'.

The repeated use of the same epithets – 'new Catiline', 'new Cromwell' – in the hundreds of addresses does not cease to amaze. The addresses, as we have seen, often bear hundreds of signatures. Many of these are written awkwardly and with difficulty by hands which are not used to holding a pen; one finds, at times, crosses instead of signatures and to some addresses are joined long lists of citizens who 'being unlettered have asked that the secretaries sign for them' (popular society of Orange, 18 Thermidor). The presence of these illiterate or semi-illiterate people at meetings of popular societies shows, to be sure, the access of new social classes to politics during the Revolution, and especially in Year II. But were they so well-versed in ancient history, did they all know who the 'old Catiline' was? Had the 'black legend' of Cromwell really experienced such a wide circulation that his name came spontaneously to the mind of illiterates for the purpose of condemning the 'new tyrant' defeated in Paris? And what are we to think of these adolescents of fifteen years of age from the company of Young Republicans of the commune of Angoulême who, so spontaneously, expressed their emotions in these terms: 'How the Mountain was great in these terrifying moments! Yes, the universe shall learn that it is above all conspiracies! Fathers of the *Patrie*, you are immortalised, you have deserved well of the human race! Remain in your place until all the scoundrels, all the tyrants, the Catilines, the Cromwells, the dictators, the triumvirs, are destroyed?'

These addresses reveal more than the spontaneous feelings of their compilers and signatories. Their very language points to the *conditions that make possible* the expression of the lofty unanimity they advertise. The clichés and stereotypes suggest a common model followed by all these addresses. This model is, moreover, quite easy to find; it is, as a matter of fact, the appeals of the Convention as well as the reports of its sessions which transmit these clichés and evidently constitute the primary source of inspiration. *The addresses speak the 'wooden language' of Year II*, the same, with a few more epithets, which had been employed to celebrate the preservation of the integrity of the 'sacred person of Robespierre'. Whatever the amount of real relief at the announcement of the 'fall of the tyrant', the addresses testify to the uniformity of language brought about by the Terror, to the unanimity commanded from above, to the conformism and opportunism acquired and internalised as political behaviour during the Terror. Those who drafted and signed these addresses were the same people who had already condemned federalism, the 'foul conspiracies' of Danton or the 'base Hébert'. (Moreover, some of the addresses draw the parallel between this 'new conspiracy' and the other older ones . . .) They had learnt well that faced with 'conspiracies' unmasked in Paris it was very risky to express any doubts; to take sides with the victors was the most elementary prudence. The monopoly of information and the stranglehold of central power over public opinion left it only one area of expression, that of increasingly extravagant rhetoric, of praise and blame.

It is, moreover, striking that the addresses presented the 'terrifying conspiracy' as a distant affair which had been acted out in Paris. After the execution of the 'triumvirs' the danger was over; the unanimous people gathered round the Convention, its 'rallying point'; the Revolution had gained a victory, the greatest (it is always the last victory which is the greatest, and the last conspiracy which is the most 'horrible'); the 'fathers of the Nation' remained in place. The people of Paris had once again been worthy of their country. The addresses passed over in silence the hesitations of the Parisian *sections*, which were, however, mentioned by Barère in his report. There were very few addresses which took the risk of stepping out of the limits outlined by the messages of the Convention and, more particularly, of denouncing Robespierre's local accomplices. Even, in this case, it was only a question of members of the Convention already 'unmasked', like Lebon at Arras, or Couthon at Clermont-Ferrand. Only once, in the Commune-Affranchie (formerly Lyon), did the popular society join to its address (bearing some 700 signatures) which recorded satisfaction at the dissipation of the 'new liberticide storm', an extract from the minutes of its meeting expressing a certain anxiety: 'What is important to avoid, is that the aristocracy should profit from our divisions. Today already [14 Thermidor] a number of strange figures were walking about our streets and their looks were sinister . . . That is true! cried the whole Assembly.'

Quite involuntarily, these addresses of allegiance pay homage, via the clichés, to Robespierre. In fact, they sometimes evoke the enormous prestige which he enjoyed. But, of course, they express indignation against this 'hypocrite' who has succeeded with incredible skilfulness to wear the mask of the virtuous and incorruptible patriot, and, consequently, to deceive the people who trusted in him. 'Our love for these men, whom we regarded as the firm pillars of the Republic, is changed into deep horror at the news of their conspiracy a thousand and thousand times too bold' (popular society of Guéret, *département* of the Creuse, 14 Thermidor). 'A short time ago all republicans would have shed torrents of tears on the tomb of a man who is today recognised as more criminal than the Cromwells, the Catilines, the Neros, and who has surpassed by his crimes, discovered in an instant, all the monsters whom nature had brought forth for the misfortune of nations' (citizens of Traignac-la-Montagne, *département* of the Corrèze).

What, on the day after 9 Thermidor, had become of the 'terrorists', the fervent supporters of Robespierre? There is no reason to think they fell silent; their voices merged with others in the uproar of popular societies and local administration, of political activists who convened the meetings, drew up the addresses, etc. To be indignant at their opportunism would be too easy (moreover, a short while after the sending of these addresses there would be no shortage of denunciations on the spot, in their own communes). This opportunism and this uniformity of behaviour and language are also one of the faces of the Terror. The addresses of congratulations sent to the Convention show up a characteristic of the period which opened on 9 Thermidor, and which we have already mentioned: the ending of the Terror begins with a language, with political behaviour and social imaginations moulded during the Terror and bequeathed by it. The disintegration of this controlled unanimity, the laying bare of the conflicts and hatred accumulated during the Terror but which had remained stifled by it, this was a condition for ending the Terror as well as its inevitable result.

At the end of Year II, no one questioned the benefits of the 'fall of the tyrant' and the merits of the 'revolution of 9 Thermidor'; as we have noticed, this *journée* constituted a common reference, it was recognised as a point of no return. Even those who began to criticise the turn taken by events, in particular the 'persecution of the patriots', did so *in the name of 9 Thermidor* and *against the 'tyranny of Robespierre'*. How could it be otherwise? To defend Robespierre would be not only political suicide but suicide pure and simple, a counter-revolutionary crime. Against such an exemplary background of unanimity, one question spreads division: *then how did it happen?*, to adopt the formula of Edme Petit in his speech at the Convention, on 29 Fructidor. The debate then provoked is above all political: the development of society and, especially, of revolutionary power, is the main issue; but the debate also involves the passions: how was it possible to establish responsibility for the actions of the Terror without fostering feelings of revenge towards the agents of the Terror? This was, despite all the *ad hoc* and *ad hominem* arguments, which slid swiftly towards the settling of scores, the first great historical debate on the Terror. Many arguments formulated in the course of this debate would, especially in the nineteenth century, be taken up by historians, more solidly supported, and also more weightily developed. The arguments exchanged were often mixed with testimony from those who had been the architects of the Terror as well as from those who were its victims. With the help of the spirit of the Enlightenment and revolutionary rhetoric, the political arguments coined for the occasion were burdened with 'philosophical' reflections, with attempts at analysis in the form of interminable speeches, which the

Convention specialised in. This debate was not limited to the Convention; it overflowed into the press, which thereby gained in freedom, and was taken up on a national scale; which commune had not had its 'terrorists' and political and personal scores to settle with them? The Convention, 'rallying point and centre of Enlightenment', quite naturally remaining the crucial setting for the struggle for power, is where speeches on the Terror were most numerous. In studying them there soon appear, as regards the *why* and the *how* of the Terror, a number of alternatives:

- the Terror was Robespierre's work and Robespierre's fault; the origins of the tyranny were to be found in the monstrous character of the tyrant himself;
- the Terror was only an accident along the way in the glorious progress of the Revolution in its struggle against its enemies;
- the Terror formed a specific system of power whose machinery and origins awaited revelation.

These responses can be classed into two groups: those which *relativise* the Terror in relation to the *circumstances* and, thereby, *depersonalise* responsibilities; and those which see in it only a monstrous crime, and seek to establish personal responsibility for unpardonable criminal acts, whatever their motivations.

This 'typology' cannot, however, be applied systematically. The debate is, in fact, far from academic; the issues are power, revenge, and, quite simply, the *lives* of those who are denounced as 'terrorists'. The responses which we have picked do not really exclude each other, but overlap and combine. No position is fixed, everything is still in movement, feeling its way: *the political experience is unprecedented and the political combination of circumstances unstable.*

### 'Robespierre's fault'

First, it will be appropriate to draw up a catalogue of the insults with which the addresses of congratulations to the Convention overflow: 'new Catiline', 'new Cromwell', 'new Nero', 'vile monster', 'wretched scoundrel', etc. – just so many clichés that are part of Thermidorean political language; so to mention the 'last tyrant' can mean only Robespierre. Let us not, however, underestimate the importance of these insults, for their very violence betrays the political climate of the epoch. The use of these clichés is a sort of ritual, one might even say a sort of collective exorcism. The 'new Catiline', the 'monster', the 'hypocrite' are all epithets which, in their way, unravel this enigmatic figure and explain his actions and criminal influence as a sort of historical and moral calamity. Robespierre appeared as a figure at one and the same time well-known and extraordinary, and 9 Thermidor is therefore presented as an unveiling and a deliverance. With Robespierre dead, countless addresses repeat, the Republic is saved.[5]

That said, the image of Robespierre is fascinating and disturbing. One text, *Portrait of Robespierre*, enjoyed enormous success: published as a booklet, it was reprinted by several newspapers. The physical portrait:

His height was five feet two or three inches; his body upright; his gait, firm, energetic and a little brusque; he often clenched his fists as if by a sort of contraction of the nerves; the same movement made itself felt in his shoulders and neck, which he agitated convulsively to right and left; his clothes were elegantly neat and his hair always carefully brushed ... his complexion was livid and bilious, his eyes cheerless and dull; frequent blinking seemed the result of the convulsive fidgeting which I have just mentioned.

The moral and intellectual portrait:

Despite all those grand words like *virtue and patrie*, he thought only of himself. Pride was the basis of his character, literary glory one of his vices; but he coveted political glory more ... Both impudent and cowardly, he concealed his manoeuvres behind a thick veil and often he pointed out his victims with effrontery ... Weak and vindictive, chaste by temperament, and a libertine in imagination, the glances of women were not the least attraction of his supreme power; he liked to attract them; there was coquetry in his ambition ... he particularly worked his enchantment on tender imaginations ... He had calculated the enchantment of his oratory and, up to a certain point, he possessed a talent for it; he stood out well on the rostrum; antithesis dominated his speeches, and he often employed irony; his style was not sustained; his delivery, sometimes harmonious and modulated, sometimes harsh and glittering, often trivial, was always tacked together with commonplaces and digressions on *virtue, crime, conspirators* ... His logic was always quite clear, and

---

[5] Let us, however, linger over the address from the Poissonière *section*, of 13 Thermidor, which takes the form of a scholarly dissertation:

Robespierre is compared to Cromwell. But Cromwell was very brave, a great general, a deep politician, he shed human blood only to strengthen his tyranny; he made the commerce and navigation of his nation prosper. Robespierre was on the contrary cowardly and craven, a talentless intriguer, ignorant in politics and administration. He spilt blood for the pleasure of shedding it. Time will make known to us his victims. Cromwell and he have only one point of resemblance: it is fanaticism and hypocrisy. Cromwell and his soldiers set out with Bibles on their saddle-bows; he quoted it unceasingly. Robespierre never stopped talking of religion, virtue, justice. His respect for the pretended mother of God and for Dom Gerle show his fondness for these mystics. Perhaps he coveted the honour of being leader of a sect in order to consolidate his despotism by religion. Robespierre had the satisfaction of being adored by his numerous disciples. Nothing equals their imbecile respect, their limitless devotion for their detestable master. Robespierre *has said so*: when they had uttered these words one had to be silent and subdue one's reason. To doubt was a crime deserving the final punishment. (AN C314; CII 12158)

Among the Jacobins the comparison of Robespierre with Cromwell or Catiline was also opposed as being too kind: 'Let this scoundrel no longer be compared to Catiline or to Cromwell, since, because of his cowardice, he does not deserve to be placed beside these two famous enemies of liberty' (speech of Mittié *fils*, session of 1 Fructidor, Year III: A. Aulard, *La Société des Jacobins*, Paris, 1897, vol. 6, p. 356).

often deft in its sophisms; but in general his mind was sterile and the range of his thinking narrow, as often happens with those who are too preoccupied with themselves.

Finally, the political portrait:

After pride the most marked trait of his character was shrewdness. He had around him only people who had serious matters on their conscience. With one word he could put them under the guillotine. He protected and caused to tremble a portion of the Convention. He transformed errors into crimes and crimes into errors ... Every time that he was attacked, it was liberty that was under attack ... he feared the very shadows of the martyrs; he weakened their influence, he would have had the dead themselves guillotined. To portray him with one stroke, Robespierre, born without genius, did not know how to create circumstances, but he could use them with skill. This was not enough for a tyrant, circumstances undid him, because they unmasked him ... and now see him one of the abhorred class of tyrants of humanity who have wished to oppress for a moment their fellow human beings, and whose memory has been consigned to the long execration of the centuries.[6]

All tyrants and all tyrannies basically resembled each other, as is shown by the parallel *between Capet and Robespierre*. The text took over, so to speak, the rumour about Robespierre-the-king, while abandoning elements of the tale (the fleur-de-lis seal, the projected marriage). Robespierre had established himself as a *virtual* king and tyrant (the insulting surname of *Maximilien the First* occurred quite often in the speeches at the Convention as well as in the press).

In 1789, there was in France a king invested with power that was unbounded in reality, limited only in appearance, maintained by ancient prejudices and much more by the authority he possessed of disposing of all the money and of all the offices of state ... In Year II, there was also in France a man whose power was in reality absolute, limited only in appearance, maintained by a popularity acquired one doesn't know how and who acquired an artificial reputation for probity and capacity, like so many other princes. This man disposed of all the offices and all the money of the Republic. As a consequence he had the support of all those who wanted to have money without earning it, and offices without deserving them.

The 'tyrant of 1789' had his Bastilles, where he enclosed all those whose knowledge he feared:

The tyrant of Year II imprisoned all those who did not wish to obey him; he treated them as suspects; they were permitted neither to write nor speak ... Both men enveloped themselves in shadows. *State secret* was their motto, and public *security* the banal pretext for all their crimes, for all their assassinations ... Both men

---

[6] *Portrait exécrable du traître Robespierre*, Paris, n.d. (1794), Bibliothèque Nationale (BN) Lb⁴¹ 3976, attributed to J.-J. Dussault. Several variations of this text can be found in the newspapers of the period. The pride, ambition and mediocrity of Robespierre would also explain his hatred for the humanities and for scholars and scientists.

brought down from the heavens the sanction of an authority which devastated the earth. One spoke of God and the life to come, the other of the *supreme god and the immortality of the soul* . . . It was forbidden to speak ill of the king in 1789, of his mistress, or the mistresses of his clerks. Anyone who doubted the divinity of the king of Year II, of his clerks or of Cornélie Copeau was punished by death.[7]

The accumulation of these accusations, slanders, insults and epithets allows us to gauge how much Robespierre was hated; it is also a sort of revenge taken on the months when the cult of Robespierre reigned, along with the glorification of his virtue and his talents. That said, to attribute to Robespierre responsibility for the Terror at the same time as presenting him as a mediocrity and an 'infamous scoundrel' was, at the very least, contradictory. The more that Robespierre was downgraded, the less the immediate past became decipherable; how to explain his popularity ('acquired one doesn't know how' said the very embarrassed Merlin) and his rise to unlimited power, if he was simply an ambitious man, devoid of any talent? And what then was to be said of all those who let themselves be subjugated by this mediocrity?

### 'A revolutionary storm'

For Lindet, to reply to the question of 'what we had been' in Year II, and so offer 'an explanation to the nation', was first and foremost a matter of demonstrating the grandiose work carried out by the Nation and the victories she had won. Year II was a heroic period, marked by the effort of all citizens and especially by the courage and sacrifices of the armies, a year when the Republic reached 'a degree of glory and power' such that no one, not even its worst enemies, could 'rob them of the trust and esteem of nations'. By the organisation of its armies, by the victories gained, the Republic had shown the whole of Europe not only that the French desired to be free, but that the Nation was powerful enough to defend its liberty against coalitions of tyrants. For the same reason, France had given the lie to the hypocritical and slanderous shouts of its enemies that it could not govern itself and was sinking into anarchy. 'You have won over the opinion of nations. They no longer ask if you have a government; they understand that to maintain the most numerous armies on earth, to cover the sea with ships, to fight and gain victory by land and by sea, to attract the commerce of the world, that is to know how to govern oneself.'

---

[7] *Capet et Robespierre*, Paris, n.d. (1794), BN Lb[41] 1155. Text signed by Merlin (from Thionville) but drafted, probably, by Roederer. 'Cornélie Copeau' was, obviously, the daughter of Duplay, the joiner who had been Robespierre's landlord. The parallel between Robespierre and Louis XVI was extended by the comparison of the former aristocrats with the 'aristocrats of Year II', the Robespierrists who defended both their 'positions' and the Terror.

The difficulties encountered and the errors committed were to be understood on the basis of this overall evaluation and in the context of these *circumstances*, that of a nation fighting for its liberty.

The representatives of the people should hand down to posterity not only their actions, their glory and success; they should also pass on their understanding of the dangers, misfortunes, and mistakes; in this way the first navigators marked the reefs they were able to avoid, and they taught their successors to navigate a safe route among the reefs that no art can make disappear, but which can without danger be approached or steered clear of, thanks to the teaching of experience.

The Terror was only one of these reefs, an accident along the way, as it were. To these circumstances, which required exceptional security measures and which fired people's passions, was added the activity of traitors and conspirators.

They attempted to divide the French, to inspire dejection, terror and despair, to weaken the feeling of recognition due to the defenders of the *patrie*, and to spread doubts about their victories; they took advantage of a great reputation for talent, energy and good citizenship . . . The measures of general security took on a forceful and severe character which brought fear to the souls of citizens and which deprived France of arms and resources; the traitors you have punished had changed its object and direction. You wished to strike at the enemies of the Revolution; they made use of your weapons and your measures to strike the weak and the useful; they spared neither the farmer nor the labourer; they could not destroy you nor make you hate, they wished to make you fear.

In the end, however, the 'revolution of 9 Thermidor' and its positive and encouraging consequences were more important than this terrorist episode. In the annals of the Revolution, 9 Thermidor would take its place in the glorious series of the *journées* of 14 July, 10 August and 31 May as well as of the military victories. The conspiracy of Robespierre was, perhaps, the most dangerous and the most treacherous, but its very treachery and the end which lay in store for it proved the successful progress made by the Nation and the Revolution. 'The *journée* of 9 Thermidor will teach posterity that in this period the French nation had gone through all the stages of the Revolution; that it had reached its end and no one could attempt to lead it astray except by the glamour of a great reputation and the appearance of good citizenship, of integrity and of virtue, which it had invoked as the order of the day.' It was enough therefore to 'tear the veil', to warn the people, although the Convention could not communicate with them freely, to give it an example of courage by striking the traitors, and it was all over for the conspirators. The conduct 'of the people, wise, great and sublime, has proved that it was impossible to lead it astray'. At the most a few citizens were seduced; the unmasked conspirators found themselves completely isolated and 'the entire people, devoted to principles and national representation, condemned Robespierre and his accomplices'. Therefore, this 'last event' was 'useful for liberty'.

One had to be able to distinguish what was right in the past and imposed by circumstances from errors, abuses and crimes. The Convention had set in train 'a surveillance plan', the carrying out of which required, in order to create the revolutionary committees, 'such a prodigious number of civil servants, that the whole of Europe could not furnish enough educated men to fill all these positions'. The project was fully justified; however, the 'enemies within' were so many that they infiltrated everywhere, in the administration and in the popular societies. For the same reason, each citizen had to regard himself 'as a sentry ordered to guard a post.' One must not, therefore, condemn en bloc the institutions which were taken advantage of, as was sometimes the case with the surveillance committees. Most of all, one must not dwell on the abuses and misfortunes which were already part of the past. To be sure, 'the Revolution has had its blemishes', but one must not exaggerate the errors committed, of which some were inevitable.

Let us not reproach ourselves, neither for our misfortunes nor our faults. Have we always been, could we have been what we would have, in fact, wanted to be? We had all been launched in the same career; some have fought with courage, with reflection; others threw themselves forward, bursting with eagerness, against all the obstacles they wanted to destroy and overturn ... Who would want to call us to account for those actions which are impossible to foresee and control? The revolution has taken place; it is the work of everyone. What generals, what soldiers have ever done in war what they should have done, and have been able to stop where cold and tranquil reason says they should have stopped? Were we not at war with the most formidable and numerous enemies? What reverses did not provoke our courage, fire our anger? What happened to us that does not happen to all men thrown an infinite distance out of the ordinary course of life? Was it not inevitable that some men should bring out the charms of equality; and that others should carry Terror and fear among our enemies?

In this way the Terror was simultaneously condemned and eclipsed; the evocation of its sad memories went hand in hand with an appeal to let them be forgotten. It did not form a true 'period' in the history of the Revolution nor a system of power. It was a *sequence*, disparate and discontinuous, of individual events, each of which should be examined separately to understand its origins, especially the circumstances which generated it. One would then distinguish the errors from the crimes, the exaggerated passions from the criminal intentions, and in this way all might be brought into proportion. But is such an examination necessary and useful for the Revolution? Does this not require that one should never look back? Lindet's text is full of metaphors which are all so many circumlocutions when he approaches particularly thorny subjects, the Terror and its agents.

The navigator surprised by the tempest is abandoned to his courage, to his knowledge, which danger makes more alert and more resourceful, if he is to save the vessel which is in his care. When he has arrived in port without shipwreck, no one asks him to justify his manoeuvres. No one examines whether he has followed instructions. When it is necessary to hurl the thunderbolt so often, can one claim to always hit the right target, and that some flashes will not deviate from the direction in which they were aimed?[8]

### 'A system of Terror'

The expression 'system of terror' had been used by Barère the day after the execution of Robespierre, but it was Tallien who would propose, a month later, in his speech of 11 Fructidor, to deal with the Terror precisely as a *system*. Again it is necessary to underline the ambiguity of this speech: Tallien launched into a philosophical and abstract analysis of the Terror, but no one at the Convention was fooled: all saw it only as a political manoeuvre. No one took Tallien seriously as a 'philosopher' (when he finished his speech, he was to receive an ironic reply on the spot: 'no doubt we must bless philosophy since studying it makes men better and just, but I note that he who, at this moment, declaims from this rostrum against the system of Terror, once spoke highly on this same rostrum of the usefulness of that system'.) Tallien, who had been one of the architects of 9 Thermidor, was, as a matter of fact, the very model of a corrupt representative *en mission*; at Bordeaux, surrounded by a whole court, he had not hesitated to send 'conspirators' to the guillotine nor, above all, to trade in the survival or release of 'suspects'. Recalled to Paris, he had sought to return to Robespierre's good graces, but without success: 'the Incorruptible' did not hide his contempt for the man who, in his eyes, had debased the Terror. After the fall of the 'tyrant' he became the very model of the 'weathervane', a *political turncoat*, that most characteristic figure of the Thermidorean political landscape. He was in the first rank of those who called for 'justice as the order of the day' from now on, as well as exemplary punishment for the 'terrorists'. His salon, where his mistress, Cabarrus, reigned (he had her liberated from prison after 9 Thermidor), was a place where political intrigues were hatched unceasingly. Although his speech of 11 Fructidor was perceived by his contemporaries as a political manoeuvre, dressed up in philosophical considerations, his reflections on the Terror deserve our attention; sometimes confused, they nevertheless provide a quite precious outline analysis and a remarkable testimony on the Terror. For Tallien was

[8] Robert Lindet, report presented, in the name of the Committee of Public Safety, on the fourth *sans-culottide*, Year II, in *Moniteur*, vol. 22, pp. 18–25.

well placed for understanding it: had he not been one of its architects before becoming one of its potential victims?

The Terror, according to Tallien, constituted a *system of power* – that 'system which Robespierre put into practice' – and not a succession of monstrous acts. To analyse this system was to understand its relationships with *revolutionary government*, with the *fear* that spread around it and on which it was based and, finally, with the *dynamics of the repression* that it produced.

The essential problem therefore was to determine 'what is revolutionary, without being tyrannical' and to 'determine clearly what is understood by *revolutionary government* ... And by revolutionary government, is understood a government *appropriate for completing the revolution or acting in the manner of the revolution.*' To confuse these two senses was to risk misrepresenting the Revolution itself. The Revolution 'is the movement of bringing to the top what was below'; in this way, the French Revolution had reconstituted the sovereignty of the people by overturning the monarchy. But this was, at the same time, to engage in an act of insurrection, an open war against tyranny, a struggle which had 'all the citizens for an army, and all the State for a battlefield'. Despite its violence, a 'revolutionary act' was not, however, arbitrary, for it was open warfare and the 'people could only act for liberty'. It was entirely different for a government installed to *complete* the revolution; it was not possible, under any circumstances, 'to continue to treat France as a battlefield'.

For a government to complete, securely and inevitably, the Revolution, it is first of all necessary that it cannot itself be a means of counter-revolution; a tyranny, even a passing one, cannot be included among the means of establishing liberty, since for it to be exercised with security and impunity for a year, a month, or a day, liberty needs to be, at least during this period, above all opposition ... The government that will be fit for completing and securing the Revolution will be one which can make the citizens love the Revolution, and make itself feared by those who betray it.

The government of the Terror was not content 'to watch over wrong actions, to threaten them, to punish them by proportionate punishments; it consists *in threatening individuals, in threatening them all the time and for everything, in threatening them with whatever the imagination can conceive as most cruel*'. The allusion was more than transparent; for Tallien the Terror did not begin with the law of 22 Prairial, already abolished, but with that of 17 September 1793, the law on suspects which still remained in force. So, the concept of *suspect* was the cornerstone of the Terror as system.

The Terror threatened and punished people for *what they were* and not for *what they had done*; for the same reason, by introducing the concept of 'suspect classes', it substituted *arbitrary power* for *justice*.

This system of Terror supposes the exercise of an arbitrary power in those who undertake to spread terror. It also supposes absolute power, and I mean by absolute power one that owes obedience or justification to no one, and which demands it of everyone else ... The system of Terror supposes the most concentrated power, the power that approaches closest to uniformity and tends inevitably to royalty.

France had been divided under this system into 'two classes: *one which caused fear and one which felt fear*, into persecutors and persecuted'. Contrary to the declarations of those in power, who formed an 'agency of the Terror', it was not deployed only against the 'suspect classes', for 'terror must be either everywhere, or nowhere'. It implied a fear that was general and pushed to extremes. It abolished the State of law.

When Tallien sketched a sort of phenomenology of the Terror and its political means in this way, he unquestionably drew upon his intense experience of one who had 'caused fear' and of one who had 'felt fear'. Terror 'degrades man and makes him like a beast; it is a shock to all his physical forces, a disturbance to all his moral faculties, a disturbance of all his ideas, an upsetting of all his feelings ... terror, being an extreme feeling, is capable of neither more nor less'. Now, a government could only spread Terror, could only 'make everyone tremble', by the threat of one punishment, capital punishment, 'only by threatening people with it ceaselessly, only by threatening everyone with it, only by threatening through acts of violence ever renewed and ever increasing; only by threatening for any kind of action, and even for inaction ... only by threatening with the always striking sight of absolute power and cruelty without rein'. The Terror, a system of generalised fear, provoked another, a system of suspicion and of informing: 'one had to place under every step a trap, in each house a spy, in each family a traitor, in the service of a tribunal of assassins'.

The system of the Terror in this way generated its own dynamic: it tended to perpetuate itself. To be sure, it had been presented as a passing authority, as a transitory measure, indispensable for ensuring the permanent triumph of the principles and values of the Revolution. However, the Terror, once established, had a tendency to assert itself not only as an arbitrary and absolute power, but also as a perpetual system. But how, in fact, could one wait for those who had employed it 'to return into the crowd, after having made so many enemies? How could they not fear revenge after committing so many crimes? How could they not take advantage of the Terror that was spread by tyranny to perpetuate that tyranny?' Thus, 'the agents of the Terror are reduced to trembling themselves'; in the end, no one escaped from fear. But even if one supposed that oppression and Terror were aimed only at protecting liberty, such power always produced perverted results; it depraved both those who employed it and those who suffered it. When this power reached the position of being able to give liberty back to the Nation, it could be that the Nation was in no state to receive it.

When it is in the name of liberty that Terror is spread, it does more than make people indifferent to liberty; it makes it hated; and it makes of this hatred not only an incurable illness but also an hereditary illness; and, under the name of prudence, fathers transmit cowardice and servitude to their children.[9]

Read out of context the speech of Tallien presents itself as the beginning of a reflection on the Terror as a *system of power*, of its political workings and its psychological principles. The speech is remarkable for its abstract character: not one reference to the precise events of the Revolution which would explain the coming of the Terror. The text, however, is strewn with allusions: the law on suspects is mentioned, without being explicitly named; there is talk of 'bloodthirsty men' without specifying them; the problem of personal responsibility for the facts and crimes of the Terror seems to be evaded. The touches of sentimentality (the Terror has debased 'relations between the sexes ... The art of making men tremble is an infallible means of corrupting and degrading women.') go hand in hand with positive suggestions that are quite vague (confirmation of the maintenance of revolutionary government until the peace, but condemnation of 'the terror which hangs over everyone' as the 'most powerful arm of tyranny' and proclamation of 'justice as the order of the day'). At the Convention, however, everyone understood this speech in its context and its true meaning. Tallien a 'sensitive soul'? Who could believe it? Just a few days ago, was he not appealing to the Convention to carry out an attack on the 'Robespierrists', in the manner of the *journée* that it had succeeded in carrying out against Robespierre himself? No one contested the principle of justice as the order of the day; but wasn't Tallien aiming at the abolition of the law on suspects? What would remain then of that revolutionary government to which he appealed? To link the crimes and the horrors of the Terror to this law, still in force, was this not to suggest furtively that 'the hour when the tyrant perished on the scaffold' had not brought an end to the Terror? Was this not a manoeuvre which allowed a reopening of the dossier on the Terror and, consequently, putting it on trial? Certainly, Tallien named nobody; he vaguely mentioned the 'Robespierrists' and he was prudent enough to underline that 'the Convention was a victim of the system of the Terror, never an accomplice'. However, Tallien started his speech just *after* a declaration of Lecointre demanding that he should be allowed to speak on the following day in order to denounce 'seven of our

[9] All these quotations are taken from the speech of Tallien at the session of 11 Fructidor, Year II, in *Moniteur*, vol. 21, pp. 612–15.

colleagues; three of whom are members of the Committee of Public Safety, and four of the Committee of General Security'. The 'great blow' was therefore to come the next day. Manipulator, intriguer, 'weathercock', this image certainly suited Tallien better than that of a philosopher and political analyst. And yet his speech of 11 Fructidor (although it is not quite certain that he drafted it himself) posed problems that no thought about the Terror could henceforth avoid.

### 'Robespierre's tail'

'It was not possible for Robespierre to do all that evil alone', claimed the pamphlet La Queue de Robespierre whose title was inspired by the anecdote circulating in Paris according to which Robespierre had said, before his death: 'You can cut off my head but I have left you my tail...'[10] The trial of Robespierre had taken place on 10 Thermidor but the trial of Robespierrism remained to be carried out: 'You have cast Robespierre down, but you have still done nothing to destroy Robespierrism', claimed, in his turn, Babeuf.[11]

La Queue de Robespierre, which had enormous print runs for the period, several tens of thousands of copies, thundered out the names of those who formed the 'tail' of this bloodythirsty reptile: Barère, Collot d'Herbois, Billaud-Varenne, members of the Committee of Public Safety before 9 Thermidor and who continued to be members after the 'great revolution'. Now, by a coincidence which no one thought of attributing to chance, these were almost the same names as those which two days later the denunciation of Lecointre presented, one by one.

The problem of responsibility among the agents of this 'system' was inescapable: 9 Thermidor was brought about from 'above', by a split in the team in power who had installed and operated the Terror; it was also a

[10]  La Queue de Robespierre ou les dangers de la liberté de la presse, by Felhémési: pamphlet published 9 Fructidor, Year II. Its author, Jean-Claude Méhée (the anagram was easy to decipher), was a curious character, one of those political adventurers who prospered under the Revolution. Born about 1760, this son of a fairly well-known surgeon became a police informer, probably in 1789. He was a spy in the milieux of the first émigrés. Having returned to France, he was, in 1792, deputy registrar of the Commune of Paris where, it seems, he encouraged the September massacres. His contacts with Tallien would have dated from this period; under his aegis and on his account, Méhée published after 9 Thermidor violently anti-terrorist brochures and pamphlets. (Might he have even written Tallien's speech of 11 Fructidor? The hypothesis is not out of the question.) He was next to occupy different positions in the service of Fouché and Napoleon, and infiltrate neo-Jacobin, Babouvist and royalist circles. He would also have a hand in the preparation of the assassination of the duc d'Enghien. Cf. O. Lutaud, Révolutions d'Angleterre et la Révolution française, The Hague, 1973, pp. 264 et seq.

[11]  Journal de la liberté de la presse, no. 10. We shall return to Babeuf as a 'Thermidorean' and his campaign against the 'terrorists' and 'blood-drinkers'. The first occurrences of the words Robespierrism and Robespierrists date from the end of Thermidor and the beginning of Fructidor.

problem of justice and of morality: to establish who was *responsible* was to point out those who were *guilty* of the executions, the imprisonments, the informing, etc.

Throughout its tortuous progress, and especially at each major turning, the Revolution had generated suspicions and had been nourished by them in turn. The Terror represented, without doubt, the culmination of this tendency which went hand in hand with a requirement to punish the 'guilty'. During the Terror, the 'suspect' became a category that was both political and legal, vaguely defined by the law of 17 September, while 'surveillance', even informing, was considered as the very expression of the revolutionary spirit which paired virtue and vigilance together. 9 Thermidor did not put an end to the 'time of suspicion' but it opened a new stage within it. From now on suspicion was fostered by the resentment, hatred and desire for revenge which were held back during the Terror and were finally given free rein.

The debate on the personal and collective responsibility for the Terror is as entangled as it is confused and endless. How should the part played by *personal* responsibility be distinguished from the part played *anonymously* by the Terror as a system of power? According to which legal and moral criteria should responsibility be established for acts which were yesterday still justified by revolutionary morality and justice? How should the 'leaders' be distinguished from the ordinary 'executants' and where should one stop in the pursuit and punishment of the 'guilty'? Did not a system of power define and, if necessary, impose individual behaviour? The debate, as it slid inevitably towards personal revenge, the settling of scores and the selection of scapegoats, necessarily opened onto the problems of the operation of the Terror, of its institutions, its workings and its personnel.

All these problems are to be found, so to speak, *in nuce* in Lecointre's denunciation as well as in the particularly stormy debate that it was to arouse during the next two days. Without any doubt, Lecointre was not 'politically minded' (when, in the course of the debate, he was accused of being a counter-revolutionary, Collot d'Herbois replied ironically that 'a counter-revolutionary would not have been so stupid as to make such a denunciation'). To the inevitably confused questions on individual responsibility, Lecointre added the confusion of his own ideas. His denunciation included seven people: Billaud-Varenne, Collot d'Herbois and Barère, all members of the Committee of Public Safety; Vadier, Amar, Voulland and David, all members of the Committee of General Security. Lecointre was a man easily influenced, and Tallien and Fréron were certainly hiding behind him. Lecointre's denunciation was skimped and poorly researched; it mixed up very general accusations and very precise facts. To put it briefly, one could sum up his accusations by arranging them into four kinds of grievance:

a) Lecointre denounced the seven members of the Committees as the architects of the Terror as a whole: they had

> repressed by the Terror all the citizens of the Republic, through signing and having carried out arbitrary orders of imprisonment, without there being against a large number of them any denunciation, any cause for suspicion, any evidence of the offences set out in the law of 17 September ... covered France with prisons, with a thousand Bastilles ... filled the entire Republic with mourning by their unjust and unjustified incarceration of more than a hundred thousand citizens, some sick, others past eighty, yet others family men, and even, defenders of the *patrie*; [they] surrounded themselves with a crowd of agents, some without reputation and the others covered with crimes; [they had] given them open powers and curbed none of their harassment and, on the contrary, supported them.

b) The seven were accused of complicity with Robespierre in the 'tyranny and oppression' exercised over the Convention and of

> having extended the system of terror and oppression as far as the members of the National Convention, by allowing and supporting, through their feigned silence, the rumour that the Committee of Public Safety had a list of thirty members of the National Convention selected for incarceration, and then *victimisation*, of having, in concert with Robespierre, destroyed freedom of opinion in the very heart of the National Convention, by not permitting the discussion of any of the laws presented by the Committee of Public Safety

of having, finally, imposed on the Convention the law of 22 Prairial, to the drawing up of which they had contributed.

c) The seven were guilty of having slowed the liberation of the Convention from the tyranny of Robespierre by their *silence*, for they had concealed his two-month absence from the Committee of Public Safety as well as 'the manoeuvres that this conspirator had employed with a view to disorganising everything, accumulating followers, and ruining the state'. On the other hand, on 8 and 9 Thermidor they had not taken the measures that were essential for striking a blow against all the conspirators, and especially the Commune.

d) Then followed a long list of the individual matters in which the seven were involved: having ordered or been responsible for numerous abuses in the working of the revolutionary Tribunal (the manipulations at the time of the judgement of Danton; the invention of the 'conspiracy of the prisons', the false evidence of the police spies, etc.); having saved some of the 'guilty', notably certain Hébertists; having employed men known to be counter-revolutionaries (among others, Beaumarchais).

The debate which followed was even more chaotic than the denunciation. On 12 Fructidor, after some general denials, the Convention decided to overrule the denunciation and 'reject it with indignation' – a motion quickly withdrawn, on the demand of the accused themselves who called for the presentation by Lecointre of all the 'documentary evidence' for his denunciation as well as the right to explain themselves on each point. So, the next day, Lecointre went through, point by point, his accusations and, for the whole day, a colossal debate was let loose. The star performers of the Convention took part as well as quite obscure deputies, in all about fifty speakers; some spoke several times, and no-one counted the 'murmurs' and interruptions. So the Assembly 'is deeply agitated' when Cambon proposed halting the debate and proceeding with the business of the day; Vadier then took over the rostrum, took out a pistol and threatened to commit suicide there and then. The Convention was, of course, used to these Roman-style gestures; had it not seen, on 9 Thermidor and on the same rostrum, Tallien shaking a dagger? Several members surrounded Vadier, and made him come down from the rostrum; another cried, touchingly, 'A vote or death.' The president put on his hat and adjourned the session, but finally, in 'the noise and the greatest confusion', the Convention went on with its discussions. These inevitably entered blind alleys. Lecointre had promised 'documents' in support of each of his accusations. But with what 'document' could he prove that 'France is covered with Bastilles'? He estimated the number of prisoners at a hundred thousand, then at fifty thousand. But again, who knew the exact number of victims? Lecointre drew largely on the file of Fouquier-Tinville who was awaiting his trial in prison. But who had made the file available for him? And what was the evidence of a Fouquier worth, himself a chief 'offender', who thought only of exonerating himself from all responsibility for his crimes during the Terror?

In the course of the debate, no one cast any doubt on the responsibility of Robespierre, of his acolytes and of the rebel Commune. But Lecointre was violently attacked for having taken his accusations too far, for in reality they went beyond the bare case of the 'seven'.[12] 'This is not a matter of bringing a few individuals to trial' (Mathieu). If these few members of the Committees who 'are nothing except through us, who have received their powers only from us' (Thuriot) were recognised as guilty, then where should the denunciations stop? The responsibility of the entire revolutionary government, of all members of the Committees, would then find itself in question. So it was recognised that 'the indictment is not confined to the seven members mentioned, but it attacks all who compose the two

---

[12] All these quotations are drawn from the accounts of the debates of 12 and 13 Fructidor, Year II; cf. *Moniteur*, vol. 21, pp. 620–42. The names of the speakers are given in parentheses. To mention some of the immediate consequences of these debates: two days later, at the time of the renewing of a third of the Committee of Public Safety (the proximity in time of the denunciation and this deadline was not, without any doubt, a matter of chance), Billaud-Varenne and Collot d'Herbois were to resign; Barère, 'selected by means of a ballot', was also replaced. On 17 Fructidor, Tallien, Fréron and Lecointre were excluded from the Jacobins.

committees and it attacks *us*' (Cambon). Seeing that the powers of these committees were extended each month, the whole Convention was arraigned: 'you are all guilty' (Cambon). The Convention would be 'in a state of suspicion in the eyes of the people' who could then wonder if 'the Convention is worthy of representing it' (Thibaudeau). To attack the Convention, to accuse it of having tolerated the tyrant and his oppression, was this not to attack the people itself? 'Since France has been oppressed, as well as the Convention, we must also indict the people for not having rebelled' (deputy not identified in the minutes). 'It is the Convention that is accused, it is against the French people that the action is brought, because it has suffered the tyranny of the infamous Robespierre' (Goujon).

The action was brought against the Convention, the Nation and, in the end, the Revolution. 'I look towards the past; I see that mistakes were made and injustice done. I seek to discover their origin, I find it in the events that are inseparable from a great revolution' (Goupilleau (from Fontenay)); 'It is the revolution which is being arraigned' (Féraud); 'They are trying to make the people believe that all that has happened, has been brought about by the Terror since the appointment of the Committees of Public Safety and General Security' (Cambon). 'Vigorous measures' had served the *patrie* well; to include them all under the name of the Terror would be to fail to take circumstances into account. 'Let us remember that things which are good in such circumstances are bad in others, and if we start proceedings over an event six weeks or a month after it happened we could make all patriots guilty' (Legendre). Should one today proceed against 'those who burnt the castles at the beginning of the Revolution or bring proceedings against the *journée* of 10 August' (Legendre)? Should one broaden the charge to include all representatives *en mission* 'for there were none who were not forced to order arrests' (Cambon)? Should the gaols have been opened when the 'brigands of the Vendée' threatened all the neighbouring *départements* (Garnier (from Saintes))? A very large portion of the arrests, and 'they must have amounted to a hundred thousand', were made by the revolutionary committees. To attribute all of these to the seven members of the Committees was ridiculous, and to condemn them outright would be counter-revolutionary (Bourdon (from the Oise)). In the name of what justice and what equality were these accusations being brought, accusations which, beyond this or that act, aimed at an entire period of the Revolution and, consequently, the entire Revolution? 'What do the charges relate to? All to things which had been carried out to enforce the law; and I ask you, if people had deviated from the law to maintain the revolutionary movement and save the *patrie*, would you send to the scaffold those who saved liberty?" (Thuriot).

The accusations bearing on the *journée* of 9 Thermidor, those of having been too slow in preparing the 'revolution' and, then, of carrying it out too hesitantly, were felt as particularly unjust, especially by the accused themselves. Weren't the seven the architects of the 'fall of the tyrant', did they not play the decisive role on that memorable day? Their speeches during the debate provided a number of details on the crisis which had torn the Committees apart in the weeks preceding the fall of Robespierre, and on the unfolding of events during the crucial days of 8 and 9 Thermidor. On the other hand, the basic questions, the explanation of the reasons which made the 'tyranny' possible, the rise of Robespierre and his hold over the Convention, were passed over in silence, drowned as it were under the floods of more or less anecdotal facts. People were content to claim that the strategy applied during Thermidor was the best, that the first occasion had been seized to 'defeat the tyrant'. 'If Robespierre had been attacked two weeks earlier, the whole Convention and liberty would have been slaughtered' (Bourdon (from the Oise)). To wait and remain silent had therefore been an act of prudence. 'It was not so much Robespierre that one had to defeat as the tyranny with which he had burdened the people, and which could have continued after his death' (Goupilleau (from Fontenay)). Certainly, there were many who would henceforth boast of having always been fiercely anti-Robespierrist. Lecointre himself maintained that he had prepared his denunciation of Robespierre several months before; but why had he, and all the others, preferred to remain silent? 'After the death of Caesar, ten thousand Romans could say they had formed the plan which Brutus carried out' (Goupilleau (from Fontenay)). To bring proceedings against 9 Thermidor was to demean the entire Convention, it was to accuse it not only of having put up with the tyrant, but of having been his accomplice, through its fear and guilty silence. To remove these troublesome memories and clear itself of all suspicion of complicity with the 'tyrant', the Convention had to forge a heroic image of itself. The small-scale story of 9 Thermidor was not enough, a glorious legend was needed:

When you were seen to overthrow the tyrant, an artillery of imposture was positioned in every corner; but let no one flatter himself for having contributed more than you to defeating him; it is your reserves of courage and virtue, it is the Convention and the entire people who have brought him down, and anyone who boasts of having played a greater part than you, anyone who would say that you could have done it earlier, deludes history and posterity. (Collot d'Herbois)

That such a debate could take place was already evidence of the extent to which the emergence from the Terror had really begun. The Convention had gained in freedom of expression. This area of liberty was also where political divisions were going to be marked out and deepened. Lecointre was not arrested; Tallien and Fréron were excluded from the Jacobins, but that no longer carried any risk. On the contrary, this exclusion encouraged sudden changes of direction and, consequently, their political careers. However, the unfolding of the debate revealed how heavily the heritage of the past still weighed. Opened by a 'denunciation', it became engulfed in the suspicion that was stirred up by the essential question of individual responsibility. The old reflexes were still sharp: Lecointre was accused of being a counter-revolutionary, in the service of the royalists; his arrest was even called for; speakers accused each other of 'making the sword of death hang over the representatives of the people', or of wanting to revive 'the system of Robespierre' and to instigate a 'new tyranny'. The Convention was compared by Tallien to an *arena of gladiators*. The debate came to an end with an official motion declaring the denunciation slanderous, 'motion put to the vote, and agreed unanimously and among the loudest applause' (motion of Cambon). The unanimity of the Convention, temporarily rediscovered, barely hid the divisions which would become more marked as the relationship of forces developed. By condemning Lecointre's denuncia-tion, the Convention not only acquitted the seven accused of responsibility for the Terror; it refused, in reality, to open the debate, for fear of implying the responsibility, one after the other, of all members of the Committees, of the representatives *en mission*, of the Convention as a whole, of the people, who had not rebelled, and of the Revolution, which legitimised the Terror. This last argument drew its force less from logic than from an appeal to considerations of joint responsibility and, especially, to the instinct of self-defence. In placing the emphasis on the feeling of collective guilt, this argument underlined the fact that there was no one, among the members of the Convention, who could honestly claim that he was not guilty, that he had not had a hand in the Terror, if not by his actions, then at least by his silence. Responsibility for the Terror was therefore shifted on to the 'loathsome tyrant' and on to the 'events inseparable from a great revolu-tion', in short, on to an anonymous and depersonalised 'system of oppression'. But to exonerate the seven denounced members implied, in reality, total solidarity with them. The dilemma – either everyone was guilty, or no one, except for an anonymous system – was morally and legally indefensible. It ignored the degrees of responsibility in an action, a decision, an order. It would offer scarcely any resistance to the dynamics of political events. Throughout the country, the hunt for the guilty, for 'terrorists' and for 'blood-drinkers', was under way. Should the Convention take on the defence of the entire political personnel of the Terror, of all the minor 'oppressors' and 'informers' at whom local revenge was aimed? Must they halt the proceedings against a Fouquier-Tinville who from his prison never stopped protesting that, in carrying out the decisions of the Committees and the Convention, he had always acted with strict respect for legality? This was no longer a time for loyalty to old allegiances, but for discord and disagreement. The logic of the political struggle demanded *both* the condemnation of the Terror as a 'system of power' and the punishment of 'Robespierre's tail', of the 'guilty' specified by name.

In the course of the debate of 12 and 13 Fructidor, the Terror had been mentioned as a *system of power*; the legitimacy of the Committees and of the laws had been discussed. Now, on 22 Fructidor the trial of ninety-four leading citizens of Nantes opened before the revolutionary tribunal, followed by that of the revolutionary Committee of Nantes. France then discovered the hideous *realities* of what the Terror in Nantes had been. We shall see that after several weeks of revelations, on 3 Frimaire, Year III, the Convention voted through, once more *with unanimity* (with two conditional ayes), the committing for trial of Carrier, directly implicated in matters at Nantes. On 7 Nivôse the Convention set up a commission to examine the revived denunciation of Lecointre and came to a conclusion on 'the conduct of the representatives of the people, Billaud-Varenne, Collot d'Herbois and Barère'. In its report, presented by Saladin, the Commission concluded that the accused had direct and indirect responsibility for the Terror, its system and its crimes.

### 'Where are we?'

#### *'Justice the order of the day'*

It is for public wisdom to harvest the benefits of your energetic virtue; it is for you to strengthen these benefits further by making all vestiges of the usurpation of national authority disappear . . . by restoring the liberty and confidence which had been taken from them by systematic manoeuvres; by substituting inflexible justice for stupid terror; by recalling true morality in place of hypocrisy, and by restoring to the tomb of executed criminals the corrupt agents and other cadaverous souls who plague the free earth.[13]

On the day after 9 Thermidor, revolutionary authority appealed to justice and officially promised to *make it the order of the day*. No one could be mistaken: this was, by the same token, to condemn *the Terror as the order of the day*, proclaimed, just as solemnly, on 5 September 1793. The 'fall of the tyrant' thus took on the significance of a decisive turning point; it should end the period which had raised repression into a system of power.

*Justice the order of the day*, a more or less vague promise for the future, had to be made concrete in the immediate present by political measures confronting the inheritance of the Terror, which could be reduced to three problems:

> what was to be done with the legal and institutional apparatus inherited from the Terror?

[13] Barère, Rapport au nom des Comités de salut public et de sûreté générale, *Moniteur*, vol. 21, p. 369.

what was to be done with the mass of detainees who populated the gaols?

what was to be done with the political personnel compromised by their participation in the terrorist repression?

The distinction is, of course, schematic: in reality the three problems are but one. This inheritance was all the more awkward to settle in that responsibility for the task rested, as we have seen, with the Convention, which had proclaimed, barely a year before, 'Terror as the order of the day', then approved the activities of the most extremist representatives *en mission*. To the inextricable problem of the moral, political and legal responsibility for the terrorist repression was added another, even more difficult. This was to separate the 'terrorist' laws and institutions, which needed to be condemned and removed, from the properly 'revolutionary' repressive apparatus which, consequently, should be retained, even if the 'terrorists' had abused it. How to draw the line, often elusive, which marked off the 'unjust and blameworthy' Terror from revolutionary justice, whose intentions were as pure as they were patriotic, despite errors of zeal in its application? To these political questions came pre-eminently political answers.

The extent and speed of the dismantling of the Terror, as a system of power inseparable from daily repression, depended largely on the speed at which the promise of *justice as the order of the day* materialised. On the day after 9 Thermidor, the slogan itself was accepted with unanimous enthusiasm; but the concrete measures, taken one by one, became very swiftly the subject of bitter confrontations, in which political forces were polarised. For some, towards the end of Year II, the policy of *justice as the order of the day* had gone too far: its champions had wrongly freed the 'aristocrats' and were oppressing the 'patriots'; they were all only 'new indulgents', '*modérantistes*', the 'new party of the right'. For others, who would soon be called the *reactionaries* but who increasingly claimed to be the 'true' inheritors of 9 Thermidor, *justice had not always gone far enough*, and those who opposed its acceleration were only disguised *Robespierrists, terrorists* or even *Jacobins*. The more this political struggle would become violent, the more this vocabulary would increase in aggression, although not necessarily in clarity. The political protagonists did not manage to free themselves from the ambiguities and uncertainties to be expected in a new political situation,[14] for which the main evidence is the setting up of a new and largely improvised legal apparatus.

---

[14] It must be added that terminological ambiguities and confusions mark the literature devoted to the Thermidorean period. Thus, a distinction is often introduced between the 'Thermidoreans' and the 'Montagnards', while forgetting that these latter, a group otherwise difficult to identify, were also Thermidoreans in that they did not contest the 'revolution of 9 Thermidor' and condemned Robespierre and Robespierrism. The phrases 'Thermidoreans of the left' and 'Thermidoreans of the right' would seem to be more apt;

The Convention first annulled, unanimously and 'to loud applause', the decree that it had passed, authorising the two Committees to arrest representatives of the people without their having received a preliminary hearing at the Assembly; for this disastrous decree '*had been sprung upon the Convention* by men who were used to deceiving justice'. Abrogating this decree, assuring each representative a minimum of parliamentary immunity, was a quite elementary precaution after the experience of the Terror (this new commitment with regard to itself was to be respected by the Convention for seven months, until the repression launched against some of its members after the troubles of 12 Germinal).[15]

On 14 Thermidor, again 'to loud applause', the Convention abolished the law of 22 Prairial, symbol and legal base of the 'great Terror'. By their loud applause the deputies seemed to want to exorcise the memory of their own vote, which had approved this 'bloody law' and which was from now on considered to be glaring proof of the 'tyranny' wielded over the Convention. In the same breath another symbol was attacked: the Convention immediately decided on the arrest of Fouquier-Tinville and his bringing to trial before the revolutionary Tribunal. And yet Fouquier had served it with great zeal and with his usual efficiency on 10 and 11 Thermidor, by taking responsibility for the legal aspects of the punishment of Robespierre and his accomplices. 'All Paris demands from you the justly deserved punishment of Fouquier-Tinville. I demand that he goes to expiate in hell the blood he has spilt. I demand against him an order for arrest.' Fréron, who protested loudly in these words, seemed to forget that in this 'spilt blood' Robespierre's was also to be found. Fouquier was to have his trial and would not fail to seize the opportunity to show that he had always respected the strictest legality.

Only on 23 Thermidor was the revolutionary Tribunal reorganised, after much indecision. Already on 11 Thermidor, voices were raised to demand the suspension of the Tribunal, which Robespierre had peopled with his creatures. 'When his holiness, for that is how his partisans called him, this catholic, or rather sacrilegious king, had pointed out the individual, the jury pronounced and the judgement was executed' (Thuriot). The suspension was decreed amidst general enthusiasm, only to be deferred some hours later. In fact, Billaud-Varenne, sent by a very alarmed Committee of Public

they suffer however from the notorious ambiguity peculiar to the left–right opposition, which would need to keep being made precise with regard to the changing political groupings of the period. Moreover, they were very rarely utilised in that period. Towards the end of Year II, political divisions settled down around the opposition Jacobins–anti-Jacobins (or even terrorists–anti-terrorists). The terminology is not uniform and satisfactory; we shall therefore employ, in what follows, mostly the terminology of the period which, in the end, brings out better both its uncertainties and its passionate climate.

[15] Session of 13 Thermidor, cf. *Moniteur*, vol. 21, p. 367.

Safety, persuaded the Assembly that the suspension of the Tribunal for which it had just voted can save only ... the 'conspirators'. Was not the Tribunal in the process of judging members of the 'rebel Commune' with the same docility it employed in executing its task before 9 Thermidor?

The utility of the institution itself was hardly put into question. On 11 Thermidor, Barère, in the name of the Committee of Public Safety, eulogised

this salutary institution, which destroys the enemies of the Republic, and clears the soil of liberty ... Great respect must therefore be paid to this institution; but the men who make it up should have attracted the complaints and attention of the National Convention. It is considered to be among your duties to revise the structure of this tribunal, but using that wisdom which perfects without weakening and which rewards without destroying.

The new organisation of the Tribunal was based, in principle, on laws previous to those of 22 Prairial, but with this difference: henceforth the Tribunal would, in making its judgements, have to come to a decision on the 'question of intent', that is to say, to pass judgement on the accused only if they had committed an offence *with counter-revolutionary intent*, other crimes and offences being a matter for ordinary criminal justice. The composition of the Tribunal was reduced to twelve judges and thirty jurors, chosen from the whole of France on the basis of proposals from representatives and renewable every three months. The accused enjoyed certain legal guarantees: he was interrogated prior to the public session, he had the help of a defence counsel, he could challenge one or several jurors; during the hearing he had a right of reply to the statement of each witness. Within the jurisdiction of the revolutionary Tribunal fell crimes against the security of the State and the National Convention, negligence and malpractices of which members of the executive commissions might be guilty, as well as judges and public prosecutors from the criminal tribunals. The special 'revolutionary' jurisdictions in the *départements*, which were conspicuous by their zeal in the Terror, were all suppressed; justice was confined only to criminal tribunals who could, however, judge certain crimes 'in a revolutionary way'.

But during the debate on this project of reform some reservations and disquiet were shown. Would it not encourage *'modérantisme'*? 'What need have you of a voluminous code which will furnish weapons for legal chicanery and provide means of impunity for the guilty? Let us bring back the Tribunal in its primitive purity, and that will be enough; in a word, remember the good results it brought about, and do not weaken its vigour.' The Convention disregarded these objections, which proposed, so to speak, a return to the 'pure origins' of the Terror. The Convention placed itself, with this reform, in a deep ambiguity: it condemned the Tribunal as an instrument of the Terror and symbol of arbitrary power, but it limited this condemnation, in principle, to the Tribunal's activity and composition after the law of 22 Prairial. The institution itself, one of the cornerstones of the terrorist apparatus, was retained. The introduction of the clause concerning intent and the proclaimed desire to respect elementary rules of procedure, including, particularly, the rights of the accused, promised nevertheless a less repressive application.[16] This renewed and reformed Tribunal was established on 25 Thermidor; in the speech inaugurating its activity, Aumont, appointed after 9 Thermidor at the head of civil administration, police and tribunals, underlined 'that it is not yet time to relax the scope of revolutionary justice, without which the supernatural courage of the defenders of the *patrie* would have gained only useless triumphs'. However, he insisted forcefully on the fact that the disappearance 'of the creatures of the tyrant opens a new page ... With them should disappear a tribunal that their bloodthirsty talent had transformed into an instrument of death, a tribunal become, under their terrible influence, the dread of innocence much more than of crime'. The renewed Tribunal would condemn no more 'batches', but up to the end of year II, it was still to deliver sixteen death sentences, some of which were for counter-revolutionary remarks, others for complicity with the Vendéans or even for acts harking back to the 'federalist rebellion'. If these sentences marked, so to speak, the continuity of the institution, others revealed, in the facts, the desire to break with the Terror and so unquestionably enlarge the space for liberty and respect for rights. Procedure had effectively changed, with in particular a preliminary investigation at the hearing, and the presence of a lawyer for the accused. In the same period, ninety-two people were acquitted (among whom were forty-two militants from the *sections*, more or less implicated in the insurrectional activities of the Commune on 9 Thermidor). The particularly wide and liberal interpretation of the 'clause concerning intent' is especially revealing of the new orientation taken by the 'scope of revolutionary justice'. Let us give just a few examples. On 24 Fructidor the public was present at the trial of a certain Catherine Breté accused of having said 'that those who had put the tyrant to death were f— and b— who deserved to die themselves'. The witnesses had attested that citizen Breté used these words only 'in a moment of bad temper' and the accused having expressed her regrets, the Tribunal acquitted her, for lack of 'counter-revolutionary intent'. On 30 Fructidor an officer who had the

---

[16] On the reform of the revolutionary Tribunal, cf. the meetings of 11 and 23 Thermidor of the Convention: *Moniteur*, vol. 21, pp. 335 *et seq.*, 448 *et seq.*; H. Wallon, *Histoire du Tribunal révolutionnaire de Paris*, Paris, 1881, vol. 5, pp. 260–74. The objections were made by Duhem who, at the Jacobin club, violently opposed '*modérantisme*' and recommended the strengthening of repression.

misfortune to cry in the street, 'Long live the king, the mess-bowl and the dumpling!' was put on trial. He could plead in his defence only a single extenuating circumstance: he was dead drunk when he made these 'counter-revolutionary remarks'. In consequence, the Tribunal severely repri-manded him, pointing out that 'a man whose blood is patriotic does not make aristocratic remarks even when drunk', but in the end acquitted him 'seeing that he had not acted with counter-revolutionary intent'. However, all these minor affairs were pushed into the background by the trial of the ninety-four men of Nantes, which marked the end of Year II and would be extended by the trial of the revolutionary Committee of Nantes and of Carrier. Beyond the accused, the Tribunal would have to judge the Terror as a system, as well as judging the Terror's supporters. Some months later Fouquier-Tinville's turn would come, another trial arousing universal interest, and which unveiled the workings of the Terror.[17]

The release of the detainees with which the prisons were bursting was not, however, entrusted to the reformed revolutionary Tribunal. This was the most spectacular measure in the efforts to translate into action the desire to 'make justice the order of the day'. From 15 Thermidor, in the first meetings of assemblies of the *sections* since the fall of Robespierre, the relatives and friends of the detainees called for them to be released, accusing the surveillance committees of having perpetrated arbitrary arrests. The Con-vention gave way to the pressure and on 18 Thermidor voted a train of measures which marked a turning point. It instructed the Committee of General Security to 'free all citizens detained as suspects for motives not covered by the law of 17 September 1793' (the law on suspects). It pointed out to representatives *en mission* that the 'unlimited power that they possess' authorised them 'to set at liberty citizens who might have been put under arrest by other representatives of the people on insufficient grounds'. The Convention finally decided that the reasons for detention and warrants of arrest would be communicated to the detainees (or to their relations and friends) by the respective authorities (Committee of General Security, representatives *en mission*, surveillance committees). This last measure aroused the opposition of certain Jacobin deputies. Fayau considered it useless: it was for the detainees themselves to produce proof of their good citizenship since 1789 and to thus cleanse themselves of the 'suspicions' which made them 'suspect'. This objection provoked a tirade from Tallien:

[17] Cf. AN W 447; W 450; cf. Wallon, *Histoire*, vol. 5, p. 321; vol. 6, p. 166. Wallon has compiled the complete lists of condemnations and acquittals given by the Tribunal from 1 Fructidor, Year II to 8 Nivôse, Year III (*ibid.*, vol. 6, p. 166). The Tribunal was permanently suppressed on 12 Prairial, Year III, after the end of the trial of Fouquier-Tinville. Following the *journées* of Prairial, repression was no longer carried out by the revolutionary Tribunal, but by the military Commission or the criminal tribunals.

'we must give the patriots who, at this moment, groan in the dungeons, the opportunity to make their innocence shine out, and perhaps, those who oppose this measure wish to prevent the people from knowing that several of these champions of the cause had been arrested without reason'. Tallien demanded the retention of 'the extraordinary revolutionary measures', but in order to strike 'the foul remains of Robespierre's faction'.[18]

The Convention decided to open the gates of the prisons. The task was enormous; under the Terror, about 500,000 people had been locked up in more or less improvised prisons; in July 1794, there were in Paris about 7,000 detainees. However, the way the releases were carried out reveals the contradictions, after 9 Thermidor, in the dismantling of the Terror. No amnesty was decreed; the law on suspects, cornerstone of the legal apparatus of the Terror, was not repealed and, consequently, the very category of *suspect* was retained. However, the clauses of this law were so vague that they lent themselves to all sorts of interpretations, either 'energetic' or 'indulgent'. The grounds for arrest were often as vague as the denunciation which had provoked it. To pronounce judgement on whether these grounds conformed to the law opened the door to arbitrary justice. Also, the Committee of General Security now disposed of an almost discretionary power of *releasing* the prisoners by referring to the same law which it had employed to imprison them. In the *départements*, the extent of the release of detainees largely depended on the more or less prominent '*modérantisme*' of the representative *en mission*.

The first releases from the Parisian prisons immediately caused a stir. They let loose a chain of reactions similar to those seen at the Convention: they kept political conflicts alive and nourished expectations as well as fears. Opposed to the hopes and enthusiasms of those who extolled 'justice as the order of the day' were the fears and mistrust of those who condemned the 'indulgence' which benefited the 'aristocrats' and other enemies of the Republic.

How the town of Paris presents a different spectacle today – compared to the one which preceded the fall of the new Tiberius. Then there reigned everywhere a gloomy silence, precursor of death; friend mistrusted friend, fathers mistrusted their children; but today cheerfulness and joy are seen on the faces of every citizen ... *Long live the Convention! Long live our worthy representatives!* This was the cry resounding yesterday in the rue de Tournon, when Tallien went to the Luxembourg to liberate a number of patriots who were detained there unjustly. The people ran up in a crowd, showered blessings upon him, embraced him, embraced those who had

---

[18] Cf. A. Aulard, *Recueil des actes du Comité de salut public avec la correspondance officielle des représentants en mission*, Paris, 1904, vol. 15, p. 678. In the same decree the Convention also demanded the communication to the Committee of Public Safety of arrests made by representatives of the people who had been and were *en mission*; it was one of the prerequisite conditions for the ending of arbitrary arrests.

just been given their freedom. 'Be calm, my friends', said Tallien, to those whom he could not yet bring out of this prison, 'you shall not sigh long for your liberty; it shall only be the guilty who shall not enjoy that gift. I shall return today, I shall return tomorrow . . . and we shall work night and day until prisoners unjustly detained are returned to their families . . .' And tears of joy and emotion flowed from every eye, and the Convention was showered with thousands upon thousands of blessings.'[19]

Affecting images, to be sure, widely circulated by that portion of the press which saw in them only the first effects of the new politics. But what was the real extent of these measures for the release of prisoners? Who were these 'unjustly detained patriots' and according to what criteria were they released? These questions were all the more pressing and embarrassing since the operation had been started in conditions which condemned it to confusion and prevented it from being open and above board. The repeated appeals to the public from the Committees of Public Safety and General Security were just as much evidence for the feverish atmosphere that followed the decree of 18 Thermidor: a crowd pressed into the ante-chambers of the Committees to extract as quickly as possible an order of release for a relation or friend. 'Soon', promised Barère, on 24 Thermidor,

the traces of personal revenge will vanish from the soil of the Republic. But the flood of citizens of both sexes at the doors of the Committee of General Security only slows down the work which is so useful to the citizens . . . We therefore invite all citizens to rely upon the civic zeal of the representatives of the people for judgement of the detainees and for providing orders of release . . . This is neither a matter of an amnesty nor clemency; it is a matter of justice, and of equal justice for all.

'The Committee [of General Security]', Vadier was claiming three days later, 'is unceasingly occupied with coming to the help of oppressed patriots; but it is slowed down in its efforts because it is besieged by aristocrats; a multitude of women obstruct it; several of our colleagues are also lodging complaints in favour of detained citizens. It is impossible that in this mass of operations some errors should not slip in.'[20]

'A mass of operations', no doubt. The strong pressure exerted on the Committees came from people with very different origins and opinions. In fact, the after-effects of the Terror were such that the victims of its successive waves could be found, mixed up together as suspects or perpetrators of counter-revolutionary crimes, in the same prison at the same time. Former princes and émigrés returned clandestinely came into contact with Kellermann, victorious general at Valmy and pacifier of the insurrection at Lyon, and Hoche, victor at Landau; the actors of the Théâtre-Français were neighbours to militant members of the *sections*,

[19] *Gazette historique et politique de la France et de l'Europe*, 23 Thermidor, Year II.
[20] Cf. *Moniteur*, vol. 21, pp. 439 and 489.

accused of complicity in the 'Hébertist conspiracy'; the ninety-four leading citizens of Nantes awaited judgement along with members of the revolutionary Committee of Nantes, who had arrested them and sent them to Paris, and who were now imprisoned for abuse of power. In five days, from 18 to 23 Thermidor, the Committee of General Security released 478 people; however, neither this number nor the list of freed prisoners were made public; the newspapers cited only rare cases and the most contradictory rumours spread. The desire to act quickly, the pressure exerted by members of the Convention themselves (they were the first to demand the liberation of members of their families, of friends or of protégés originating from their *départements*), a quite summary procedure, the concentration of power of release in the hands of the Committee of General Security alone, supposed to examine each case according to badly defined criteria, explain the disordered 'mass of operations'. Hence the abuses and unfortunate mistakes which caused a scandal – such as the release, denounced by Vadier, of the former Duke of Aumont who, following the decree of the Convention granting liberty to all workers on the land, had passed himself off as Gui, a labourer of Aumont.[21]

Apart from these unfortunate errors, which were more or less inevitable, it was the whole policy of release as practised by the Committees that swiftly raised doubts and opposition. On 23 Thermidor, during the discussion of the plan to reorganise the revolutionary Tribunal, the Convention adopted the proposition of Mallarmé, a Jacobin deputy, which required the Committees of Public Safety and General Security to have 'printed, every five days, the list of citizens they have released'. The vote occurred without debate, along with other amendments, as if the Assembly did not perceive the consequences of its decision. The storm broke three days later, on 26 Thermidor. The atmosphere was very tense, as the evening before the assemblies of the *sections* had been in uproar: again the revolutionary committees had been denounced, along with their 'bloodthirsty policy' before 9 Thermidor, and a complete change of personnel had been called for; but, on the other hand, violent criticisms had been made of 'the aristocracy and *modérantisme*' that were raising their heads. The debate at the Convention, quite chaotic as was too often the case, unfolded in two

[21]  Laurent Lecointre, in his pamphlet *Les Crimes des sept membres des anciens Comités*, Paris, Year III, pp. 154 *et seq.*, estimated that in a month the number of detainees in Parisian prisons went from 8,500 to 3,500. However, the record of the prisons on 13 Fructidor established 5,480 detainees; a month later, on 14 Vendémiaire. this number had diminished by more than a thousand (4,445). Cf. Saladin, *Rapport au nom de la Commission de vingt-et-un*, Paris, Year III, p. 105; AN AF II,73; Wallon, *Histoire*, vol. 5, p. 450. We give the overall figures on the numbers of detainees according to the estimates of D. Greer, *The incidence of terror. A statistical interpretation*, Cambridge, Mass., 1935, and of G. Lefebvre, *La Révolution française*, Paris, 1968, pp. 417 *et seq.* To the number of prisoners should be added at least 300,000 suspects under house arrest.

phases. There were firstly the attacks of several Jacobin deputies – notably Mallarmé, Duhem, Chasles, Levasseur (from the Sarthe) – against the 'aristocracy' which was the only party to profit from the policy of releasing prisoners. The two exemplary cases – of the Duke of Aumont and the Duke of Valentinois who showed off in public places, proud of their freedom – were vehemently denounced. The Committee of General Security had itself recognised that these were obvious errors which had 'escaped their vigilance' and isolated occurrences whose importance should not be exaggerated. In making so much of these mistakes, the Jacobins were not content to demand the rigorous enforcement of the decree on the publication of lists of freed prisoners. They also demanded the immediate arrest of all those who had solicited similarly mistaken releases. Among these was again mentioned the case of Kellermann who found himself among the first prisoners to be set free. Now, this release, contrary to previous cases, no longer gained unanimity. It is moreover striking that the whole of this debate, like those which will follow, lacking precise figures on the numbers set free, oscillates between two extremes: some put forward generalisations that were as hasty as they were concise ('aristocrats are being freed'), while others stressed individual cases, which too often only made the discussion yet more passionate. Carnot, alerted by the attacks against Kellermann, ran from the hall of the Committee of Public Safety, to explain his release. Supported by several representatives, he did not hesitate to praise Kellermann. He was a good patriot and republican, an excellent citizen and soldier, a victim of the jealousy of Robespierre and not a 'traitor'. The matter was referred to the Committee of Public Safety but, at the same time, the debate entered its second phase: the decree, voted three days ago, requiring the publication of the list of released prisoners was called into question again. Voices were raised, claiming that this decree had been rushed through and that its proclamation 'had spread terror in all hearts' (Merlin (from Thionville)). Tallien, who was at the same time taking steps to obtain the liberty of his mistress (they will be crowned with success a week later), violently criticised the decree. Of course, it was possible that 'some patriots had been deceived in the case of some individuals' and had demanded their release. That, however, was not the point; the liberation of prisoners must be energetically continued: 'I prefer to see today twenty aristocrats at large than to see one patriot in irons. What's this, the Republic with its twelve hundred thousand armed citizens in fear of a few aristocrats!' In the prisons were innocent men, snatched from their families without any valid reason, uniquely on the basis of vile denunciations. To publish the list of released prisoners, was this not to draw up a new proscription for the use of those who dreamt only of establishing themselves in Robespierre's now empty place? 'Successors of Robespierre, do not hope for victory, the whole of the Convention is determined to perish here or annihilate all tyrants, whatever mask they hide under.' This tirade was greeted with enthusiasm ('yes, yes, cried all members as they rose simultaneously'); nevertheless, the Convention hesitated, and even confirmed the contested decree. Tallien then replied with a counter-proposition – 'Since it is intended to print the list of those who have been set at liberty, I demand that there also be printed a list of the names of those who had them imprisoned; the people must know its true enemies, those who denounced the patriots and had them incarcerated' – an obviously rabble-rousing motion that was, however, also promptly adopted, which put the fat in the fire. In the general confusion, several voices were heard crying: 'It's civil war!' In full disarray, 'so as to emerge from the political confusion which must destroy liberty and equality', the Convention annulled, finally, *both* the decrees it had just adopted. The debate and the vacillation are very revealing both of an unstable political situation and of the polarisation of political positions which will finish by sweeping it away. The Convention was caught up in its own contradictions: 'to tear away the veil that should hide certain government operations' was to risk compromising everyone, those who had just left prison and those who remained; those who called for the release of detainees and those who had signed the letters of denunciation and the orders of arrest (sometimes, in fact, these were the same people). The demand for ensuring that the policy of release was open and above board was revealed, in the end, to be a double-edged sword; to apply it was to run the risk of letting loose a process with uncontrollable consequences, perhaps leading to civil war. The lists of freed prisoners and of those who solicited their release, especially members of the Convention, were never published; but, during the winter of Year III, émigrés published at Lausanne a list naming the 'blood-drinkers' of Lyon for punishment and lynching.[22]

The news coming from the *départements* could only stir up the conflicts and passions. Already towards the end of Thermidor there began to flow into Paris, to the Convention and especially to the Jacobins, alarming addresses and complaints; not only was the aristocracy raising its head, nobles and priests were being released, the assemblies of popular societies were being invaded by royalists and counter-revolutionaries, but in addition the 'purest patriots' were being oppressed, persecuted: they were incarcerated while suspects came out of the prisons. 'Each day members of the Convention receive distressing accounts of what has happened in

---

[22] Session of the Convention of 23 Thermidor, *Moniteur*, vol. 21, p. 448; session of 26 Thermidor, *ibid.*, pp. 484–7. A pamphlet presenting the *Liste générale des Dénonciateurs et des Dénoncés, de Lyon et diverses autres communes* was published by émigrés in Lausanne, in 1795. It was a true catalogue of people to be killed. Cf. Fuoc, *Réaction*, p. 83. In Paris there was published the *Tableau des noms, âges, qualités et demeures des principaux membres des jacobins* (by Francastelle, Year III), a sort of guide to the 'Jacobin hunting'.

large communes since 10 Thermidor . . . All the patriots are accused of being supporters of Robespierre and they are oppressed in a manner as unjust and barbaric as in 1791 and 1792.'[23] Towards the middle of Prairial, these complaints started arriving daily; delegations from popular societies and revolutionary committees presented themselves at the Convention and at the Jacobins; the families and friends of 'oppressed patriots' sought support, some from the deputies of their *département*, others from ex-representatives *en mission*. The Jacobins were not content simply to listen to those who petitioned them for help; they took upon themselves the necessity of having the 'oppressed patriots' released and quite often appointed 'official defence lawyers' instructed to intervene, in particular cases, with the Committee of General Security. In the last ten days of Fructidor and at the beginning of Vendémiaire, counter-addresses came in reply to these addresses and petitions, often from the same places: they protested to the Convention against defamation and declared firmly that the complaints came only from some terrorists and partisans of Robespierre, or, quite simply, from thieves and embezzlers who had been unmasked. Their arrest was only an act of justice at which all good citizens rejoiced, and also a measure of protection with regard to the 'revolution of 9 Thermidor' which could not tolerate the continued activity, intriguing and conspiring of all these 'blood-drinkers'. The risk had then existed of a return to the Terror. The source of the complaints and addresses – to which we shall return – against the 'oppression of patriots' is evidence that towards mid-Fructidor the new direction, and especially the purging of political personnel, was already well under way in the country, particularly in the *départements* where the Terror had caused great havoc and where its after-effects were so much more serious and difficult to resolve.

Why this 'war of petitions'?

The first complaints against the 'oppression of patriots' began to reach the Convention while the flood of congratulations for its heroic action against the 'tyrant' and the 'rebel Commune' had not yet run dry. These were, however, the first cracks in that glorious unanimity, a paradoxical sign that the fall of the 'modern Catiline' was really beginning to register in local political realities. The unanimous enthusiasm with which the political personnel established in power during the Terror had received the news of the fall of Robespierre had, at least at first, only revealed an opportunism engendered by this same Terror. This had added yet more confusion. As we have noticed, on the day after 9 Thermidor, the country awoke fiercely anti-Robespierrist: no resistance, not even any doubt about the 'frightful conspiracy'. However, in the capital about sixty of those who took sides

[23] Speeches by Chasles and Réal at the Jacobins, 26 Thermidor. Cf. Aulard, *Société des Jacobins*, vol. 6, pp. 336–7.

with Robespierre and the 'rebel Commune' had been outlawed and executed in the 'batches' of 10 and 11 Thermidor; on the days that followed dozens of militants suspected of having supported the Commune had been arrested and were awaiting judgement. In other words, at Paris, from the day after 9 Thermidor, the political enemy had been pointed out and was not limited to the 'triumvirs' alone. On the other hand, in the *départements* (apart from a few exceptions, notably in the Pas-de-Calais, where Lebon had been denounced before 9 Thermidor) the 'conspiracy' was associated only with the distant Robespierre. His unanimous condemnation also betrayed the desire of those who held 'offices' (or, at least, of a portion of the terrorist personnel) to take the lead and to avert any eventual suspicion of their collusion with the 'tyrant'. Not one representative *en mission* showed the least hesitation on learning the news from Paris. At the very most a feeling of surprise, of amazement, rapidly overcome:

No sooner had the mail brought the unexpected news of the conspiracy of the two Robespierres and their accomplices than we were immediately struck with amazement: 'What! we said to each other, were they also traitors! By what sign shall we now recognise the patriots, the true friends of the Republic?' ... We did not hesitate, citizen president, to make our choice. The popular society, the constituted authorities of this commune, instantly let out a cry of horror against these lying souls; they admired the constancy and energy of the National Convention ... Let them perish, the impostors, the tyrants of opinion and of liberty.[24]

From now on, each *département*, each town, in order to bring the Terror to an end and 'make justice the order of the day' had to conduct its own 9 Thermidor on the spot, to attack its own agents of the Terror, and denounce them as so many 'Robespierrists'. In doing so, they not only overcame the time-lag in relation to Paris, but they overtook the capital. For in condemning as slanderous Lecointre's denunciation of the seven members of the Committees, the Convention seemed to show a desire not to pursue those responsible for the Terror beyond the 'nucleus' initially indicated on 9 Thermidor. Now, these first 'purges' in the *départements* necessarily extended these responsibilities beyond a restricted Parisian group; they did not attack the *direct* accomplices of the 'conspiracy of 9 Thermidor', who were nonexistent outside Paris, but the local terrorist personnel and, consequently, their Parisian protectors, notably the Jacobins. As a repercussion, they again launched accusations against the Terror as an overall system of power, which could not be separated from all those who were its agents, who had profited from it and who from now on could no longer escape justice.

---

[24] Forestier, representative *en mission* in the Allier, to the National Convention, writing from Cusset, 16 Thermidor; AN C 311; cf. Aulard, *Recueil des actes*, vol. 15, pp. 644 *et seq.*

The Convention and its Committees often gave the initial impetus for starting the purges and arrests (for example, the Committee of Public Safety required the arrest of the members of the tribunal of Orange)[25] but it acted above all through the representatives *en mission*. From 18 Thermidor, when the Convention decreed that missions to the *départements* should not last longer than three months, the representatives were systematically replaced by moderate members of the Convention, to whom the Committees entrusted the release of detainees along with the purging of the constituted authorities, the popular societies and the revolutionary committees. By deciding, on 7 Fructidor, to proceed to a fundamental reform of the latter, the Convention in fact itself indicated the main directions to be taken in the coming purges. The debate which preceded the vote on this decree reveals the desire to be rid as quickly as possible of the most compromised personnel of the Terror, as well as the hesitations and contradictions characteristic of the political circumstances at the end of Year II.

The revolutionary committees (or surveillance committees) that spontaneously arose after 10 August 1792 on the initiative of the popular societies and municipalities gained in importance in 1793 to the point of becoming a particularly deadly instrument of the Terror. The law on suspects required the revolutionary committees to draw up, each in its own *arrondissement*, a list of suspects, to issue warrants of arrest against them and to have their papers put under seal. During the winter of 1793 (14 Frimaire, Year II), the powers of these committees were again increased: they were made responsible, conjointly with the municipalities, for applying the revolutionary laws and the measures of general security (especially the issue of certificates of good citizenship), and *all* their members were henceforth appointed by

---

[25] You know that several members [of the tribunal of Orange] were denounced for having individual links with the vile triumvirate whom the National Convention has just brought down and destroyed, and for having received specific instructions from them. You must, moreover, have already acquired definite views on the conduct of these members, and without doubt you have taken all the measures required by general security and the benefit of the *patrie*. (Committee of Public Safety to Perrin and Goupilleau, representatives in the Gard, Hérault and Vaucluse, 8 Fructidor, Year II, AN AF II, 37; cf. Aulard, *Recueil des actes*, vol. 16, p. 344)

The popular society of Orange had however congratulated the Convention on its victory over 'Catiline-Robespierre' ('May this terrible lesson bring terror and fear to the hearts of any bold men who would imitate his example'), while expressing its gratitude for ... the establishment of the revolutionary Tribunal:

'We have already shown, citizen-representatives, our gratitude for your having established within our walls a popular commission ... Exterminating all supports of tyranny, pursuing and punishing crime wherever it appears, correcting seduced weakness, protecting lost innocence, returning persecuted republicans to the *patrie*, these are the foundations of all the judgements it has handed down. (AN C 316; CII 1269)

The commission of Orange, as is well known, had been a model of terrorist repression; the procedure that it had followed inspired the law of 22 Prairial.

the representative *en mission*. The exorbitant powers of these committees, their abuses and their frequent conflicts with the representatives *en mission* made their reorganisation necessary after 9 Thermidor. The Convention decided not to completely deprive itself of their services by suppressing the institution itself. It was content to restrict their field of activity, to impose a stricter legal framework so as to put an end to their arbitrary power and, finally, to change their personnel. The most important measures were contained in the law of 7 Fructidor: suppression of revolutionary committees in the communes which were not the chief towns of their districts and had fewer than 8,000 inhabitants; the committees preserved the right to issue warrants for arrest but were required to interrogate the accused within twenty-four hours and let them know, within three days, the grounds for their arrest; each committee was composed of twelve members, appointed by the representative *en mission*, and half of the members were to be replaced every three months. In the course of the debates relating to this law, which lasted three days, several amendments were proposed. They provide enlightening evidence of the mistrust and rancour accumulated against the committees, especially as this evidence comes from former representatives *en mission* and is the fruit of their experience of collaboration, often in conflict, with these committees. Among these amendments, let us note that: citizens who could not read or write were not to be admitted to the committees, because they had to draw up reports and carry out interrogations; 'no bankrupt' could be a member, for there had been too many cases of 'immoral individuals arresting their creditors'; it would be forbidden for 'a father and son or two relatives, to the fourth degree inclusive, to be members of the same committee', in order to keep them from being dominated by a clique; the committees should be obliged to keep a record of their operations, for several could not 'explain the reasons for the arrest of the citizens they had imprisoned'; they would be banned from authorising the release of prisoners, for 'there are some who had citizens arrested and who then negotiated with them the price they required to give them their freedom'. Perhaps the most revealing proposal – it was in fact rejected – aimed to grant legal protection to members of the committees not reappointed to their posts:

By the new organisation of the revolutionary committees you deprive more than five hundred thousand individuals of their employment. Among these public servants there are some who without doubt are not beyond reproach, but it cannot be hidden that most of them united to save the Republic. Well, citizens, the members who will leave the revolutionary committees should be put under the special protection of the nation. If you do not adopt this measure, these citizens will become the object of *private passions, of revenge and hatred.* You must know little about the human heart if you think that anyone who has had his father, relative or friend thrown into gaol or led to the scaffold on the denunciation of a revolutionary committee will not keep up his hatred against the members of these committees, and will not seek for a dramatic revenge, if you do not curb these resentments. Citizens, these passions will operate with even more force in the little towns and could light the fire of civil war. To avoid this misfortune, I propose to decree that new revolutionary committees may not issue warrants of arrest against members of previous committees for actions previous to the termination of their office.

This speech by Ruelle was particularly pertinent and farseeing: he anticipated the foreseeable consequences of the reorganisation of the revolutionary committees and of the purging of the constituted authorities and popular societies. The Convention rid itself of a large part of this personnel without great regret, more or less aware that it was thereby inaugurating, inevitably, a period in which political conflicts and personal, individual and family revenge, would blend inexorably to the point of becoming completely intermingled.[26]

The purges in the *départements*, as we have seen, were entrusted to the representatives *en mission* and made their responsibility. These then had as their mission, as it were, to watch over and control an explosive material, and set off the detonator at the moment considered most opportune. For if central authority was encouraging the purges, its initiative linked up with the expectations of moderate local élites, often distanced from power, if not persecuted, during the Terror and who were increasingly aware of the opportunities offered to them by the new political circumstances. The Terror had, of course, aggravated political passions and then fed on this aggravation; it asserted itself however as a system of power only to the extent that it had succeeded in *politicising traditional* social and cultural

[26] On the reorganisation of the revolutionary committees, cf. *Moniteur*, vol. 21, pp. 547–9, 581–3, sessions of 3 and 7 Fructidor. We have referred only to certain aspects of this reform; other measures were: the reorganisation of the committees of Parisian *sections* (twelve committees instead of forty-eight, with one committee per *arrondissement* of four *sections*), a reform which weakened the power of the *sections*; the rejection of Chasles's proposal to proceed to the election of new committees (this would be contrary to the 'principles of revolutionary government' and would surreptitiously introduce an 'appeal to the people' once preached by the Girondins). The high number of 500,000 people who were affected by the reform was exaggerated. In fact, there were many communes where revolutionary committees had never functioned or were incomplete. Barère estimated the total number of committees in the country at 21,500 (cf. B. Barère, *Mémoires*, Paris, 1842, vol. 2, p. 324). In the course of the debate, the figure of '500,000 civil servants' was not contested. As we have noted, the Convention, during its debates on the Terror, often lacked precise figures; it fell back either on particular cases or upon more or less vague and hasty generalisations. The reformed and 'purged' revolutionary committees – who retained a portion of their personnel from the time of the Terror – served authority quite faithfully and efficiently in its 'anti-terrorist' and 'anti-Jacobin' actions. Cf. M. Bouloiseau, 'Les Comités de surveillance de Paris sous la réaction thermidorienne', *Annales historiques de la Révolution française*, 1973, vol. 10.

divisions, local antagonisms and conflicts, thereby fostering their *political violence*. From which follow two aspects of the Terror: on the one hand, it smothered and evened out through its violence the diversities, differences and divisions inherited from the past, in the name of its *single* unifying and centralising political programme; on the other, its politics, language, institutions and violence accompanied regional and local conflicts, down to the smallest commune or village, and then became intermingled with very old cabals and intrigues. This specific structure of the Terror, these two registers, make it, moreover, a privileged time and place for the analysis of the complex relationships between the revolutionary political field of action, modern and unifying, and traditional *mentalités* rooted in regional and local characteristics.[27]

The activities of the representatives *en mission* could only strengthen these characteristics of the Terror. The unlimited powers they possessed were, of course, the very expression of the centralising aim of the revolutionary government. However, the representatives arrived in *départements* that they did not know well; they were condemned to surround themselves with local political militants and, consequently, come under their influence; to carry out the national plan they had of necessity to cut to the bone of local conflicts and antagonisms, sometimes very brutally and arbitrarily. So they were seen to be more or less implicated not only in the conflicts which tore apart the local authorities and popular societies, but also in the cliques and intrigues that they discovered often after the event. Their powers being unlimited, the exercise thereof necessarily betrayed the political and ideological choices of this or that representative, and, quite often, his personality, his passions, fantasies and phobias (the Committees of Public Safety and General Security in fact sometimes intervened in the most flagrant cases of abuse of power and political extremism). The 'reign' of each representative thus marked the Terror with a specific imprint and, especially, generated an entire clientele greedy for 'offices'. The ending of the Terror in the *départements* was to take, in its turn, very different routes; it would depend, for one thing, on the extent of the Terror, on the situation then created and on the policy followed by the representative *en mission* responsible for 'making justice the order of the day'. Since the institutions remained almost unchanged, the new policy was revealed by the release of certain detainees, by the dismissal and, usually, by the arrest of those who had shown especial zeal in the exercise of terrorist power, and indeed the

---

[27] Colin Lucas has made a remarkable analysis of the relations of continuity and rupture between the violence and conflicts under the *ancien régime* and under the Revolution: cf. 'Themes in southern violence after 9 Thermidor', in G. Lewis and C. Lucas, eds., *Beyond the Terror*, Cambridge, 1983, pp. 152–94. Cf. also G.Lewis, *The second Vendée. The continuity of the counter-revolution in the department of the Gard, 1789–1815*, Oxford, 1978.

arrest of those on whom hatred and resentment focussed. Inevitably, these measures had repercussions in Paris: the persons arrested were not slow, through their families and political friends, to alert their former protectors, the representatives of the *département* concerned or the Jacobins. It was this that would cause the flow, from the *départements* to the capital, of deputations and petitions carrying news as alarming as it was confused: patriots were being oppressed, the aristocracy and *modérantisme* were raising their heads, said some; these alleged patriots were only intriguers, embezzlers, 'blood-drinkers', Robespierrists, who wanted to escape their just punishment, retorted others. Thus, as we have seen, events in the *départements*, through a full network of political affinities but also of friendships, influences and clientele, contributed to the polarisation of political positions in Paris, particularly in the Convention and at the Jacobin club.

Only a study of local situations, which would go a long way beyond the plan of this book, would permit understanding the exact extent of this first wave of arrests of 'terrorists' and establish its distribution by *départements*. In fact no one, to tell the truth, worried too much at the time about knowing such facts. It was the moment neither for exact figures nor for nuances, but for clear-cut stereotypes. These corresponded, at the very best, to extreme cases; now, the complex reality of the daily Terror, lived through at the level of a small town, was made up of confused situations where it was difficult, even impossible, to distinguish *a posteriori* between excess of zeal and abuse of power, between the 'energetic' exercise of revolutionary justice and arbitrary violence which amounted to a violation of common rights.

Who then was being imprisoned towards the end of Year II? At the time this question was violently debated in the Convention and at the Jacobin Club, in the press and in the 'groups', in Paris and in the *départements*. No overall reply could encompass the multitude of concrete cases. The very terms in which the question was formulated – 'good patriots oppressed', 'blood drinkers', 'intriguers', 'plunderers' – already implied one reply. These terms expressed one of the stakes of the political confrontation in progress: to win acceptance in public opinion and in the collective imagination for one cliché or the other, and, consequently, reduce the complex realities to these idea-images. Towards the end of Year II the triumph of the idea-image of the 'terrorist' and 'blood-drinker' began, a movement which was to accelerate rapidly in the first months of Year III under the impact of several factors with converging results: the Jacobin disturbance in Marseille at the beginning of Vendémiaire, the denunciation of 'vandals' and of 'vandalism' and, especially, the revelations on the Terror at Nantes produced by the trials of the revolutionary committee of Nantes and of Carrier. The requirement to make justice the order of the day converged more and more with a definite political choice: the political personnel of the

Terror was *judged guilty* from the very fact of having *participated in power that was itself guilty* and 'wicked'. The image of 'blood-drinker' thus justified the *policy of revenge* as the one effective means of dismantling the Terror. It was political revenge, of course; but also cultural and social revenge, against all these ignorant people, issued from the 'rabble', propelled by the course of events, for a moment, into politics, and even raised to the exercise of power.

What Michelet wrote about the wave of hatred which submerged the Jacobins could pertinently be applied to the resentment against all the terrorist personnel:

They were accountants who could not give an account . . . This terrifying power of arresting whoever they wished made people (even the purest) believe in the existence of vile, hateful things. Seeing the cowardice, the trembling docility of those they did not arrest, shameful bargains were imagined . . . To those who could do anything, hatred and imagination without any proof attributed everything . . . To their past brutalities, to their pride, to their fury, people replied with outrage; they said to them: 'Turn out your pockets.'[28]

### 'Freedom of the press or death'

Where is the Convention then? . . . The *journée* of 9 Thermidor has only kept France from having an acknowledged master. In fact, it had one for more than a year; but that *journeé* was not a true revolution. You could have, or rather, you should have supplemented it since then; but where are the laws you have passed to restore to the nation its usurped rights? Where are the decrees exterminating those shameful institutions, institutions more monarchic than those established under the tyrants? What use is it to destroy the man if all that he created remains? *The press has been regained, but it is we who have carried it by assault, with the weapons of reason in our hands.* We have been reduced to carrying out this outrage to public reason from the necessity of proving that the freedom to declare one's thought is a legitimate right. This has been turned into a problem in your chamber. You gave hardly any sign of tacit approval for this freedom, and at the first resistance which you were seen to make against this eternal and indefeasible right, it remained unclear, in the judgement of many, if your tolerance in this respect has not been commanded by the strength of the general will, which despite you seems to decree the protection of free writers.[29]

The publication of 'these strong truths addressed to the Convention' in a journal whose very title claims the freedom of the press is in itself a demonstration of the effective re-establishment of this freedom towards the end of Year II. Of course, Babeuf's narrative of this reconquest is too

---

[28] Michelet, *Histoire du dix-neuvième siècle*, p. 97.
[29] Babeuf, *Journal de la liberté de la presse*, no. 10, on the Festival of the Virtues, first day of the *sans-culottides*, Year II.

heroic, but it is incontestable that after 9 Thermidor the changes that came in this domain are among the most spectacular. There is a striking contrast with the muzzled press of the Terror, as cheerless as it was unanimous in the display of its enthusiasm, and content to take up and paraphrase official discourse. Publications multiplied, newspapers and booklets increased in variety of political opinions and in polemics. The tyranny of yesterday was denounced and, like justice, freedom of expression was 'made the order of the day'. The claiming of freedom of the press and opinion became the object of a bitter debate, revealing the difficulties and contradictions inherent in the process of emerging from the Terror. This debate, which took place in the Convention, at the Jacobins and in the press itself contributed to the acceleration of the process and the press asserted itself in its turn as an important factor in this acceleration.

A dozen days after 9 Thermidor, the claim for full re-establishment of freedom of the press was heard at the Convention; from the beginning of Fructidor, this question had unceasingly occupied the Jacobins. This freedom was claimed first of all for the innocent victims of the Terror. It fell to them to present publicly the misfortunes they had encountered and the horrors they witnessed. To tell the truth on the very recent past was the essential measure preventing its return.

It is enough to cast our eyes over what has taken place for more than a year, to see that freedom of the press has been destroyed. It is not enough to have the existing laws, since it is clear that they have been violated; there has to be a certain and indestructible guarantee, and we should no longer fear being guillotined for having written such and such a thing at such and such a time. If we are to properly detest the regime which has just ended, I believe it is necessary to make its disgusting effects visible; it is in the portrayal of the evils that people were made to suffer in the prisons that the indignation of good citizens should find its sustenance.[30]

Freedom of expression had been stifled throughout the country, and it was only through this that the 'tyranny' of Robespierre could be established and exercised. The 'tyrant' was above all criticism; to criticise him was to risk one's life; it was the same with criticism of his acolytes and the innumerable violations of the laws. The re-establishment of freedom of expression and, especially, of the press was a fundamental guarantee of republican institutions. So the unanimous condemnation of Robespierre's tyranny found its logical extension in freedom of the press and of opinion; re-establishing it, as well as putting it fully into practice, were all conditions of the re-establishment of justice which the Convention had 'made the order of the day'. To empty the gaols of the victims of the Terror, to denounce the

---

[30] Réal, speech at the Jacobins, meeting of 28 Thermidor, Year II; cf. Aulard, *Société des Jacobins*, vol. 6, p. 342.

guilty – those 'knights of the guillotine' – by name in the press, to protect the citizens against abuses and arbitrary power, these were the three facets of a single and even noble cause.

Without the adoption of this motto, *Freedom of the press or death*, without its full execution, we are no more than abject slaves of the whims and despotic moods of the first man who, invested with authority, can turn it against us with impunity, and use it to crush us. No, no, liberty has never had a real existence in a country where all mouths can be closed, all pens broken, where even thought can be enchained. The natural right of every individual to express his own thought freely no longer exists today in France ... Ah! no doubt it is time that the frightful regime of violence, of repression, of tyranny, should fall and be for ever destroyed; it is time that man, the equal of every other man, should enjoy without distress, without fear and without reproach, the right to express his desires, to give his opinion, to resist slander, and to declare what he thinks of individuals and things. It is only by guaranteeing this precious liberty that you will be able to find a secure shelter against all the blows of arbitrary authority.[31]

'Freedom of the press or death!': the slogan was, of course, not new. Tallien was only taking over for his own use the words Danton used to defend Marat against the attacks of the Girondins in February 1793 ... The rhetorical exaggeration went hand in hand, in fact, with declarations which remained quite vague and abstract. 'Freedom of the press or death' certainly; but no one was threatening with death or prison those who *after* 9 Thermidor denounced the 'modern Catiline' and his 'tyranny', and no voice was raised to defend Robespierre. The possible adversaries of freedom of the press were referred to only very allusively; at the end of Thermidor, Tallien was still calling on the Jacobins to make this freedom the principal object of their activities and so consolidate the unity of all the enemies of tyranny.

Very swiftly, however, in the second and third *décades* of Fructidor, freedom of the press became the centre of conflict and debate. The touching slogan, 'freedom of the press or death', divided public opinion more and more. In fact, the debate was about the role which should be taken by public opinion and, particularly, the press in the political arena of the period after the Terror and about the use that the press was beginning to make of this rediscovered liberty, following the relaxation of government control. The spark had been put in the powder keg – as we have seen – by the pamphlet *La Queue de Robespierre* published on 9 Fructidor, the very day that Fréron made his saga-speech on freedom of the press. What did *La Queue de Robespierre* have to say?

*Let freedom of the press come*, and then the questions that people ask themselves everywhere, but quietly: 'Was it possible that Robespierre did all that evil by

[31] Tallien, speech at the Jacobins, meeting of 1 Fructidor; *ibid.*, pp. 354–5.

himself, alone?' will be asked openly and loudly. It is not surprising that *Robespierre's Tail*, the Barères, the Billauds, the Collots become agitated as soon as freedom of the press is called for: 'Ah, citizens, beware of the mania for discussion, people already do too much discussing throughout the Republic.' Just like all the tyrants of the past, they call for urgent measures to be taken against the 'prattling of the press' and its dangerous consequences. Thus we shall 'discuss no more' the innocent victims, gunned down in Lyon on the orders of Collot; no evil tongue shall contest 'the gentleness and mercy' of Billaud-Varenne and no one will recall that Barère was, by turns and according to circumstances, aristocrat, captain of the Feuillants, Jacobin and ally of Robespierre, to become today his mortal enemy.[32]

The success of the pamphlet was immediate. It associated, in effect, the defence of freedom of the press with the struggle against the 'tail' left by Robespierre, the 'successors of the last tyrant'; the exercise of this freedom would consist above all in the denunciation of the crimes committed yesterday and of the desire to camouflage them today; direct and violent personal attacks corresponded best to collective expectations, to the feelings of revenge and retribution. A pamphleteer could therefore easily find both political protectors and a public. *La Queue de Robespierre* was to stir up in its turn a number of lampoons in the same vein: *Fight for your tail*; *Give me back my tail, since you have my head*; *Cut his tail off*. All these titles were bawled out by street-hawkers, had 'enormous sales' and enjoyed 'close public attention'. Their growing number as well as their wide circulation bore witness to the new political climate and to a new relationship of forces. There is a revealing anecdote which delighted the press: one street-hawker who was shouting at the top of her voice, 'Here is *The Jacobins unmasked*', in the garden of the Tuileries was arrested by a Jacobin and brought before the Committee of General Security; the Committee on this occasion paid 'formal tribute to freedom of the press by giving the unjustly arrested woman a voucher to compensate her and by detaining the man who had arrested her'.[33]

Towards the end of Fructidor, this political development was again emphasised by the publication of three new newspapers which, so to speak, took possession of the terrain left open to the press. In close succession, appeared (or reappeared) Babeuf's *Le Journal de la liberté de la presse* (17 Fructidor), Tallien's *L'Ami du citoyen* (reappearance on 23 Fructidor); Fréron's *L'Orateur du peuple* reappeared on 25 Fructidor. Apart from the individual differences of each of these papers, their similarities and affinities, their common political orientation stood out. They intervened actively in political debates, quickly and clearly took up positions on subjects in the news. The preferred subjects and the lines of attack were the same as in the

---

[32] Felhémési, *La Queue de Robespierre*.
[33] *Gazette française*, 30 Fructidor, Year II; the same anecdote, in a slightly different version, appears in the *Courrier républicain*, 30 Fructidor, Year II.

speeches of Tallien and Fréron at the Convention: denunciation of the horrors of the Terror and glorification of the benefits of the 'revolution of 9 Thermidor'; the work of the latter should be extended by 'energetic measures' which would, in particular, make 'justice the order of the day'; to have defeated the 'tyrant' was not enough, the right thing now was to destroy 'Robespierrism', the system and its agents. These political attacks converged, but above all a new tone, combined with verbal violence, nourished on old fears and the spirit of revenge, stirred up people's fury.[34]

The change made itself felt everywhere in the newspapers, if only because of the publication of the animated and contradictory debates of the Convention. Even the *Bulletin de la Convention* and the semi-official *Moniteur* began to look like fire-brands when they published, for example, accounts of the debates on Lecointre's denunciation. At the end of Year II, one could see also the beginning of a Jacobin counter-offensive in the press: so, on 29 Fructidor, Chasles, a Montagnard member of the Convention, and the printer Lebois launch *L'Ami du peuple*, in homage to Marat's paper. Now, from its beginning, the new journal embarked on a very clumsy polemic which was going to last several weeks and deserves our pausing over. An admission of weakness, it is also evidence of the disarray provoked by the reversal of public opinion. In fact, the audience enjoyed by the anti-terrorist pamphlets and newspapers which, in asserting the freedom of the press, attack the 'blood-drinkers' and the 'Robespierrists', led *L'Ami du peuple* to make a subtle and paradoxical distinction, thanks to which the

---

[34] These few, very brief observations scarcely pretend to analyse these papers, their content or their role in political life, or their development. Such an analysis remains to be carried out, as well as a detailed study of the Thermidorean press. It would be especially necessary to stress the particularities of each of these three papers, and especially Babeuf's. As is well known, having reached the 23rd issue (14 Vendémiaire, Year II), he was to change the title to *Le Tribun du peuple, ou le défenseur des droits de l'homme en continuation du Journal de la liberté de la presse*. When reading *Le Journal de la liberté de la presse* in the light of the future development of its editor, the historians of Babeufism were especially interested in the precursory signs of this development. However, towards the end of Year II, its similarities with the papers of Tallien and Fréron were stronger than the differences. Babeuf, moreover, expressed his admiration for Tallien and Fréron, 'athletes of the revolution', 'champions of the group of the defenders of the rights of man'; Tallien, in turn, spoke highly of Babeuf, 'one of the writers who since 10 Thermidor had displayed the most energy' (*L'Ami des citoyens*, no. 4, 14 Brumaire, Year III). At the end of Year II Babeuf's thought was confused; it exuded hatred against 'king Maximilien', 'Robespierrism' and 'Robespierrists'; it nourished hopes of the likely consequences of the 'revolution of 9 Thermidor' – elements which quite naturally united it with the other 'athletes' of this revolution. Unlike Fréron and Tallien, old campaigners of revolutionary politics who adroitly played their cards as defectors from the camp of the 'knights of the guillotine', Babeuf was conspicuous by his great political naivety. His writings on the massacres of Nantes and the Carrier affair were to bring striking evidence of the fantasies and contradictions through which his politics developed.

publicist attempted to rationalise a development whose meaning escaped him.

Opinion is the queen of the world. A trivial and hackneyed truth, but it is the order of the day, and will provide material for useful reflections. For too long *public opinion* has been confused with the *opinion of the people*. The *public* is not the people; and the people rarely thinks like the public. This kind of paradox will soon be an established truth. *Since 10 Thermidor public opinion is in a state of counter-revolution.* Why is the counter-revolution not yet completed? Because the opinion of the people is there, serving as a dyke for public opinion. While the aristocracy is active and makes a lot of noise, the people, calm and passive, observes, reflects and is silent. The silence of the people, as we know, is not without eloquence nor its inaction without effect.[35]

This was only one of the paradoxical effects of 9 Thermidor which 'offers very strange contrasts and results'. On the one hand, 'it saved the Republic by the return of liberty, it restored to national representation its dignity, to opinion its energy'; but on the other hand, 'it has infected the Republic with the noxious emanations of the aristocracy, escaped from the cesspool of the prisons; it has rung the alarm bell of defamation and revenge against patriots; it has neutralised revolutionary spirit and action'. At the same time, the newspaper makes itself the interpreter and the spokesman of this 'silence of the people' and that with a very menacing tone. 'It is not' it continues on the same day, 'by the hypocritical gestures of adulation and lies, by congratulations and speeches, that the people expresses its opinion. Its true language is the one it used on 31 May, after the completion of the constitution of '93 and at the great hours of the revolution.' Tallien would find it easy enough to refute 'these sophisms' and to 'denounce this distinction' between public opinion and the opinion of the people:

You claim that since 10 Thermidor, public opinion is in counter-revolution. What! You call counter-revolution this deep horror for tyranny, which appears in all hearts, this unanimous cry raised against the men of blood, against the rascals and embezzlers. What! It is counter-revolutionary to desire the reign of justice and to reunite around the National Convention; in this case there are in France 24 million counter-revolutionaries.

To reject *public opinion* and invoke the *opinion of the people* was merely a 'Jesuitical *distinction*' (Chasles was a defrocked ex-canon) proposed by people who could no longer hide and against whom the people gave its verdict.

The people want justice and not tyranny. The people want the punishment of crime, where it is encountered. The people reject barbarity, injustice and immorality with

[35] *L'Ami du peuple*, no. 5, 12 Vendémiaire, Year III; no. 19, 6 Brumaire, Year III.

horror. Go into the workshops, into the suburbs, into the public squares, in short wherever the people meet, ask them about Carrier and Lebon and everywhere a unanimous voice shall convince you: public opinion is the people's opinion.[36]

To set oneself up in arbitrary fashion as interpreter of the people, opposed to the public, was to make this bogus distinction the basis for a 'new aristocracy' which aimed to seize the expression of public opinion for itself alone.

The polemics and the attacks in the press are particularly characteristic of the passionate political climate that set in at the emergence from the Terror. The press, far from escaping from this climate, contributed to the sudden rise in temperature. It became a particularly formidable political weapon by taking up and exciting the political passions which tore apart the Convention and public opinion. Whatever the intellectual quality of the political press, which sank too easily into invective, informing and settling of scores, the gain in liberty, compared to the period of the Terror, was indisputable.

The situation was *de facto* a new one, as a result of the reversal of political circumstances, but it was *not* new *de jure*.[37] The Convention, as we have seen, took, in the weeks following 9 Thermidor, a series of measures modifying the legal apparatus established during the Terror. But it did nothing similar as far as the press and its legal basis were concerned. Now, the latter was particularly ambiguous. The Terror represents an especially sombre period in the stormy history of freedom of the press under the Revolution. As a kind of basic principle, the Constitution of 1793 officially confirmed the freedom of the press: 'The right to manifest one's thought and opinions, either through the press, or in any other manner, the right of peaceful assembly, the free exercise of cults, cannot be forbidden. The need to set out these rights assumes either the presence or the recent memory of despotism.'[38] However, the Constitution of 1793 was, immediately after its proclamation, enclosed in an 'ark' and its application postponed until the end of the war. It therefore changed nothing in the *de facto* situation, which continued to worsen with the strengthening of the Jacobin dictatorship. Already on 9 March 1793 the Convention, under pressure from the Mountain, voted through a law requiring the journalist deputies to make a

---

[36] *L'Ami des citoyens*, no. 14, 14 Brumaire, Year III (article signed by Tallien). On 1 Brumaire, Year III, the newspaper became a daily and abandoned its subtitle *Journal patriotique* while substituting for it *Journal du commerce et des arts par Tallien et une société des patriotes*. Méhée *fils* was in practice the editor. Cf. E. Hatin, *Histoire politique et littéraire de la presse en France*, Geneva, 1967, vol. 6, pp. 237 *et seq.*

[37] It is in fact quite symptomatic of the state of public opinion to see the appearance, from Floréal, Year III, of Richier-Sérizy's *L'Accusateur public*, a newspaper which barely hid its royalist opinions. However, no newspaper dared to take up the defence of the 'new Catiline' or his 'system'.

[38] Article 7 of the Declaration of the Rights of Man and the Citizen, *Les Constitutions de la France depuis 1789*, edited by J. Godechot, Paris, 1979, p. 80.

choice between their mandate and their newspaper. It was a discriminatory
measure against the Girondins, and especially against Brissot and Gorsas
whose newspapers enjoyed a very great popularity. 'The rights of man are
no more; all natural laws are trampled under foot; one night has overturned
the work of four years: individual liberty, the freedom of the press ... A
faction that wishes to reign among shadows has banned thinking deputies
from enlightening their citizens', declared Brissot the next day in *Le
Patriote français* (no. 1306), as he announced that he found himself obliged
to abandon the editorship of his newspaper. On 29 March 1793, the
Convention decreed that anyone who called for a return of the monarchy or
attacked private property would be punished by death. After the *journée* of
31 May, the Girondin press disappeared; it was decreed by the law on
suspects that 'all those ... who either by their conduct, or by their
connections, or by *their words or writings*, show themselves partisans of
tyranny and federalism, and enemies of liberty, are considered suspect'. On
17 October, another law dealt with the personal responsibility of the editors
of any writing containing criticism of the Convention and the Committees.
The condemning to death of several Girondins was based on their opinions
expressed in the press as journalists. The little that remained of freedom of
the press disappeared with the repression that swept down upon *Le Vieux
Cordelier*, a newspaper which was, as it happened, defending freedom of
expression with great courage, and upon the Hébertists, along with whom
sank *Le Père Duchesne*. The only titles left were scrupulously controlled by
Jacobin authority which, moreover, subsidised some of them. This press
spoke with but one voice and was content to repeat the discourse prevailing
at the Convention and the Jacobins. Despite this zeal, mistrust of journalists and the press continued and did not cease to be shown on the rostrum
of the Jacobins and at the Convention.[39]

If, after 9 Thermidor, the Committees took hardly any initiative in
abolishing the laws on the misdemeanours of the press nor in proposing
new guarantees of freedom of expression, authority nevertheless relaxed its
stranglehold. It was, in fact, impossible to maintain it. The 'fall of the
tyrant' had brought down the barriers, as is shown by the energetic and
contradictory debates at the Convention and at the Jacobins; the press, by
gaining in vigour and liberty, made in its turn new breakthroughs. Liberty
was regained but it remained very fragile; hence the importance of the
initiative proposing, by legal and institutional guarantees, to confirm it and
protect it against any domination.

Fréron's speech of 9 Fructidor on unlimited freedom of the press is

[39] A recent restatement of the history of the press under the Terror and, in particular, of the
repression of journalists, can be found in H. Gough, *The newspaper press in the French
Revolution*, London, 1987.

remarkable for the ideas that he put forward, but also for his silence. For this largely explains the resistance which he was to run up against. Like many other texts of this period, this speech is first of all valuable as an analysis, made in the heat of the moment, of the workings of the Terror and of the lessons that could be drawn to prevent its return. Like so many other speeches, this text is also a weapon in a carefully prepared political offensive. A simple comparison of the dates already reveals a tactic, even a political manoeuvre which we have already mentioned: Fréron spoke on 9 Fructidor, the very same day that *La Queue de Robespierre* was published; on 11 Fructidor Tallien delivered his speech on the 'system of the Terror' and on justice as the order of the day; on 12 Fructidor, Lecointre drew up his indictment against the seven members of the Committees.

Fréron began with a general discussion of the place that 9 Thermidor held in 'the immense chain of events occurring in France'. Now, in this 'short space of five years, which will together preoccupy the centuries under the general name of the French Revolution', 9 Thermidor was set down as the fourth revolution, after those which attacked in succession the nobility and clergy, the monarchy and, finally, federalism. This fourth revolution was, perhaps, the most difficult to carry out, for the enemy was then the most treacherous and most hidden. A comparison with the English Revolution (Fréron thus took over for his own use the standard French view, which had been in place since 1789) proved the repetition of this kind of experience in any revolution as well as the superiority of the French Revolution. More fortunate than England, because it was more enlightened, because it was more deserving, France should be a great example: 'it should have a Cromwell, but it should not have a master'.

For Robespierre was, to be sure, a new Cromwell, yet more dangerous and ambitious. It was for history to draw up 'the life of the tyrant Robespierre, his complete portrait', but the workings of his system of tyranny were here and now to be stripped bare. In this system, 'artistically graded, he had undertaken, under the pretext of revolutionary government, to place the Convention above principles, the two Committees above the Convention, the Committee of Public Safety above the Committee of General Security, and himself above the Committee of Public Safety'. It was in this way that he suppressed freedom of expression and did so at the very heart of the Convention, 'where freedom of opinion should have taken refuge when it had been exiled from all the earth' and where 'it was necessary to sacrifice one's life to have an opinion contrary to Robespierre's'. The whole machine of the Terror: the system of 'the most vile spying'; the gaols overflowing with innocent prisoners; the fabricated 'plots'; and, finally, 'a tribunal of assassins', imposed a deathly silence on the Convention and the whole country.

To draw up this description of the 'system of terror and blood', was it not 'to take the risk of accusing the National Convention in the eyes of France, and France itself in the eyes of Europe and humanity? ... Should we not blush as well as groan for the many excesses and evils we have suffered?' But only treacherous men, the accomplices and successors of the 'tyrant', disparaged the Convention, on the pretext of denouncing collective responsibility. In Fréron's text a leitmotiv of Thermidorean discourse can be found: exoneration of the Convention from any responsibility in the Terror; restoration of confidence in itself and raising of its prestige. 'The tyrant, who oppressed his colleagues even more than the nation, was so surrounded with the semblance of the most popular virtues; the respect and confidence of the people, which he had usurped by five years of unremitting hypocrisy, formed around him a rampart so sacred, that we would have jeopardised the nation and liberty itself if we had abandoned ourselves to our impatience by attacking the tyrant earlier.' (The Convention received with prolonged applause these words of moral comfort which it needed so much ...)

The Convention was divided in its opinions on the death of Capet and these divisions weighed heavily on the course of events; the Convention showed its unanimity in voting for the death of the new tyrant. This unity in face of the common danger had already inspired the first 'noble acts', which had 'halted tyranny and punished some for its awful disturbances ... Let us hurry to turn this restoration of our feelings and souls to advantage and complete the legislative work that the Republic has called for at the Convention.'

The re-establishment of freedom of the press was therefore a contribution to the carrying out of two important objectives: the correction, in the immediate present, of the abuses created by the Terror, and, in the longer term, *the completion of the Revolution* through the working of the Convention. The bloody period belonging to the past had bequeathed a fundamental lesson.

The tyrant had stifled both freedom of discussion, by which the Convention could have denounced him to the nation, and freedom of the press, by which the nation would have denounced him to the Convention. This terrifying example teaches us to what extent freedom of the press is necessary for frightening, unmasking and halting the plots of the ambitious.

But Robespierre himself had not dared openly to say that it was no longer permitted to publish. Thus no law had been dragged out of the Convention to suppress freedom of the press and remove from the people 'the enjoyment of the first of the rights of man', that of 'the unlimited freedom to think anything, say anything, write anything, print anything'. The Convention had never forgotten that the Revolution began 'with the enlightenment which the press disseminated under the very eyes of the despots'. However, the 'last tyrant ... as artificial as he was cruel' acted in such a way that 'the axe was suspended over all the heads that might have made use of this freedom ... And how right he was to believe that this crime was necessary for him to carry out all his other crimes; to put liberty into retreat it was absolutely necessary for him to force into retreat the enlightenment which had been its origin.' So, although never formally abolished, freedom of the press no longer existed. Hence the urgency of both its official confirmation and its active re-establishment.

Fréron then came to discuss the role of a free press in the future perfecting of republican institutions. Since 1789, one of the essential problems at the heart of constitutional debates was that of the means to be devised which would ensure the advantages of direct democracy for a *modern* people, for whom that form of democracy was out of the question, if only because of its size and the large number of citizens.[40] Now, it fell to Fréron to make the connection between this, so to speak, classical subject of discussion of democratic institutions and freedom of the press. Democracy presupposed, on one hand, that the law was the expression of the general will, but the representative system had as its inevitable consequence that the laws became the real expression of the mind and wish of some hundreds of members of the National Assembly. Now, thanks to a free press, 'this defect of representation is removed, or at least corrected'. Through the press, the whole Nation, if it did not contribute to the votes of the Assembly, could actively contribute to the deliberations that preceded them.

Through [the press] the representatives and the represented keep moving towards unity, and democracy exists in a nation of twenty-five million men, although there be only eight hundred legislators.

In this way the Revolution would accomplish something unprecedented in history, something considered until now as 'chimerical' even by men of genius, that was, 'giving to representative government the essential features of the purest democracy'.

It was only by returning to its founding and unalterable principles that the Convention could draw all the lessons imposed by the disastrous experience of the Terror, as well as construct a new political arena for the future. Now, as far as the freedom of the press was concerned, this fundamental principle left no doubt and permitted of no provisional measures:

[40] On the importance of this issue in the constitutional debates, and in particular for the definition of the democratic political arena, cf. B. Baczko, 'Le Contrat social des Français: Sieyès et Rousseau', in K. M. Baker (ed.), *The French Revolution and the creation of modern political culture*, vol. 1: *The political culture of the Old Regime*, Oxford, 1987, pp. 493–515. (English translation in *Journal of Modern History*, September 1988, vol. 60.)

*Freedom of the press does not exist if it is not unlimited; any boundary in this area destroys it.* This very day, therefore, let this fountainhead of enlightenment, which kept springing from freedom of the press, be reopened, over this sanctuary of the laws as well as over the whole extent of the Republic, and, in the light with which it will surround us, let us debate all the great questions of organisation which are not yet decided, or which have not been decided to the satisfaction of patriots, the most enlightened of France and the sages of the universe.

Of course, unlimited freedom of the press was not without risks; this 'beacon of humankind' could become a harmful instrument in 'the hands of some incendiaries'. These were, however, minimal risks if they were compared to the advantages offered by freedom of the press. The decree, proposed by Fréron in conclusion to all these arguments, was quite vague; it was an official declaration confirming the principle of unlimited freedom of the press and condemning any attempt to return to the methods of the Terror.

The press is free; it shall suffer no breach nor retroactive action, at any time, for any reason, nor under any pretext. Any legislative body, any government committee, any executive power that, by decree, order or taking the law into its own hands, will prevent or impede the freedom of the press, will put itself and declare itself, by that alone, in a state of conspiracy against the rights of man, against the people and against the Republic.[41]

Fréron's speech communicated more than it actually stated and this was the sense in which it was understood. Beyond the glorification of great principles, discussions of the future, of democracy, the rhetorical flights, the public took it to be offering proposals of political currency. It was a month after 9 Thermidor, *a time of generalised suspicion*; intrigues, underhand blows, dubious manoeuvres are imagined everywhere. The speech of a man like Fréron could not avoid this, and rightly so. Fréron glorified the freedom of the press and held out bright prospects of an improvement in republican institutions; however, he said nothing of the revolutionary government in force 'until the peace', and, consequently, nothing of the emergency regime which was suspending constitutional rights. To confirm freedom of the press and declare it unlimited, outside the supervision of 'any Committee', was this not already to call into question again the very principle of this government? Fréron aired his opinions on the importance of the press for the effective functioning of representative government; he did not, however, even mention the popular societies. If the press was to be, in some way, the substitute for direct democracy, the popular societies would thereby lose the very reason for their existence. And to grant to the press an exceptional role in the functioning of republican institutions

[41] All quotations are taken from the speech of Fréron on unlimited freedom of the press: cf. *Moniteur*, vol. 21, pp. 601–5.

seemed to be a ruse to make it a counter-power in face of the Assembly and, consequently, elevate journalists, these 'hacks', into forgers of public opinion, equalling or even surpassing in importance the representatives of the people. Fréron exalted the sublime principle of freedom of opinion and speech; but no one forgot the use he had made of it himself in his *Orateur du peuple*, his poisonous pen, his shameless rabble-rousing, the meanest personal attacks, which he had justified by appealing, as it happened, to freedom of the press. Fréron glorified the unity of the Convention, rediscovered and confirmed on 9 Thermidor, but in the Convention's corridors the rumour ran that Tallien along with Fréron was preparing a coup, a 9 Fructidor which would follow 9 Thermidor. Was not the celebration of unity the best means, tested many times, of hiding a political cabal? To appeal to unlimited freedom of the press at the very moment that the street-hawkers were 'shouting' in Paris *La Queue de Robespierre*, was this not to make the principle, presented as sacrosanct, a simple pretext for the better preparation of political revenge?

The Convention was not sparing in its 'repeated and unanimous' applause for Fréron's speech, but it refused to vote through his draft bill and sent it to the Committee of Legislation, a better way of burying it. The objections and reservations raised during the debate were many. Of course, no one contested the principle of freedom of the press itself. On the contrary, those who most opposed acceptance of the bill kept underlining the 'sacred' character of this principle. Deputies, mostly from the Mountain, put forward several reservations. Formal reservations first: the principle having been officially declared in the 'code of the rights of man' and never repudiated by the Convention, even at the harshest moments of the 'tyranny', its confirmation was simply superfluous. Then reservations on the vagueness of the bill: it was not enough to proclaim the freedom of the press; all the experience of the Revolution proved that such a proclamation had to be accompanied by certain restrictions concerning, in particular, abuses and libels, which should be punished. But then, how to bring in these restrictions without thereby calling into question the *unlimited* freedom of the press? On the other hand, wouldn't this freedom, with the right to criticize, represent the best protection against all abuses? Classic arguments and disagreements, so to speak; in fact, they resurfaced each time the successive assemblies debated bills on the press. The Convention should therefore both acknowledge the freedom of the press – which it had already done in the Constitution – and restrain it, by defining *for whom* it existed, and by fixing, in *detail*, limits not at all acknowledged by the Constitution. To this were added arguments more specifically linked to the political situation: the country was not in 'an ordinary period'. By following the Declaration of the Rights of Man to the letter, the Convention would never have decreed the creation of the surveillance committees, and yet it unanimously considered them necessary (Cambon). On the other hand, from the definition of *liberty* or *freedom* as *undefined* would it follow that the Royalists and the Vendéans could put forward and publish their political ideas and, in particular, attack 'innocent and upright men over their political actions' (Amar)?[42]

After the debate on Lecointre's denunciation and the rush of new anti-Jacobin libels, the suspicions and fears which were put forward in the conditional tense during the debate on Fréron's bill become certainties amongst the Jacobins. Fréron and Tallien *desired* freedom of the press in order to camouflage their intrigues and to give aristocrats, royalists and Vendéans the opportunity to speak. The undefined freedom of the press could only destroy the Republic because it was incompatible with revolutionary government. By expelling Fréron, Tallien and Lecointre, the Society of Jacobins unmasked the slanderers; the revolutionary laws placed limits to liberty, limits required for the protection of this very liberty: 'I fully expect that there will be an attempt to make people believe that the Jacobins do not want freedom of the press; this is false. The Jacobins reject only undefined freedom, which cannot be reconciled with revolutionary government.'[43]

However, the climacteric of Year II was passed without any restriction being imposed on the press and the attacks against the 'terrorists' only increased. The trial of the revolutionary committee of Nantes and of Carrier as well as the attacks against the Jacobins reached their climax. The Montagnards and the Jacobins, exasperated by the newspapers and the innumerable pamphlets which hounded them with accusations of wanting to save the 'drowners', decided to counter-attack. The episode, in itself minor and without major consequences, is not only evidence of the outburst of passions which freedom of the press provoked, it also throws light on certain traits of the political culture of the Revolution.

On 18 Brumaire, Year III, at the end of a stormy session at the Convention, Cambon went so far as to accuse Tallien of being a 'slaughterer' responsible for the September massacres, and a thief, who had shamelessly embezzled public money, while he was now elevating himself in his newspaper into a moral censor. Following this exchange of civilities, Goupilleau (from Fontenay) proposed that the Committees should re-examine 'the question so many times debated, whether a representative of the people can be at the same time a journalist'. In support of this proposition he argued:

By what right does an individual come here to elevate himself into a universal tribunal? What! One can slander and be let off by saying: I was wrong! I declare that

---

[42] *Ibid.*, pp. 605–6.
[43] Cf. Aulard, *Société des Jacobins*, vol. 6, pp. 407 *et seq.* (session of 17 Fructidor), pp. 417 *et seq.* (session of 19 Fructidor), pp. 517 *et seq.* (session of 5 Vendémiaire, Year III).

any faker of libels, any journalist who is at the same time a representative of the people, is in my eyes the most contemptible of men. A representative should be either at the Committee or the Convention and, at times when he cannot be at either of these two posts, he should be occupied in thinking over matters which will be discussed at the Convention. He should not be carrying out a vile traffic in slander, nor calculating if, by speaking evil of this or that individual, he will sell six thousand more papers than if he did not mention him.

Fréron and Tallien were certainly the targets more than anyone else. The proposal, which found support on the benches of the Mountain, curiously revived the law of 9 March 1793, which we have already mentioned, and which decided precisely on the incompatibility of the two functions: being a journalist and a representative of the people. The image of the representative who consecrated all his time and all his thoughts to his function was, of course, demagogic, and everyone knew it. This demagogy exploited, however, a commonly accepted stock of ideas and perceptions on the demarcations of the two fields to be respected: that of mainly political and public activities constituted by the representative Assembly and where the general will was expressed, and the field of opinions and individual interests, where, in the nature of things, cliques and factions formed and to which the press belonged. In March 1793, the Jacobins used this argument against the Girondins by accusing them of attacking the Convention in their papers, thus placing themselves outside it and forming a 'faction'. Now, curiously, in Brumaire, Year III, the same argument would be turned against the Jacobins. The response to Goupilleau was not only to remind him that the Convention was obliged to annul this decree of March, for it had felt that it was unjust and dangerous; but, in order to find out if a representative of the people should in fact consecrate all his time and all his thought to the Convention, so as to contribute to the better clarification of the general will, he was also questioned on the subject of membership of a *particular, even exclusive*, society: How can one be both a representative of the people and criticise the Convention *from outside*? In other words, how can one *both recognise the Convention as the single rallying point and be a Jacobin*?[44]

### How can one be a Jacobin?

On 9 Thermidor the Convention carried out *its* revolution and did so *unanimously*. This unanimity was expressed in the cries of *Down with the Tyrant!* as well as by the outlawing of Robespierre, his acolytes and the Commune, declared to be in revolt against national representation, the

---

[44] Cf. *Moniteur*, vol. 22, pp. 459–60. The session ended in chaos, jeers and insults. Goupilleau himself withdrew his proposition.

single legitimate authority. This victory and this new epoch, opened by the 'happy revolution', were thus placed under the sign of the Convention as the one and only 'rallying point'. This assumed, however, a Convention that was itself united, which would experience no more deep divisions or discord, once the 'conspirators' were eliminated. This also assumed that there would exist *only one centre of authority*.

In the days and weeks that followed 9 Thermidor, the Convention adopted a succession of measures intended to reinforce its active role in the exercise of authority. The Convention ensured a minimum security for its members by adopting legal measures preventing their arbitrary arrest (these would be added to in Brumaire, Year III, at the time of the Carrier affair). The Convention also protected itself against any eventual reappearance of a counter-power in the form of a new Commune of Paris. It thus drew on the lessons of 9 Thermidor as well as of the previous *journées*, notably that of 31 May when it had been besieged and threatened by cannons aimed at it. Deprived of a municipal council, either elected or emanating from its *sections*, Paris would henceforth be administered directly by central authority or by agencies named by that authority. Another decree reduced the number of Parisian revolutionary committees from forty-eight to twelve, one per *arrondissement* of four *sections*, their control becoming in this way easier. Finally, the Convention took measures to affirm its real power over its own committees, in particular over the Committees of Public Safety and General Security. Its first move, on 11 Thermidor, was to decide on the renewal of the Committees by quarters each month, each member having to wait a month before being able to return. The more fundamental recasting of the organisation of the Committees and their respective powers came later, at the end of a wide debate. Cambacérès had, perhaps, brought out best of all the stakes involved. The Convention was proceeding between two reefs: the abuse of power and its relaxation. It was a matter of preventing 'the return of the state of oppression from which we have just emerged', while maintaining the principles of revolutionary government, this 'palladium of the Republic ... on which depends the salvation of the *patrie* and our individual existence'. To reorganise the Committees was therefore to give to the Convention itself a 'revolutionary constitution'. Its unshakeable base, a guarantee against any return of tyranny, resided in the confirmation of the very principle of the representative system: 'The Convention alone is the centre of government ... it *alone* has deserved the confidence of the people ... The Convention *alone* should have legislative power; it is a right which the sovereign people has entrusted to it alone and which it is not free to delegate.' The Committees would therefore no longer have the power to interpret the laws; their decrees would be limited simply to carrying them out. Government action should be swift and uniform, hence the need to entrust the exercise of government to a few chosen members, by granting them all the authority necessary for attaining their aims but by containing this power within precise limits. The new organisation of the Committees marked in effect both continuity and a break with regard to the period preceding 9 Thermidor. The Committee of Public Safety was retained but its powers were limited. The 'executive commissions', a kind of ministry, were made independent of it and subordinate to the respective committees elected by the Convention; the Committee of Public Safety also lost the right of presenting to the Convention the list of members proposed for other committees. Similarly, the Committee of Public Safety found itself deprived of a large part of its powers relating to public administration and justice, to the benefit of the Committees of General Security and of Legislation. Government power was thus decentralised to the benefit of the Convention and its different committees. The Committee of Public Safety nevertheless retained the direction of military affairs, of diplomacy, the right to requisition people and goods, and to arrest civil servants and officials. This decentralisation remained relative: on the one hand, the Committee of Public Safety was often to transgress its powers; on the other, the Committee of General Security gained enormously in importance: with it above all would lie the responsibility for 'making justice the order of the day', for releasing people arrested before 9 Thermidor and for carrying through repressive action against the former terrorist personnel. Likewise, the Committee of Legislation's involvement in the exercise of central authority increased.[45]

While rebalancing the exercise of power between the Assembly and its Committees, the Convention hardly envisaged, even for a moment, calling into question the unlimited character of its own power. Nor did anyone at the Convention think that the 'revolution of 9 Thermidor' would provide the opportunity to apply the Constitution which since August 1793 had been officially enclosed in its 'ark', while waiting for better days. When, four weeks after 9 Thermidor, the club of Evêché, where Babeuf was active, demanded 'a strengthening and extending' of the revolution against the 'tyrant' by proclamation of the unlimited freedom of the press and by the election of revolutionary committees at the time of the approaching decadal assemblies, this demand was indignantly rejected by the Convention. The refusal and condemnation of the very idea of 'having recourse to the people'

---

[45]   Cf. *Moniteur*, vol. 21, pp. 473–4 (speech of Cambacérès on 24 Thermidor) and pp. 458 *et seq*. Cf. Aulard, *Recueil des actes*, vol. 16, pp. 310–20 (text of the decree relating to the Committee of Public Safety and the other committees of the National Convention, on 7 Fructidor, Year III). Cf. also the commentary in J. Godechot, *Les Institutions de la France sous la Révolution et l'Empire*, Paris, 1951, pp. 279–81.

were unanimous and enjoyed the total and 'energetic' support of the Jacobins. The latter even decided to send their members to assemblies of *sections* likely to support this motion (which was in fact maintained by the Muséum *section*). Their motion was denounced as a disguised attack on the Convention and revolutionary government, under the demagogic and counter-revolutionary pretext of restoring the electoral rights of the people.[46] By contrast, the right example was set by those countless addresses which congratulated the Convention for 'its revolution', which called on the 'wise legislators', 'fathers of the nation', to remain and pursue their work, thus confirming the uncontested and uncontestable legitimacy of the national representation, as well as its unshakeable unity with the people.

So 9 Thermidor seems to confirm and reinvigorate the image of a people, *one* and *united*, knowing only one *centre*, its 'rallying point', the Convention. All this imagery was carefully cultivated and exploited by authority. Now, at the end of Year II, this imagery inevitably fell apart. The 'rallying-point', the Convention, was more and more divided and yet managed neither to admit its divisions nor overcome them. Did it in fact constitute the 'only centre' ? Nothing is less certain. To bring the Terror to an end, it was necessary to resolve the strictly political problem posed by the role of the Jacobins in the structures of power bequeathed by the Terror, as well as in public life as a whole.

'We should be but one family. Anyone who does not wish to be free will be chased from its bosom; for we are all brothers. The Jacobins are the Convention! The Convention is the people! And the Society is eternal as Liberty!'[47] In appealing to the Jacobins with these words, on 11 Thermidor, Collot d'Herbois had difficulty concealing, under this incantatory formula, a very severe reprimand. In fact, the day after 9 Thermidor, the Jacobins found themselves very badly placed; in the night of 9 to 10 Thermidor, the Society had taken up, as we have noticed, a very ambiguous position. The

---

[46] Cf. *Moniteur*, vol. 21, p. 694 (session of 20 Fructidor). The Convention *unanimously* decided to put aside the petition of the Club demanding 'unlimited freedom of the press and the selection of civil servants by assemblies of the people'. Billaud-Varenne, who, since his denunciation by Lecointre spoke quite rarely at the Convention, found it useful to attack the Club and to propose entrusting the Committee of General Security with this affair: 'The electoral club has always been a hotbed of counter-revolution. It took part in Hébert's conspiracy; today when a new conspiracy seems to be forming the club pushes it forward; for it must be noted that *the speaker did not know how to read* (*sic*!). For Billaud then, Babeuf was only an accomplice of the 'new conspiracy' hatched by Fréron and Tallien; the Club's proposition aimed only at undermining the revolutionary government. The Jacobins in fact called upon their members to go to the assemblies of the *sections* to oppose the petition of the electoral Club (cf. Aulard, *Société des Jacobins*, vol. 6, pp. 386–7). The Club had been finally closed in Brumaire, Year III, on the pretext of seditious activities.

[47] *Ibid.*, pp. 305; 355 *et seq.*

assembly had, first, supported the Commune; but as events developed to the detriment of the latter, the assembly of the Society became more and more hesitant, and, above all, the numbers of those present declined. Finally, at dawn, Legendre, at the head of a small detachment of the National Guard, emptied the hall, locked the door, and solemnly handed the keys to the president of the Convention. What a symbolic gesture! and corresponding, in a way, to the outlawing of Robespierre and his acolytes. In fact, the exceptional power held by Robespierre in the system of Montagnard dictatorship, and particularly during the Terror, depended largely on the strategic position that he occupied: his political and moral authority was exercised *both* at the Convention and at the Jacobins. His position, then, hinged on this and by occupying it, Robespierre seemed to embody and combine in himself alone the two principles of legitimacy which revolutionary government appealed to – the representative system and direct democracy. The political talent of Robespierre consisted, among others, in his remarkable ability in handling simultaneously the two levers of power available to him thanks to his key position on the Committee of Public Safety and in the group directing the Jacobins. Robespierre ensured the subordination of the Jacobins, of the mother-Society and of the affiliated societies to the decisions of the Committee of Public Safety, but it was at the Jacobins that he first sought discussion and approval of the decisions and bills which the Convention was then content to ratify. So the representatives whom he denounced at the Jacobins harboured no illusions on their political future, or even, simply, their future. On 8 Thermidor, Robespierre reckoned that he could still play effectively on these two keyboards, by repeating in the evening, at the Jacobins, the indictment which he had just delivered, in the morning, at the Convention. The enthusiastic support of the Club must have provided him on the following day, 9 Thermidor, with a powerful instrument for putting pressure on the Convention. But, for the first and last time, the machinery of power seized up, and then broke.

The victors of 9 Thermidor had therefore many reasons to mistrust the Jacobins. The reasons which led them to return the keys and have the hall reopened have never been made explicit but they can be guessed at. They had to do with the authority and prestige of the Society as well as the functions it had acquired as part of the essential machinery of power. On the day after 9 Thermidor it was difficult to imagine the continuity of revolutionary government without the support of the Jacobins and, consequently, of the affiliated societies. On the other hand, the political and technical experience accumulated during the Terror, especially the experience of the representatives *en mission*, showed that to manipulate the popular societies was sometimes a delicate affair, but that thanks especially to the purges, they eventually came round to following meekly the policy of central authority, however sharp the turning.

'May this example [that of Robespierre]', said Billaud-Varenne in the course of the first session of the Jacobins after 9 Thermidor, 'teach you never again to have an idol. You were victims of La Fayette, of Brissot, of a host of other conspirators ... Rally around the Convention which, at these stormy moments, has displayed the greatest character. It will show mercy to no conspirator and virtue will always be the basis of its operations.'[48]

This political strategy of rallying the 'regenerated' Jacobins to the Convention would, however, be swiftly compromised by a development that no participant had expected.

On the day after 9 Thermidor, it looked as if everything should turn out for the best. Of course, the Jacobins who met on 11 Thermidor, in their reopened hall, were few and shaken by recent events. It was, however, members of the Committee of Public Safety, the very architects of the 'fall of the tyrant', who called upon them to 'regenerate themselves' and encouraged them to resume their activities. So the Society was not sparing in its declarations of allegiance to the victorious Convention and condemned the vanquished, particularly those among its own members who had chosen the camp of the 'tyrant' and of the 'rebel Commune'. It did not even hesitate to deny them, after the event, their status as Jacobins, to which they were appealing. The 'true' Jacobins were those who precisely *were not* in the hall, in the Rue Saint-Honoré, during this memorable night (or who, let it be added, decided in good time to leave the Club). Unanimously, the Jacobins, reunited on 11 Thermidor, decided to 'go *en masse*' to the Convention where their deputation made the following speech:

Citizens, you behold the true Jacobins, who have earned a place in the esteem of the French nation and in the hatred of tyrants; you behold the men who took up arms to fight the treacherous magistrates, the usurpers of national authority. True Jacobins, when the moment of alarm comes, have no special meeting-place; it is wherever the force and watchfulness necessary to fight the conspirators can be found. The monstrous assembly of conspirators who have fouled our soil was composed of men who did not have cards of membership, who were devoted to their infamous leaders; but we, we have marched with our *sections*, to defeat the new tyrant.[49]

[48] *Ibid.*, p. 300. On the double legitimacy of representative system and direct democracy, cf. Furet, *Penser la Révolution*, pp. 85 *et seq.*
[49] *Moniteur*, vol. 21, p. 358; Aulard, *Société des Jacobins*, vol. 6, p. 361. Tallien, who presided over the session, let it be believed that he accepted this distinction between 'true' and 'false' Jacobins. He praised 'this famous society ... whose services to the Revolution will be written on every page of our history'. He did not, however, restrain himself from launching a jibe by recalling that this same Society was 'sometimes led astray by scoundrels' (*ibid.*).

The Society proceeded to the readmission of those of its members who had been excluded during the 'tyranny' of Robespierre and who then played a leading role during the 'revolution of 9 Thermidor': Fouché, Tallien, Dubois-Crancé. It did not tire of abusing Robespierre:

Behold then Robespierre, that tiger corrupted by the taste of blood, the blood which circulates for liberty, behold him vanished in the twinkling of an eye from this place where he came to gorge himself ... Republicans will no longer suffer the bitterness of hearing his machiavellian accents point out everywhere, in the most innocent groups of men, conspirators, intriguers, traitors. Ah! thanks be unto those who did in fact conspire and intrigue against him and his guilty conspirators.

The 'true Jacobins' were so many victims suffering from his tyranny. The silence of those who remained quiet during 'six months when the tyrant openly violated the rights of man' in the very heart of the Jacobins was not a conformist attitude but, on the contrary, a heroic act:

On this rostrum, where we were showered with the epithets of scoundrels and traitors, because we had the courage to remain calm, and to not give way to the prompting of that ignorant rabble who covered over the hypocritical ranting of the tyrant with scandalous shouts ... As soon as the moment favoured us, we spoke out; we did better yet, we acted.[50]

A special commission was charged with examining the actions of former members of the Society and with renewing the cards only of those who could demonstrate irreproachable behaviour through the night of 9 to 10 Thermidor. A month after these events, when the purges seemed already over, the Society prided itself, in an address, on having brought together 600 members who 'had not been tainted by any blemish; all were at their post as citizens on the night of 9 to 10 Thermidor ... Those who on this forever memorable night dishonoured our places in this chamber, were false Jacobins whom the despot had introduced, vile slaves whose victims we had often been, but never their accomplices'.[51] Now, the Jacobins never published the details of the number of their 'false members' who were excluded, nor of the number of those who remained members. It is known, however, that at its peak, before 9 Thermidor, the Society consisted of more than 1,200 members. Despite this reduction, which in fact was to continue, the Society gradually took up again its labours: regular meetings, correspondence with affiliated societies, speeches to the Convention. The accounts of the meetings of the Jacobins were again published in the *Moniteur* and in other newspapers, along with those of sessions of the Convention. Everything proceeded, then, as if these accounts comple-

[50] *Ibid.*, pp. 305 *et seq*; pp. 335.
[51] *Adresse de la Société des Amis de la Liberté et de l'Egalité, séante aux Jacobins, à Paris,à toutes les Sociétés qui lui sont affiliés*, Paris, n.d. (Fructidor, Year II): BN Lᵇ 40/786.

mented each other, as if, after 9 Thermidor, the position occupied by the Jacobins in the public realm, especially in relation to the Convention, had not changed at all. But these appearances poorly concealed the conflict which was already becoming manifest four weeks after 'the night forever memorable' and which would continue to increase.

It was, in fact, to the Jacobins that the pleas of terrorist personnel against the 'persecution of patriots' began to flow; it has been noted that numerous petitions arrived at the mother-Society from the affiliated societies while deputations came forward to the bar. The Society, having discussed the plea, appointed, if necessary and according to its usual practice, the 'official defence lawyers' authorised to plead the just cause of the victims before the Committee of General Security. After 13 Fructidor and the rejection by the Convention of Lecointre's denunciation, the Society gained in energy and pugnacity. Some of its members, denounced and rehabilitated, notably Billaud-Varenne and Collot d'Herbois, continued to play an important role in the work of the Jacobins; regularly present at meetings, they often spoke and took part in the work of the commissions. On the other hand, the lampoons that accompanied all of the campaign of denunciation, especially *La Queue de Robespierre*, violently attacked the Jacobins as instigators of the Terror. On 17 Fructidor, following a particularly stormy meeting, the Society decided to exclude Lecointre, Tallien and Fréron. Carrier, who was becoming more and more active, asserted that the Society wished by this exclusion to give even more vigour to its criticisms, which it had already expressed, of the 'evils which have afflicted the Republic since the fall of the tyrant'. In fact, the Jacobins, in their meetings as well as in a special address presented to the Convention (on 8 Fructidor), had called for a fight against the *modérantisme* which is raising its head' under the pretext of a re-establishment of justice; to this end, they supported the motion to publish the list of people released from prison; they criticised all those who, in the wake of Tallien and Fréron, called for unlimited freedom of the press while at the same time encouraging the disparagement of 'energetic patriots'. On 14 Fructidor, there was an accidental explosion at the powder-factory of Grenelle which claimed several victims. The Society was not slow to draw a parallel between this catastrophe, the 'persecution of patriots', the liberation of 'suspects' and the anti-Jacobin pamphlets; it saw in all this so many links of a vast conspiracy against revolutionary government. Those members of the Convention who were also members of the Society, and who continued to sit in the Mountain (whose benches, however, grew emptier day by day), defended the positions of the Jacobins and the Society itself in debates. But it was usually secondary figures like Duhem or Chasles who took the floor; the star performers of the Society, in particular the members of the Committees, often kept silent.

Now, all this taking up of positions among the Jacobins, with each one meant to be more 'energetic' than the last, and which, taken all together, should be evidence of the determination and strength of the Society, turned against it and became demonstrations of its impotence. The expulsion of Fréron and Tallien is flagrant evidence of this. In fact, times had changed since 9 Thermidor: the two excluded men left the chamber laughing; Tallien embraced Fréron to applause from part of the galleries where the cry could be heard: 'They don't give a damn!' To be denounced at the Society or be excluded from it no longer carried any risk; it meant neither exclusion from public life nor proscription. On the contrary, it only stimulated new attacks against the Jacobins as well as new defections. The list of members of the Convention who, after 9 Thermidor, still frequented the Society and who then turned against it became longer each day: Legendre, Dubois-Crancé, Léquinio, Thirion, Bentabole, Merlin (from Thionville) ... Jacobin addresses to the Convention, far from receiving immediate approval as before, were often received with mistrust and hostility by large portions of the deputies and the galleries. On the occasion of one of these 'energetic' addresses the president himself, Merlin (from Thionville), former Jacobin, did not hesitate to remind the delegation of the Society that it was the Convention who had overturned the 'tyrant' on 9 Thermidor, while 'some perverse people' were still defending him from the rostrum of the Jacobins. Once, the intervention of 'official defence lawyers' named by the Society was sufficient to remove from difficulty, even from prison, anyone who benefited from the protection of the Jacobins; from now on, these 'defenders' had no need to unpack their arguments, for the members of the Committee of General Security did not even find time to see them. In reply to the denunciation of 'aristocratic plots' an entire press now responded with counter-denunciations of 'Jacobin conspiracies'; even the explosion at Grenelle was blamed on them; the anti-Jacobin press portrayed it as the result of their sinister machinations, devised to bring back the Terror. When Tallien was 'assassinated' (on 21 Fructidor, an unknown man wounded him lightly on the arm with a knife; for several days, the Convention had bulletins on his health read to it), suspicions were openly raised, in the press as well as at the Convention, that the Jacobins had inspired, even planned, this attempt. In the same way, they were the permanent target of the newspapers and lampoons, which accused them of having been 'blood-drinkers' and informers during the Terror, who now sought to escape the sword of law, under the pretext of the 'regenerating policy' of the Convention. One episode, chosen from several others, is a good illustration of the new situation. On the day of the fourth *sans-culottide*, at the Palais-Egalité (previously the Palais-Royal), a fight broke out between two 'groups': some cried 'Long live the Jacobins!', others attacked them with the cry of 'Long live the Convention! Down with the Jacobins!' Duly alerted, the Committee of General Security did not intervene to defend the insulted Jacobins; one of its members was to declare that the whole affair was of no interest . . .[52]

So each day the Jacobins suffered a bitter experience: what they believed to be the *power of their word* was only the secondary effect of the fact that during the Terror *they voiced the word of power*. From the moment that they no longer held the monopoly of this word and that power no longer supported what they had to say, their word was condemned to increasing impotence – an impotence all the more glaring in that the Society would never succeed in recognising it and would seek to make up for it by the piling up of more and more 'energetic' declarations and protests, by a threatening but increasingly empty rhetoric, founded on the heroic past of the Jacobins, their just deserts and services rendered to the Revolution, their unshakeable loyalty to the great revolutionary principles. The combined effects of this impotence and these threats turned against the Society. The verbal violence, more and more obviously in contrast with the political choices of authority, made the Jacobins the 'rallying-point' of all those dissatisfied with these choices. Quite quickly the Jacobins took on the functions of an *ideological authority* intended to legitimise only resistance to the dismantling of the institutions created by the Terror and to take on the defence of terrorist personnel against the repression which swept down upon them. As a result, Jacobin discourse could only stir up the fears and hatred bequeathed by the Terror, while the obvious signs of the Society's weakness focussed feelings of revenge against it. The Jacobins were attacked as the very symbol of the Terror, the people responsible for its past excesses and advocates of its return, while they, in their turn, took a leading part in the 'war of speeches', by calling openly for a struggle against the '*modérantisme*' and 'aristocracy' which were persecuting the 'patriots'.[53]

So conflict between the Jacobins and the majority in the Convention became inevitable. The overheated atmosphere of the Convention was the same as that which accompanied the brawls at the Tuileries and the Palais-Egalité.

The people no longer want *two authorities*, cries Merlin (from Thionville), it wants the reign of the *assassins* to end . . . I denounce to you here the assassins of my country, those who, in the legislative Assembly, voted beside me for principles, and who today beside me vote on the opposite side. I denounce to you these men, who

---

[52] Cf. *Courrier républicain*, 30 Fructidor and third *sans-culottide*, Year II; *Moniteur*, vol. 22, p. 4; Aulard, *Société des Jacobins*, vol. 6, pp 489–91. We have noted above another similar episode.

[53] In particular, the Society had the address of the popular society of Dijon distributed: this was a true call for the return of the Terror, to which we shall come back.

have had the audacity to speak in a Society which strongly contributed to overturning the throne, but who, having no more thrones to overturn, wish to overturn the Convention ... (*Yes, Yes!* Applause.) ... People, if you wish to conserve liberty, if you wish to retain the Convention, *the single centre where you can join together* ... arm youselves with your authority and, with the law in your hand, pounce upon this *lair of brigands*.

A popular society, asserts Bentabole, has no right to send anything to the armies before the Convention has given its opinion ... It is a question of knowing if a society which has, so to speak, supreme control over public opinion, if this society is not carrying out an act which puts the country into danger when it undertakes to begin a proscription of the representatives of the people. I ask if, when the people sent me here, it wanted me to be censured by a *private organisation* for the opinion that I expressed in the Assembly of representatives of the nation?

In the time of Robespierre, Legendre explodes, representatives of the people were hounded from the Jacobins for opinions that they had expressed in the Convention; today deputies are still hounded from the Jacobins for their opinions in the heart of the Convention ... (At the Jacobins) ham actors are on the boards, and Robespierre is in the prompter's box ...[54]

As often in revolutionary debates, beyond the unchained passions and the burning issues of current events, questions began to be raised about the essential characteristics of revolutionary institutions and authority. At the end of Year II, this debate is evidence of the awareness that the political arena, modified by 9 Thermidor, but nevertheless created by the Terror, was only provisional and needed to be compared with the founding principles of the Revolution and the representative system. The attacks against the Jacobins were necessarily to be seen in a larger context: how to conceive and organise the political arena which should succeed the Terror? Should the ending of the Terror be accomplished *with* the Jacobins and, more widely, the popular societies, or *against* them? These questions, however, entailed others, both wider and older: what should be the role of the popular societies in the functioning of power? Did these societies consist simply in meetings of their members or should they have an existence, an activity and a political authority of their own? Was the people to exercise its sovereignty, source of all legitimate authority, uniquely through its representative institutions, or through forms of direct democracy as well, such as the intermediary role of multiple popular societies?

New questions, old questions. New, in so far as they betrayed preoccupations born of the very recent political practices of the Terror, where the popular societies, and especially those affiliated to the Jacobins, had become a real body of the state, escaping the control of the Assembly. Old questions, insofar as the Convention, in the conflict which set it against the Jacobins, seemed to take over the arguments which the Constituent

---

[54] *Moniteur*, vol. 21, pp. 724–5 and 727; vol. 22, pp. 58–9.

Assembly had already, in 1791, urged against the Society of Friends of the Constitution: the Society abused freedom of association by forming a 'political organisation' contrary to the very principles of representative government; its members arrogated to themselves the 'privilege of exclusive patriotism' and thereby elevated themselves into a real counter-power; they aspired to real dictatorship by concealing it under the different forms of direct democracy. There is remarkable evidence for the persistence of a whole set of political and institutional questions, even of an entire vocabulary, in the speech, on 24 Fructidor, Year II, of Durand-Maillane, spokesman of the Plain and one of the founders, in 1789, of the 'historic Jacobins', the Society of Friends of the Constitution. He was not slow to contest the legality of the very existence of the Jacobins, by comparing them with a sort of corporation, against the spirit of republican institutions.

You suppressed all the corporations because they were by their nature opposed to republican institutions; you did not even spare the guild of pharmacists and others of this kind ... I demand that we examine whether there is no danger for liberty in enduring the existence of the *corporation of the popular society of Paris along with the forty-four thousand which are affiliated to it* and which are in correspondence with them.

The comparison of the Jacobins to a guild of apothecaries is certainly a stylistic device aimed at provoking laughter. But in attacking the *Jacobins* as a *political corporation*, it turned against them the principles of 1789 and, more generally, opposed these founding principles to the political practices of Year II. It was, finally, a transparent allusion to Le Chapelier's law, voted through in September 1791 at the end of the Constituent Assembly. This law aimed in some way at setting rigorous controls on the rights and activities of the popular societies according to the same principles as those that were the basis for the suppression of the corporations.[55]

The September text has often been neglected by historians who give precedence to another of Le Chapelier's laws, the one of 14 June 1791, banning 'workers' associations', in order to demonstrate the 'bourgeois' character of the Revolution. Now, these two texts were closely linked: in Le Chapelier's mind, they both applied the same liberal principles, which were the basis of the new Constitution, to all kinds of political association.

Durand-Maillane's allusion was not simply a rhetorical device. There exists, in fact, a *structural analogy* between the questions that the Constituent Assembly asked itself at the end of its labours and those which the Convention began to raise at the end of Year II. In short, the problem could

---

[55] *Ibid.*, vol. 21, p. 728; Aulard, *Société des Jacobins*, vol. 6, p. 441 *et seq*. The number of 'forty-four thousand affiliated societies' advanced by Durand-Maillane is, obviously, exaggerated and polemical; it was only a way of saying that the Jacobins wished to spread their tentacles into every commune by establishing popular societies within them.

be defined like this: the popular societies had played an important role in the period of revolutionary instability and violence, but their functions should be redefined after the *completion* of the Revolution, in a new political domain with stable institutions. After 9 Thermidor, to paraphrase Tallien's formula, already quoted, it was necessary to distinguish between a *government which made the revolution* and one which *wished to complete the revolution*. Now, Le Chapelier's report remains a document of great importance; in particular it offers one of the first analyses of the Jacobin phenomenon and its relations with representative government, such as they were perceived in 1791.

Le Chapelier had presented his report on the behalf of the Constitutional Committee, on 29 and 30 September 1791, the eve of the winding up of the work of the Constituent Assembly. Obviously, this move had an immediate political objective: the elimination of the popular societies from the political contest, especially the Jacobins, those 'extremists' wishing to proceed with and radicalise the Revolution. The acceptance of the Constitution as well as the 'Feuillant crisis'[56] which the Jacobins were going through seemed to offer a particularly favourable moment for carrying out this plan. But Le Chapelier's preoccupations went beyond these immediate aims; they meant to *conclude*, finally, the Revolution by implementing new institutions, and by making the *representative system* function in the form of a constitutional monarchy. Now, to establish this system and, consequently, carry out the principles of 1789, required legislation covering the activities of the popular societies, a point on which the Constitution remained vague. Le Chapelier did not conceal the complexity of this task in insisting principally on two points. On the one hand, the originality of the revolutionary changes in France stemmed from the fact that the advent and triumph of the principles of 1789 could be ensured only by extra-parliamentary means (if not extra-legal) and, in particular, by the increasing activity of many patriotic societies. On the other hand, the activities and mode of operation of these societies, and especially of the Jacobins, became so extensive and took such a turn that they concealed the gravest dangers for the representative system. The activities of the political societies, simultaneously *political and extra-parliamentary*, were, in Le Chapelier's view, opposed to the recognition of the elected Assembly as the single embodiment of the sovereignty of the nation. The pursuit of these activities could only end in anarchy under the pretext of wanting to prolong the Revolution. Both *liberal and conservative*, Le Chapelier thus formulated the political and institutional dilemma: either the Assembly of representatives of the sovereign Nation exercised authority within a rigorous and stable framework of representative institutions, or

---

[56] *Feuillants*. A club formed in 1791 after a schism among the Jacobins. Among its members were Barère and Sieyès. A chief aim of the club was to obtain a constitutional monarchy.

the activities of various extra-parliamentary associations, which were all so many factions, undermined the representative system by substituting for it a sort of direct democracy plunging the country, through ever-increasing demagogy, into a revolution without end.

The popular and patriotic societies, insisted Le Chapelier, were

spontaneous institutions ... created by enthusiasm for liberty and which, in that stormy time, had the fortunate effect of rallying hearts and minds, of forming common centres of opinion, and of making known to the opposing minority the enormous majority that desired the destruction of abuses, the overturning of prejudices, and the establishment of the rights of man ... When a nation changes the form of its government each citizen is a magistrate; everyone deliberates and should deliberate about public affairs, and everything that encourages, everything that ensures, everything that accelerates a revolution, should be put to use; it is a momentary fermentation that must be kept going and even increased, in order that the revolution, no longer leaving any doubt, encounters fewer obstacles and comes more swiftly to its end; but when *the Revolution is terminated*, when the constitution of the empire is complete, when it has delegated all public powers, summoned all the authorities, then it is necessary, for the salvation of this constitution, that everything returns to perfect order, that *nothing hampers the action of the constituted powers*.

Of course, the Declaration of the Rights of Man and the Citizen, as well as the Constitution, officially established the free communication of thought and opinion, as well as the freedom of citizens to assemble peaceably and to address petitions signed individually to the constituted authorities. But the free enjoyment of these rights could only continue according to the *principles of representative government*, these also established by the Constitution. Now, these principles were categorical: 'the very nature of the government that we have adopted' had as a consequence the exclusion of the existence, even if provisional, of any body that was intermediate between the citizens and their representatives (and any delegated authority), for the members of such bodies inevitably arrogated to themselves exclusive privileges and rights, contrary to the principles of liberty and equality. These maxims were valid in all domains of social life, notably in commerce and industry; they should be all the more respected in politics:

There are no powers other than those constituted by the will of the people, expressed by its representatives; there is no authority other than that delegated, there can be no action other than that carried out by its representatives entrusted with public office. It is in order to maintain this principle in all its purity, from one end of the empire to the other, that the Constitution has dissolved all corporations, and recognises only a single social body and individuals.

If one compared these principles with the practices adopted by the Societies of Friends of the Constitution, that is, the Jacobins, one would be convinced that they raised themselves up against the Constitution and destroyed it instead of defending it and that they 'place themselves in the same category as a corporation ... much more dangerous than the old ones'. This held as much for their programme as for their modes of operation. 'To take on a public existence', to accept certain citizens as members and refuse others, to lavish praise and blame on citizens, to hand out diplomas and certificates – all this in the name of patriotism and the general will – was to grant oneself 'a sort of *exclusive privilege of patriotism* which produces accusations against individuals not members of the sect and hatred against societies not affiliated', divisions that any good citizen should seek to extinguish and which 'spring up again at every moment, with the help of bizarre and corporative associations'. Founded on 'exclusive patriotism', a network of associations was formed which 'extends its branches over the whole empire' by a system of affiliations, of political correspondence and 'a kind of metropolis', a system with grave consequences and contrary to the Constitution. In fact, it was in the nature of these societies 'to seek to acquire some exterior influence' by laying claim to a monopoly on patriotism, and by appealing to the Nation and its general interest; so they tended to 'gain influence over administrative and judicial acts'. They had also been seen to order public officials 'to come and give an account of their conduct', sent their deputies to get involved in judicial enquiries, sent commissioners 'entrusted with missions which could only be conferred upon constituted authorities'. In other words, the Jacobin societies arrogated to themselves the right of substituting for representative and legitimate institutions their own political practices, which appealed to a sort of *direct democracy*. Now, men gathered in assemblies would always have greater strength than isolated citizens, and their assemblies risked subjugating the nation. 'If these societies are able to have some influence, if a man's reputation is at their disposal, if, formed into corporations, they have from one end of the country to the other branches and agents of their powers, then *the societies will be the only free men*.' It was therefore necessary to ban the affiliation of societies; it was necessary to prevent them from 'usurping part of public power', and from exercising 'any influence on or inspection of the actions of the constituted powers and legal authorities.' This especially implied that societies should not have a right to *collective petitions*. The right to petitions was a 'natural right' and, because of this, was not to be delegated. Now, the practice of delegating it to presidents, secretaries and other members of a society was only a form of abuse which profited, in the end, a few leaders. Societies could therefore have no other existence than that of

meetings of friends ... to learn, to discuss, to communicate their knowledge ... but their meetings, their interior actions should never step across the threshold of their assemblies; no public function, no collective action should draw attention to them

... Everyone wants *the Revolution to be ended*. The time of destruction is over; there are no more abuses to overturn, nor prejudices to oppose; we must from now on improve this building, for which liberty and equality are the corner-stones.[57]

Le Chapelier's criticism of Jacobinism reveals what separated him, as well as other more or less conservative liberals, from the Jacobins, but it also hides a certain stock of political views common to both sides. Le Chapelier's position was rigorously liberal: society was composed of individuals who were free and equal in rights; the task of government was to protect and ensure respect for their natural and civil rights. The representative system effectively ensured the coherence and unity of the social body insofar as it ensured the sovereignty of the Nation and allowed the general interest to be clarified, while respecting the free play of individual interests. Now, the pretension to 'exclusive patriotism' turned the Jacobins into a 'political corporation' and perverted the representative system, since it served as a shelter for particularisms and strengthened them; it justified the recourse to forms of extra-parliamentary action, contrary to the law; it contributed to the break-up of the social body by multiplying divisions and conflicts. Any division of the social body into interest groups or exclusive associations was, for Le Chapelier, fundamentally evil, for it reproduced, in another guise, the old estates, privileges and corporations. For this reason, it was contrary to the principles of 1789, to the liberty and equality of citizens as well as to the sovereignty of the Nation whose unity was brought about by and was expressed by representative government. A liberal and an individualist, denouncing the perversion of the representative system by the recourse to direct democracy, Le Chapelier rejected, for the same reasons, any *political pluralism*. Hence his mistrust of *political associations*: a single political association would aspire, by reason of its 'exclusivism', to monopolise power; the existence of several associations, condemned to confrontation with each other, would lead to anarchy. His whole argument is

[57] All the quotations are taken from the report of Le Chapelier of 29–30 September 1791; cf. *Moniteur*, vol. 10, pp. 7–11. The decree accepted by the Constituent Assembly did not suppress the popular societies but banned them from any 'political existence', affiliations, publication of the minutes of their debates, collective petitions, the carrying out of any inspection of or influence on the actions of the constituted powers. One might say that the law proposed to reduce the patriotic societies to their historic origins, to enclose them in the framework of 'societies of thought'. Robespierre, in opposing this law, insisted on the right of association recognised by the Constitution; there would therefore be nothing anti-constitutional in the affiliation of several legal societies. For Robespierre *the Revolution was not terminated* and the patriotic societies were at the service of *the revolution in motion*. They brought together the purest and worthiest patriots to watch over corrupt people and intriguers, some of whom sat in the Assembly (*ibid.*) Several questions about the formation of Jacobinism have been clarified in M. L. Kennedy, *The Jacobin clubs in the French Revolution. The first years*, Princeton, N. J., 1982. Discussions of Le Chapelier's report and the revolutionary political arena have been stimulated by B. Manin's article, 'Montesquieu et la politique moderne', *Cahiers de philosophie politique*, 1985, no. 2–3.

certainly aimed at the Jacobins, their organisation, their forms of action and their aspirations. But he was close to Jacobinism, as a political doctrine and practice, in his strong hostility to *all political pluralism* and in his glorification of a *unified political arena*. In 1791 the Jacobins, thanks to their ideology and organisation, were already asserting themselves as the political force best suited to making the most effective use, in the struggle for power, of a *unitary conception of the political arena*. Against Le Chapelier and the liberal conservatives the Jacobins defended freedom of speech, the right of association and of forming a national network of affiliated societies. They claimed this right for 'good patriots' alone, for those who united the Nation and not for those who divided it. This right would be, all things considered, *their exclusive right* only, insofar as they brought together precisely all 'pure' patriots. Political and moral 'purity', this key concept of Jacobinism, was a criterion that excluded any idea of pluralism. In fact, 'pure patriotism' did not acknowledge diversity but only an extreme purism; it condemned *a priori* the existence of *different patriotisms*. 'Pure patriotism' implied a *multiplicity of patriots* but not of patriotisms; it condemned the existence of different political or social programmes and groupings. In its eyes these would be only a source of conflicts and factions, which would threaten to break the unity of the nation and, consequently, ruin its sovereignty. The will to have both the unity of the nation and 'pure patriotism' triumph implied *exclusion* as a regulatory mechanism of public life and political action. This hostility to pluralism increased in the course of the struggle against the Girondins and during the Terror. The Jacobins defended the right of association as a principle, but on condition that it be exercised in a political arena from which division would be excluded, and, consequently, where there could exist only a single association whose legitimacy would reside precisely in its patriotic 'purity' and the virtue of its members. In this way the Jacobins set themselves up as a political and moral *authority*, as guardians of purity and fidelity to the founding principles of the Revolution. Their relations with representative power were necessarily ambiguous and this ambiguity was at the origin of their force as much as of their political weakness. Jacobinism recognised only a single source of legitimacy: the sovereign and unlimited will of the people, and this sovereignty resided in national representation. Hence the legalism of Jacobinism and its respect for the representative system, on which Robespierre particularly insisted. But the people, single and indivisible, also *directly* invested the popular societies with authority outside of and over the representative forms of public life – not as government institutions but in their capacity as political and moral authority called, at the same time, to *counsel and watch over* the constituted authorities. The legislation of 1791 on the popular societies, voted through on Le Chapelier's proposal, was never applied. The dynamic of the Revolution worked in favour of the Jacobins who ended up by gaining effective control of power, and in particular of the Convention, while not becoming merged with the constituted authorities.

Now, 9 Thermidor overturned the relationship of forces between the Jacobins and the Convention. At the end of year II, the conflict which arose between the Society and the Assembly therefore brought out a *structural political problem*, in circumstances particularly unfavourable to the Jacobins. Compromised by their complicity with the system of the Terror, even identified with terrorist power, the Jacobins could less and less easily lay claim to moral purity and to a patriotism above all suspicion. Furthermore, their own ideal of a unified political arena was skilfully turned against them. It was now the turn of the anti-Jacobin members of the Convention to condemn the Jacobins as agents of division, as an exclusive 'political corporation', to claim the full exercise of sovereignty for national representation. Certainly, the Jacobins of Year II were not those of 1791; the stakes and the political protagonists had radically changed. The fact that, despite these changes, the essence of the argument formulated by Le Chapelier (who had been guillotined in April 1794) should be taken up again proves how certain characteristics of the political culture of the Revolution and of revolutionary political *mentalités* remained, beyond all the spectacular changes of direction. In fact, the creation of the democratic arena in 1789 did not entail, and this was the case throughout the Revolution, the *working out of a pluralist political system*. In this sense Jacobinism was both the expression and the perversion of the concept of the political arena as unified. The Revolution invented a democracy which, by an apparent paradox, joined together individualism and a true cult of unanimity, representative government and the refusal to allow any interest other than the 'general interest' to be represented, the recognition of freedom of opinion and the mistrust of divisions in public opinion, the desire for a transparent political life and the obsessive search for 'plots'; in short, a democracy which, in politics, mixed modernity with archaism. Quite often the political protagonists shared this concept of democracy, which was, in the end, fairly crude and this was the case even in the divisions that tore them apart. They never succeeded, at any stage of the revolution, *in agreeing to disagree*, in recognising that conflicts in a society are at the origin of its working and not a vice to be eradicated. This is a particularly striking example of the *mixture of the traditional and the modern* in the political concepts, institutions and workings of the Revolution, which marked all its experience with its seal. As a result, *exclusion* swiftly became the regulatory mechanism of the political game; the adversary was excluded in the very name of the fundamental unity of the Nation, of the People, or of the Republic. This principle is, moreover, appropriate to the functioning and preservation of traditional communities, where unity and solidarity tend to be confused with unanimity. The persistent obsessions of the revolutionary imagination, particularly the plot and the hidden enemy, could only nourish, through hatred and suspicion, the idea-image of *healthy exclusion*. The emergence from the Terror was certainly not a period which encouraged evolution towards political pluralism. The desire to re-establish the principles of the representative system did not only go hand in hand with the idea of excluding political adversaries; it united with the *furies of revenge*. So the Jacobins were stupefied to see the political machinery, of which they had thought themselves the masters, violently turn against them.

The most violent indictments against the Jacobins were drawn up at the time of the debates at the Convention and at the Society, which were occasioned by the decree of 25 Vendémiaire, Year III (16 October 1794) aiming to dismantle the Jacobin network and reduce the mother-Society to impotence. (In fact, a Jacobin member of the Convention, Lejeune, would not fail to make the comparison between the draft of the new decree and the shackles which 'Le Chapelier and his partisans, in the days of degradation and infamy' wanted to impose on the popular societies.) The speeches were particularly aggressive and violent, richly furnished with real knowledge and a lived experience of Jacobinism as a mode of thought and of political action. In fact, the star performers were political defectors, former Jacobins who knew what they were talking about when they turned against the Society.

What did they have against the Jacobins? Apart from bias, one recurrent accusation becomes clear: the mother-Society and its network of affiliated popular societies elevated themselves into a *parallel power*, even a *counter-power*, in face of the Constitution and the constituted authorities. The Jacobins contributed to the fall of the monarchy but they then opposed free government. The Terror was not possible without the domination of the Jacobins and the experience of 9 Thermidor was a powerful indictment of them.

At the time of the happy revolution of 9 Thermidor, when the people sees that you [the Convention] have taken back the reins, that you wish to bring back justice, it turned towards you, it held out its hand to you, and it felt that without the help of the Jacobins, Robespierre and his accomplices would never have succeeded in dominating you. Now, since the societies knew how to seize government from you and put it in the hands of a man whom they had placed above the Convention and above the people, you should recognise that they cannot be watched too closely. You ought to watch carefully an institution that overturns both despotism and liberty with the same success. (speaker not identified in the verbal transcript)

To watch over the popular societies, and especially to ban affiliations, was to put an end to a situation in which there had sprung up, beside the Convention, '*another centre* that misleads public opinion, that takes away from the representative system the confidence and respect which it deserves' (Bentabole). The correspondence network uniting the popular societies around the Jacobins had perverted the very principles of representative government. Therefore, no one knew any more where the 'rallying-point' was, nor where the sovereign people was. 'I only see the people in the primary assemblies; but I see *a sovereign rise up beside representative government*, a sovereign whose throne is here, at the Jacobins, when I see collections of like-minded men correspond ... I shall say to the people: choose between the men you have named to represent you and the men who have raised themselves up beside them' (Bourdon (from the Oise)). The Jacobins presented the popular societies as the very expression of the will of the people and, because of this, as the guarantors of republican institutions. This would, however, substitute for the representative system a direct pseudo-democracy, and, consequently, substitute for the sovereignty of the entire nation a usurped authority, exercised by a faction *in the name of the people*. 'The people is not in the societies. Sovereignty resides in the sum total of the nation; it is not, as has been said, upon the popular societies in general that society rests; the guarantee of liberty rests on the nobility and the energy of the feelings of the sum total of the French' (Thuriot). The Declaration of the Rights of Man and the Citizen as well as the Constitution of 1793 included the right of association as well as the right of petition. The Jacobins protested against the violation of these rights by the new legislation, but this should be seen as only a decoy. Those who understood the internal workings of the societies and especially the representatives who had carried out missions in the *départements* knew perfectly well that to claim the right of correspondence and collective addresses was only a pretext for defending the dominant position and the political privileges acquired by a small group to the detriment of the majority of citizens. 'For five years, we have wanted a representative republic. What are the popular societies? A collection of men, who, like monks, choose among themselves ... Aristocracy begins where a collection of men, through its correspondence with other collections of men, leads to the triumph of opinions other than those of the national representatives' (Bourdon (from the Oise)).

Whether 'aristocracy' or 'corporation', it was a *de facto* inequality which the Jacobins had introduced. 'People, how do you view the men who wish to put themselves above the laws, men who communicate among each other like citizens, who wish to be more than other citizens, who wish to communicate like a corporation?' (Reubell). The collective addresses served only to hide what really went on in the societies. It was claimed that the people expressed itself through these addresses; now, 'five or six citizens do not represent the people' and yet in how many popular societies was it the case that it was only their committees, the president and a few members, who took the decisions and signed the petitions, and this in the name of the entire society and consequently, of the people (Bentabole)? The representatives *en mission* came up against these ringleaders many times and had to proceed to the purging of the popular societies. The time had come to bring order everywhere – a task all the more urgent so that no one was deceived: many popular societies were dominated by agents of the Terror who would prefer its return, in order to escape justice. 'Citizens, your enemies have poisoned your popular societies and *sections* with men unknown to those who began the Revolution in 1789, men who want only plunder, only disorder, only murders, only assassinations: they are men who must be returned to the dust, and it is this that is asked of you' (Bourdon (from the Oise))[58]

By multiplying the quotations, one can size up the role of the ex-Jacobins and terrorists in the offensive against the Society, in the 'unmasking' of the machinery of its working and of the power it had acquired. To accuse the Jacobins of all evils, to present them as the principal support of Robespierre yesterday and as 'the lair of brigands' today, was also a way of discharging the Convention of any responsibility for its own activities during the Terror. It was only, in its turn, another victim of the 'tyrant' whom it had just defeated, as of the Jacobins, whom it was going to defeat.

Faced with this campaign contesting the legitimacy of their political activities and undermining the very bases of their activity, the Jacobins were caught in a dilemma.

Like all political discourse after 9 Thermidor, that of the Jacobins necessarily refers to the 'fall of the tyrant' and to the 'happy revolution'. So, the Jacobins could not assert in full the role they had played in the past, especially in the exercise of power during Year II. This would in effect be to accept responsibility for the Terror and put their adversaries in the right. But neither could the Jacobins deny their past; they glorified unceasingly their unconditional devotion to the Revolution, their vigilance, their struggles and sacrifices. Loyalty to this tradition precisely ensured their collective identity; it also endowed their pretension to express themselves in the name of the people and, consequently, to assume an autonomous political role in relation to the Convention, with a sort of legitimacy. The Jacobins could not define themselves as an opposition force, in conflict with the new politics of the Convention, precisely because their own set of

[58]    All these quotations are taken from reports of the debates on the decree of 25 Vendémiaire. Cf. *Moniteur*, vol., pp. 255 *et seq.*; Aulard, *Société des Jacobins*, vol. 6, pp. 571 *et seq.*

concepts excluded the possibility that an opposition *party* could be established. All their unitary rhetoric, which had been shown to be so effective in the past, had accused *others* – their political adversaries – of forming such associations, *factions* guilty of ruining the unity of the people and its indivisible will. To declare themselves an opposition force was to justify immediately the whole anti-Jacobin campaign which denounced the Society precisely as a 'political corporation', elevated under the Terror into a second illegitimate 'rallying-point'. In order not to expose themselves to such attacks, the Jacobins therefore insisted strongly on their republican legalism, their unconditional respect for the Convention and the law. They defended themselves against accusations of having the slightest intention of 'raising a new political throne', of arrogating to themselves the smallest fragment of power that by rights belonged to the Convention, and to the representatives of the sovereign people. They were doing no more, they argued, than *enlightening* and instructing the people, by bringing some understanding to the Convention and the revolutionary government, and by debating the great political problems and the decisions to be taken. This was the sacred duty they carried out by virtue of the legitimate rights of all citizens – those of freedom of association, of speech and of petition, guaranteed by the Constitution. In reality this was translated into the desire to keep permanent *watch over* the Convention, by a whole series of pressures and even of threats, formulated in the petitions addressed to the Convention or in the addresses distributed through the country via the network of affiliated popular societies. Everything carried on, then, as if the Jacobins hoped to re-use the political tactics which had ensured victory for them over the Girondins, in the spring of 1793. But in Vendémiaire of Year III, this repetition underlined the weakness of the Jacobins: the relationship between forces was hardly to their advantage and they did not even think of giving their proclamations an effective extension, by making an appeal to the 'risen people'. They had neither the notion of nor the means for such a policy, which would involve open rebellion against the Convention and the revolutionary government. At the end of Year II the Jacobins no longer retained the monopoly on their own methods of political action. So the Convention, in order to bring to heel the local popular societies linked to the Jacobins, proceeded, through the representatives *en mission*, to 'purge' them, a well-worn method from the time of the Mountain's dictatorship. In the Convention, the fiercest adversaries of the Jacobins were the recent defectors who were not ignorant of how fearsome a political stake was involved in the claim to express the will of the people; from now on they carefully reserved this right for the Convention and fiercely denounced as a 'terrorist' imposture the Jacobin attempts to lay claim to it.

Nothing is perhaps more revealing of the impasse in which the Jacobins found themselves than their attitude with regard to the memory and heritage of Robespierre. The power of Robespierre was based, as we have seen, on the pivotal position that he occupied both in the Convention and at the Jacobins. At the Society, Robespierre held full moral, political and intellectual authority, which he exercised particularly in the spring of Year II. He was at nearly all the meetings, which he transformed into a sort of permanent school of republican virtue and revolutionary spirit, and of which he was himself both the interpreter and the embodiment. This great authority allowed the Jacobins to assert themselves as a superior authority in morality and politics. Now, from the moment of Robespierre's fall, the Society barely hesitated to loathe him, to claim to be victim of his 'tyranny', and to reject with indignation the accusation of being his 'tail'. And yet, at the end of Year II, in the difficult moments which succeeded 9 Thermidor, the Society more than ever needed a 'leader' to impose authority. The place once occupied by Robespierre remained empty; no one wanted to or could occupy it, for it was precisely the 'throne' of a tyrant.

One episode shows this clearly. When the decree of 25 Vendémiaire on the popular societies was reported during a session of the Society, 'a mournful silence reigned in the chamber and tears were shed'. Lejeune, a deputy who had courageously criticised the decree and defended the Society, launched a dramatic appeal to Billaud-Varenne and Collot d'Herbois, these historic leaders who symbolised the grandeur and energy of the Society before 9 Thermidor and who, besides, had played a decisive role during the 'last revolution'. He reproached these 'men of talent', whom nature had endowed with the 'gift of speech', for having kept a guilty silence during the debate at the Convention: 'I am astonished at the silence kept for the last two months by these same men who, not long ago, stood every day at the rostrums of the Convention and of the Jacobins. You spoke then of the rights of the people, Billaud and Collot; why then are you silent today when it is a matter of defending them?' The two members thus challenged replied, very embarrassed, that, 'in view of the state of the Convention', their interventions could only harm the cause of the people and of the Society. Their silence was hardly a sign of weakness; they reminded their audience that they were silent during the three *décades* which had preceded their denunciation of Robespierre and the fall of the 'tyrant'.[59] This silence contrasted vividly with the fervour and verbosity of the man who, after 9 Thermidor and up to the trial of the revolutionary committee of Nantes, was very active front-stage at the Jacobins, condemning '*modérantisme*' and the 'persecution of patriots': Jean-Baptiste Carrier.

[59] Cf. the accounts of the sessions of 25 and 27 Vendémiaire: *ibid.*, pp. 588 *et seq.*

## 'Where are we going?'

'We are giving an account of ourselves to the Nation. We remind ourselves what we have been, what we are; we declare what we should be. France hears and judges us.' In his report, presented in the name of the Committee of Public Safety on the day of the fourth *sans-culottide*, Year II, Lindet provides replies to these three questions which the Convention dramatically asked itself at the end of Year II: where have we come from? where are we? where are we going?

Lindet's report aimed to bring an official conclusion to Year II, to draw up the balance-sheet as well as to formulate a policy for the future. It was unanimously adopted, amidst the greatest enthusiasm, by the Convention. This unanimity marks a pause in the political struggles at a particularly symbolic moment, the celebration of the end of the republican year. Five *décades* after 9 Thermidor, Lindet wished to gain the widest assent of the Convention and, consequently, of the Nation, to the political plan put forward by his report. Lindet drew up a vast inventory of problems with which the country was faced; he analysed the experience of the policy inaugurated on 9 Thermidor, he scrutinised the horizon of expectations and hopes which surrounded this experience and, to conclude, he sketched a vision of the future, a sort of utopia on which should open the 'new period' of the Revolution. A text born of a momentary combination of circumstances, it is only a sort of instant snapshot; thanks, however, to the fullness of the problems raised, his lucidity and also his illusions, this report clarifies Thermidorean politics as a whole. We shall content ourselves with extracting a few essential points.

'A spirit of destruction hovered over France': the most urgent, but also the most complex problem, to emerge on the country-wide scale, as well as in each town or village, was *to liquidate the heritage of the Terror*, to make good its devastation. This was a particularly heavy inheritance, which weighed upon all areas of collective life. The Convention must therefore continue the work begun on 9 Thermidor when it made 'justice the order of the day': free the innocent; bring about a rebirth of public confidence and security; extinguish the 'torches of hatred and discord'; put an end to the suspicions which had for too long disturbed people's minds; re-establish the rights of man and the citizen, especially freedom of opinion and freedom of the press. Lindet insisted particularly on the damage and persecution suffered by the arts, the sciences and letters. He took over for his own purposes the speech by the Abbé Grégoire against vandalism and, in particular, as we shall see, the attacks launched by the Abbé against *Robespierre-the-vandal*. Despite all these prejudices, the arts had nevertheless magisterially contributed to the victories of the armies as well as the economic progress of the country. 'If they have made this rapid progress, despite Robespierre's rages, what will they not do when they share the advantages of liberty and equality! They were the first to proclaim the rights of man; must it be the case that they cannot appeal to them?' Lindet lingered long over the economic problems for which, in fact, he was particularly responsible in the Robespierrist Committee of Public Safety, before 9 Thermidor. Commerce was in ruin; agriculture had, of course, made 'incredible progress: never has such a large extent of earth been cultivated and sown', but it was also in crisis. The fault did not lie only with neglect and ignorance but, again, with Robespierre, with his 'destructive spirit', with his premeditated plan of subjugating France through Terror. ('Commerce today presents ruins and debris ... Robespierre wished to destroy it ... It was necessary to ruin the silk industry, and he forced the abandonment of the cultivation of mulberry trees, one of the principal resources of the *départements* of the south; he had oils transported abroad to destroy your soap factories.') The large commercial and port towns were plunged in desolation; they were the victims of a disastrous policy that sought to regulate everything as well as of a repression as cruel as it was systematic. There was a barbaric plan to destroy Lyon; on the pretext of counter-revolution businessmen were imprisoned, factories closed, workmen sent away.

Turn your eyes to Commune-Affranchie; bring a halt to the demolition of buildings and houses; bring the citizens back into their workshops; they are made to create and not to destroy. These are not payments that you are being asked for; ensure freedom of export ... and Lyon will emerge from the ruins. Let Marseille remember the means by which it achieved its glory and its prosperity; elevated passions have made it forget the advantages of its situation, its interests and its needs. This commune, whose commerce was so splendid and so beneficial ... survives only through the help that the government sends it ... At Sette they were regarded as counter-revolutionary, the businessmen who sacrificed their fortunes in order to carry out a decree of the Committee of Public Safety, which required them to send out exports in order to discharge the Republic of a portion of its commitments ... All resounds here with the sound of the misfortunes which have afflicted the commune of Nantes. What could commerce do among so many disasters and so much persecution ... The integrity, the misfortunes [of Nantes] call for encouragement.

In order to turn the page for ever on the Terror, a system contrary to the founding principles of the Republic, there must be an 'official declaration that any citizen who employs his days usefully in the labours of agriculture, in the sciences, the arts, commerce, who establishes or maintains manufacturing businesses, *cannot be disturbed nor treated as a suspect*'. It was necessary, finally, to put an end to the war of the Vendée, to establish peace and order in the *départements* of the West. Of course, force and weapons would be resorted to, if necessary. However, military measures alone would not be enough to bring this disastrous war to an end. The final victory of the Republic was to be won, in the end, in Paris, by the putting into practice of a new policy, one that broke with the Terror.

The example of courage, of integrity, of union which you will give here, should also be the principal influence on the *départements* of the West. The ostentation, the luxury and the crime of certain generals shall be forgotten; the army will respond to your expectations, and the people will recognise only avengers in the soldiers of liberty. The calm that you will establish here, the great principles that you will sanction, and with which the representatives and the generals will show themselves imbued, will bring an end to these frightful troubles that desolate such a beautiful country, which you should reconquer for liberty. It is by enlightenment, by the force of principles, by reason, by an army terrible to the rebels, protective of good citizens, that you will complete this conquest.

The restoration of liberty, confidence and justice were essentially political problems, for which political solutions must be sought. In the same way, the economic problems needed, first and foremost, political responses: it was necessary to regain for the Republic the confidence and support of all those who ran commerce and manufacturing. Under the Terror they were too often considered to be suspect from the single fact that they were rich. So a future could be considered only if the measures taken after 9 Thermidor were extended and amplified. In this sense, Lindet's report is a 'Thermidorean' text; he exalts 9 Thermidor as a turning point, a point of no return in the history of Year II and, therefore, of the Revolution. Lindet not only contributed to the working out of these measures; in his report, he took up nearly all the questions over which the Convention and its Committees had kept tearing themselves apart since 9 Thermidor, and in doing this he seems to bring off a gamble: to present the policy, so tortuous and hesitant, of the Convention, during the last five *décades*, as the carrying out of a coherent and consistent political strategy. The new measures, which he announced in his report, aimed in the same direction, that of dismantling the Terror in all areas of social life, and, consequently, of liberalising them: easing the procedure for the handing out of certificates of good citizenship; elimination of irregularities in this area by committing the municipalities and committees of the *sections* to giving the reasons in cases of refusal and by installing an appeals procedure; examination of all complaints relating to arbitrary arrests as quickly as possible and, if necessary, immediate release of the innocent; promotion of commerce, especially exports; finally, a series of measures relating to public education, to which we shall return.

By not avoiding the difficulties raised by this unprecedented enterprise, that of dismantling the Terror, Lindet aimed to reassure. The task to be accomplished would succeed on condition that the Republic did not fall under the influence of extremisms and that it thereby avoided the great danger that risked jeopardising the emergence from the Terror. It was necessary, first, to avoid revenge. Of course, 'errors, mistakes, abuses of power, arbitrary acts' had been committed, but were they not so many 'evils inseparable from a great revolution'? Now, they must not be confused with crimes. So the right action to take was to reassure the members of the dissolved revolutionary committees, as well as the civil servants who were returning to their work, that even if they had committed, in good patriotic faith, some errors, the Nation would protect them against any attempt at vengeance: 'They have defended the sacred cause of liberty and, in a time of storm, they made use of a great power which was created by necessity. The Nation does not wish that those who directed and launched the thunder against its enemies should be struck and consumed by it.' On the other hand, those who had committed *crimes* should be severely punished, as required by law and justice. Lindet also denounced the extremism of those who 'have only embraced revolution for the sake of the crimes that they would be able to commit', these 'monsters . . . who had usurped the title and reputation of patriots'. Finally unmasked, they sought now to present themselves as so many 'persecuted patriots', to alarm the popular societies, to excite passions and suspicions. They attempted to present the just punishment awaiting them as a threat directed against all patriots. Lindet alluded to the anxieties which appeared in the popular societies as well as among the political personnel of the Terror, and on this point his view is firm:

If there are crimes, if there are atrocities which require prompt atonement, you will not impose silence upon the courts ... Are not the citizens who have been seen sharing the alarm of the guilty going to detach themselves from them? Will they not abandon the cause of these criminal imposters? France will soon see crime and imposture isolated, begging for support and failing to find it.

The Nation would know how to 'repress and contain through its power' all those who would endeavour to bring about a rebirth of new disturbances in the country.

It was especially necessary to prevent the rebirth of old factions and the formation of new ones. For that, it was necessary to bury the past, its memories, however painful they were, its old discords: 'Let us make our fellow-citizens forget the misfortunes inseparable from a great revolution; *let us say to them that the past is no longer ours, that it belongs to posterity.*' The ending of the Terror should not, in any case, degenerate into a settling of scores, into a pursuit of the guilty; the allusion to Lecointre's recent denunciation of the members of the former Committees is transparent.

The only valid strategy for the future consisted in the largest possible *rallying together* of Frenchmen. Lindet insisted especially on factors which were so many symbols of *national unity*. There was, first, the victorious army.

Twelve hundred thousand citizens in arms, the avant-garde of the defenders of liberty, extend our frontiers into Spain, the Palatinate and Belgium. Everyone yields to their courage; our enemies, struck with terror, hurl themselves into retreat, accuse their leaders, their tyrants, and pray secretly for their conquerors. Peoples sacrificed to the pride of kings, who alone suffer the calamities of war, see in the French only the avengers of the rights of man.

There was, next, the people; a people sovereign and free, certainly, joined together in public affairs; but, above all, it was *the people at work*, who refused no sacrifice for the *patrie* at war in order to ensure the victory of its armies.

The French have discovered resources in their productivity. Constant work has preserved us from the misfortunes we had so many reasons to fear . . . What a picture to offer to posterity, that of a people who make a continual sacrifice of the wages of its labour, its clothing and its own supplies to the *patrie*, who forget themselves for the *patrie*, and recommence each day with sacrifices which transcend human forces.

The people under the banners and the people at work ensure, together, *national greatness*:

Your enemies can no longer obscure nor veil your glory. They can no longer rob you of the confidence and esteem of nations . . . You have reminded men that they were all equal, that they were all brothers. They have rushed to the aid of each other, they now see themselves only as a single family, and *France, closely united, has become the first, the most powerful of nations.*

This unity was hardly conceived as exclusive; on the contrary, the Republic should open itself to all those who had taken a wrong turning along the tortuous roads of the Revolution:

It is not for yourselves alone that you have founded a Republic, it is for every Frenchmen who wants to be free; you may exclude only bad citizens . . . You are too aware of your situation not to know how many citizens have gone astray on the routes of the Revolution . . . Doesn't the same blood flow in the veins of these valiant young men and women, who expect from you the liberty of their parents, as the worthiest prize of their labours and victories?

The image of national greatness, of 'energetic and hard-working France', thus ensured a unity in Year II, beyond the vicissitudes of the Terror, the struggles and the quarrels.[60]

---

[60] Lindet endeavoured to employ a rhetoric and vocabulary of national union in his report. So he avoided terms like the Mountain, the Jacobins, the *sans-culottes*, etc. The social imagery and vocabulary of year II used for expressing and exalting 'revolutionary energy' thus found themselves condemned, even exorcised, and this change of language says much about the road taken since 9 Thermidor. In his report, Lindet proposed to come to terms

The calls to both national and republican unity found their extension and, after a fashion, their justification in the *educational utopia* sketched by Lindet at the end of his report. The most effective means of 'attaching the people to the Revolution' was to *enlighten* it. A means, unfortunately, too much neglected, and the responsibility for this fell, once more, on Robespierre: like any tyrant he considered ignorance and prejudice his natural allies. How otherwise to explain the fact that 'the shadows of ignorance' had not yet been dispersed by 'knowledge and instruction'? Why did the French not yet possess, in every cottage, 'the much-needed works in which they would learn their rights and duties'? The Republic still lacked an

with the principal problems raised in the debates of the Convention since 9 Thermidor. In his recourse to a rhetoric of unity, Lindet seems to be inspired by the observations of Edme Petit on the perversion of revolutionary language during the Terror. Edme Petit, representative of the Aisne and a surgeon, was close to the Girondins but had escaped the repression which followed the 'journée' of 31 May. On 28 Fructidor, Year II, Edme Petit gave a long speech to the Convention in which he examined the factors that had favoured 'Robespierre's tyranny' and, consequently, the regime of the Terror. 'How did it happen? What were the causes of this phenomenon, frightening for liberty? Yes, citizens, these are the questions which the interest of the people demands we resolve in the very presence of the people.' The originality of Edme Petit's analysis consisted particularly in the importance he attached to the perversion of revolutionary principles through a language that was itself perverted.

No doubt Robespierre spoke of liberty, of equality; but this was so that everyone submitted to Robespierre, so that Robespierre had no equals; no doubt he spoke of patriotism, but this feeling was nothing else, according to him, than the love due to him and the respect one should have for his agents; no doubt Robespierre spoke of the Republic but this Republic was Robespierre himself, it was Couthon, it was Saint-Just. He spoke of truth; but almost without ceasing he used lies to do harm and he never told the truth when it could be harmful ... Let us remember that, beginning with the word Revolution, *they removed from all the words of the French language their true sense*. Let us remember that having brought in confusion, uncertainty and ignorance everywhere, *they introduced into the language a crowd of new words*, of names with which they described as they pleased the men and things they wanted to be loved or hated by the deceived people ... Let us remember that these speeches were re-read and repeated in bombastic style in all the affiliated popular societies, that is to say, societies which were under the power of this too famous Society, which in turn had fallen under the power of Robespierre; and we will have an exact picture of the way in which the infernal morality of Robespierre and those like him was propagated.

Hence the proposition of Edme Petit to ban all members of the Convention, under pain of suspension until the restoration of peace, from using in their reports or speeches 'words invented to excite confusion and division in the Revolution and in the Republic', beginning with the words *Montagne, Plaine, Marais, Modérés, Feuillants*, etc. Hence also another proposal, complementary to the first: to require the Committee of Public Instruction to give the words that made up the French language their true sense and, thereby, 'give back to republican morality its true energy'. Edme Petit's speech, while developing these pertinent points on the functions of language in the working of the Terror, paradoxically displays an illusory faith in the quasi-unlimited possibilities of revolutionary power to direct and modify language, to restore to words and unifying symbols their 'true sense'. In the same speech Petit also proposed a decree committing all deputies to publish an account of their wealth and profits since 1789. The Convention followed Edme Petit neither in his hopes nor in his suspicions, and proceeded with the business of the day (cf. *Moniteur*, vol. 21, pp. 750–9: session of 25 Fructidor). Petit's text is the first to provide consideration of the specific language of the Terror (continued by La Harpe, among others) and is interesting evidence on political culture at the end of Year II.

'educational strategy' worthy of it and the Committee of Public Instruction should take responsibility for drawing one up as swiftly as possible. But here and now urgent measures were required. On the model of the Ecole de Mars, it was necessary to create a special School which would train, at high speed and by employing unprecedented methods, the army of teachers which the country so badly needed. The forthcoming creation of the Ecole Normale would thus be an original as well as an effective response to the crucial problem of any reform of public education: how to train, as quickly as possible, the teachers of a new people? It was also necessary to 'fill the unoccupied moments of the decadal festivals by producing, for each *décadis*, 'booklets' which would provide 'a catalogue of the work [of the Convention] and of principal events ... Let them include advice, rules of conduct; let them radiate love of labour, morality and public honesty; let a pure and easy narrative attract and interest.' In this way, revolutionary power would accomplish its educational mission, would be in permanent contact with the citizens, and itself enliven the festivals, not by 'the pomp of a futile spectacle but by education'. France would then become populated with 'new men'; it would come closer to the model provided by the Valais and praised by Rousseau, where the people united harmoniously, in a peaceful life, in love of liberty, work and enlightenment. 'In the Valais every inhabitant knows how to cultivate his field, the arts and the sciences; every house has a collection of the best books, the most ingenious tools of the different arts and crafts, and agricultural implements, all of which the owner knows how to use.'

In this country which had hardly begun to emerge from the Terror and which found itself in the middle of a war, what citizen would not see himself in this vision of a new France, reconciled with itself, enlightened and peaceful, working and free? The recourse to utopia (or, if you will, the flight to utopia) allowed the present, and the crisis and conflicts marking the end of Year II, to be perceived as a fleeting moment. To reinvigorate the teaching mission of the Revolution was to return to its sources and so fill, through education, the gap that had opened between the founding principles of the Revolution and the history which had been their realisation.[61]

[61] Lindet thus vigorously took up the educational preoccupations and hopes that marked every political debate after 9 Thermidor. The transformation of the Terror into 'vandalism' encouraged the reanimation of revolutionary power's educational vocation and work. Revolutionary rhetoric now found a privileged place for its employment in the glorification of the hoped-for benefits of education, the only effective remedy against an eventual return of the Terror. We shall be easily pardoned for giving a sample:

What have I heard, Senators of the Republic? The patriots of the campaigns demand, desire a new victory; for five years repulsed from a new promised land by an invisible and sacrilegious hand, they burn, they sigh ardently for public education, with the cry of despair, the tears of emotion and the tenderness of gratitude. The hour presses; we are coming out of the storm ... let us calm anxieties, console the mass of citizens, and with a paternal hand let us pour into the labourer's hut, under the

So, for Lindet, with 9 Thermidor 'the French nation had gone through all the phases of its revolution'; it had completed, so to speak, a complete cycle of its history. The righting of the abuses of the Terror consisted in 'the return to rules and principles', to its original values. Yet this journey was not wasted: the people emerged from it enriched with experiences that were, certainly, very painful, but steeled, war-hardened and energetic, knowing how to distinguish true virtues from deceptive appearances. Lindet knew perfectly well that the post-Terror period, begun on 9 Thermidor, could not be a 'restoration', a simple return to a previous situation, to a political and institutional model made in the past. A return to constitutional monarchy was, evidently, excluded; but also excluded was a return to the situation before 31 May 1793 (this date still served as a reference-point; the 'rehabilitation' of the Girondins and, consequently, the return of the imprisoned deputies were not yet envisaged). A return then to the beginning, but in the sense of the fundamental values and founding principles of 1789. Their re-establishment should however go hand in hand with the preservation of the institutions of 1793: revolutionary government until peace and retention of the popular societies whose mission was to enlighten the people. In other words, Lindet would propose both to *return* to the principles of 1789 and to *retain*, as lasting acquisitions of revolutionary experience, the institutions and *élan* of Year II, minus the terrorist practices. Aware of the difficulties and obstacles to be overcome, he still believed this to be a realistic programme: as if there existed no contradiction between the principles of 1789 and the institutions and values of 1793; as if the 1789 values themselves had not suffered in any way from the terrorist ordeals of Year II; as if authority possessed infallible criteria, which were also generally shared, for separating 'crimes' from 'abuses'; as if, finally, the 'sovereign People' and, therefore, revolutionary authority could avoid the difficult distinctions between the 'pure' and the 'impure', virtue and vice, in the history of the Revolution, in its past and in its future.[62]

thatch of poverty, the bountiful dew of education. Agitators and alarmists, desolated by our brilliant successes, attempt to degrade, to slander national representation; they know very well, these perverse men, that liberty, nourished by public education, fortified by good behaviour, shining out like the star of day, will show itself in majesty to the peoples of the earth, embellished with the palms of triumph and immortality. (Giraud, at the session of 22 Fructidor, Year II, in *Moniteur*, vol. 21, p. 708)

Compared with such pinnacles of rhetoric, the vision of France transformed into a country of peaceful and virtuous mountain-dwellers, imagined by Lindet, seems quite modest. At the end of Year II and the beginning of Year III an enormous step forward would in fact be taken in the forming of new republican élites: the creation of the Ecole Normale, announced by Lindet, and the foundation of the Ecole Centrale des Travaux Publics (later called the Ecole Polytechnique): cf. B. Baczko, ed., *Une éducation pour la démocratie. Textes et projets de l'époque révolutionnaire*, Paris, 1982.

[62] All the quotations taken from the report of Lindet are from the text published in the *Moniteur*, vol. 22, pp. 19–27.

The Convention received the report of Lindet with enthusiasm and approved it unanimously. The day after, however, it seemed to forget this fine unanimity in order to give way to its factional divisions. Lindet's report is a document remarkable for its lucidity as well as its illusions. It is distinguished by its sense of the State's responsibilities, and by its desire to master unchained passions. The unanimity of its adoption seemed, for the space of a moment, to bring about the impossible unity of the Thermidorean Convention. Lindet's plan proposed, in order to ensure the future of the Republic, the largest possible rallying of the French, which would be carried out to the exclusion of all extremisms that would like to come back to the Terror or attack the gains of Year II and of the revolutionary government. In this respect, Lindet's report outlined a *centrist programme*, but it did not begin a new stage in politics; at the very most, it marked a pause. Its centrism represented a *point of view* and not a *political force*; this was not the time for an impossible rallying together but, on the contrary, for the aggravation of political conflicts and contradictions. That this point of view should be presented in the name of the Committee of Public Safety was only the result of a combination of circumstances and a fleeting relationship of forces. In fact, the procedure of the renewing of the Committee of Public Safety each month, applied for the first time on 15 Fructidor, created a very delicate balance in the heart of this Committee. The unanimity with which the report was accepted was therefore a sign of weakness and not of strength.[63]

The report was passed on the last day of Year II. The solemnity of the session certainly favoured its adoption as a balance-sheet and as a programme. Symbolic moments secrete their own illusions: the fleeting instant is experienced as a lasting moment, hopes seem certainties, the ephemeral becomes stable and solid. Lindet hoped and believed that the painful experiences of the Terror would give way to the dawning of a dynamic unity. By adopting his report, the Convention seemed to agree with him and opted for an emergence from the Terror which would be carried out 'by decreeing forgetfulness', to use Quinet's phrase.[64] It was, however, only one of those rare moments when the symbolism of utopia

[63] On 15 Fructidor the Convention proceeded to the first renewal of the Committee of Public Safety; a quite complex process (selection by lot and withdrawals, in particular of Billaud-Varenne, Collot d'Herbois and Tallien) resulted in the retention of certain members of the former Committee (among others, Robert Lindet, Carnot and Prieur (from the Côte d'Or) and the introduction of new men (Merlin (from Douai), Delmas, Cochon and Fourcroy). Cf. J. Guillaume, 'Le Personnel du Comité de salut public', *La Révolution française*, 1900, vol. 38, pp. 297–309.

[64] Cf. E. Quinet, *La Révolution* (edited by C. Lefort), Paris, 1987, p. 604. Mona Ozouf has given a remarkable analysis of this 'impossible forgetfulness', which could not be imposed by decree and whose contradictory influence marked the history of the Thermidorean Convention, in 'Thermidor ou le travail de l'oubli', in her *L'Ecole de France*.

and unity seemed to get the better of the divisions and denunciations, the denigration and violence.[65] For it was, in reality, no longer a time of union and rallying together, but for *polarisation* and *confrontation*. The political and symbolic heritage of Year II, even reduced to what Lindet wanted to keep of it, no longer united, but divided; the principles of 1789, with regard to the problems raised by the ending of the Terror, no longer brought people together, but stirred up conflict. The end of Year II demonstrated that *the heritage of the revolution was not single, but plural*. It became the source of political conflict.

'It is necessary to put an end to suspicions ... to re-establish France', insisted Lindet in his report. He proposed to emerge from the Terror without a spirit of revenge. This deliberate originality was the mark of his greatest weakness and condemned him to defeat. Lindet's report tried vainly to exorcise hatred and suspicion, to prevent passions and feelings becoming enmeshed. Lindet's political plan, or rather his gamble, referred back to the unity achieved by the Convention and the Nation on 9 Thermidor. The period after the Terror should only lead back to the unity symbolised by the unanimous cry: 'Down with the tyrant!' The Terror had divided the citizens so that the 'tyrant' and his acolytes might reign. By regaining its liberty, by returning to its original values and principles, by recognising only one 'rallying-point', the Nation should cement its unity in forgetting the 'tyranny' and in the passion for liberty.

Lindet believed he was inaugurating a new era, while, yet once more, the Revolution was encouraging the myth of the fundamental unity of the Nation, of the people, and, consequently, itself. At the same time, it

[65] Already on the following day, the day of the fifth *sans-culottide*, the festival of the pantheonisation of Marat brought out into the light once more the ambiguities and contradictions in which the Thermidorean Convention was plunged. There was no symbol which would not cause division. For a Fréron claiming kinship with him, Marat symbolised the persecuted journalist, therefore, the freedom of the press; Fréron, more-over, imitated, as we have seen, the verbal violence of Marat by turning it against the Jacobins and terrorists. But Marat was also, if not especially, a symbol of violence, the instigator of the Terror, the man who was involved in the September massacres and who had demanded 'a hundred thousand heads' to save the Revolution. The ceremony of the pantheonisation of Marat was marked by a clear unease (cf. the subtle analyses of Mona Ozouf, *ibid.*). Two *décades* later, on 20 Vendémiaire, the Convention proceeded to the translation to the Pantheon of the ashes of Rousseau; the festival went under the banner of peace, of a return to Nature and a homage to the Enlightenment. But to place the manes of Rousseau next to those of Marat, was this not to blaspheme, to offend the author of *Emile* and *La Nouvelle Héloise*? On 19 Nivôse, Year III, a hundred days after the pantheonisa-tion, the bust of Marat was removed from the chamber of the Convention; three weeks later, a bust of Marat is overturned at the Feydeau theatre by the *jeunesse dorée*, an act which set off the smashing of busts in all public places, in Paris and the *départements*. On 7 Ventôse, Year III, the remains of Marat left the Pantheon and were removed to the cemetery of Sainte-Geneviève, after his bust had been symbolically thrown, also by the *jeunesse dorée*, into the sewer of Montmartre. On the black legend of Marat in the Thermidorean period, cf.J.-C. Bonnet, *La Mort de Marat*, Paris, 1986, pp. 170 *et seq.*

continued to employ the *regulatory mechanism* of its working, namely the *exclusion* of defeated political adversaries, who were classed as the seditious, the enemies of the Republic. 9 Thermidor would treat the unchaining of passions by the single remedy appropriate for this moment of collective life: revenge.

It was, in fact, the language of suspicion that best expressed the fears and hatreds bequeathed by the Terror. Hatred aimed at the 'terrorists', the agents and political personnel of the Terror, all those whom public opinion condemned in advance for having participated in *the exercise of an iniquitous power*. Fear roused the spectre of the return of the Terror, of new massacres; the press, the anti-Jacobin pamphlets, the first revelations of the mass drownings at Nantes and the tales of released prisoners, the innumerable rumours, stirred it further. Revenge became personal and collective, social and cultural, against all these 'scoundrels' and 'cut-throats', 'knights of the guillotine' and 'murderers', pillagers and thieves, the ignorant and insolent, who had cornered all the 'offices' and who for a time had the upper hand over the 'honest people'. These fears and hatreds were reversed in the case of the Jacobins, with their anguish at being persecuted: the abrupt reversal of political circumstances, which had become more and more chaotic, and the first attacks against the 'patriots' created a climate of fear and insecurity among the Jacobins. In both camps, fear was stirred up by the verbal exaggeration typical of the Revolution, but particularly in these first weeks after 9 Thermidor. The emergence from the Terror enlarged the area of liberty, especially freedom of speech and the press. This increase in fear lest the Terror should return is striking to the historian who knows from hindsight the state of weakness in which the Jacobins then found themselves. It is true that contemporaries were first of all sensitive to the rhetorical violence of the speeches delivered at the Society. For, at the session of 21 Fructidor, had not Duhem proposed, in order to 'rid, once and for all, the Republic of all aristocrats and counter-revolutionaries', the pure and simple replacement of 'the waves of blood and ... the manifold punishments' with the massive deportation of all nobles and priests, 'this foul crew of gangrenous beings ... these plague-ridden lepers'?[66] We should not forget that, having barely emerged from the Terror, the political protagonists were still aware of the extent to which the language of violence could anticipate violence itself, could promise and prepare it, if the circumstances were right. This mutual distrust was all the greater in that the

[66] Session of 21 Fructidor, Year II; cf. Aulard, *Société des Jacobins*, vol. 6, pp. 423–5. Carrier lent his full support to the motion: 'Yes, citizens, yes, the time for false pity, for guilty indulgence is past; it is right that the salvation of the people, which is the supreme law of the patriot, should silence this frightful *modérantisme, which will finish by slaughtering us pitilessly, if we have the weakness to listen to it any longer.*'

relative political liberalisation eased the spread and circulation of rumours and fears. Paris teemed with 'persecuted patriots' and their relations who came to seek help and protection from the Jacobins, while bringing alarming news of what was happening in the *départements*; on the other hand, the rumours of a 'new conspiracy' by the Jacobins provoked movements of panic, as would be shown by the history of the Jacobin riot in Marseille, on 5 Vendémiaire, Year III.

The period after 9 Thermidor could not, therefore, be a time for the working out of new regulatory mechanisms for political life. Of course, the Convention took certain precautions against the eventual return of 'tyranny', notably the reorganisation of the structure of central authority, but this period, turned as it was towards revenge, favoured neither political pluralism nor tolerance. The appeals to national unity, whatever their intentions or source, did not calm matters; instead, they redoubled mistrust and suspicion. In fact, the symbolism and depiction of the *unity* of the Nation or of the people had been employed, since 1789, as a formidable weapon in political struggles, always announcing often bloody purges. The slide towards Jacobin and Montagnard dictatorship had come about through the exclusion of successive opposition groups in the name of the unlimited sovereignty of the people, *one and indivisible*. In the same way, the emergence from the Terror would be effected by the exclusion of the 'terrorists' and repression would be legitimised by 'justice as the order of the day' and carried out in the name of the people united against tyranny. The majority in the Convention turned on the Jacobins a rhetoric and an ideology that the latter had themselves worked out. This was not a political manoeuvre, but the recovery by the 'Thermidoreans', who were often products of the Mountain, of a portion of the Jacobin legacy.

Because of this absence of fundamental political innovation, it could be said that if the report of Lindet closed Year II, *it did not inaugurate Year III*. This year, decisive for the Thermidorean political experience, opened in reality under the auspices of the *official address* launched by the Convention on 18 Vendémiaire, barely twenty days after the adoption of Lindet's report.

Your most dangerous enemies are not the satellites of despotism whom you are accustomed to defeating ... The inheritors of Robespierre and of all the conspirators whom you have brought down are active everywhere, with the intention of shaking the Republic. Hidden under different masks, they seek to lead you across disorder and anarchy into counter-revolution. Frenchmen taught by experience, you can no longer be deceived. Evil has recommended the remedy to you ... No popular authority, no assembly can be identified with the people; no one should speak or act in its name ... Every act of government will bear the marks of justice; but this justice will no longer be presented to France as emerging from the cells, all covered in blood, in the way the vile and hypocrite conspirators have portrayed it ...

Frenchmen, avoid the men who keep speaking of blood and scaffolds, these exclusive patriots, these fanatical men, these men enriched by the Revolution, who fear the action of justice and who count on finding salvation in confusion and anarchy.[67]

It would be worth quoting the text in its entirety; it is a real call to vengeance and revenge against the Jacobins and the former terrorist personnel. The attacks against 'exclusive patriots' announced the bringing to heel of the popular societies, beginning with the mother-Society, the Jacobins of Paris. The address contained all the elements of the policy that Thermidorean authority would eventually adopt. Retribution was first conceived as legal and contained strictly within the limits of the law. The verbal violence of these appeals, however, gives a premonition of the fragility of these limits.

It is quite enthralling to follow how from day to day this turn-around took place, a change of direction which led to a political option radically opposed to the unifying political strategy proposed by Lindet. In fact, the political choice announced by the address of 18 Vendémiaire was in no way the fruit of an overall political strategy, worked out beforehand; the Thermidorean majority did nothing but improvise answers, point by point, to the concrete problems posed by the development of the political situation. However, by *reacting* in this way to events, it laid itself open to an escalation of repression and violence, of suspicion and resentment. The effects of these jolts and the passionate political reactions combined and complemented each other to such an extent that they seemed to form a new political phenomenon. Its outlines were still fluid, but the whole was already sufficiently distinct for a need to be felt for a new word to define it: the anti-Jacobin and anti-Terrorist *reaction*. It is not our intention to rewrite that political chronicle; let us be content with mentioning some important points which establish the context of the address of 18 Vendé-miaire and, at the same time, throw light on the route taken by authority at the beginning of Year III.

Through this address to the French people, the Convention wished to intervene in an 'energetic' manner in a sort of 'war of addresses', for which the Convention had been the battlefield for the last month. We have quoted the addresses to the Convention which, after 9 Thermidor, congratulated the 'fathers of the *patrie*' for having thwarted the dreadful conspiracy of the 'new Catiline' – addresses which were unanimous in their support and enthusiasm (it hardly matters whether this admirable unanimity is the reflex result of the unity imposed by the Terror or of a real relief at seeing the

[67] *Moniteur*, vol. 22, pp. 201–2; address of 18 Vendémiaire, 'La Convention nationale au peuple français'. This address was also accepted unanimously . . .

dictatorship fail). We have also seen that towards the middle of Fructidor the last addresses of congratulation for 9 Thermidor reached the Correspondence Committee of the Assembly, at the same time as the first petitions denouncing the return of the '*modérantisme* which is raising its head', and 'the persecution of patriots'. So the popular society of Dijon, which had approved 9 Thermidor, made a number of proposals to the Convention, on 7 Fructidor, to combat the *modérantisme* which 'invokes justice just as Robespierre invoked virtue'. The Convention should organise district revolutionary committees as quickly as possible, it should authorise them to 'recommence the arrests of suspect persons according to the law of 17 September', it should invite all citizens to 'pass on reasons for suspicion against this or that individual', and should re-examine the law which ordered 'consideration of the question of intent'. This same text, which sounds like a call for restoration of the Terror, had also been sent to the Jacobins, to all the affiliated societies as well as the Parisian *sections*.[68] Now, this address did not only find support amongst the most radical *sections* in Paris; the Jacobins gave it an enthusiastic reception, had it printed and ensured an even wider circulation (sending it to the armies and all the affiliated societies). From that moment, nearly every day, the Convention was inundated with very similar petitions and pleas which, according to rule, were sent at the same time to the mother-Society. The Convention replied, we have seen, by accusing the Society of elevating itself into a 'parallel centre' of power, itself fabricating all these addresses, then sending them to the *départements* where their 'terrorist' accomplices imposed them upon the societies, in particular by arrogating to themselves the right of signing a 'collective petition'. In their turn, the representatives *en mission* incited the constituted authorities, the popular societies, and the inhabitants of the commune to carry out a sort of counter-campaign of addresses which called upon the Convention to preserve 'justice as the order of the day', and punish the 'thieves', the 'villains' and other partisans of Robespierre. One even sees counter-addresses arrive from societies which in the space of two or three *décades*, had recanted, had radically changed their position and now denounced those who had 'taken advantage' of them (this was the case especially in Bourg-en-Bresse, Auxerre, Sedan, Marseille). One can easily imagine the 'purges' suffered in these towns, between the sending of the two addresses. The society of Dijon itself, 'purged' by representative Calès, finally retracted, on 3 and 4 Brumaire, its address that was judged, 'amidst the most unanimous applause', 'frightful'

---

[68] Concerning the popular society of Dijon and its immense power, which 'made everyone tremble' during the Terror, as well as its address of 7 Fructidor, Year II, cf. L. Hugueney, *Les Clubs dijonnais sous la Révolution*, Dijon, 1905, reprinted Geneva, 1978, pp. 153 *et seq.*

and 'vile'.[69] This outbreak of a reflex unanimity is an incontestable gain in freedom of expression, acquired in a relatively short time. But these polemics and controversies showed also that the new freedom revealed divisions and conflicts that were peculiar to the 'real country' which was disengaging itself from the Terror. One episode of this 'war of addresses', on 11 Vendémiaire, reveals the bitterness of the confrontations provoked nearly every day by the reading of correspondence. It was to serve, moreover, as a pretext for the working out of the official address of the Convention calling for an end to this 'war'. On that day, Thibaudeau denounced the manipulation and the manipulators who hid themselves behind the addresses condemning 'modérantisme' and the 'persecution' of patriots. He relied on a concrete example. The previous day, the Convention had had before it the address of the popular society of Poitiers in which 'we tell you that the aristocracy and modérantisme raise their heads, and that all patriots are being persecuted'. Now, Thibaudeau, himself a deputy of Vienne, went to examine this address. (It should be added that several members of his family had been arrested during the Terror; he himself had feared for his liberty; evil tongues did not fail to insinuate, later, that to provide proof of his loyalty he came to the Convention, during the Terror, dressed in a 'carmagnole' that was a little dirty and wearing a red bonnet...) He had ascertained that this address had been written some weeks before and that it was 'signed by only seven individuals, and that of these seven individuals there is one who had died five weeks before. Moreover, these seven individuals are scoundrels who have been removed from office by the representatives of the people and who have stolen the belongings of detainees.' And Thibaudeau concluded: the Correspondence Committee was a party to manoeuvres and manipulations (another representative would not fail to denounce, on the same occasion, the 'Robespierrists' who had infiltrated this Committee); but, more seriously, this was an attempt 'to control the changes of public opinion'. It was therefore necessary 'to stabilise this opinion', more especially as the report adopted by the Convention to 'direct its behaviour' (Lindet's report) had not sufficiently

[69] Ibid., pp. 206–7. There was even a demand to 'call the citizens together to the sound of a trumpet' to make them sign this repudiation. The censure of this 'shameful address' was proposed by a certain Sauvageot, leader of the Dijonnais Jacobins; he had been ... the instigator of the first address and was known, under the Terror, as 'the little king of Dijon'. This belated repudiation would not however save him: in Germinal, Year III, he was arrested and charged with abuse of authority and with making arbitrary arrests (ibid., p. 218). Le Messager du soir of 6 Frimaire was to record with great satisfaction the retraction by the purged clubs of Dijon of their previous appeal, 'a rallying sign for all terrorists'. This appeal of the popular society of Dijon was to inspire an 'anti-vandal' and 'anti-terrorist' play, L'Intérieur du Comité révolutionnaire, to which we shall return.

clarified the situation: its 'principles' had been obscured by 'considerations that were too general'.

> Tell your three Committees to prepare an address to the French, in which these principles will be put forward simply, distinctly and positively. If anyone dares to suggest, in the popular societies or anywhere else, principles opposed to those you have proclaimed, they will be banished ... If some rogues libel each other and squabble over the influence they wish to exercise, if they fight for their lives against the punishment they have deserved, it is up to the majority of the National Convention whom they wish to seduce, whom they wish to have share their passions, to show themselves firm, to put an end to all these excesses.[70]

An example of this 'firmness' would be given by the Convention the following day; after a violent attack by Legendre against Collot, Barère and Billaud-Varenne, referred to as 'traitors', the Convention decided to return to the examination of their responsibilities during the Terror, and, in particular, of their complicity with Robespierre. The Convention thus opened the debate that it had decided, barely a month earlier, to bring to a definitive conclusion ...

So it turned out once more that the two questions: where are we coming from? and, where are we going? were inextricably entwined, and that the dismantling of the Terror, without revenge or the settling of scores, was only an abstract and theoretical possibility. But it was the 'news from Marseille' especially, very opportunely presented to the Convention on the same day by the three Committees (of Public Safety, of General Security, and of Legislation), which brought the proof, if any were needed, that

---

[70] *Moniteur*, vol. 22, pp. 132–3. In his pamphlet *Histoire du terrorisme dans la Vienne*, Paris, n.d. (Year III), Thibaudeau himself clarified this episode as well as the particular context in which his attacks against the 'terrorists' and 'scoundrels' of Poitiers were to be placed. To characterise the reign of the Terror in Vienne, Thibaudeau evoked an image which took on a symbolic value: 'The guillotine has been in Poitiers a long time; it was still there some days after 9 Thermidor. The terrorists had dug a ditch under the scaffold, at the foot of the tree of liberty; its roots, they said, should grow and spread in the blood of its victims' (*ibid.*, pp. 52–3). The address proposed by Thibaudeau was meant to constitute a particularly 'firm reply' to the *Rapport du Comité de correspondance de la Société des Jacobins*, of 5 Vendémiaire, which had been 'printed, put on walls, distributed and sent out to all affiliated societies, the armies and the forty-eight *sections* of Paris'. The report, while not daring to make an explicit condemnation of the policy of the Convention, nevertheless outlined strong criticisms. Thus it was claimed that after 9 Thermidor *a cruel reaction made itself felt*, as was shown by the 'multiple addresses' which were sent by affiliated societies from all corners of the Republic. The report vigorously denounced those who claimed that a million men were providing for the other twenty-four million in France. This was a tranparent allusion to a speech of Dubois-Crancé made during the third *sans-culottide*, who, in order to denounce the evil effects of the Terror on the economy, had spoken of a 'million' people nourishing 'twenty-four million' others. It would be fully exploited by the Jacobins; they appealed to the 'twenty-four million' whom they were defending against 'one million'. In this way they presented the stakes of essentially political conflicts as social antagonisms, opposing the people, poor and hard-working, to the 'million' rich profiteers of the Revolution.

ending the Terror could be carried out only through open confrontations and at the price of an anti-Jacobin 'reaction'.

The Marseille affair, which goes back to the second *décade* of Fructidor, deserves recapitulation – but this has to be brief since it is impossible for us to describe the particularly complex history of the Terror in the Midi, in which it was only one episode. On several points it demonstrates the overall development of the political situation in the country, but also of the relations between the situation in Paris and the specific problems that the emergence from the Terror raised in the *départements*. On 20 Fructidor two new representatives *en mission*, Auguis and Serres, arrived in the Midi, determined, as they put it in a report to the Committee of Public Safety, to liberate the Midi 'from the monsters who were governing it and keeping it under the oppression of terror and arrogant crime'. Immediately, conflict became inevitable with the Marseille Jacobins from the celebrated 'club of the rue Thubaneau'. Of course the latter had enthusiastically congratulated the Convention for the 'fall of the tyrant' on 9 Thermidor, but they very quickly showed their disquiet in face of the turn taken by the political situation. So, in their meetings they denounced '*modérantisme*', the release of 'aristocrats' and 'suspects'. They sent a delegation to Paris to make representations to the Convention and the Jacobins. Another 'delegation' ('ten deputies, each armed with a sabre and a pistol') was hurried to a meeting with the new representatives *en mission*. The latter moved swiftly to the release of detainees (about five hundred in a week) and denounced as terrorists, to the Committees of the Convention, the Marseille Jacobins as well as the constituted authorities which the Jacobins dominated. On 26 Fructidor they had a certain Reynier arrested – one of the leaders of local Jacobinism, a defrocked priest, holding the offices of teacher and secretary of the revolutionary committee of Marseille; they had intercepted a letter of his calling for a new '2 September'. The Jacobins saw in this arrest an act of direct aggression against the Society as a whole, a new episode in central authority's opposition to the people of Marseille. They greeted Auguis and Serres with boos and call for a 'levy *en masse*'. On 28 Fructidor, Reynier, who was to be taken to Paris, was snatched from his escort, as he was leaving the town, by a hundred Jacobins. The representatives denounced this incident as an unmistakable case of revolt and a challenge thrown down to the Convention and revolutionary government. They proceeded to the 'purging' of the local authorities and informed the Convention of this 'affair' in the most alarming terms. Now, in Paris, in the last days of Year II, this news from Marseille could only cause a disturbance. Right in the middle of the 'war of addresses', after the very vigorous interventions of the delegation of Jacobins from Marseille at the Convention and the mother-Society, there was a rumour that an armed battalion, made up of Marseille

Jacobins, was coming to Paris in order to proceed to a new 10 August, but this time against the Committees of the Convention. Babeuf, in his *Journal de la liberté de la presse*, alarmed public opinion by declaring that the troubles at Marseille had been provoked by the Jacobins in order to assassinate the Convention. Faced with these rumours and the influx to Paris, from several *départements*, of terrorist personnel who felt threatened and came to seek refuge with their families and friends, the Convention decided, during the meeting of the third *sans-culottide* (therefore the day before the adoption of Lindet's report), to proceed to the expulsion from the capital of all people who were not residing there before 1 Messidor (this measure foreshadowed the law of *grande police* which was to be adopted on 1 Germinal, Year III, and which ordered all 'terrorists' to return to their domiciles). At its session on the fifth *sans-culottide*, therefore the day after the acceptance of Lindet's report, the Convention decided that it would itself intervene in the affairs of Marseille. It outlawed Reynier, called its representatives to proceed to the arrest of the instigators of the rebellion, to place seals on the papers of the Jacobin society and to carry out a 'purge'. The order to close the club arrived in Marseille on 4 Vendémiaire, and the representatives *en mission* issued orders of arrest against thirty-five Jacobins suspected of having participated in Reynier's release. On 5 Vendémiaire, at one o'clock in the morning, they proceeded to the first arrests (the president of the Jacobins, Carle, climbed onto the roof of his house, which was surrounded by soldiers, and hurled himself into the void). In the town, a riot broke out. A crowd of about four hundred people surrounded the house occupied by the representatives; one of the 'club members', a certain Marion, entered the building and demanded, 'in the name of the sovereign people', the immediate release of all the arrested Jacobins. The representatives tried, first, to disperse the gathering, then they had the troops who surrounded the area intervene and put ninety-six people (including thirteen gendarmes) under arrest. On 7 Vendémiaire Marion and four gendarmes were condemned to death by a military commission; before their public execution they sang the 'Marseillaise'. About 250 people were charged (the trials were to drag on until the end of Year III); the local authorities as well as the club itself would be radically purged.

During the session of 12 Vendémiaire, the Convention was informed of these events; it examined the reports of the two representatives *en mission* as well as the triumphalist and vengeful appeals launched by the new authorities of the town. 'War on all traitors!' proclaimed the surveillance committee of Marseille.

Representatives, it is our duty to inform you of the troubles which have disturbed our commune on the fifth of this month . . . We are carrying out the most scrupulous enquiries to discover the authors and motivators of this freedom-threatening rebellion ... We have finally succeeded in stripping them of the mask of patriotism under which they insulted national representation, turned the people aside from their true principles, and degraded them, so as to achieve more surely the counter-revolution they were plotting and which they would have certainly brought about, if the eye of surveillance had not seen their perfidious intentions. Let them tremble, these traitors! National justice will pursue them, and its sword will avenge the guilty for us.

The newly appointed municipal officers of Marseille were even more explicit and violent:

Representatives, they are no more, these mad rulers, who would continue Robes-pierre's system. Eternal gratitude be unto you, representatives, you alone could defeat this frightening colossus; you alone could deliver Marseille, the entire Republic, from this bloodthirsty caste that wanted to make everything a victim for its ambition ... Representatives, you can count on these virtuous men who were able to protect themselves from the poison of revolt; the scourge of the enemies of the people, they have made a solemn commitment to crush them, and they will use only the means provided by the law, by the labours of the Convention, which they will never cease to recognise as the centre of supreme authority, the rallying point where all should converge.

The Convention passed a decree approving the measures of its representa-tives and declared that the troops which had blocked the revolt had deserved well of the *patrie*.[71]

The riot of Marseille has sometimes been seen as a foreshadowing of the *journées* of 12 Germinal and 1 Prairial in Paris. The analogy, however, hardly seems valid. The crowd in Marseille was, in the end, noisy rather than violent. It was much less desperate than the Parisian crowd: famine, that powerful mobilising factor in the spring of Year III, did not exist in Marseille. The crowd of Marseille was composed almost entirely of men; contrary to Paris, women accompanied by children did not take part in the mob. In this sense, the crowd at Marseille showed more clearly its political colours: the Jacobins formed its kernel and barely hid their very 'federalist' mistrust of the representatives of central authority who became involved in their affairs. Whatever the reason, the Jacobin riot in Marseille, only a minor accident on the road, played an important role in the determination of the Convention's policy. In effect, it strengthened their will to react firmly against the Jacobins, even to fight them, once and for all. It certainly

---

[71] On the Jacobin riot of 5 Vendémiaire and its context, cf. G. Martinet, 'Les Débuts de la réaction Thermidorienne à Marseille. L'émeute du 5 vendémiaire', in *Actes du quatre-vingt-dixième Congrès national des sociétés savantes*, Nice, 1965, Section d'histoire moderne et contemporaine, vol. 2, pp. 150–66; M. L. Kennedy, *The Jacobin club of Marseille, 1790–1794*, Ithaca, N.Y., pp. 128 *et seq.*; M. Vovelle, 'La Révolution', in E. Baratier (ed.), *Histoire de Marseille*, Toulouse, 1975, pp. 275 *et seq.* See also Aulard, *Recueil des actes*, vols. 16–17.

influenced if not the content, then at least the particularly virulent language, of the official address to the French people of 18 Vendémiaire.[72] A week later, on 25 Vendémiaire, the Convention would pass its decree on the popular societies, banning any 'affiliation, combination, federation, as well as all collective correspondence between societies, whatever name they were known by'.

In the space of a month, the corner had been turned and the reply to the question: *where are we going?* had been formulated in terms of revenge. The decision of the Convention, taken at the same period, on 22 Vendémiaire, to speed up the trial of the revolutionary Committee of Nantes, would consolidate this political choice and reinvigorate the desire to dismantle the Terror. For, beyond the revelations on the massacres of Nantes, this trial would foster the overall images, the symbols of the *Terror* and the *Terrorist*. This trial had an immense influence upon the disintegration of the conquering social imagery of Year II, on the decline and fall of the Jacobins as well as on the growing repression against the political personnel of the Terror.

The appeal to the French people of 18 Vendémiaire imposed silence on the discordant voices in the addresses which arrived at the Convention. It did not slow down the flood of these but, on the contrary, provoked a new wave. Between 1 and 15 Brumaire the Convention received more than five hundred addresses which glorified it in unison, with rediscovered unanimity.

For a moment we could fear the spread of the incendiary principles to which the intriguers of Marseille sought to set light; for a moment we could fear the continuation of Robespierre's reign of blood. We have heard the proclamation of the Convention. We have applauded the feelings of justice that inspire it and from this moment we have sworn anew to live for the Republic and to remain inviolably attached to Republican principles and the Convention ... Our centre is the Convention, let the traitors, the intriguers, the oppressors and the knaves die'. (popular and reformed society of Rodez, address arriving 14 Brumaire)

The address to the French people has reached us: three times it was read at the tribune, three times it was accompanied and followed with tumultuous and widespread applause. Woe betide those who read it without being moved, woe betide those whose wild and corrupt souls like to feed on tears and blood; they are certainly the successors or the accomplices of the triumvirs ... Continue, citizen-representatives, to make yourselves worthy of the honourable mission which has

---

[72] The particularly violent language of this address expresses a 'reaction' in the 'war of addresses' and to the Marseille riot, but it reveals also a new relationship of forces in the heart of government: on 15 Vendémiaire, Lindet and Carnot had left, owing to their length of service, the Committee of Public Safety; the Committee of Legislation, which was dominated by prominent partisans of a policy of revenge, had been associated in the drawing up of the address.

been entrusted to you by a great people. Strike the enemies of the *patrie* without rest, have no pity for the agitators, the anarchists and the rogues. (popular and reformed society of the commune of Beaune, *département* of Doubs, address received on 12 Brumaire)

What a beautiful day this is, when the French people, ecstatic with admiration, sings the triumph of virtue amid the brightest joy ... Legislators, our happiness would have been extreme, if you had been witnesses of our enthusiasm, if you had heard the praise and applause that crowned the reading of your address to the French. The principles that you develop there are ours. We abhor the terrorists, we swear implacable hatred for them ... Fathers of the *patrie*, receive our homage, remain at your post! (inhabitants of the commune of Villefranche d'Aveyron, address dated 30 Vendémiaire)

Your address to the French people annihilated, without return, the reign of the Terror, that reign which legitimised the devastation of families and the assassination of Frenchmen; the patriot breathes at last; if any man of ill will believed that the day of 9 Thermidor was to his benefit, let him read your address: he shall find there the patriot protected and the certain fall of the enemy of the *patrie* if he does not in good faith unite himself with the great family. Tyrants, tremble! You will seek in vain to disunite us! The French will be only a people of brothers and friends. (popular and reformed society of Port-Malo, address arriving on 14 Brumaire)[73]

Do these speeches and this language express the spontaneity of anti-terrorist feelings? Do they not rather prolong the political conformism of before and after 9 Thermidor? In reality, the two phenomena combine. The Convention recognises itself all the more clearly in the addresses of allegiance and congratulation which it receives, addresses which paraphrase its own message 'amidst enthusiasm and applause' and which echoes its own language.

[73] Cf. AN C 325 CII, 1404; 1410; 1411. Lindet, in his speech in Brumaire, Year III, on the denunciation of the former members of the Committees, suspected manipulation and spoke out against 'these addresses, these petitions that are claimed to be the manifestation of public opinion'. Cf. R. Lindet, *Discours prononcé sur les dénonciations portées contre l'ancien Comité de salut public et le rapport de la commission des 21*, Paris, n.d.(Germinal, Year III), p. 117.

# 3    'Horror the order of the day'

### A series of trials

The silence that was maintained over such appalling acts is not the least curious characteristic of this strange period. France may have suffered from the Terror, yet one can say that she ignored it, and Thermidor was first of all a deliverance; but then it became a discovery: through the months that followed, people passed from one surprise to another.[1]

Cochin seems to be surprised at this real or feigned 'ignorance' of the realities of the Terror by a country which, however, relived them daily. With an intensity which had varied according to local circumstances, the Terror had been present everywhere. If not always in the form of 'appalling acts' of mass repression, then at least in the shape of an unending procession of constraints and oppression: the lists of 'suspects', the searches of people's homes, the emergency taxes, the chicanery necessary to obtain 'certificates of good citizenship', the arrogance and brutal domination, in thousands of towns, of those who but yesterday hardly dared raise their heads. The silence kept on the realities of the Terror was one of the elements of the 'system' itself. More exactly, under the Terror, people never stopped talking about it, but *language was monopolised by terrorist discourse*, by its rhetoric, its symbols and its ideology. On the rostrum of the Convention, in the newspapers, during the meetings of popular societies, speakers excoriated the 'enemies of the people', the 'conspirators' and *'modérantisme'* until they ran out of breath. The *Bulletin du Tribunal révolutionnaire* regularly published accounts, sometimes of trials, often of hastier procedures; the lists of those condemned to death constituted a daily item of the *Moniteur*, complementing the accounts of sessions at the Convention and the Jacobins. In Paris and several other towns, the guillotine functioned in a public square (at the very most, it had been moved from the Place de la Révolution towards the outskirts), and the spectacle offered by the scaffold

[1] A. Cochin, *Les Sociétés de pensée et la démocratie*, Paris, 1921, p. 118.

always attracted its share of regulars. The precise function of the Jacobin discourse on the Terror was to justify its purpose by sublimating it through symbolism and impassioned uproar, so as to hide the hideous reality: the rumbling of the carts carrying the condemned; the sharp blows of the guillotine's blade; the dirt, promiscuity and epidemics in the overpopulated gaols; but also, in everybody, the repression of fears and anxieties which deeply troubled their minds without them being able or daring to express themselves openly, although these fears were regularly kept alive by rumours produced by the daily repression. 9 Thermidor was not immediately the 'day of deliverance'. The first mass release of detainees, the suppression of the terrorist law of 22 Prairial and the reorganisation of the revolutionary Tribunal followed soon after the largest 'tumbrils' of the Parisian Terror when, on 11 and 12 Thermidor, the 'Robespierrists' were led to the scaffold. True deliverance could come only with the freeing of speech: only then would fears and hatreds be expressed in public, only then would the suffering experienced be unveiled, through 'revelations'. The first of these revelations, in particular on the 'conspiracy of the prisons', was made on the rostrum of the 'reformed Jacobins'. Réal, who had just been released from the Luxembourg prison, gave an account of his own experiences and called for the whole truth on the Terror to be told.

To fully detest the regime which has just finished, I think it is necessary to make clear its disgusting effects. It is in the portrayal of the evils which people were made to suffer in the prisons that the indignation of good citizens should find its sustenance. I leave to the citizens whom persecution had plunged in other prisons the task of making known the horrors they witnessed; for myself, I am going to tell you what took place in the Luxembourg. I do not believe, as has been said in certain reports, that *the Revolution is a virgin whose veil should not be lifted.* A regime of iron, a state of death, the gloomy distrust on all faces, deeply imprinted in the prisoners' souls, because of the spies among them, whose occupation it was to draw up the lists and provide fodder for the revolutionary Tribunal; the physical and moral state of the prisoners, all declared that the Luxembourg was only a vast tomb intended to bury the living.[2]

Through these 'revelations' the ideological discourse which justified the Terror, like the symbolic system that it employed, found itself confronted

[2] In the rest of his description Réal provides some examples of the atrocities; now, 'this frightful portrait excites cries and gestures of horror; some citizens *express the desire that the speaker should not continue these revolting descriptions*'. These protests and the debates they sparked off illustrate the political and ideological stakes which, in the very heart of the Jacobins, were represented by the unveiling of the hidden face of the Terror. In the end Réal would continue his tale. Cf. Aulard, *Société des Jacobins*, vol. 6, pp. 343–5. Let us note here that Réal would play an important role in the trial of the ninety-four citizens of Nantes and, after that, in the trial of the members of the revolutionary Committee of Nantes, by taking on their defence.

with very brutal realities. These 'revelations' allowed a collective psychological liberation to break out, and also generated an intense *counter-symbolism*. The 'surprises', the tales of horror, the memories which surged across the country after the fall of Robespierre, became an often determining factor in the great political choices which were required at the end of Year II: for they did not only add new horrors to those already known; they were not content with condemnation of the 'last tyrant'. This had become, to an extent, a ritual. Each new tale raised the problem of the Terror and that of the *terrorists* but also the problem of their *responsibility*. The 'revelations' were not only exorcising the fear of the past; they stirred up the hatreds of the present. The desire for vengeance went beyond the personal cases of Robespierre and his acolytes executed after 9 Thermidor, to embrace the entire political, administrative and legal personnel, implicated – directly or indirectly – in the exercise of the Terror. The accusations were often directed against a particularly cruel gaoler or a particularly zealous or fierce member of a surveillance committee. But had they not themselves acted in accordance with emergency laws? Why should they now be the only ones to pay for a 'system of power' in which they had only been a cog? Here one kept coming across the obsessive question: how to limit *personal* responsibility for the misdeeds of the Terror, without it reaching all levels of power, from the lowest to the highest, from a gaoler to a member of the Convention?

The trials of the revolutionary Committee of Nantes and of Carrier were the first great political trials of the 'terrorists'. On 10 Thermidor Robespierre and his acolytes had been executed without other form of trial; faced with rebels decreed to be outside the law, the procedure was reduced to simply establishing their identity. The revolutionary Committee of Nantes, for its part, had the right to a regular trial, with a Public Prosecutor and a defence. There was not one *trial*, but *a series of trials* which formed a whole.

The vicissitudes of revolutionary history had the paradoxical result that, after 9 Thermidor, as many lives were saved among the victims of the Terror at Nantes as among their executioners, as many among the leading citizens of Nantes, whose cases were referred to Paris to be judged there for conspiracy and treason by the revolutionary Tribunal, as among the terrorists of Nantes who had imprisoned these citizens, and then found themselves accused of counter-revolutionary activities and been imprisoned in Parisian dungeons.

The details go back to the time of the mission of Jean-Baptiste Carrier. On 21 October 1793 (11 Brumaire, Year II) he arrived in Nantes as representative of the people *en mission* with the army of the West. He was furnished, as were all other representatives *en mission*, with unlimited powers to save the Republic, conquer its enemies, ensure republican order, punish traitors, and mobilise all resources required by the armies – tasks that were particularly formidable in a region where the war of the Vendée was raging. Two days later, a rumour ran like a powder trail in the popular society of Vincent-la-Montagne: a 'federalist plot' was being prepared in Nantes; it aimed at seizing the representative *en mission*, then handing the town over to the Vendéans. In this 'plot' the most important citizens and businessmen of Nantes were implicated. On 24 Brumaire, the revolutionary Committee, which had fabricated and spread the rumour, drew up a list of 132 'plotters'; two days later, Carrier countersigned the order for their arrest and transfer to the revolutionary Tribunal in Paris. On 7 Frimaire (27 November 1793) the convoy of the 132 leading citizens of Nantes reached Paris on foot; they arrived only after a journey of forty days. Only ninety-seven survived. The conditions of the journey had been particularly severe, for it was mid-winter. In Paris, on their arrival, they were divided between several prisons and hospitals. Three more prisoners died.

During this time, the tide of terrorist repression was at full force in Nantes and had taken a particularly savage form: mass executions by firing squads, mass drownings, arbitrary imprisonment. The town was going through a dramatic period: after the defeat of the remains of the Vendéan army at Savenay, thousands of prisoners were sent to Nantes, shut up in warehouses and hospitals transformed into prisons, while waiting to be tried by a military commission; thousands of refugees, mostly women and children, sought refuge in Nantes, hoping to escape from the repression that battered the country like a road-roller. A food crisis soon broke out, felt most severely in the prisons, where the conditions were unspeakable. An epidemic of dysentery and typhus broke out in its turn (in the town, thanks to a collective panic, people spoke even of plague). The repression did not only strike at the Vendéans: in the town the pursuit of suspects and counter-revolutionaries was constant. Collaborators of the Vendéans were seen everywhere; attacks were made on families suspected of having émigré relations and keeping up their links with them. 'Revolutionary taxes' were levied and their payment demanded from one day to another; they hit 'the rich' most of all, the 'monopolists' who were held to be responsible for the shortages. The climate of suspicion, informing and arbitrary arrests was made heavier yet by the conflicts between the different authorities, each with badly defined powers, who fought for dominance: the constituted authorities whose powers were increasingly reduced; the military command (Nantes was a military town); the popular society Vincent-la-Montagne, with extremist Jacobin tendencies, which practised a sort of direct democracy, keeping its 'vigilant eye' on the authorities denounced as 'laxists' and accomplices of the 'suspects'; the revolutionary Committee, which was largely identical with the leaders of the popular society and whose task was 'revolutionary surveillance' of the town as a whole; the 'Marat company', a sort of special police, in the service of the revolutionary Committee, recruited from the most 'reliable' elements; and, finally, exercising his supreme and unlimited power above all these, Carrier.

The representative *en mission* took his own initiatives, cut through conflicts of authority, directed and guided the repression himself and, finally trusting only in himself, gathered around him his own network of agents, spies and companions. This situation, aggravated by the war of the Vendée which, despite all the victories, was not coming to an end, and by the economic crisis which paralysed the port, could only encourage high-handedness and abuse of power, conflicts, informing and general insecurity. In a town of around 80,000 people, these feelings were very widely shared, and in no way according to 'class divisions'. If both the new and the old élites in power were particularly exposed to the dangers of this unstable situation, it was the whole town that heard the salvoes of the firing squads, that breathed in the nauseating smells from the Entrepôt, where prisoners piled up, and from the quarries near the town, where the executed piled up, and that saw the bodies carried along by the Loire.[3]

Carrier's mission in Nantes lasted more than four months; he was recalled on 19 Pluviôse Year II (8 February 1794) by the Committee of Public Safety, who, while congratulating him for the work he had carried out, advised him to take a rest, before other tasks were entrusted to him. The recall of Carrier had been motivated, in reality, by the report of 'young Julien', special representative of the Committee of Public Safety and a man trusted by Robespierre – a report all the more damning because, owing to a misunderstanding, Carrier had given the emissary of Robespierre a very bad reception: he had believed he was dealing with a person of minor importance (Marc-Antoine Julien was only nineteen) and an accomplice of the Vincent-la-Montagne society (the stormy relations of the representative with this society were at that moment going through a delicate phase).

The combination of the three scourges, war, plague, and famine, threatens Nantes. Not far from the town an innumerable crowd of royal soldiers was shot, and this mass of bodies, piled on top of each other, and combined with the pestilential exhalations of the Loire, all polluted with blood, has corrupted the air ... An army is within Nantes, without discipline, without order, while scattered bodies are sent to the slaughter. On one side the Republic is plundered, on the other it is killed. A people of generals, proud of their epaulettes, and the gold embroidery on their collars, enriched with appointments which they have stolen, whose carriages

---

[3] It is clear that I do not claim to sum up in these few short lines the very complex situation in Nantes during the winter of Year II. An excellent account, which aims to unearth the truth from the legends, a particularly delicate task in the case of the Terror at Nantes, can be found in two comprehensive works: P. Bois (ed.), *Histoire de Nantes*, Toulouse, 1977, pp. 260–81; J.-C. Martin, *La Vendée et la France*, Paris, 1987, pp. 206–47.

bespatter the *sans-culottes* on foot, are always at the feet of women, at the theatre or at parties and sumptuous dinners which are an insult to the general famine ... Carrier is invisible to all constituted bodies, to the members of the club and all the patriots. He has it said that he is ill and goes off into the country in order to avoid the work that the circumstances demand, and no one is duped by this lie. He is known to be well, and in town, it is known that he is in a seraglio, surrounded by jeering sultanesses, and with epaulette-makers serving him as eunuchs; it is known that he is accessible only to people on the staff, who ceaselessly fawn upon him, and slander patriots in his eyes. It is known that he has, everywhere, spies who report to him what is said in private committees and in public assemblies. Conversations are listened to, letters intercepted. No one dares speak, nor write, nor even think. Public spirit is dead, liberty no longer exists. In Nantes I have seen the *ancien régime*.[4]

Carrier's departure and the arrival of new representatives, Bô and Bourbotte, were enough to bring to Nantes an atmosphere of settling of scores. The revolutionary Committee denounced two close collaborators and accomplices of Carrier, Fouquet and Lamberty, who served him as spies. Both were equally responsible for the drownings; they would, however, be tried and condemned to death for having attempted to release Vendéan women illegally ... On the other hand, the new representatives decided to deal severely with the revolutionary Committee, accused of theft and arbitrary violence. Arrested on 24 Prairial (12 June), its members were sent, on 5 Thermidor, to appear before the revolutionary Tribunal of Paris (joined with them was Phelippes-Tronjolly, former president of the revolutionary criminal tribunal of Nantes). Almost simultaneously, the ninety-four leading citizens of Nantes, dispersed in several prisons, were brought together at Plessis, as if Fouquier-Tinville were preparing to try them.

There is hardly any explanation as to why the trial of these ninety-four men of Nantes was not held earlier nor why they rotted for months in prison. During his trial, Carrier would claim the credit for having delayed their trial by intervening with Fouquier-Tinville, which is manifestly false. Between his recall to Paris and 9 Thermidor, Carrier had other worries: he was especially preoccupied with his own life, not with those of the citizens of Nantes whom he considered as a bunch of federalists and counter-revolutionaries. Once returned to Paris, Carrier was more or less implicated in the 'Hébertist plot'; but though he did not fall there and then, he

---

[4]  E. B. Courtois, *Rapport sur les papiers trouvés chez Robespierre*, Paris, Year III, pp. 358–9; cf. also A. Lallié, *J.-B.Carrier, représentant du Cantal à la Convention*, Paris, 1901, pp. 247 *et seq*. In the rest of his report, M.-A. Julien is a little more moderate: he recognises Carrier's merits, especially for having 'in a short time, crushed *négociantisme*, thundered with force against the mercantile, aristocratic and federalist spirit'. The evidence of Julien is certainly biased and incomplete; the 'pure Robespierrist' that this boy of nineteen was at the time shares, to a large extent, the contradictory vision of the Terror characteristic of Robespierre himself. Arrested after 9 Thermidor, young Julien would be a witness for the prosecution in Carrier's trial.

nevertheless felt himself threatened. In the eyes of Robespierre, who had complete confidence in young Julien, Carrier was another example, along with Barras, Fréron or Fouché, of a representative *en mission* who had soiled the Terror by his behaviour in the field: luxury, theft, extortion, tyranny, arbitrary violence, etc. Now Robespierre, the day before 9 Thermidor, was still thinking of 'purging the Terror', to make his realities conform to his principles. The Hébertist links of Carrier made him even more suspect in Robespierre's eyes. To avoid the danger, Carrier apparently had a hand in the preparation of the anti-Robespierrist plot. Legend has it (but there are several surrounding Carrier) that Carrier was in the first row of those who, on 10 Thermidor, followed the cart leading Robespierre to the scaffold and that he cursed him.

The delay in the trial of the citizens of Nantes could have been due to purely 'technical' problems: congestion of the revolutionary Tribunal (for ninety-four people was a very large 'batch'; later Fouquier-Tinville would also claim the credit for having delayed this trial through lack of evidence). 9 Thermidor therefore saved the heads of the ninety-four men of Nantes, as well as Carrier's. The ninety-four from Nantes were not released in the days following 9 Thermidor. Their trial (along with that of Phelippes-Tronjolly, as co-accused) opened only in the last days of Year II, on 22 Fructidor (8 September 1794). The indictment took up the original charges: conspiracy against the Republic, adherence to or help for federalism, royalist sentiments, links with émigrés, manoeuvres aiming to discredit *assignats* and to cause famine. Goulin, Chaux, Grandmaison and Bachelier, former members of the revolutionary Committee of Nantes, were taken from the prisons where they rotted while waiting for their own trials in order to give evidence for the prosecution. Carrier also gave evidence as a witness.

At the end of Year II, now that *justice had been made the order of the day*, the trial took place in a context quite different from when the charges were formulated during the winter. It took a surprising turn. From the beginning, it was transformed into a trial of the revolutionary Committee of Nantes, a denunciation of its terrorist practices; the case was brought against the Terror in general, and against Carrier in particular, who embodied the Terror and the unlimited power that the Convention had delegated to him. The accused, and particularly Phelippes-Tronjolly, turned into accusers, and interrogated the witnesses on their actions in the name of the revolutionary Committee: the mass drownings, the thefts, the acts of personal vengeance, the holding of the innocent to ransom ... The accused witnesses defended themselves badly: they denied some acts, while admitting others, but each sought above all to discharge himself of any responsibility and to compromise the others. Did not Carrier himself declare indignantly that he knew nothing of the drownings and firing-squads? He had not 'the least notion of all these horrors and acts of barbarism'. At the end of five days of hearings, when the revelations on the Terror at Nantes followed those on the suffering that the accused had undergone during their journey from Nantes to Paris, the defenders changed their role: their defence pleas became so many indictments. Without doubt, said Tronçon-Découdray, one of the defending counsel, it was necessary to

bring down the aristocracy and *modérantisme*, but we should not lose from sight the *modern Machiavellians* ... Some of the accused had momentarily gone wrong, most fought for the fatherland and are covered with honourable scars. Foul assassins have profaned liberty: the tribunal should be an example to Europe; you should show the coalition of tyrants what a true patriot is and how justice supports him. Last October a revolutionary committee was established in Nantes: it has traded in the life and honour of its citizens. It was composed of vile men, without morals ... The citizens were surrendered to men full of the maxims of Robespierre, they have spilt torrents of blood; they continually invented new conspiracies in order to accuse the citizens and have them killed; they said that it was necessary to slaughter all the prisoners *en masse*.

The verdict of the tribunal, given on 28 Fructidor, was no surprise. If eight of the accused were acknowledged as accomplices 'of a conspiracy against the Republic', like Phelippes-Tronjolly, 'the acknowledged author and accomplice of federalist acts and decrees', the Tribunal brought into play the famous clause on intent, introduced after 9 Thermidor: no one committed these reprehensible acts 'wickedly, with counter-revolutionary intentions'. As for all the other accused, the Tribunal was unable to find any proof of misdemeanour. All the accused were acquitted. The verdict was greeted with enthusiasm: 'Scarcely has the president ceased to speak than the chamber of the tribunal resounds with universal cries of *Long live the Republic!* All hearts are moved, all the spectators gaze upon on the unfortunate men of Nantes, given back to the *patrie* and freedom after such long suffering.'[5]

So the first trial came to an end; its progress and its verdict ushered in unavoidable consequences. The press gave very wide publicity to the trial of the men of Nantes, by dwelling especially on the crimes of the revolutionary Committee and, particularly, on the drownings. Carrier's name had been printed and spoken a hundred times. On 8 Vendémiaire, Year III (29 September 1794), the case of Carrier, who sat with the Mountain and was quite feverishly active at the Jacobins, was mentioned in the Convention for the first time, linked with the atrocities committed during the Terror at Nantes. Carrier replied, by publishing some days later his *Rapport sur les*

[5] Cf. AN W 449, no. 105, pièce 90. *Bulletin du Tribunal révolutionnaire*, Year III, part 6, p. 86; *Moniteur*, vol. 22, pp. 48–50; Wallon, *Histoire*, vol. 5, pp. 345 *et seq*.

*différentes missions qui lui ont été déléguées.*[6] Meanwhile, and with a certain slowness, the revolutionary Tribunal prepared the trial of the members of the revolutionary Committee of Nantes; on 17 Vendémiaire, the charges were drawn up by Leblois, public prosecutor. However, the decisive push came from the Convention. On 22 Vendémiaire, therefore four days after the proclamation of the *Adresse au peuple français*, a call for revenge we have already referred to, Merlin (from Thionville) informed the Convention of new documents on the mass drowning of women and children in the Loire and exclaimed: 'the Convention should, if it were possible, invent new punishments for these cannibals'. Thereupon, the Assembly voted through the motion requiring the revolutionary Tribunal to 'prosecute without delay the affair of the revolutionary Committee of Nantes, *as well as all those who shall be implicated in the same affair*'. The allusion to Carrier is clear, as well as the manifest political determination to make this trial an advertisement, even an exemplary case of repression against all 'terrorists' and 'blood-drinkers'.

The revolutionary Tribunal must prosecute all these assassins, without exception; the people must see the guilty struck down where they are found; the Tribunal must, without delay, prepare its case against the revolutionary Committee of Nantes, and must bring to justice all these monsters who have ordered the crimes which have been committed in that part of the country. It must not be kept from us, citizens – if a superior authority had not ordered these crimes, they would not have been committed. Let us not suffer the system of these men to continue any longer, for this would be to ensure for these monsters, these blood-drinkers, impunity for their crimes.[7]

The indictment was exceptional in its violence.

All that is most barbarous in cruelty; all that is most treacherous in crime; all that is most arbitrary in authority; all that is most frightful in extortion, and all that is most revolting in immorality, make up the indictment of the members and commissioners of the revolutionary Committee of Nantes. In the most remote annals of the world, in all the pages of history, even in the centuries of barbarism, one can hardly find deeds with which to compare the horrors committed by the accused ... These immoral beings sacrificed honour and probity to their passions; they spoke of patriotism, and they crushed its most precious bud; terror preceded their steps, and tyranny sat amongst them ... The Loire will forever roll bloody waters, and the foreign sailor will only tremble as he lands on the coasts covered with the bones of victims slaughtered by barbarism, and which the indignant waves will have spewed up on the shores ... Innocent victims, children hardly out of the arms of nature, were picked out by these new Caligulas ... TAKING A BATH, that is how these men

---

[6] Printed by order of the National Convention, Paris, Year III; BN L$^e$ 3982.

[7] Cf. *Moniteur*, vol. 22, pp. 226–8; speeches of Merlin (from Thionville) and of André Dumont. Both seem to be familiar with the indictment, ready, as already mentioned, several days beforehand. Cf. AN W 493, no. 479, plaquette 3.

described a crime Nero blushed at having committed once on a single person, and which they, more cruel and more wicked, committed many times and on thousands of unfortunate souls.[8]

The tone and verbal violence perfectly maintain the tradition of the institution and strangely recall the rhetoric of Fouquier-Tinville, who was waiting, in his turn, to be charged. (History, through the traces it leaves in the archives, sometimes takes on a strangely explicit symbolism; the charges against certain members of the revolutionary Committee of Nantes were drawn up by Leblois, the public prosecutor, on paper which carried as a heading ... 'Antoine Quentin Fouquier, public prosecutor of the revolutionary Tribunal, established in Paris by the National Convention'. The new public prosecutor was content simply to cross out the name of Tinville and write in his own, by hand. We know that this is to be explained by the shortage of paper and the very swift succession of events. But still, what a fine symbol of the continuity of the institution which successively served to establish the Terror and to 'pronounce revolutionary judgement' on the terrorists ... It in fact changed the people it accused more swiftly than its language.)[9]

The authorities gave the widest publicity to this indictment; it was not only taken up in several newspapers, but published in the form of a pamphlet and posted up in towns, in several thousand copies. In an overheated atmosphere, the second trial, that of the revolutionary Committee of Nantes, opened on 23 Vendémiaire. From the first day, the accused adopted a more or less concerted strategy; they rejected outright certain accusations, and shifted the responsibility for their crimes onto Fouquet and Lamberty, the acolytes of Carrier who, it should be remembered, were condemned and executed in Nantes; they minimised the guilt of other actions by referring to the circumstances of civil war in which they were carried out. But the major argument they put forward in their defence aimed at Carrier: they were all only carrying out Carrier's orders, who was the one who had unlimited powers. On 1 Brumaire, one of the accused, Goulin, exclaimed emotionally: accusations rain on our heads; the author of our anguish, 'the man who electrified our minds, guided our movements, tyrannised over our opinions, is free ... It is essential for our cause that Carrier should also appear at the Tribunal. Call upon the whole of Nantes: everyone will tell you that Carrier alone provoked, urged, ordered all the revolutionary measures.' The galleries, overflowing at each hearing, did not remain unmoved; the public kept crying: 'Carrier! Carrier!' Likewise, after

[8] Cf. AN W 493, no. 479: 'Acte d'accusation fait au cabinet de l'accusateur public, ce 17 vendémiaire, l'an trois de la République française, signé Leblois'.
[9] Cf. for example AN W 493, no. 479, plaquette 3, no. 17: indictment against Louis Naud.

some testimony that revealed revolting horrors, the public cried: 'Vengeance! Vengeance!' The president, to restore calm in the gallery, declared that the Committee of General Security was being informed each day of the progress of the trial. (In this, too, the Tribunal remained faithful to a well established tradition of the Terror, that of the closest collaboration with the Committee which influenced the trial from behind the scenes.)

Carrier, like any member of the Convention, had enjoyed a sort of parliamentary immunity since 9 Thermidor which could be withdrawn only by the Convention. On 9 Brumaire (30 October), the latter embarked on a complicated procedure, relating to the eventual committing to trial of a deputy. The following day a commission of twenty-one members was appointed, chosen by lot, to deal with the Carrier case. Now the third act of the affair of Nantes began: on 21 Brumaire, the Commission gave its report and concluded 'that there are grounds for the prosecution of representative of the people Carrier'. He could present his defence; nevertheless the Convention decided on his provisional arrest, while awaiting the remainder of the preliminary investigation and, in particular, the bringing together of all the evidence for the prosecution. During this time, tension mounted; a mass of pamphlets attacked both Carrier and the Jacobins, who were accused of wanting to keep him from justice; scuffles broke out in town, particularly in front of the Jacobin club. On 21 Brumaire, in the evening, the Jacobin club in the Rue Saint-Honoré was attacked by the *jeunesse dorée*, and on the next day the Convention decided to suspend the sessions of the Society. On 29 Brumaire, the Convention had before it the address of the citizens of Nantes which, in appealing to 'justice as the order of the day', demanded that Carrier's case be brought as promptly as possible before the revolutionary Tribunal. It was a long and vehement indictment. The Convention decided to have it printed.

Representatives of the French people, you who are already convinced that it is not by Terror, whose frightful domination can arise only amidst crime and informing, that one can consolidate successful government ... our hearts, unbosoming themselves in your paternal breast, are filled already with hope and joy ... But what then do they want, those ferocious men, always so quick to send the innocent before the criminal courts, to accuse those who unmask them ... Citizen-representatives, faithful to our vows like you, we denounce to you the infamous Carrier; his crimes arise on every side against him; everything here bears witness to them; we denounce him to the national representation that he wished to degrade, we denounce him to the entire people whose faith he has betrayed ... But, citizen representatives, you cannot hide it from yourselves, Carrier is only the lieutenant of a faction for whom the happiness of the people seems a misfortune; this faction which wanted to enslave liberty under piles of bodies, assassinate virtue, insult genius by destroying the monuments of the arts, outrage nature by debasing its most beautiful productions, by wanting to degrade humankind, this implacable faction which detests all that is beautiful and great, and for whom humanity itself is a crime. Ah, representatives of the French people, take care lest this faction should employ any means to postpone Carrier's punishment, so they can destroy the witnesses who might confound him, or shield from judgement a criminal whose revelations it fears.[10]

On 1 Frimaire, Carrier finally began to reply before the Convention to the charges of the Commission of Twenty-one; on 3 Frimaire the Convention voted by a roll-call for Carrier's committal, almost unanimously (of 500 votes, 498 were for the decree, with two conditional ayes). Carrier was arrested immediately and on 7 Frimaire he took his place among the accused before the revolutionary Tribunal.

And so the last act opened. Now that Carrier was one of the accused, the Tribunal, which had already been sitting for forty-two days, had to take up the trial again almost from the beginning; the principal charges had to be redefined and it was necessary to establish Carrier's responsibility in relation to that of the other accused. The hearings were extended until 26 Frimaire, the day when the verdict was given: Carrier and two members of the revolutionary Committee, Grandmaison and Pinard, were condemned to death (and guillotined the same day) for crimes committed 'with criminal and counter-revolutionary intent'. The Tribunal found the twenty-eight other accused guilty of crimes and atrocities: complicity in drownings and shooting-squads, theft, extortion, setting aside a share out of oppressive taxes, arbitrary acts, oppression of citizens by Terror, etc. However, by deciding that they did not commit them 'with criminal and counter-revolutionary intent', the Tribunal acquitted them and set them free. Two other accused were acquitted because 'they were not convicted of having executed the arbitrary orders of the Committee'. The acquittal of the accused whose crimes had been demonstrated every day of the trial provoked a nice row. Two days later, the Convention decreed a complete change of the members of the revolutionary Tribunal and decided to send the case of the acquitted to the court of criminal justice.

So, between the trial of the ninety-four citizens of Nantes and the execution of Carrier almost a hundred days had passed: a hundred days during which hundreds of witnesses filed before the revolutionary Tribunal; the accounts of the hearings had been published in the *Bulletin du Tribunal révolutionnaire*, in the *Moniteur* and other newspapers; the results of the ballot by roll-call relating to the indictment of Carrier were sent to local administrations and the armies. A hundred days during which the country had been literally bombarded with revelations whose significance went beyond the tragic hours of the winter of Year II in Nantes. Other trials were to follow, including that of Fouquier-Tinville (Germinal–Floréal, Year

10 Meeting of 29 Brumaire, *Moniteur*, vol. 22, pp. 543–6.

III). They would never have as much influence as the trials of the revolutionary Committee of Nantes and of Carrier on the turn of events taken by the ending of the Terror. The trials raised larger problems than were imagined at the beginning. They contributed to creating an unatonable feeling of horror against the Jacobins and the terrorist personnel. 'Justice the order of the day', that Thermidorean slogan, meant not only the release of the innocent; the trials also associated with it a requirement to *punish the guilty*, at all levels of power, up to the Convention itself. The trials made the *right to vengeance legitimate*. Starting with the example of Nantes, they began a disastrous and hateful evaluation of the Terror, as well as of the collective responsibility of its personnel. In that, they contributed largely to the compromising, even destroying, of the revolutionary imagery of Year II. The trials, finally, accelerated the move from the question: *How to dismantle the Terror?* to the problem: *How to terminate the Revolution?*

### The 'major measures' and everyday terror

'Fouquet and Lamberty, Carrier's faithful agents, made the whole town of Nantes tremble; not only did they make terror the order of the day, but also horror', declared one of the accused, Pierre Chaux, during the trial of the revolutionary Committee.[11] The Terror in Nantes, especially during Carrier's mission, still poses problems for historians today. The uncertainties are many: estimates of the number of victims vary; the extent of the repression, and the respective functions and responsibilities of its protagonists are poorly measured – those of the representatives *en mission*, especially Carrier, of the revolutionary Committee, of the special police established by Carrier, with Lamberty and Fouquet at the head; of the two military commissions, Bignon's and Lenoir's, who condemned 'bandits' to death after a procedure reduced to establishing their identity. Uncertainties remain also on the ambivalent attitude of the town itself with regard to the repression; certainly it suffered the Terror, but to what extent was it an accomplice, approving, if only tacitly, the 'cleansing' of the town of these thousands of 'bandits' whom it was necessary to feed at a time of shortages and who were piled up in temporary prisons, true centres of epidemic?[12]

[11] *Procès criminel des membres du Comité révolutionnaire de Nantes . . . instruit par le Tribunal révolutionnaire . . .* Paris, Year III, 'chez la veuve Toubon', second part, p. 243.
[12] It is not our task to reopen the files on the Terror at Nantes. By way of illustration only, let us mention some of the uncertainties, beginning with the figures. The number of *direct* victims of the Terror, that is to say, of people executed, is the subject of several estimates. So, for the number of mass drownings: during the trial, Phelippes-Tronjolly spoke of twenty-three; Michelet who, during his stay at Nantes, carefully took information from the surviving witnesses, arrived at a number of seven; Alfred Lallié, who did not hide his hostility to Carrier and the terrorists of Nantes, estimated that there were twenty. Gaston

At the time of the trials of the Revolutionary Committee and of Carrier, these uncertainties are even greater; all the more so because this spectacular trial was badly run by Dobsent, the president of the Revolutionary Tribunal. Of the 240 people called to give statements at the Tribunal as witnesses, 220 replied when their names were called. Several witnesses made statements for many hours, and several times at that, in successive phases of the trial. The charges concerned fourteen people; the verdict condemned thirty-three accused. In fact, in addition to Carrier who was held to be jointly responsible, the Tribunal decided, in the course of the hearings, to arrest witnesses whose interrogation had shown they were accomplices of the accused in the perpetration of their crimes. To the chaotic character of the trial is added today the confusion of the different accounts. Besides the quasi-official version of the *Bulletin du Tribunal révolutionnaire*, there were published in the newspapers, as well as in separate works, other versions of the proceedings. There are many differences between these versions, even contradictions, which it is often impossible to resolve. However, for the majority of contemporary readers these differences between the different versions of the horrors were secondary. In their minds, the different estimates of the victims mentioned by the witnesses, as well as the exaggeration to which they succumbed in recounting the atrocities, had only a cumulative effect: they complemented and added to each other.[13]

Martin, very lenient towards Carrier, counted only eight. The estimates of the number of the drowned varies from a few hundred to about twenty thousand (this last number is unlikely; the most probable estimate is between two and five thousand; so the discrepancy remains huge). Bignon's commission probably condemned to death not fewer than 2,600 Vendéans; but some guesses raise the figure to 3,500. Between Brumaire and Pluviôse, more than 200 people were guillotined in Nantes, that is to say an average of two a day. However, averages have scarcely any meaning in this kind of situation: in fact, on some days several dozens of the condemned were executed. The estimates relating to the *indirect* victims of the Terror, notably those dead in prison, are yet more uncertain; they have to be counted in thousands: from January to August 1794, there were 12,000 burials and it was necessary to open a dozen new cemeteries. Michelet states that the repression of the Vendéans enjoyed the support of a large portion of the population of Nantes:

All of them (Vendéan prisoners and refugees) were ill with a contagious diarrhoea which took hold of the town. The decrees were unambiguous: kill them all. They were shot. But the dead killed the living. The epidemic increased: two thousand inhabitants of Nantes died in a month. The anger was great in Nantes ... The lower classes of Nantes said it was necessary to throw all this Vendée into the Loire. The two authorities of Nantes, representative Carrier and the revolutionary Committee, in close rivalry, watching each other, ready to accuse each other if one or the other showed the least sign of indulgence, *followed the rage of the people*, and substituted (without regard for the law) mass drownings for firing-squads. (Michelet, *Histoire du dix-neuvième siecle*, p. 115)

The works of P. Bois and of J.-C. Martin, cited in note 3 above, present the contemporary state of research on the Terror at Nantes. Cf. also two extreme and contradictory points of view: Lallié, *J.-B. Carrier* and G. Martin, *Carrier et sa mission à Nantes*, Paris, 1924.

[13] Cf. Phelippes dit Tronjolly, *Réponse au rapport de Carrier, représentant du peuple sur les crimes et dilapidations du Comité révolutionnaire de Nantes*, Paris, n.d. (Year III); A. Velasques, 'Les Procès de Carrier et du Comité révolutionnaire de Nantes', *Annales*

Concerning the realities of the Terror at Nantes, the trials do more than provide overwhelming evidence; they add a completely phantasmagoric imagery which emanates from the Terror. The trials became, so to speak, a site of collective psychic liberation, while the hearings contributed to the enriching and spreading of this phantasmagoric universe. The statements of the witnesses exude a mixture of fear and hate, and it is often difficult, even impossible, to tell where the truth lies in what is reported by individual and collective memory. The witnesses became the echo of rumours and of hearsay, a year after the events. Since our investigation bears especially on the *role of these trials in the formation of anti-terrorist 'mentalités'*, on their role in the ripening and strengthening of the anti-terrorist reaction, the overall imagery of the Terror, as it actually spread, becomes interesting, including its excesses. Michelet knew how to describe the impact of the trials on public opinion:

It was an immense Dantesque poem which made France redescend from circle to circle into the still hardly known hells of the very people who had crossed them. We see again and pass over these gloomy regions, this great desert of terror, a world of ruins, of spectres. The masses whom the political debates did not interest at all, *were* fascinated by this trial. Men, women and children, all, from the highest to the lowest, dreamt of these drownings, saw at night the foggy Loire, its depths, heard the cries of those who slowly sank.[14]

The impact of the revelations concerning the Terror at Nantes had as much to do with the little trifles of the 'ordinary Terror' as with the evidence of the great 'horror as the order of the day'. In fact, one heard at the Tribunal the description of the 'major measures', which brought about the horrifying circumstances of the Terror at Nantes: the mass drownings, the shootings by the thousand, often without trial and without consideration for women and children; but also the banality of a repression common to all regions of France: the overpopulated cells, the exactions and extortion exercised by the surveillance committees faced with 'suspects' (or those who

*historiques de la Révolution française*, 1924, pp. 454 *et seq*. There are at least four versions of the accounts of the hearings: 1. the version of the *Bulletin du Tribunal révolutionnaire* (Clément version); 2. the version of the *Journal du soir* (Gallety version); 3. an abridged version in the *Moniteur*; 4. the version published 'chez la veuve Toubon' (cited in note 11 above). For the purposes of this study, it seemed to us a waste of time to draw attention to the more or less important differences between these accounts. So, to reduce the length of the notes we content ourselves, in what follows, with indicating between parentheses the name of the witness (or of the accused) whose statement we are quoting.

[14] Michelet, *Histoire du dix-neuvième siècle*, pp. 102–3. As if he were fascinated by this person who united republicanism and cruelty, Michelet has different formulas to describe him: 'With Carrier it was above all the *baroque, bizarre and gloomy apparition* that was disturbing', *ibid.*, p. 103, note 1. In the same pages, Michelet mentions the effects of other trials against the 'terrorists', but he attaches a particular importance to the trial of Carrier and of the revolutionary Committee.

were only 'suspected of being suspect') who were asking for certificates of good citizenship; the excessive 'revolutionary taxes'; the little thefts (several bottles of wine) during a 'domiciliary visit' which, entirely naturally, implied a careful search of the cellar, etc. But, by a strange game of mirrors, the everyday harassment, corruption, and bullying, which were inseparable from the Terror suffered by all, were suddenly as if increased by the concurrent description of the horrors of Nantes. 'The major measures' gave them a quite different meaning, increasing people's fears, their feeling of having run risks and, consequently, their hatred. The Terror of Nantes underlined, as it were, the fact that the most minor bullying and harassment might have been only the antechamber to death by drowning or shooting. All of them, members of revolutionary committees wherever they were, who had not resisted the temptation to take advantage, even in a minor way, of their power or to show their arrogance with regard to the 'rich' and the 'predators' – were they not from now on practically executioners, virtual Carriers? Thus, the great tale of the Terror at Nantes, put together during the days before the Tribunal, began by exciting horror at abuses committed elsewhere, and then soon, through identification with the martyrs of Nantes by all those who had only had their property or liberty encroached upon, repulsion for the whole of the Terror.

Thousands of pages have recorded the often repetitive statements of the witnesses, for ever going back over the same facts. But, from one statement to another, details were added, even exaggerations, as dread went into retreat, as people shook off their fears, as they sought the sensational, as hatred and then vengeance rose to the surface. Several statements are characterised by the accumulation of horrors which the witnesses claimed to have seen or, more often, heard about. Moreover, eye-witness reports are often confused with rumours and hearsay. Some overall images of the Terror and of the terrorists emerge from the whole and mark out the lines of force of the anti-terrorist imagination.[15]

[15] Let us recall the names of the men facing charges, which return many times in what follows. 1. Jean-Jacques Goulin, member of the revolutionary Committee of Nantes, born in Saint-Domingue, aged 37, inhabitant of Nantes; 2. Pierre Chaux, aged 35, born in Nantes, residing there, merchant and member of the revolutionary Committee; 3. Michel Moreau, called Grandmaison, aged 39, born in Nantes, residing there, member of the revolutionary Committee; 4. Jean-Marguerite Bachelier, aged 43, born in Nantes and residing there, notary, member of the revolutionary Committee; 5. Jean Perrochaux, aged 48, born in Nantes, residing there, building entrepreneur, member of the revolutionary Committee; 6. Jean-Baptiste Mainguet, aged 56, residing in Nantes, pin-manufacturer, member of the revolutionary Committee; 7. Jean Lévêque, aged 38, born in Mayence, member of the revolutionary Committee of Nantes and residing there; 8. Louis Naud, aged 35, born in Nantes, residing there, cooper, member of the revolutionary Committee; 9. Antoine-Nicolas Bolognie, aged 47, born in Paris, residing in Nantes, member of the revolutionary Committee; 10. Pierre Gallon, aged 42, born in Nantes, residing there, refiner; 11. Jean-François Durassier, aged 50, born in Nantes, residing there, broker for unloading ships

Two images, which take on the value of symbols, together sum up the Terror at Nantes. The first is that of the bloody Loire, covered with bodies, rolling its poisoned waters. This image appeared in the indictment: 'The Loire will forever roll bloody waters, and the foreign sailor will only tremble as he lands on the coasts covered with the bones of victims slaughtered by barbarism, and which the indignant waves will have spewed up on the shores.' During the trial this theme returned, repeatedly, enriched with ever more horrifying details. 'I declare that I have seen, on the shores of the Loire, the naked bodies of women spewed up by this river; I have seen piles of bodies of men eaten by dogs and birds of prey; I have seen bodies still attached to submerged barges and half-floating on the surface' (statement of the woman Laillet). Supreme sign of the indignation of offended Nature, the river threw back the bodies onto the banks. 'I have seen the banks of the Loire covered with dead bodies; I have seen on the banks the bodies of children of seven or eight; I have seen the body of a naked woman still holding her child in her arms; I have seen the naked corpses of young women and young men' (evidence of Lambert, sculptor of Nantes). 'I saw on the banks of the Loire, as far as Paimbœuf, an infinity of corpses, of which many were naked women, and which the riverside municipalities were obliged to bury' (statement of Baudet, ship-builder). In its most stereotypical form the image was taken up and put on record in the famous book on the atrocities of the Terror by Prudhomme, which fed collective memory for several generations.

A man who could be trusted assured me that for a long time, and for an extent of eighteen leagues, the Loire, from Saumur to Nantes, was *all red with blood*. Swollen by the immense crowd of corpses that it rolled in its waters, it spread terror to the ocean, but all of a sudden a violent tide pushes back those frightful monuments of so many cruelties to the walls of Nantes. The whole surface of the river is covered with limbs floating here and there which the greedy fish fight over and tear apart. What a spectacle for the people of Nantes ... who banned the consumption of water and fish.[16]

The other image is that of a town of 80,000 inhabitants completely terrorised, given up to the arbitrary domination of a band of 'blood-

coming from Saint-Domingue; 12. Augustin Bataille, aged 46, born at Charité-sur-Loire, textile worker, residing in Nantes; 13. Jean-Baptiste Joly, aged 50, born in Angerville-la-Martel, *département* of Seine-Inférieure, brass-founder, residing in Nantes; 14. Jean Pinard, aged 26, born in Christophe-Dubois, *département* of the Vendée, residing in Petit-Marc, *département* of Loire-Inférieure. These latter five were commissioners of the revolutionary Committee. Cf. 'Acte d'accusation', AN W 493, no. 479, plaquette 3.

[16] L. M. Prudhomme, *Histoire générale et impartiale des erreurs, des fautes et des crimes commis pendant la Révolution française à dater du 24 août 1787*, Paris, Year V, vol. 6, pp. 337–8. Prudhomme suggests a figure of 100,000 for the victims of Carrier, a number reached 'by an approximate calculation based on prisons, illnesses, etc.' Yet, Nantes was a town of about 80,000 inhabitants.

drinkers' and thieves, where the dregs of the populace took its revenge on honest people. Fear fell upon the town, like a covering of lead.

It cannot be repeated too often, terror was the order of the day; this town was struck by the most overwhelming stupor; a person who believed himself innocent one evening could not be certain of being recognised as such the next day; it would be difficult to paint the worry, the anxiety of mothers, of wives, when they heard the rolling of vehicles, in their neighbourhoods, at eight o'clock in the evening; it seemed to them that they and their husbands were going to be snatched from their homes to be plunged into the cells. This was the fear of Nantes, and Carrier and the Committee were alone its authors. (statement of Lahenette, doctor at the Charité in Nantes)

The number of people arrested is 'incalculable': 'it is principally on people with talent, probity or riches that the Committee carried out its Inquisition' (same witness);

the Committee of Nantes had incarcerated almost all of those who had money, talent, virtue or humanity. It had tolerated what was called in this town *sabrings*; this kind of operation refers to when seven or eight prisoners would come out of the Committee to be taken to the Entrepôt. The guards, finding that it was late and the journey too long, massacred these unfortunates under the windows of the Committee. (statement of Georges Thomas, medical attendant)

In this town, paralysed by the fear of making any complaint, plagued with the odour of corpses, activity in the port and in business, which kept it alive, was paralysed. 'Probity, virtue, talent and wealth were then so many reasons for proscription and virtue has been assassinated by crime. Following the principles of the Héberts, the Chaumettes, the Roussins, the Robespierres and other *vandals*, they assassinate commerce, in order to enslave France' (statement of Villemain, businessman of Nantes).[17]

The river brimming with corpses inevitably evokes the mass drownings. Their exposure was one of the great moments of the trials. The mass drownings alone summed up the horrors of the Terror of Nantes. The charges against the Committee stated that there existed 'material proof only that there was one operation of this kind' but, it added, 'there is available the confession of several of the accused who, torn by remorse,

---

[17] One of the accused, Bachelier, attempted, at the beginning of the trial, to justify the policy of repression. This policy called for preventative measures and proposed to mobilise the *sans-culottes* against the 'rich'. (On this last point, Bachelier used a terminology: 'class of the rich', 'capitalists', etc. which deserves notice.)

Carrier kept repeating that the rich favoured the war of the Vendee; that the 'predators' were in contact with them; that the rich gave no help to the poor; that there was a counter-revolutionary hotbed in Nantes ... The entire class of the rich was suspect in the difficult circumstances in which we found ourselves; it was therefore also necessary to strike the person who had the power to destroy, as well as the person who had both the power and the will. But few patriots were arrested; we mainly came down hard on the formerly noble and priestly classes, on the capitalists who would do nothing for the *patrie*; but the true *sans-culottes* were spared.

have been forced to admit that there were *four to eight* of them'. The estimates of the number of drownings and the drowned would change from one hearing to another: 4,000 brigands drowned and 7,500 shot at the Gigant quarry (statement of François Coron, soldier of the Marat company); three or four drownings in which 9,000 victims perished (according to the statements of Affilié the younger, ship's carpenter, who took part in the building of barges, and of Moutier, blacksmith of Nantes who claims to have seen 'all the drownings' which took place in his neighbourhood); 'twenty-three drownings and innumerable victims', according to Phelippes-Tronjolly; Lamberty and Carrier had praised their worth by declaring that '2,800 have already passed through the national bath' (statement of Martin Naudille, previously inspector of the army of the West). The Tribunal made no effort to verify this information, not even by confronting witnesses with one another. For historians these estimates pose almost inextricable problems; for contemporaries they were swept away by the overall image and the horror of the crime, the picture of these barges sent to the bottom with their cargo: women and children, priests and 'brigands'.

To speak of the mass drownings is inevitably to evoke the 'republican marriages', an image which has enduringly marked collective memory. Reproduced in many engravings, from Year III, the 'republican marriages' had the power to impress the imagination; they became the symbol of the horror of the drownings. From the first day of the trial of the Committee, these 'republican marriages' (also called 'revolutionary marriages') were mentioned as the 'ultimate refinement of cruelty'. 'It consisted in tying, under the armpits, a quite naked young man to a young woman, and throwing them in the water' (statement of Lahenette, doctor at the Charité, in Nantes). The description reappeared several times in the course of the trial and had several variations: the executioners stripped the men and the women and tied them, both naked, by the arms and wrists; then they were put on the boat where they were beaten with 'large sticks' and pushed in the Loire; 'that is called "civic marriage"' (statement of Thomas, medical attendant, reporting the tale of a drunken boatman who was present at this killing). According to another version, the 'republican marriages' showed not only cruelty but also the perversion of the executioners who delighted in the crude and the obscene. 'I have heard of these republican marriages which were carried out by attaching an old man to an old woman or a young man to a young woman; they were left, quite naked, for half-an-hour in this attitude; they were hit on the head with a sabre and then were thrown in the Loire' (statement of Fourrier, director of the revolutionary almshouse). It seems rather doubtful that these 'republican marriages' were carried out in a systematic manner. No crudeness or gratuitous cruelty can be excluded during these drownings, but all the tales of 'republican marriages' are founded on hearsay, and not at all on eyewitness accounts or the admissions of anyone taking part. Repression and terrorist pillage seemed to require that the victims were inevitably stripped and thrown in the river two by two, so that death mowed down the people of Nantes in a cortège of obscenity and perversion.

The 'major measures' were not limited to the drownings. If the victims did not disappear into the Loire, then it was into common graves (especially those dug at the quarries of Gigant, very close to Nantes). The victims, especially the Vendéan prisoners, were executed there by means that were, so to speak, more 'classical', less spectacular: the guillotine and weapons. During the trial there was relatively little mention of 'mass guillotining' because the victims had been condemned at the end of a legal process, although a summary one. And their cases had not come before the revolutionary Committee but before the revolutionary Tribunal. The idea of carrying out the mass drownings came from the relative slowness of the Tribunal; several witnesses mention Carrier's bouts of fury against the Tribunal, his orders to pass judgement and apply the guillotine more quickly, without useless legal 'chicanery'. The mass shootings of Vendéans taken prisoner in battle, weapons in hand, sometimes allowed the liquidation of more than 200 in a day, after Bignon's military commission had simply recorded their identities; these, however, raised much less indignation than the drownings.[18] To read the statements, one could believe that the town became used to the massacre of prisoners, through respect for a legality reduced to its simplest expression. No one dared, it is true, contest this semblance of legality, for this would have amounted to denouncing the Convention which had decreed this swift process. During the hearings, one comes especially upon failures to observe the fragile revolutionary legality and flagrant cases of arbitrary power and savagery in the repression. So, throughout the trials, there recurred the question of the eighty Vendéan cavalry who, after the defeat of Savenay, had come to Nantes with the

[18] That these executions had been entrusted to the 'black hussars' traumatised people's minds, all the more because of the rumours of the horrifying brutalities of these troops, especially with regard to women. One hears an echo in one of the statements. On 28 Pluviôse,

an officer called Ormes comes to call for armed force in support of five pretty women whom some Americans have arrested, and whom they insult in every manner. Several men are provided, they go to the lair of the Blacks, they hear their captives groan. These women, with one voice, ask to be taken away. 'They are our slaves, reply the Americans to our request; we have won them with the sweat of our bodies, and they will be taken away from us only by force ...' A fight was about to begin when the armed force, out of prudence, preferred to withdraw. ... Two days after this event, the Americans, without doubt having had their fill of their captives, send them back; one of the unfortunate women had been obliged to receive a hundred men; she had fallen into a kind of stupidity and could not walk. A few days later, I hear a fusillade; I ask what it is; someone tells me that they are the women of the Americans who have just been shot. (statement of J. Commerais, mirror merchant)

No mention of this episode, nor of an analogous case, was made in the other statements.

intention of giving themselves up and laying down their weapons. Yet, Carrier had personally given the order to shoot them, without trial. It was only one episode among all the atrocities but it took on great importance, because several witnesses agreed (although rumour finished by pretending that Carrier had shot as many as 500 cavalry) and because Carrier had the imprudence to sign the orders of execution himself. The Convention had them brought by special courrier from Nantes and these lists constituted evidence of capital importance.

The case of the Vendéans was to be placed, moreover, in a larger context, often mentioned during the hearings. Did not all these atrocities explain the continuation of the war of the Vendée despite the republican victories? Carrier was thus accused of having prolonged the war by maintaining repression to the cruel point that it prevented the Vendéans from capitulating.

After the affair of Savenay I saw four of our soldiers leading brigand cavalry in large numbers; I heard them admit their errors, declare the sharpest regret and offer to give themselves up on condition of keeping their lives ... If they would have mercy on them, and on those who remained in the Vendée, they would take it upon themselves to bring in their leaders with feet and hands tied, and persuade the majority of their communes to come and place themselves under the flags of the Republic. If these advantageous proposals had been accepted, there would be no more question of the Vendée, but the men of blood, the accomplices of the despots, were very far from co-operating with measures likely to strip them of the powers with which they had been invested ... So I had the grief of seeing about a hundred of these brigands massacred, pitilessly shot ... and this cruel business was carried out the day after the arrival of these misguided men, in contempt of the proclamations which promised them security and protection. (statement of Girault, ex-barrister, ex-member of the Constituent Assembly)

Naud, one of the accused, completed this statement; he had in fact transmitted this offer of surrender to Carrier: 'I allow myself to solicit mercy for our brothers deceived by fanatics and counter-revolutionaries.' 'Stuff that', cries Carrier. 'Don't you see that it's a trap? You don't know your job; they are fooling you by this pretended submission; they want to overthrow the town. You are useless cowards who don't know how to face the enemy. No mercy; all these scoundrels must be shot.'

The horrors of the repression in the Vendée were mentioned every day: the inhabitants of Bouquenay and the neighbouring hamlets were called together on the pretext of giving them certificates of good citizenship and were shot (statement of Renet, battalion commander); the corpses of shot women remained piled on each other for several days and the 'cannibals' called them, laughingly, 'the Mountain' (statement of J. Delamarre, paymaster general of public expenses in the *département* of Loire-Extérieure; statement of Bourdin, blacksmith of Nantes). The prisons, if one was not taken away to be drowned or shot, were true killing grounds.

Having received the order of the military commission to go and ascertain the pregnancy of a large number of women detained at the Entrepôt, I found a great quantity of corpses spread here and there; I saw children shivering or drowned in buckets full of excrement. I pass through immense rooms; my expression makes women tremble; they see no men other than their executioners ... I ascertain the pregnancy of thirty of them; several were seven or eight months pregnant; some days after I come to see these women ... I tell you, my soul broken with grief, those unfortunate women had been thrown in the waters! These pictures are heartrending, they afflict humanity; but I owe to the tribunal the most faithful account of what I know. (statement of Thomas, medical attendant)

This focussing upon the accused and, more generally, upon the agents of the Terror, of all the hatred that the trial brought to the surface, denies any ideological motivation in the accused: there are very few statements from witnesses that grant them, by way of attenuating circumstances, 'exaggerated revolutionary feelings' or that consider them as misguided souls. On the other hand, the accused argued their 'revolutionary intentions' all the while granting that they were deceived. The stakes were high: the Tribunal was required to give judgement while taking into account the 'intentional clause', the revolutionary or counter-revolutionary motivations of the incriminating acts. But the problem is, as one can see, not entirely a legal one. Beyond the nominal attacks and accusations a sort of collective portrait of all the accused was sketched out, and, consequently, of the terrorist personnel. The individual differences were effaced and confused in the overall image of a band of wicked men, of 'blood-drinkers', of 'cannibals' who unscrupulously terrorised the entire town. Their only motivations had been hatred, cruelty, greed and other ignoble feelings. Slaughterers, they were first of all downright scoundrels, thieves and rogues. The Revolution did not call them; they called upon the Revolution with their desire to take hold of power, to enrich themselves and satisfy their worst desires. The charges drew up this portrait from the start:

Under the mask of patriotism, they dared commit every outrage; they assassinated virtue to crown crime; they knowingly perpetrated all kinds of extortion ... These immoral beings sacrificed honour and probity to their passions; they spoke of patriotism, they stifled its most precious seeds ... Far from extinguishing and ending an unfortunate war which rent the heart of the country, they fanned its fires by their cruelties; they served the aims of our treacherous enemies who, to subjugate us, employ all that vileness suggests, who, unable to attack republicans from the front, seek out in the Republic's bosom the despicable slaves who hide the most wicked souls and the most corrupt hearts under the mask of patriotism.[19]

[19] 'Acte d'accusation', AN W 493, no. 479, plaquette 3. There is no need to stress the consequences of this characterisation, where morality joins with politics. Far from being revolutionaries, as they pretended, the accused became counter-revolutionaries, in the service of the 'enemy', allies of the Vendéans. At a stroke, the 'intentional clause' no longer applied to them. We shall have to return to this transformation of the 'terrorists' into agents working for Pitt or the royalist émigrés in Koblenz.

The accused were only the visible portion, now forever unmasked, of a vast company of evildoers. The proof was that during the sessions of the Tribunal several witnesses would also be unmasked and arrested; that Carrier, although denounced as the instigator of the mass drownings and shootings without trial and of other atrocities, sat on the bench of the accused only from 7 Frimaire onwards, forty-two days after the opening of the trial of the revolutionary Committee.

The images of the 'terrorists', which were widely circulated by the Thermidorean political language, were confirmed by the statements of the witnesses. *Blood-drinkers, cannibals*: these were not just epithets or metaphors; the witnesses claimed that the accused really did drink blood and behave like cannibals. The statements contain remarkable examples of the blurring of divisions between memories of the Terror of Nantes and the fantasies working at a deep level on these traumatised minds. We shall give only a few examples of the workings of this collective imagination.

François Coron, ex-attorney, soldier of the Marat company, brought overwhelming evidence on the preparations for the mass drowning, in the night of 24 to 25 Frimaire, at Bouffay where he went with others of the Marat company. To this he added *what he had heard*, rumours that ran through the town. 'I was told that the fruit of a woman about to give birth was snatched from her, put on the end of a bayonet and thrown into the water.' The 'terrorists', by speaking, in their turn, of the atrocities committed by the Vendéans, used analogous images: women ripped open, so many barbarous acts expressing the desire to destroy the enemy, including his possible descendants. These stories, which are impossible to verify, bear witness to the intensity of the hatred on both sides: the enemy is described as the author of the cruellest and the most archaic violence. The same witness declared that Goulin had announced, on the rostrum of the popular society: 'Take care about receiving moderates among you, false patriots; you must admit only *revolutionaries, patriots with the courage to drink a glass of human blood*.' Goulin protested in vain 'that his remarks had been poisoned' and that he had wanted to paraphrase the celebrated words of Marat saying that he 'would have liked to be able to slake his thirst in the blood of all the enemies of the *patrie*'. The epithet of *blood-drinker* turned out to be correct; the band of enemies of humankind it described had sealed its unity by a rite charged with a secular symbolism, that of the sabbath and a pact with the devil. Another witness, other symbolic acts: Pinard said that he had brought back chalices and ritual objects from one of his expeditions against the Vendéans; now, Carrier had required him to drink some mysterious brew from this chalice, while reproaching him for not having killed enough of 'all these brutes'. Jean-Baptiste O'Sullivan, aged thirty-three, master of arms, named by Carrier as adjutant of the Place de Nantes, stated as witness, on the subject of the drownings at the Entrepôt, that Carrier had told him that the citizens of Nantes were counter-revolutionaries and that he would have 150,000 men come to exterminate the people of Nantes. The president, however, posed a question to him on his own exploits. 'Did you not take part in bleeding brigands by the neck using a knife with a very narrow blade? Did you not boast about it by saying: "I have watched carefully how a butcher does it; I pretended to talk with these brigands; I made them turn their heads as if to look at the fish; I cut their throats with the knife and it was all over."' The chamber reacted with 'groans of horror'. O'Sullivan explained that, having taken part in the war with the 'brigands' and seen their atrocities, he might have said, 'in a moment of indignation' that 'if I had the brigands in my hands, I would make them bleed with my knife, and that would revenge my brothers ... but I am incapable of carrying out the blood-letting mentioned, and which I could not listen to without shuddering myself.' He was immediately arrested and joined the accused on their bench.

A quite special place fell to the Marat company in the evidence. It enjoyed enormous, almost unlimited power. 'It had the right to make domiciliary visits, to incarcerate according to need, without the decision of the Committee.' The Committee would simply give a list to the Marat company, who went to the home of the individuals listed and imprisoned them, just on the basis of a note and sometimes even in the street, 'just on suspicion'. The men of the Marat were, so to speak, the link between the 'major measures' and the everyday Terror: with members of the Committee they carried out the mass drownings, but they also robbed and pillaged the 'rich'. They held the important citizens of the town to ransom and threatened to send them to the Entrepôt, from which they would emerge only to 'drink a large mouthful'; they placed seals on apartments and shops which they would then pillage. For so many crimes to be perpetuated, it was necessary for the most immoral beings to join together.

A company called the Marat company, formed either by the Committee, or by representative Carrier, a company composed of corrupt beings and, so to speak, the sewer of the town of Nantes, was the faithful instrument of the barbarity of the Committee; these men, on whose foreheads the seal of reprobation was printed, acquired a number of partisans; they exercised the most tyrannic domination and dishonoured as they wished, in the minds of the despots invested with the right of life and death, the honest citizens who had the misfortune to displease the supreme agents of the Committee.[20]

It was further claimed that the revolutionary Committee had this company recruited according to quite specific criteria. The most wicked

[20] *Bulletin du Tribunal révolutionnaire*, trial of the ninety-four citizens of Nantes, p. 162 (résumé of several statements); cf. also Wallon, *Histoire*, vol. 5, pp. 360–1.

were admitted and, at each nomination, Goulin asked: 'Is there no one more wicked, for we need men of that kind to show the aristocrats reason ... These are fine b— – are there any more wicked?' (Statement of Phelippes-Tronjolly. Goulin, interrogated by the president, categorically denied these accusations as 'improbable': he had been the first to propose that the choice of candidates be put to the vote and had himself eliminated several among them.) As if this method of recruitment did not carry all the necessary guarantees, the Marat company swore a special oath: 'I saw a poster entitled *Marat oath*. This poster was worded in a way to make all good citizens tremble. Through this oath friendship was renounced, parenthood, fraternity, the tenderness of a father or son; the feelings most appropriate for honouring nature and the social body were sacrificed' (statement of Lamarie, sculptor and municipal officer in Nantes; the text of this poster, presented during the trial, employed revolutionary rhetoric and emphasis to call for devotion to the *patrie* and the Revolution, without taking into account any private interest). Scoundrels, they were so many *vandals*, uneducated and unlettered people to whom talent and the arts were repugnant. To be sure, *Pierre* Chaux, one of the leaders of the Committee, had found it useful to change his name and call himself *Socrates* Chaux; he would however have done better 'to sign himself *Scoundrel* Chaux' (statement of Bô, representative of the people). The Marat company 'destroyed superb paintings; they spared one which represented death; they said [to the prisoners] with a cruel irony: *reflect on this painting!* while saying to the female prisoners that *they were good for sending to the bottom of the Loire*' (statement of widow Mallet, tobacco merchant; she also complained that, on the pretext of requisition, they had stolen from her gold, silver and 700 *livres* in *assignats*). Goulin and Pinard were accused of having signed an order whose execution permitted the extortion of more than 3,000 *livres* in silver, jewels and watches, from the Labauche family (sentenced to imprisonment with hard labour since it had children suspected of being émigrés). Pinard did not deny having arrested this family which had been pointed out to him as 'brigands', nor having kept a portion of their money in agreement with the Committee, but he indignantly rejected the accusation that he signed the requisition order. The proof that this was only a slander was that he could not read or write (statements of Guignon and Pinard on the Labauche affair).

The case of a certain Dhéron, the 'ear-cutter', sums up, perhaps best of all, the inextricable oscillation operating between the real facts, macabre and horrifying, and the spectres to which they gave birth. During the hearing of 1 Frimaire, citizen Layet asked the Tribunal to hear her so that she could 'state an important fact'. She gave evidence, in effect, that after the rout of the Vendéans 'a certain Dhéron presented himself to the popular society *with the ear of a brigand which he had attached to his hat with a cockade; his pockets were full of these ears, and he gave himself the pleasure of having the women kiss them*'. The witness added that she knew of more 'barbarous circumstances' relating to the 'morality of the accused' but that she did not dare tell them, fearing a lack of respect for the Tribunal. Having thus sharpened curiosity, she did not need much persuasion and completed her statement. 'This same Dhéron *also had his hands full of genital parts, which he had had the cruelty to tear from the brigands while massacring them and with which he also wearied the sight of the women.*' Some days later the Tribunal proceeded to the examination of the said Dhéron, inspector of military supplies, as ... prosecution witness against Carrier. In effect, Dhéron accused Carrier of various atrocities; it was he who gave the order to have shot all the commissioners delegated by other representatives *en mission* and who wished to share supplies between Nantes and other towns. 'I'll be b— if I allow all the grain of the Vendée to be carried off; have these brutes shot for me!', this was Carrier's reaction, although he refused to confirm this order in writing. Dhéron was then interrogated on his own exploits. During a confused interrogation, in which other witnesses intervened, Dhéron 'has been convicted of presenting himself *before the popular society with the ears of brigands and genital parts that he made the women kiss*'. Moreover, he admitted that he had had assassinated children of thirteen and fourteen who were grazing their sheep. (In his defence, Dhéron added that children of this age were often bearers of ammunition and spied on republican troops; he also praised his own courage and the services he had rendered during the fights with the 'brigands'.) The Tribunal immediately decided to have him moved to the bench of the accused, charged with several atrocities and assassinations blamed on the revolutionary Committee. At the end the Tribunal would consider in its verdict the charge of having assassinated children and of having 'carried in public on his hat' ... the ear of a man whom he had killed (while confirming that he had not done it 'with counter-revolutionary intent'; he would therefore be acquitted).

The spectacle of Dhéron, child-killer, carrying in public an ear on his hat, like a hunting trophy, is macabre and terrifying. To transform this image into one of Dhéron forcing women to kiss the genital parts torn from the Vendéans required the work of a morbid imagination, spurred on by public rumour. In this way death and cruelty, sexuality and perversion find themselves inextricably joined. The story of Dhéron is an extreme case, but not an isolated one, for a number of examples could be quoted where the same elements and tendencies of morbid imagination can be found. In the course of the trial there recur tales of 'orgies' and sexual violence which would have found a prominent place in the novels of the 'divine Marquis'. Thus Robin, with his accomplice, a certain Lavaux, another of Carrier's trusted men, had female prisoners put on board a boat in order to 'slake their brutal passions upon them, and then they sabred them and drowned them' (statement of Chaux, co-accused with Robin). The men doing the drowning made themselves 'very familiar with the women whom they forced to serve their pleasure, when the women were to their liking and, as reward for their complaisance, these women obtained the precious privilege of being saved from drowning. One of the men, used to finding the women docile, said to me one day: *tomorrow I will come to wake you in the night, I'll say that I am Mandrin and you will let me in*' (statement of Victoire Abraham, widow Pichot). Perrocheaux was also accused of having required the 'girl Brétonville to permit his indecent desires'; it was only on this condition that he promised to have her father released (Perrocheaux rejected the accusation, stating that it was the mother of the girl who had offered him 'the enjoyment of her daughter and he had rejected these offers, remarking to this citizen that she dishonoured her position as a mother' (statements of Sophie Brétonville and Perrocheaux). Several times the case of Lamberty, factotum of Carrier, was mentioned; he was one of the organisers of the mass drownings, who had been condemned and executed at Nantes, after Carrier's departure, for having taken 'a beautiful Vendéan countess and her chambermaid off one of those boats' and saved their lives 'in order to enjoy them' (statement of Naud, co-accused).[21]

In this catalogue, no one would be surprised that Carrier surpassed all the others in his cruelty, debauchery and perversity. His 'orgies' are mentioned throughout the trial, as much by the witnesses as by the accused. It was claimed that on his orders young girls of less than seventeen were taken out of the Entrepôt and sent to his country house to make up his 'seraglio', the 'victims of his voluptuousness' (statement of Clairval, postal employee). With other women whom he had requisitioned, he gave himself up to 'his ordinary debauches' and to 'the most dissolute orgies' (statement of Villemain, businessman in Nantes), and he also gave the order to have

[21]   Michelet treats this episode at length, while presenting it in a completely different light. The 'lady, who was only too well known' (but he does not reveal the name), was 'a Vendéan who belonged to the queen, and who spoke only of the queen'. Now, Lamberty fell in love with her and as a 'man of action' dared to save her and take her to his home. It was a 'mystery of love, pride and fury' for, in the end, 'she had not refused, this proud lady, to follow him, to live with him. Bringing death as her dowry, she accepted his devotion, wanted him to die for her ... He died for her alone. He had the funereal happiness to possess her for forty days' (Michelet, *Histoire du dix-neuvième siècle*, pp. 115–16). In this way the episode of the 'beautiful countess' is transformed into a romantic love story, a story of passion which overcomes social divisions and political hatred. Michelet does not give his source; did he make use of the tales of the erudite Dugast-Matifeux of Nantes, an ardent republican whom he often visited during his stay in Nantes? Michelet otherwise passes over in silence the zeal and exploits of Lamberty during the drownings but praises his unwavering courage in the struggle against the Vendéans and his devotion to the Republic: *ibid.*, pp. 117–18; cf. Martin, *Carrier*, pp. 274–5.

about a hundred prostitutes drowned (statement of Jean Drieux, landlord). Three women 'awoke the lewd desires of Carrier . . . He sacrificed them to his lust and when he had his fill of them, he had them guillotined' (statement of Phelippes-Tronjolly; even the president found it worth remarking to Tronjolly that he 'pushed his observations and his anxieties too far'). The story of a dinner on the Dutch boat which Carrier had given as a present to Lamberty and which was used for the drownings often recurs: on it Carrier gave 'a splendid dinner, with twenty places, for his men' (with or without girls, depending on the version). One of them, called Legros, still had his moustaches red with blood; they sang Jacobin songs and drank 'to the God-botherers who had been sent to the bottom'. Lamberty amused the guests by describing how he had sabred escapees from the drowning. Carrier himself read out the report which he had sent to the Convention on the drowning of the priests; he had cried 'Kill! Kill!' and said that he had never felt such great pleasure as in looking at the grimaces of the dying priests (statements of Jean Sandroc, head of the transport division; of Jean Gauthier, cutler, soldier of the Marat company; of Robin, co-accused).[22]

The stories of the perversity of Carrier, in the collective imagination, had the precise function of sketching his image as a *monster*. Carrier crystallised within himself the 'major measures' and the everyday Terror. He spoke only of 'stuffing' and of 'brutes'; during a meeting of the popular society, he drew his sabre and cut the candles; he knew only the words 'kill', 'guillotine', 'stuff into the water', as a response to every plea. The witnesses and the accused, members of the Committee, joined together to accuse Carrier of being the person responsible for all the atrocities and monstrosities of the Terror in Nantes. 'Carrier requisitioned terror, death, the Loire, the guillotine and counter-revolution', exclaimed Chaux who went on to ask: 'Did we then appoint a representative of the people to assassinate the people?' Naud, another member of the Committee, declared: 'Carrier himself came to our Committee to treat us as counter-revolutionaries. We were fathers of families; Goulin was not, but he was the agent and blind instrument of Carrier who destroyed him and destroyed us all.' On 1

---

[22] Carrier in fact had a mistress in Nantes, the wife of Le Normand, director of the almshouse of the Ursulines. After the recall of Carrier to Paris, she followed him, accompanied by her husband. Cf. A. Velasques, 'Etudes sur la Terreur à Nantes', *Annales historiques de la Révolution française*, 1924, pp. 150 *et seq.* Velasques reports, following the documents, several rumours which were current in Nantes, on this 'three-way marriage', and notably on 'La Normand' who 'was openly called Carrier's whore'.

One day, he [Carrier] said to La Normand: 'I've been offered a superb woman who wants to request my protection to have mercy on her; I said to the man who told me this: Is she beautiful? Have her brought to my house.' Then La Normand said to him, 'I will go with you to see her.' I heard it said to her that Carrier had this woman brought to the château of Aux (on the banks of the Loire) and the following day at four o'clock, he and the women would leave for Aux and that they would have the pleasure of making her drink a good cup of watery tea. (*ibid.*, p. 165)

Brumaire, in the name of all the accused, Goulin demanded Carrier's appearance before the court: 'The man who electrified our minds, guided our movements, tyrannised our opinions, directed our actions and peacefully contemplated our alarm and despair. No, justice calls for that man who showed us the abyss into which we blindly threw ourselves at his voice, and is now cowardly enough to abandon us on its edge; it is crucial for our cause that Carrier should appear at the Tribunal.' Through these rumours, statements and phantasmagoria, as the hearings progressed, Carrier the *person* each day found himself more and more at the centre of the trial of the revolutionary Committee. But, in time, the trial evolved: soon it was no longer a matter of coming to terms with Carrier the person but with Carrier the *problem*.

Had Carrier been, in fact, anything other than the link between the local Terror and central power, the Convention and its Committees? While the trial enabled each person to recognise in the Terror the misdeeds of which he had been the victim, the dismantling of the terrorist system extended, and phrased in new terms, the question of responsibility: should prosecutions be limited to all the local agents of the banality of the Terror, or should it be broadened to include all the former members of the Committees, representatives *en mission*, members of the Convention – forerunners and emissaries of the great national Terror? Should there be a trial of the Terror at Nantes or a trial of Year II, of the Convention and, consequently, of the Revolution?

### A trial of the Revolution?

The Terror had been the first calamity; a second, which destroyed the Republic, was the trial of the Terror.[23]

This was Quinet's comment on the great terrorist trials, particularly those of Carrier and of Fouquier-Tinville, who were in his eyes only minor agents of the Terror, simply 'cogs' in the workings of the 'system of Terror'. What did he mean by 'calamity'? Quinet, it seems, was close to the position defended by Lindet in his speech of the last days of Year II: it was necessary to emerge from the Terror *without revenge* and, according to Quinet's strong formula, 'to decree forgetfulness'.[24]

Was it really possible – politically and psychologically – to emerge from the Terror, to break that 'engine' without *publicly declaring the truth about the Terror*, without making known its hideous realities? And once the file on the Terror was half-opened and freedom of the press ensured, how could the trial of the Terror not be extended? It is not for the historian to make

[23] Quinet, *La Révolution*, p. 628.     [24] *Ibid.*

conjectures about an emergence from the Terror, without a trial of the terrorists or revenge, which does not actually occur in the reality he is studying. At the very most he will see in Quinet's desires and regrets an expression of the complexity of the situation to which the Thermidoreans had to respond with urgency, and which the historians of the last century had to explain. We have seen what the major stages of the dismantling of the Terror were and how it became a process with its own logic, almost a meshing of gears. One of its key moments was the trial of Carrier, since to prosecute him came down to putting on trial *the very principles of the Terror* and their application in the war of the Vendée. Carrier, moreover, did not vent his anger only on the members of the revolutionary Committee of Nantes, accusing them of having transgressed his orders and directives and of indulging themselves on their own authority in acts as horrifying as arbitrary; he also charged the Committees of the Convention with responsibility, and even the Convention itself, which had entrusted him with the unlimited power he possessed. Carrier, in his defence, argued that all he had done, in the end, was to apply the policy set out by the Convention, by rigorously conforming to its principles and by regularly informing it of his actions. That the trial of Carrier should be broadened into a trial of the Revolution was an evident risk, for the terrorist of Nantes was not only, in the eyes of public opinion, the 'monster' denounced in the course of the trial, he was also a very 'energetic' Jacobin. Let us not forget that after 9 Thermidor, Carrier in fact remained a representative of the people in full exercise of his function which, by definition, carried the requirements of probity, virtue and patriotism; a very active member of the Convention: he attacked Tallien in particular by demanding that he give an explanation of the 'conspiracy' that he fomented on 10 Fructidor; he proposed the expulsion from Paris of all the *muscadins*;[25] he demanded the deportation of all aristocrats; he spoke in the debate on the new organisation of the Committees, etc.; – a militant Jacobin who gained in importance and played a leading role in the purged Society. He was especially notable for his extremism and his clear-cut positions: he proposed the exclusion of Tallien, Fréron and Lecointre from the Society; on several occasions he denounced the 'system of *modérantisme* which is being put in place'; he called on the Society to present itself *en masse* at the Convention to 'help it to crush the aristocracy'; he protested against the slanders aimed at the Jacobins and exhorted them to reunite to combat their enemies; he was part of the commission charged with preparing an address of the Society inspired by the famous address of the popular society of Dijon; he made barely concealed threats against 'the aristocrats who raise their heads' ... Until his

---

[25] *muscadins*. The extravagant and affected young people who dressed outrageously to contrast themselves with the *sans-culottes*.

own trial, Carrier was, at the Convention, a Montagnard (or rather, a man of the 'Crest', as the few who still claimed to be members of the Mountain were now called), and at the Society an 'advanced' Jacobin. Retrospectively, it remains difficult to grasp his character: even on the most individual level, he could not avoid being transformed by his mission. He was not only an *agent* of the terror, but also its *product*.

His name is found everywhere: in reports of sessions of the Convention, in reports of sessions of the Jacobins and, finally, in reports of the hearings of the revolutionary Tribunal, three headings, which, in this period, are close to each other in all the newspapers; he is discussed unceasingly in the 'groups' in the Tuileries and the Palais-Egalité; dozens of pamphlets are published about him. Carrier is therefore at the heart of the conflicts and political manoeuvres; he polarises passions.

The Convention quickly bumped up against the problem of lifting Carrier's parliamentary immunity (the terminology is a little anachronistic). The day after 9 Thermidor, it granted itself, as we saw, minimal legal protection in order to secure itself against a new 31 May or a new 9 Thermidor: it had banned its Committees from arresting representatives of the people without previous agreement of the Convention; it had not, however, specified the procedure to be followed in the case where a representative *en mission* was denounced. From 2 to 7 Brumaire, it laboriously worked out this procedure. This legal and political debate reveals a general mistrust – each member, because of his actions under the Terror, feared that the procedure might be turned against himself – and the anxiety to protect oneself against the 'tyranny' of a group over the Convention. The procedure worked out was, therefore, relatively complex: any denunciation of a member of the Convention should be first examined by the three Committees together (of Public Safety, of General Security and of Legislation). If the Committees, after examination, found the denunciation well-founded, the Convention would proceed to the nomination, by drawing lots, of a Commission of Twenty-one who would examine, in their turn, the denunciation; then, if necessary, they would propose that the Convention come to a decision, with voting by a rollcall, as to whether there were grounds for accepting an order of indictment and for making the accused appear before the Revolutionary Tribunal. The procedure granted legal guarantees to the accused and, in particular, the right to present his defence publicly, before the Convention. The discussion on the establishment of the procedure was vitiated from the beginning – those taking part *knew* that it was a matter of defining the ways and means that would shortly be applied to Carrier, without his name once being mentioned. The Convention voted a law which did not pronounce judgement on a particular case. This legalism proves what progress had been made in effectively making 'justice the order of the day' and bears witness to the firm will to go forward, to lay the Carrier case before the Convention and, consequently, to bring him before the Tribunal.[26]

In fact, for all those who wished to increase the anti-Jacobin 'reaction', dismantle the apparatus of the Terror, punish the militants, *and last but not least*, take their revenge in complete legality, the Carrier case was a godsend. The Convention seemed to want to strike several birds with one stone: condemn Carrier the representative *en mission* for the crimes of Nantes; strike a blow against the Society by prosecuting Carrier the Jacobin; and, finally, wash its hands of any responsibility in the Terror – thus avoiding a trial of the Revolution – by amputating one of its members, one who had been elevated into a symbol of the Terror. On this last point, the Convention could argue that Carrier had not *really* informed it of the repressive measures put into train to combat the 'brigands'. It was one thing to have approved at the time, in the course of meetings where exaltation and revolutionary rhetoric were mixed with fear, reports alluding to the Loire – this 'revolutionary river' which had swallowed up priests and brigands – but it was quite something else to learn, in the autumn of Year III, thanks to the accounts of the hearings, the realities of the Terror of Nantes ... all of which was to count without Carrier's reaction. From the beginning of the campaign aiming at his indictment and appearance before a court, Carrier was firmly resolved to defend himself and to identify his cause with that of all the 'persecuted patriots', even with the cause of the Republic and the Revolution. Taking advantage of the procedure decreed by the Convention, he published several versions of his defence, expressed as so many counter-attacks; he defended himself before the Convention, rejecting the report of the Commission of Twenty-one point by point; he again outlined his arguments on 3 Frimaire, the eve of the vote whose result would be disastrous for him; he would not capitulate, and would defend himself again before the Tribunal against the other defendants who accused him. This defence, beyond his shrewd tactics and his sincere convictions, followed a political logic which reveals an extraordinary ideological burden.[27]

---

[26] *Moniteur*, vol. 22, pp. 314–15; 361–7.
[27] We shall refer in what follows to the following documents: *Rapport de Carrier représentant du peuple français sur les différentes missions qui lui ont été déléguées*, Paris, Year III, AN AD XVIII A 15; *Suite du rapport de Carrier représentant du peuple français sur sa mission dans la Vendée*, Paris, Year III; *Discours prononcé par le représentant du peuple Carrier à la Convention nationale, dans la séance du soir du 3 frimaire*, AN AD XVIII A 15. These documents present the outlines of Carrier's defence; to these should be added the long refutation of the report of the Commission of Twenty-one at the meeting of 2 Frimaire; cf. *Moniteur*, vol. 22, pp. 561 *et seq*. In what follows the references to these documents are given in the text, after the respective quotations.

Carrier adopted several converging lines of defence: a) he refuted all the accusations *en bloc*, as slanders without any written proof, and with only dubious evidence; b) he shifted the responsibility for certain crimes and offences onto the revolutionary Committee which acted in its own right, and with whom he broke his links; c) he 'relativised' the Terror in Nantes and the Vendée by recalling the extraordinary circumstances, to which the redefined norms and criteria of a year later, in a quite different political situation, could not be applied; d) he attributed responsibility for the acts of which he was accused, especially the systematic recourse to violence, to the Convention which had ordered them: in prosecuting him, the Convention would thus put itself on trial; e) he presented the campaign of which he was the object as a link in a vast counter-revolutionary conspiracy, aiming to attack him first, then, increasing step by step, the revolutionary government, the Convention and, finally, the Republic.

On the first point, Carrier's task was relatively simple. The report of the Commission of Twenty-one took up the accusations made during the trial by the witnesses, where it was difficult to pick out the facts in their statements from rumours, the reality from fantasy. So Carrier had an easy time in showing that he had never given the order for having the prostitutes drowned. 'Vile slanderers, show me my orders, my decrees, I shall prove to you that I meant those women for sewing the gaiters and breeches of the defenders of the *patrie*. The whole town of Nantes is my witness ... My colleagues, who replaced me, called them to the same task. Could they have done so if I had had the barbarity to have them killed?' (*Rapport*, p. 23); similarly for the mass drowning of children. The witnesses who claimed this could produce no written proof, while it could be established that the public prosecutor

has called as witnesses all the scum of the aristocracy of Nantes, the accomplices and correspondents of brigands, he has called brigands and Chouans.[28] Certainly, at the present time people are amazed at the frightening pictures which every day are drawn at the Revolutionary Tribunal; but don't people see that the aristocracy is creating and increasing the phantoms only to terrify credulity, alarm feelings and sacrifice innocence and patriotism? (*Suite de rapport*, pp. 9–10, 19–20)

It is possible that he had too much confidence in the revolutionary Committee of Nantes; but where else could he find the support to carry out his mission, if not in this Committee which he had not appointed and which was already formed before his arrival?

Carrier was playing with fire. He did not deny the stated facts, such as the

[28] *Chouans*. Counter-revolutionary partisans from Brittany and Normandy who formed an insurrection alongside the rebellion of the Vendée.

mass drownings. He only refused to take responsibility, since *written proof*, orders signed by himself, were lacking. This tactic would finish by rebounding against him for, as we have seen, the Convention would have documents *signed* by him brought from Nantes, documents that carried the proof that he had given the order to shoot, *without trial*, a group of Vendéan cavalry, women and children, and that he had given the order to release one of his agents, Lebatteux, arrested on the orders of another representative *en mission*, Tréhouard, thus going beyond his powers. Signed evidence was rare, but it confirmed some of the evidence and thereby permitted the presumption of the truth of all the other evidence. Besides, how could one believe that *all of Nantes knew* that the drownings were going on, and that only Carrier was not informed? He was, furthermore, the only one who could bring them to an end, even if he had not given the order for them.

Carrier was too skilful a jurist not to perceive the weaknesses of this line of defence. From now on, he was bent on compromising this or that witness, in order to draw the conclusion that the others were equally 'brigands'. He exalted his own merits during his mission, his exploits during confrontations with the 'brigands' and, especially, he laid stress on his unceasing efforts to save Nantes from famine and epidemic. To the image of a 'bloody monster', he opposed the praises with which the people of Nantes covered him:

If the measures that are being exaggerated today had really been carried out, why did those people, who today turn them into images with which to frighten anyone who does not see the perversity of some men, keep silent for more than a year ... I was seen at all the public festivals among the people and with the people ... Citizens, constituted authorities, not one person in the city of Nantes brought me any complaint, any protest. The terror, it is said, commanded silence; but I never noticed that it was established in Nantes; I always saw around me, every time I presented myself in public, a crowd of citizens eager to show their satisfaction in seeing me among them ... People speak of the misfortunes of Nantes; but what then of the evils afflicting Nantes during my mission! What! I provided provisions for this commune for six months, without receiving any help from the government; ... I preserved it from all invasion, all attacks from the brigands; the people of Nantes, assembled for a public festival, covered me with civic crowns two weeks at the most before my departure; I accepted them on behalf of our brave defenders. (*Suite du rapport*, pp. 7–8;12)

Carrier seemed to sincerely believe in the spontaneous enthusiasm the people of Nantes had shown for him. To the image of the 'ferocious man' he opposed the evidence of his electors in the Cantal, who bore witness to 'my humanity, my good deeds and my burning love for the *patrie* and for liberty' (*Rapport*, p. 32: attached to it was an address from the popular society of Aurillac, signed by two hundred and fifty members, and accompanied by a list of the names of about fifty citizens who voted for it 'and who could not sign', confirming that 'Cantal honours itself for having given representative Carrier to the Nation').

Carrier developed a *political* line of reasoning. It was first necessary to *see events in relative terms*, to put them back into the political and historical context of the war of the Vendée. This meant there was a lot of talk of revolutionary atrocities, all exaggerated; on the other hand, the *Vendéan atrocities* were forgotten. To the horrors mentioned during the trial, Carrier opposed, so to speak, 'counter-images' that were even more horrifying.

Foul agents of a counter-revolutionary party, you show the brazenness of crime but now you are unmasked. The people will see that you have been influenced by only a few events which avenged them on well-known enemies of the Republic, and that you did not shed a single tear, write a single line on the massacres committed by the counter-revolutionaries, on the even greater massacres they would have permitted themselves had they triumphed. (*Rapport*, pp. 25–6)

Carrier poured out Vendéan horrors and atrocities: the 'cannibal priest' celebrating mass surrounded by blood and corpses (*Rapport*, p. 26); a constitutional priest impaled alive after the most sensitive parts of his body had been mutilated and he had been nailed, still alive, to the tree of liberty (*Rapport*, p. 26); the women who threw themselves out of the window with their children and whom the brigands knifed in the street (*Rapport*, p. 27); eight hundred patriots cut into pieces at Machecoul, buried still alive, only their arms and legs showing, while the brigands tied up their women, forcing them to watch the sufferings of their husbands; then the brigands nailed them in their turn, along with their children, to the doors of their houses (*Suite du rapport*, p. 23); the patriots whose noses and mouths were stuffed with cartridges, which were then lit in order to make them die in dreadful torment (*Suite du rapport*, p. 23). Carrier adopted for his own purpose the image of the Loire full of blood:

With piteous voices you grieve over the blood which, according to you, reddened the Loire and the ocean. But one can see what led you to exaggerate this image which has the power to move you to pity for them [the executioners of the republicans]; it is that in fact ten thousand brigands, who were at war with us, were thrown in. They were firing upon our brave soldiers in order to cross the Loire with weapons in hand, return to their homes, and perpetuate the war of the Vendée; our cannons, by breaking up their embarkation, plunged them in the Loire ... This is how my enemies have portrayed, with all imaginable fervour, the loss of a few enemies of the Republic, and maintained complete coldness, complete indifference on the massacre of so many republicans. (*Rapport*, p. 29)

If patriots sometimes 'at the sight of so many atrocities undertook reprisals that were a little violent' (*Suite du rapport*, p. 25), these illegal excesses were inevitable and understandable. It was a question of reprisals provoked by the abominable cruelties of the 'brigands'; and one must never forget that there were 'evils inseparable from revolutions', all the more so as it was also a civil war, 'the longest, the most disastrous war that has ever existed on earth' (*Suite du rapport*, p. 28). Only the result counted: the defeat of the Vendéans. 'When the pilot beset by the storm brings his ship to port, is he asked how he set his course?' (*Rapport*, p. 31). The *moral criteria* appropriate in a time of peace were hardly to be applied to exceptional periods of wars and revolutions. To complain of excesses *after* the victory, 'when calm has returned', to judge the *means* without taking into consideration the *ends* which dictate them, was to ignore justice in politics:

It would be cruel, it would be the last of injustices, to judge a citizen, a representative of the people, according to *the present laws and regime, on acts of the revolution* which took place a year ago: it can only be done, it should only be done according to *the laws and circumstances in which he carried out his operations* ... Take yourselves back to those unfortunate times which the graving tool of history would have difficulty in etching; form a true idea of it ... and say what you would have done in my position; could you have, would you have known how to prevent all the evils, all the excesses which took place? (*Suite du rapport*, p. 16; *Rapport*, p. 19)

Had the Convention itself not applauded the news announcing the victory at Le Mans when 'the entire Catholic army was routed; priests, nearly all the women, nearly all the children, fell under the blows of the revolutionaries' (*Suite du rapport*, p. 5)? Carrier gave many other similar cases where the Convention applauded, approved and decreed the publication in its *Bulletin* of news which announced victories, their cost in human lives and in goods destroyed, at the same time as it confirmed its orders to 'crush' the brigands and to apply, with full severity, the supreme law, *that of saving the Republic*. The Convention should therefore take the responsibility for its acts and their consequences. By persecuting those who executed its orders, *the Convention was putting itself on trial*.

Take good care, my case is *the plank which will save or destroy national representation* ... *It is the Convention itself that is being proceeded against*, since it approved and ordered by decree the measures taken everywhere by representatives of the people who were *en mission*. It was a good as well as a wise policy to bring the frightful war of the Vendée to a prompt end; that was the desire strongly expressed by the will of the National Convention, the will of the French people manifested in loud cries; its safety and the triumph of political liberty imperiously demanded it; I fully co-operated in carrying out this important task, and yet today I am drenched with all the bile of slander, harassed, defamed for *matters of detail* in which I did not take nor could take any part. *Are they not strange, the vicissitudes of the Revolution* ... What could my intentions have been? Most certainly I had none, other than that of saving the Republic ... The brigands of the Vendée ... were outlawed; the Convention *ordered that they should all be exterminated* within a specific period; it approved the measure of having them shot as soon as they were captured; to disapprove of it today, to put on trial those who carried it out, is to put the Convention itself on trial, since it decreed the measure ... *My intentions were yours, if I made a mistake, the error is common to all of us*; you cannot convert it into a crime. (*Suite du rapport*, p. 29; *Discours ... du 3 frimaire*, pp. 11–15)

Carrier, hammering out this last argument, showed that at the heart of the debate had arisen the fundamental question of the *very legitimacy of revolutionary violence*, of the sovereign and unlimited will of the people. From now on, no one would be able to escape the case brought against the Revolution: not, today, representative *en mission* Carrier, nor, tomorrow, the members of the former Committees, the other representatives *en mission*, all those who 'could not prevent the necessary evils' carried out in Lyon, in Marseille, in Toulon (Fouché, Collot, Barras, Fréron ... ). Already people began to bring proceedings against the *journée* of 31 May. Why not, then, accuse the whole army of the West which carried out the order to shoot the brigands? And the other armies which carried out the Convention's order not to take English and Hanoverian prisoners? And then the men of 10 August: did they not kill the Swiss guards *after* the victory of the people? And finally the victors of the Bastille who killed intendant Bertier after the 'affair of 14 July'? Behind 'the intrigue', Carrier unveiled an infernal logic:

This is to put *the Revolution itself on trial* with this insidious and counter-revolutionary manner of separating the facts and the events of the revolution from the revolutionary crises which brought them about ... This is to put the entire people on trial, since it carried out all the revolutions, since it is involved in the evils which are inseparable from them: let the people then be judged, let them be punished *en masse*! It is putting liberty itself on trial, since it could defend itself only by *a continual, energetic and revolutionary struggle* against its enemies, and by the union of patriots committed to protecting and maintaining it. (*Suite du rapport*, p. 27–9)

Carrier's argument followed, on this point, the paradigmatic revolutionary speech. Without doubt, he saw himself as no more guilty than the other 'terrorists', ex-representatives *en mission* who were now hounding him. The action that people wanted to bring against him could therefore only be explained by occult reasons which sprang from a 'conspiracy' . The same 'plot' that aimed at him meant to also bring down the popular societies, the Jacobins and all the 'advanced patriots'. Concluding his last speech before his peers, Carrier exclaimed:

The Convention has clearly seen that it is the trial of royalism against liberty, of fanaticism against philosophy. The trial brought against me unites these two features. It is a crowd of royalists, of fanatics from Nantes and the Vendée who roar against me ... Take good care, citizens. In party conflicts, as in the stormy fortunes of the Revolution, the passions, the opinion of the moment, lead always to unfortunate excesses: the return to calm makes one regret the consequences, but regrets are belated and unnecessary. Reason and philosophy have rehabilitated the memory of Calas;[29] but we have only sterile tears to give to his tomb.

Until 22 Brumaire, the date of the closing down of the Jacobins, Carrier seemed to believe that once more political logic and prudence would carry the day, that they would dictate to the members of the Convention the closing of the file on their collective responsibility ('even the president's handbell is guilty in this chamber', he had said). He reckoned that the instinct of solidarity would come into play, particularly as the Convention was to find itself, yet once more, under pressure from the Jacobins and the popular societies, maintained by the deputies of the Mountain.

However, this political tactic, whose premises were not entirely erroneous, turned against Carrier. For the same analysis of the political stakes reached opposite conclusions: it was necessary for the Convention to reject all collective responsibility and, at the same time, accuse Carrier alone to the utmost. The reports of the police showed clearly that in 'groups' and in the *sections* the Carrier affair was the subject of passionate discussions. 'Some, in considering this affair, fear that it will ensure impunity for crimes inseparable from great revolutions; others see the unequivocal intention to prosecute the crimes of the Revolution, in order to have a pretext for prosecuting the Revolution itself; this is the true source of all the debates in the groups.'[30] To condemn Carrier came down to putting an end to this wavering of a part of public opinion and to replying to the expectations of the many people who saw in this condemnation the most elementary justice. Carrier could possibly count on the support of the Jacobins and of the 'Crest'. For anyone who wished to accelerate the liquidation of the power of both parties, the dreamt-of opportunity was provided by the trial of the Jacobin Carrier. The majority of the Convention rallied to this strategy. For the behaviour of the Convention was no longer that of Fructidor, Year II: it could reopen the file on responsibility for the Terror, insofar as the relationship of forces had radically changed.

After the Convention's decree, the Jacobins were in an impasse; the Society could no longer correspond with other popular societies nor, consequently, discharge its responsibility as mother-Society. Participation at meetings, by members as much as by the public, continued to diminish (towards the middle of Brumaire it was reduced to some three hundred people); the Jacobins were denounced in the press, their club was described as a 'lair of brigands' according to the expression of Merlin (from Thionville). The appeal of 18 Vendémiaire, which denounced the 'exclusive

---

[29] *Calas.* Jean Calas was tortured and executed in 1762 on the spurious grounds that he had killed his own son to prevent him converting to Catholicism. The miscarriage of justice was widely publicised by Voltaire.

[30] Report of 19 Brumaire, Year II, in Aulard, *Paris pendant la reaction*, vol. 1, pp. 228–9.

patriots' as advocates of a re-establishment of the Terror, was aimed at them. The isolation of the Jacobins increased; fewer and fewer representatives attended their meetings. The Jacobins no longer had a coherent political strategy with which they might oppose the policy of anti-terrorist vengeance, to which the government was more and more committed. It was futile for them to denounce the fact that they were being compared to 'terrorists', for it was to them alone that flowed the complaints from the 'persecuted patriots' and from the Terror's personnel in the *départements*, who were the victims of the repression. They kept denouncing the too great freedom of the press which benefited only the 'aristocrats' and the 'counter-revolutionaries', but these attacks stirred up anti-Jacobin articles and pamphlets. What then was to be done with Carrier? He was *one of them*, one of the prominent figures of the declining Society, one of the last 'advanced' members of the Mountain. The Society was the target of the attacks against him. But the revelations on the Terror at Nantes and the role Carrier had played there, as well as the opening by the Convention of the procedure for committing a representative *en mission* to trial, made him the very symbol of a 'blood-drinker'. The Society did not decide to abandon him completely: this would be to capitulate before the anti-Jacobin attacks and abandon the cause of all 'persecuted and slandered patriots', of which Carrier became at the same time a symbol, and this would deprive it of the support of the last militants. But to engage itself too openly in the defence of Carrier was to pose, in the face of public opinion, as supporters of the mass drownings and shootings and encourage the 'Jacobin-hunt'.

In Brumaire, the Carrier affair occupied the Jacobins more and more. During the sessions of the Society they criticised the development of the trial of the revolutionary Committee: the accused found it difficult to defend themselves, while there was a queue of witnesses supplied with passports issued by the Chouans. They denounced the 'lampooners', the 'disguised aristocrats' and the 'muscadins' who, in slanderous pamphlets as well as in the 'groups', threatened the Convention by insinuating that 'the people will rise up if it does not hand Carrier over to them'.[31] Tension was very high during a session on 13 Brumaire. What happened exactly? It is difficult to establish the facts. For some weeks, the official account published in the *Journal de la Montagne* and taken up, more or less faithfully, by the *Moniteur* (and also by the *Annales patriotiques*) no longer tallied with the versions and rumours published by the anti-Jacobin press. With the meeting of 13 Brumaire, these differences were flagrant. Whatever the truth of the matter, the version from the anti-Jacobin press found the largest audience, even at the time of the Convention's debates. So,

---

[31] Cf. Aulard, *Société des Jacobins*, vol. 6, pp. 629 *et seq.*; *Journal du Perlet*, no. 770.

according to the *Messager du soir*, one of the orators (Bouin) had proclaimed that

the patriots have all the more reason to defend Carrier in that it is their own cause they are defending. Which one of us is there ... who in the *départements* or in the *sections* has not been compelled, in order to save the *patrie*, to take rigorous measures against the *muscadins*, the moderates and the Brissotins?[32] He therefore invites all *energetic revolutionaries to make a rampart of their bodies for Carrier*.

The *Journal de Perlet* attributed to Crassou, president of the meeting, the following words:

It seems to him that *these proceedings are less a trial of Carrier than of all revolutionary men and all the Jacobins*. He thinks that it is against them that there is a grudge, and that consequently they should mutually defend each other. He does not believe that the people is thinking of rising up, should the Convention absolve Carrier ... He invites the Jacobins *to set against the horrors blamed on Carrier* a portrayal of those committed by the brigands.

But all the newspapers, including the *Journal de la Montagne*, agreed in quoting the allusive and threatening words uttered by Billaud-Varenne: 'the lion is not dead when he sleeps, and when he awakes he exterminates his enemies.'[33]

These remarks appeared in the context of very great confusion: the slow pace of the procedure of the Commission of Twenty-one which was late in presenting its report on Carrier, rumours of the preparation by the Jacobins of a 'plot' against the Convention,[34] scuffles, more and more violent, in the 'groups', provoked by the *jeunesse dorée* who have taken up the 'Jacobin-hunt', while shouting *Long live the Convention!* and a press campaign, more and more virulent, against the Jacobins.

The press and, more generally, the non-periodical sheets (pamphlets, brochures) which attacked the Jacobins are of very poor quality: they aim not to convince, but to stir up people's passions. Insults take the place of

---

[32] *Brissotins*. Followers of Jacques Brissot, a leader of the Girondins.

[33] *Messager du soir*, no. 809; *Journal de Perlet*, no. 773; Aulard, *Société des Jacobins*, vol. 6, p. 631.

[34] Several newspapers noted 'alarming news' on the insurrection which was being prepared in the Faubourg Saint-Antoine: it was even claimed that 20,000 red bonnets had been purchased, as 'rallying signs' (cf. *Journal de Perlet*, no. 783). At the Convention, on 16 Brumaire, there was discussion of a mysterious letter from Switzerland, intercepted by the Committee of General Security, which mentioned the counter-revolutionary strategy of setting the Convention against the popular societies, of putting the latter into a 'state of revolt against national representation, and stirring them up through their most influential members' (*Journal de Paris*, no. 47). Duval, in his memoirs, reported the rumour, spread by, amongst others, Fréron, according to which the Jacobins were prepared to attack the Convention under arms and slaughter all members who wished to end the reign of Terror: Duval, *Souvenirs thermidoriens*, vol. 2, p 16 *et seq*.

argument, as their titles show clearly enough: *The Jacobins are s— and France is saved; Robespierre's private parts left among the Jacobins; While the beast is in the trap, he must be killed; The rampart of Carrier dragged in the mud or what the Jacobins of the Mountain are worth; Reserved seats to see Carrier on the day he shall go the guillotine, with a description of the dinner that his most intimate friends will eat on the same day.*[35] This is only a symptom of the persistence, throughout the Revolution, of the production of pamphlets that are vulgar and of doubtful quality, which coexists with moving declamations and rhetorical outbursts. A sort of correspondence is established between the two registers: the pamphlets simply translate the sublime and the moving into vulgar and improper language. But the anti-Jacobin pamphlets had become very effective instruments for forming public opinion. The monopoly of speech, held by the Jacobins during the Terror, was permanently broken. To be sure, the pro-Jacobin press only just managed to keep going, deprived of government subsidies. If reports of the sessions of the Jacobins continued to be published in the majority of newspapers, the grandiloquent speeches which were delivered there were mocked everywhere. The word of the Jacobins *no longer represented ideological authority*, as was the case during the Terror. It still claimed to be legitimised by the people, but this hollow pretension was now derided. The Jacobins found it difficult to come to terms with this reversal of roles, with

[35]  By way of a sample, here are two extracts.

> What then is the secret reason that makes them exhort each other to make their bodies into a rampart for Carrier? Personal interest or delirium? Is it fraternity? These reasons perhaps all go together, the fraternity of crime, interest in their own safety and the delirium of fear. Before coming to a decision on this, ask yourself this simple question: would a man of honour, a really virtuous man, support a wicked man? Those who do not blush to support him are they then men of this kind? Examine your heart, I am sure that it will reply without hesitation: no, and there you have what the Jacobins of the Mountain are worth. *Le Rempart de Carrier*, n.d., n.p., (Paris, Year III)

And here is the second example:

> (Air: *Allons enfants de la patrie*)
> A combination of iron and fire
> Strikes the Lyonnais indiscriminately,
> Collot punishes with this carnage,
> Those whose jeers he endured;
> All fall, innocent and guilty;
> Buried half-alive
> We've seen their quivering bodies
> Move and lift the sand.
> Join Carrier in the crime, monster of cruelty, Collot, (*bis*) you deserve no better than he.
>   *Carrier a commencé la marche, suivez messieurs*, n.p., n.d. (Paris, Year III).

Finally, let us mention a Jacobin attempt to pastiche pamphlets of this kind to avoid their effects. So, under the alluring title, *Their heads tremble! Your turn after Carrier, messieurs Barère, Collot d'Herbois, Billaud-Varenne, Vadier, Vouland, Amar. And all of you who were members of the former Committees of Public Safety and General Security*, n.p., n.d. (Paris, Year III), the reader finds a satirical text which derides the accusations made against 'energetic patriots'.

the resurgence of public opinion that legitimised the word of the anti-Jacobins. Their disarray was well expressed in the fallacious distinction noted earlier by Chasles between the 'opinion of the people' which remained silent but pro-Jacobin, and 'public opinion' which was expressed loudly but, alas, was 'counter-revolutionary' . . .

The press campaign was redoubled in its violence by the appearance *of a new political protagonist*: the *jeunesse dorée*. Its muscular intervention was the *coup de grâce* for the Society of the Rue Saint-Honoré. The historian today has a better knowledge of the history of the *jeunesse dorée*, its social composition, its forms of action, thanks to certain works.[36] The *jeunesse dorée* (or the *muscadins*) were recruited, above all, among the middle bourgeoisie, in particular from the milieu of the law courts. It was composed of 'young people' who, on different pretexts, avoided military conscription and filled, as clerks, the offices of notaries and barristers, as well as the offices of local and central administration (where they sometimes worked alongside former militant *sans-culottes* seeking refuge in military administration or in the apparatus of the Committee of General Security). The *jeunesse dorée* was characterised especially by its political views as well as by the forms of its organisation. After 9 Thermidor, it embodied the anti-terrorist and anti-Jacobin reaction, and translated the desire for revenge into action (one found, moreover, the relations or friends of victims of the Terror in its ranks; to be part of this group was a sign of glory). More or less socially homogeneous (but one also found among them some 'aristocrats' like the famous Marquis de Saint-Huruge, one of the political adventurers produced by the Revolution), the *jeunesse dorée* was not, however, politically homogeneous. It possessed no positive political strategy (so one found moderate republicans and monarchists of various colours among them, as well as opportunists who follow Thermidorean power); its homogeneity came solely from its forms of organisation and action. They were commandos armed with sticks, iron bars, cudgels or whips, forming regimented bands who numbered, as a whole and at the moments of their greatest effectiveness, about two to three thousand people. At the beginning of Year III, these bands took possession of the public arena left unoccupied by the relaxation of the police and political control of terrorist power. So the *jeunesse dorée* was able to occupy the *cafés* (including the Café de Chartres, at the Palais-Egalité, where a sort of headquarters was established), the *street* (notably the places where the 'groups' formed to discuss politics, at the Tuileries, the Palais-Egalité, before the Convention, etc.), the *rostrums* of the Convention, the *assemblies* of the *sections*. The *jeunesse dorée*

---

[36] Especially F. Gendron, *La Jeunesse dorée. Episodes de la Révolution française*, Quebec, 1979; reprinted Paris, 1983.

operated through detachments which, according to a 'battle plan' established in advance, attacked precise objectives: a 'Jacobin-hunt' in the 'groups' and in the assemblies of the *sections* where they provoked scuffles and confusion; sacking of cafés claimed to be 'Jacobin'; attacks, with beatings, of the street-hawkers of Jacobin newspapers or pamphlets as well as of booksellers who sold them; and action soon followed in the theatres where the commandos booed actors compromised by their 'collaboration' with the 'terrorists', or in public places where the *jeunesse dorée* destroyed the symbols bequeathed by Year II (busts of Marat, Phrygian bonnets, etc.). In Nivôse, Year III, *Le Réveil du peuple* became the hymn of the *jeunesse dorée* and the commandos forced people in public places, especially in the theatres, to sing this call to vengeance. The *jeunesse dorée* thus represents a specific form of *revolutionary violence*, and one which, from several angles, is unprecedented. It is easy, however, to establish that on several points it turned inside out the technical *experience*, so to speak, of the use of violence, thoroughly tested by the *sans-culottes*. But it was not arranged according to residential areas nor, consequently, as belonging to a *section* or to a popular society. Command was secured through 'leaders' and not through clubs; their places of assembly were different from those which were hallowed by revolutionary tradition. The forms of violence were sometimes imitated, sometimes new (boos in the theatres, breaking of busts, obligatory repeating of songs, etc.). The *jeunesse dorée* became a sort of auxiliary force of the Committee of General Security, which let it carry on or even incited it to act; at certain critical moments, the Committee mobilised and directly commanded the detachments of the *jeunesse dorée* (notably during the *journées* of Prairial, when the Committee distributed weapons to the 'young people' in order to help pacify the Faubourg Saint-Antoine). The resistance offered by the Jacobins and the revolutionary activists of the faubourgs to the *jeunesse dorée* was all the weaker in that they no longer enjoyed the protection of power.

On 19 Brumaire, about a hundred 'young people' attacked the meeting hall of the Society, throwing stones and bottles; the brawl was repeated the following day. On 21 Brumaire, in the evening, some three hundred 'young people' assembled to attack the seat of the Jacobins in the Rue Saint-Honoré, to the cries of *Long live the Convention! Down with the Jacobins!* Along the way the crowd increased and there were at the end 2,000 people attacking the Club; the President was obliged to adjourn the meeting, the Jacobins (scarcely one hundred ...) emerged to spittle, and blows from the feet and fists of the 'young people'. The women had their skirts pulled up and were whipped, to the laughter and insults of the crowd. The Committee of General Security let this go on until the early morning, before sending a patrol, which took over the keys and closed the door of the Jacobin Club – as if it were repeating the scene of the night of 9 to 10 Thermidor. This time, however, the closure would be final. With the Constitution guaranteeing the existence of the popular societies, the closure was presented as a provisional suspension of the meetings, a simple police action imposed by the desire to maintain public order. This is how the Society came to an end. The Assembly had adopted the decree on the closure of the Jacobins almost without debate, and unanimously (except for one vote, that of a minor member of the Convention, Marbeau-Montant). And only a 'very small number of deputies' took part in the vote. The closure of the Jacobins was the fall of a symbol and marked the end of an epoch.[37]

Carrier, therefore, accelerated the end of the Jacobins; it was inevitable that this would bring about, in its turn, his fall. On 21 Brumaire, the Convention had decided that Carrier would be placed under house arrest, under the guard of four gendarmes. The vote by a rollcall, which began on 3 Frimaire and lasted until four in the morning, sealed Carrier's defeat. The Convention rediscovered, once more, its unanimity; it voted through the decree of indictment by 500 votes with two conditional ayes.

There were relatively few representatives who, in giving the reasons for their votes, mentioned the charges brought during the trial of the revolutionary Committee of Nantes. Of course, the mass drownings were mentioned ('a genre of punishment as new as it was horrifying', said Laurent; 'the most barbaric and cannibalistic acts', exclaims Elie Dugène), but only one representative alluded to the 'republican marriages'. One deputy (Léquinio) would have the courage to declare that in the course of his stay at Nantes (three days) he 'did not see any orgies'. Couturier (from Moselle) stated that 'it is not the drownings, nor the shootings nor even the clack-valves[38] supposed to have been invented by Carrier that lead me to make up my mind, because the mode of destruction of the enemies and brigands who are against the Republic can be judged criminal only by their good or bad intentions'. The orders to execute without trial the Vendéans who wanted to surrender were often mentioned; but more frequently still the fact that Carrier, in going beyond his powers, and in annulling the orders of Tréhouard, committed an 'offence against national representation' worthy of the 'tyrants of the Committee of Public Safety'. According to Patrin (from Rhône-et-Loire), 'the atrocities committed by Carrier are frightful, they make nature tremble and call down the vengeance of the

---

[37] Cf. *Moniteur*, vol. 22, pp. 489 *et seq.*; Aulard, *Société des Jacobins*, vol. 6, pp. 643 *et seq*; Aulard, *Paris pendant la réaction*, vol. 1, pp. 226 *et seq.*; *Journal de Perlet*, nos. 813, 814, 815; G. Walter, *Histoire des Jacobins*, Paris, 1946, pp. 347 *et seq*; Gendron, *La Jeunesse dorée* pp. 46 *et seq.*

[38] *clack-valves*. 'Holes were punched in the sides of flat-bottomed barges below the waterline, over which wooden planks were nailed to keep the boats temporarily afloat. Prisoners were put in with their hands and feet tied and the boats pushed into the center to catch the current. The executioner-boatmen then broke or removed the planks': Simon Schama, *Citizens*, London, 1989.

laws upon his head. But his greatest crime, in my eyes, is the offence against the sovereign power of the people in prohibiting the recognition of our colleague Tréhouard as the representative of the people.' Other members of the Convention refuted the argument of Carrier according to which the Convention had, with his indictment, indicted themselves. Bentabole declared:

It is vain for anyone to seek to persuade you that when the National Convention sees itself forced to deal severely with a man who has thrown himself into the party of revolution, it is to attack the revolution ... The Convention should hasten to announce to all the nations that, when innocent blood is shed, no one can elude vengeance by taking shelter in a glorious revolution, for a glorious revolution cannot be supported by crime and will be the triumph of virtue.

On what was to follow Carrier's indictment and trial, whose fatal result seemed scarcely to raise any doubt, a difference of opinion appeared: for some, it was only the first measure, and the logical consequence of the condemnation of Carrier was the opening of other similar proceedings, in particular against former members of the Committees. This was, for example, the meaning that Lecointre gave to his vote. 'Carrier's crimes concern, just as much and even more, the majority of members of the Committees of government who knew of them, permitted them, tolerated them for six months, without having checked, punished or denounced them to the National Convention ... These last crimes are as much their crimes as Carrier's, although this does not make Carrier any less of a criminal.' On the other hand, the embarrassment among the members of 'the Crest' was clear; they voted *yes* while at the same time expressing their reservations and demanding that this indictment should be the last and should put an end to denunciations of the representatives of the people: 'I hope that the imperturbable and pure justice of the National Convention will watch over what follows the denunciations which multiply against its members', declared Billaud. Romme, who presided over the Commission of Twenty-one and whose position had been hesitant for a long time, finally gave a favourable vote, specifying his desire that all those who were recognised as guilty of 'slanderous declarations' should be the object of rigorous prosecution and that 'the debates which are going to take place at the Tribunal should be printed and distributed at the Convention and that no other writing on this affair should be laid before the public'.[39]

The unanimity of the Convention expressed, in the end, its *deep divisions*.

---

[39] Cf. *Moniteur*, vol. 22, pp. 589–96; AN C 327 CII 1430–1431. Having no intention of analysing the vote as a whole, we have not taken up here other problems raised by the explanations given by members of the Convention (for example, the doubts expressed on the value of certain witnesses, the absence of papers signed by Carrier, etc.).

On the announcement of the result of the vote Carrier tried to end his life (he was prevented by the gendarme who was watching him) and he died courageously (this counted for a lot in the eyes of spectators sensitive to moving gestures, after having seen thousands of the condemned pass through the 'little window'). His last words, in face of a huge crowd assembled around the scaffold, were 'Long live the Republic!' The Thermidorean press could hardly disguise its disappointment: it would have preferred him to die a coward's death.

Neither Carrier's death nor the trial of the revolutionary Committee of Nantes produced any satisfactory reply to the question: why all these horrors under the Terror and, more generally, during the war of the Vendée? Did they have to be seen as the work of 'bloodthirsty monsters' who had seized power and imposed their tyranny? Or was it necessary, rather, to deplore the fact that certain 'evils' were inseparable from any great revolution and from any civil war? There were other explanations that revealed more about the obsessions of the revolutionary imagination. First of all, the old explanatory schema of an aristocratic and royalist plot was rediscovered. Although it would seem *a priori* that this schema was badly suited to the interpretation of the Terror in Nantes, one cannot underestimate its roots in the revolutionary imagination nor its malleability. Several minor publicists were, therefore, not slow to unveil the diabolic plot, planned by the coalition of tyrants: by means of crimes and misfortunes they hoped 'to make the French people repent of having desired to open their eyes to enlightenment and pick the fruit of the trees of liberty'. They thus aimed at making 'this nation of gentle manners revolt from the spectacle of horrors' with the intention of then throwing upon the revolutionary government the responsibility for all the crimes and misfortunes. This would explain, in particular, the crimes of Carrier and other wicked men who, under the mask of exclusive patriotism, hid their true face as agents of William Pitt. In the same way Fouquier-Tinville, by his wicked and criminal acts, sought only to debase the Revolution, and therefore to re-establish royalty. This story renewed the tale of Robespierre-the-king a little, but always reverted to the same explanatory structure of history: the worst enemies made the best allies.[40]

---

[40] Baralère, *Acte d'accusation contre Carrier présenté aux Comités réunis, à la Convention nationale et au peuple français*, Paris, Year III; Dupuis, representative of the people, *Motifs de l'acte d'accusation contre Carrier*, Paris, Year III; Buchez and Roux, *Histoire parlementaire de la Révolution française*, vol. 34, p. 27: 'Acte d'accusation contre Fouquier-Tinville'. Leblois, in this indictment, took up several Thermidorean clichés: Fouquier had planned to 'depopulate France', and to drive out above all 'genius, talent, honour and industry'.

Another interpretation deserves dwelling on a little longer: the one developed by Babeuf in his writings devoted to Carrier and his trial.[41]

Babeuf categorically denied the thesis according to which the Terror was imposed by 'circumstances' and that the terrorists acted only in order to save the country. He himself took up all the horrors presented throughout the trial. Responsibility for the Terror did not lie with some monsters and scoundrels who had taken over power (even if Carrier was a monster, as was shown by 'the less equivocal evidence'). In reality, it was necessary to unveil all *the hidden circumstances* which coincided to give these 'natural carnivores' the latitude to act with the agreement of those who 'dabble in the administration of society'. So it was not the war of the Vendée which provoked the setting up of the Terror, contrary to the declarations of the former Committees. This war existed only because the group in power wanted it. 'It is necessary to snatch away ... the veil which has prevented discovery until now of the fact that there existed an insurrection in the Vendée only because some despicable people in power wanted it, and because it was part of their frightful plan.' The people of the Vendée were peaceful, with simple manners, and for whom it would have been enough to hear the good republican word, preached by devoted patriots, to win them over to the true cause. Why then war? The key to the enigma was given by the discovery of the 'system of depopulation and of a new division of riches among those who remain; [this] explains everything, the war of the Vendée, war with abroad, proscription, mass guillotinings, killings, drownings,

---

[41] G. Babeuf, *On veut sauver Carrier! On veut faire le procès au tribunal révolutionnaire. Peuple prends garde à toi!*, n.d., n.p. (Paris, Year III); G. Babeuf, *Du système de dépopulation ou la vie et les crimes de Carrier. Son procès et celui du Comité révolutionnaire de Nantes. Avec des recherches et des considérations politiques sur les vues générales du Décemvirat dans l'intention de ce système; sur sa combinaison avec la guerre de la Vendée et sur le projet de son application à toutes les parties de la République*, Paris, Year III. We shall not analyse the place of these texts in the evolution of Babeuf's ideas. They certainly reveal a moment of great confusion. Scarcely out of prison, Babeuf expressed, after 9 Thermidor, all his hatred against Robespierre, the revolutionary government and the Jacobins. He did the same in his *Journal de la liberté de la presse* which was, along with Fréron's *L'Orateur du peuple*, one of the most vehement 'Thermidorean' papers. Babeuf condemned the Terror but wished also to understand how such a 'despotate' could arise in the course of the Revolution. At the same time he seemed to believe that 9 Thermidor marked a first return to true revolutionary principles, especially to the exercise of liberty in a sort of direct and decentralised democracy. The revelations brought by the trial of Carrier and the revolutionary Committee of Nantes deepened the confusion of his ideas even further. From our perspective, these texts are particularly interesting because of this confusion: *Du système de dépopulation ou la vie et les crimes de Carrier*, a fairly rare text, has not raised much interest for two centuries. It was republished only on the occasion of the bicentenary by R. Secher and J.-J. Bregeon (Paris, 1987). D. Martin devoted a paper to 'the depopulation system' at the symposium *La Légende de la Révolution*, in *Actes du colloque de Clermont-Ferrand (juin 1986)*, edited by C. Croisille and J. Ehrard, with the collaboration of M.-C. Chemin, Clermont-Ferrand, 1988.

confiscations, *maximum*,[42] requisitions, largesse to certain individuals, etc.'
At the beginning, therefore, there was the strategy conceived by Robespierre, who had decided,

having done his calculations, that the French population was to a certain extent
exceeding the resources of the soil ...[43] that there were too many arms for the
execution of all the works of essential utility ... Finally [and this is the horrible
conclusion] that the overabundant population could rise to such an extent [we lack
a detailed statement from these splendid legislators], that a number of the sans-
culottes would have to be sacrificed ... and that it was necessary to find the means.

Other concerns were attached to this objective: property had fallen into a
small number of hands and it was necessary to redistribute it to ensure
equality; now, that could not be done without excessive taxation of the rich
and 'without first taking all properties into government hands'. Robespierre could succeed only by 'sacrificing the big owners and by setting in
motion a terror so powerful that it was capable of persuading others to
submit to it willingly'. This 'immense unveiled secret' explains, then, all the
mysteries: the 'curses against other nations', the 'anthropophagy', and the
Vendée turned into the field for experiment for 'a vile and unprecedented
political goal: *to weed out the human race*'. This diabolical plan had already
cost France a million inhabitants. Moreover, it was not limited only to the
Vendée and war outside the borders; there existed also a 'serious plan' to
organise famine in Paris, the most effective means of 'depopulating France'.
This explained the fact that 'the Republican hosts, transformed into legions
of Erostrates and into horrifying human butchers, armed with a hundred
thousand torches and a hundred thousand bayonets, slaughtered a
similar number and burnt as many unfortunate agricultural havens'. It was
in 'revolutionary government that one must seek all the evils of the
Republic'. The Convention carried the heaviest responsibility: it formed
and supported this government; it gave its agreement to laws that were
'burning and slaughtering, it sanctioned so many others of the same
carnivorousness, that one must believe the truth of what it says, that
Robespierre alone was stronger than all its members together'. The
discovery of this Machiavellian plan would permit, therefore, the punishment of those who were really guilty, the men who served the 'despotate'
and whose crimes called for vengeance. But this 'fortunate and justificatory

---

[42] *maximum*. The fixing of prices in 1793–4, to control the highest prices at which a merchant
could sell his products.
[43] Babeuf seemed to agree with this Malthusian idea which he attributes to Robespierre: it
would be substantiated by 'the only reliable measure, a survey of the total produce of the
rural economy ... since all the possible arts are incapable of producing between them a loaf
of bread more'. However, according to Babeuf, the response to this problem could and
should be peaceful and egalitarian.

key to the enigma' above all grants innocence to the Revolution; the unveiling of the conspiracy and its 'terrible system' ensured that it would rediscover its original purity.[44]

This recourse to a phantasmagoria in an attempt to get to the bottom of the story makes for a hallucinating text, but it is easy to recognise within it, mixed together and confused, the great fears which haunted the *ancien régime* and the new spectres engendered by the Revolution: shadowy conspiracy and plot; the famine pact; the Terror as a plot conceived by occult forces and put into action by 'cannibal monsters'. It is remarkable for its development of an obsessional logic which leads to the perception, even though it is an hallucination, of the Terror as a system of power ready to exclude, and therefore to eliminate, thousands, even millions, of citizens with the sole aim of ensuring the realisation of revolutionary objectives.

The trial of the Terror was becoming the trial of the Revolution: not the French Revolution as a historical phenomenon, since one of its phases was from now on this very demand for truth, which led to the analysis of the connections which linked the principles of 1789 to the massacres of Nantes and civil war; but the Revolution as a demiurgic figure of the imagination of Year II. And so, expressing satisfaction at the closing of the Jacobin Club, a Thermidorean newspaper wrote this terrible sentence: 'They shall no longer drown us, they shall no longer shoot us, *they shall no longer turn their guns on the French people in order to make it better*.'[45] The closing down of the club was the event that marked the dismantling of the symbolic and political heritage of the Terror. There were others: the return of Girondin deputies, the redoubled denunciations of members of the former Committees, the elimination by the *jeunesse dorée* of the symbols of Year II – red bonnets and busts of the 'martyrs of liberty'. It could not stop there: soon the Constitution of 1793 was implicated. In attacking terrorist imagery, Thermidor faced political and cultural problems, for the Revolution, inheritor of the Enlightenment, had not only led to 'tyranny', it had also engendered a monstrosity which contradicted both its origins and its objectives and which it wanted to banish for ever: *vandalism*.

---

[44] The principal source in support of Babeuf's discovery of the 'key to the enigma' was a pamphlet by J. Vilatte, *Causes secrètes de la Révolution*, Paris, Year III, in which certain passages, very freely interpreted, suggested the idea of the 'infernal plot' to Babeuf. Vilatte, co-defendant in Fouquier's trial, was condemned to death, despite his denunciation of Robespierre.

[45] *Gazette historique et politique de la France et de l'Europe*, 25 Brumaire, Year II.

# 4    The vandal people

## Our ancestors, vandals?

In 1912 Alphonse Aulard returned from his visit to Avignon, incensed. The guide, as he described the monuments to the tourists, kept emphasizing the destruction and devastation committed during the Revolution. Having checked the evidence, Aulard established that the Revolution had nothing to do with this destruction: it had been carried out under the Empire or even under the Restoration.

See what the lessons of official guides are worth. Their chatter is believed only by the credulous. But this is to say that it is believed by the majority. Every day, in some national building and in every region of France, there is an official fellow who, under orders or not, pours contempt on the Revolution, presents our ancestors as vandals, as brutes, and this when it is proven that the Committee of Public Safety, the Commission of Arts, the Committee of Public Instruction made every effort in 1793, and in the Year II, that is, in the middle of the Terror, to maintain and defend the heritage of art in France, and made these efforts with the most competent and most enlightened concern.[1]

Aulard's indignation is perfect evidence of the scale of the passionate debates aroused by 'revolutionary vandalism' within an entire historiography, in whose eyes the history of the Revolution was 'a story of origins, therefore a discourse on identity'.[2] At the time of the cultural offensive of the Third Republic, 'revolutionary vandalism' acquired a quite special importance. If historical polemics sometimes take a Homeric turn, it is because the stakes involved are much greater than appears from their subject: the monuments, the works of art or the libraries destroyed during the revolutionary period. That there was destruction, no one disputes; moreover, no one proposes to defend it, nor apologise for it: this is unthinkable at a period devoted to the cult of Progress and Civilisation. If there is a bitter debate on the extent of the destruction and, especially, in

[1] A. Aulard, 'Boniments contre-révolutionnaires', article published in *La Dépêche de Toulouse*, 2 December 1912, reprinted in *Révolution française*, vol. 63, 1912.
[2] Furet, *Penser la Révolution*, pp. 18–19.

order to find out who is responsible, if some seek to make a detailed inventory of the destruction and to demonstrate that it was hardly the result of chance but of a premeditated plan, while others declare that the destruction was no greater under the Revolution than at other times of war and disturbances and that as much, if not more, was destroyed later ('yes, under the Restoration!' exclaims Aulard with satisfaction) and that it came about by accident and was contrary to the revolutionary cause and policy, this is because they all seek to defend or denounce precisely the 'fore-fathers'. Did the schoolteachers of the Third Republic have vandals as their ancestors? What then of their civilising mission and, consequently, of the civilising work of this Republic, so proud of its revolutionary origins?

To reread the polemics of the end of the nineteenth and beginning of the twentieth century – and as far as one can stand back from the problem of 'ancestors' – one is struck by the fact that the respective theses of those who denounce 'vandalism' and of the champions 'of Republic and Revolution' are more complementary than contradictory.[3] Provided that the argument is limited to what is at its heart, that is to say, the question of the destruction of cultural assets and of the responsibility that would then lie with the revolutionary authorities (but, as we shall see, the discourse on vandalism since the Revolution is hardly limited to this question alone), one would be tempted to think there is reason on both sides.

Did successive revolutionary authorities want to preserve cultural assets, works of art, books, old manuscripts from destruction and deterioration? Did they set in train a policy of conservation as well as institutions to carry out this policy? Yes, certainly. There is a long list of decrees from successive Assemblies which legislate on measures relating to the conservation of books, charters, furniture, paintings, monuments. Once nationalised, these objects should be carefully catalogued and deposited in warehouses reserved for the purpose. The first measures dated from November 1789; supplementary measures were taken in 1790 (October), in 1791 (May–June), in 1792 (September), etc. In December 1790 the Commission of Monuments was created, composed of savants, scholars, bibliographers and artists, instructed to look after 'the conservation of monuments, of churches and houses now national property' and, especially, to take care of the monuments to be found in Paris as well as 'repositories of charters, title deeds, papers'. In the middle of the Terror, in October 1793, a month after the law on suspects, the Convention voted through energetic measures against the abuses which were going on in the country and which were causing the 'destruction of monuments, of scientific and artistic objects,

---

[3] Let us mention, as an example, on one side, G. Gautherot, *Le Vandalisme jacobin. Destructions administratives d'archives, d'objets d'art, de monuments religieux à l'époque révolutionnaire*, Paris, 1914; and, on the other: E. Despois, *Le Vandalisme révolutionnaire, fondations littéraires, scientifiques et artistiques de la Convention*, Paris, 1885.

and of the arts and education'. The Commission of Monuments, thought to be ineffective (but also 'unreliable' politically), was replaced by a new organisation, the temporary Commission of the Arts. The Montagnard Convention demanded that it should 'carry out all decrees concerning the conservation of monuments, objects of science and the arts, and their assembly in suitable repositories'; it demanded the application of new methods to ensure the efficient conservation of monuments and that this be done 'throughout the whole of the Empire'.[4] This list of orders, decrees, measures, and institutions could easily be lengthened.

Were, however, the successive revolutionary authorities responsible for the destruction? Did they, if not inspire it, at least tolerate it? Without any doubt, and there is ample proof. The same long list of decrees, orders, etc. repeating the same appeals and admonitions already shows to what extent they remained ineffective, if not unsuitable for the situation. All these measures against the defacement of monuments were required as a consequence of other decisions of the revolutionary authorities, which inevitably put these cultural assets in danger. The nationalisation of the assets of the clergy, the confiscation of the assets of émigrés as well as the sale of these alienated goods, were all measures that of necessity led to the forced removal of entire libraries, of collections of charters and paintings, their piling up in improvised and unconverted storehouses and this, in turn, led to unavoidable damage, to say nothing of the thefts and the wild speculation in works of art and precious manuscripts. The sale, at bargain prices, of cloisters and châteaux left them open to demolition. The famous decree of 14 August 1792 on the suppression of 'signs of the feudal system' with its requirement not to 'leave any longer under the eyes of the French people, monuments raised to pride, to prejudice and to tyranny', condemned countless works of art and monuments to destruction. To be sure, the Convention introduced restrictions, but a month after the decree the enormity of the destruction that it had brought about was so evident that it was necessary to add new restrictions, provisions, admonitions. And yet, in the summer and autumn of 1793, a whole series of decrees condemned all coats of arms and 'emblems of royalty' in all houses, parks, enclosures, churches, etc. And what is to be said of the dechristianising wave, of all the bells and roofs removed, the church towers destroyed in the name of Reason and of 'holy Equality', the defaced statues, the cult objects melted down?

It is objected, from the Republican side, that most frequently this was

---

[4] F. Rücker, *Les Origines de la conservation des monuments historiques en France (1790–1830)*, Paris, 1913. The reports of the hearings of both Commissions bear witness to their untiring efforts to confront these immense tasks; cf. *Procès-verbaux de la Commission des monuments*, published and annotated by L. Tuetey, Paris, 1902–1903; *Procès-verbaux de la Commission temporaire des arts*, published by L.Tuetey, Paris, 1912.

only a question of abuses denounced precisely by revolutionary government itself, that the dechristianising wave lasted a short time, that sculptures and altars were defaced or destroyed in large part by revolutionary
armies carrying out a savage dechristianisation which was itself quickly
halted, that certain measures, finally, were imposed by 'exterior circumstances', the army lacking bronze to cast its cannons. These arguments,
more or less valid, hardly contradict those advanced by the 'denouncers' of
vandalism. Is not the iconoclastic wave to be understood in the context of a
policy launched by the élites of power, started from 'above' and hardly
followed 'below'? Were the brave *sans-culottes* who indulged in this
iconoclasm not encouraged – notably in Year II – by authority and did not
the sanctions remain a dead letter? Did people not continue to engage in
financial speculation and, therefore, to calmly destroy (the example of
Cluny is the most striking), throughout the period of the Directory when
'external circumstances' did not exist?

Neither of the opposing sides seems to attach any importance to the
Thermidorean period, when nevertheless the discourse that denounced
vandalism asserted itself. For some this is because they are reluctant to give
any credit to the 'reaction', which would then have the merit of stopping the
destruction, as the Revolution in its 'heroic' hours had a very strong desire
to be the protector of the arts and culture. Moreover, the cultural creations
of the Thermidorean period – such as the Ecole Polytechnique, the Ecole
Normale and the Museum of French Monuments – accord with the
extension of initiatives begun during the Montagnard period. The 'detractors' of vandalism minimise the importance of Thermidor for quite
different reasons. Thermidor, in the final reckoning, denounced vandalism
without really stopping its flow. The same spirit of devastation, inherent in
the Revolution, ran right through it, and the only difference from one
period to another was the intensity of this spirit. Nothing was reconstructed
after Thermidor, and Lenoir's Museum of French Monuments was, at the
very most, a cemetery of mutilated sculptures, where so-called preservation
was, very often, only another means of mutilation. The polemical speeches
on vandalism agree, nevertheless, that the will to destruction was more
asserted than effective. After all, Lyon, a town condemned to disappearance by the Convention, still exists ... Some see in this the proof that verbal
violence is more important than action and that the Revolution, even if it
sometimes fell into excesses which were always required by 'external
circumstances', finally succeeded in overcoming them. Others find in this
the confirmation of a will to destruction which, lacking time and material
means, could not be fully carried out. If it had been possible, France would
have been deprived of all its cultural heritage.

Both sides demonstrate only the internal contradictions of the Revolution's cultural policy. From the beginning, it paraded a cultural vocation which gave birth to hopes and dreams and also caused setbacks. It professed to be the daughter of the Enlightenment, the single legitimate heir of the 'educated mind'. In consequence, revolutionary power granted itself the role of *administrator*, if not of the entire national cultural heritage, then at least of the part which found itself, as a matter of fact, *nationalised*. (This nationalisation occurred as a result of different political and social measures – confiscation of the assets of the clergy and émigrés – but didn't these measures also have a cultural dimension? Could they be understood apart from this aspect?) It was the duty of the authority representing the Nation to place these cultural assets at the nation's service and no longer to restrict them to a handful of privileged people, to be the protector of the arts, to establish them, therefore, in a *cultural* arena which would then conform with the democratic *political* arena. The successive revolutionary governments claimed this duty and responsibility loudly and constantly; and they promptly stumbled against all the practical difficulties that the efficient administration of nationalised cultural assets presents: a lack of premises, of competent personnel who are loyal to the new regime, lack of financial resources, etc. Upon this deficient infrastructure was grafted, especially during the 'heroic' period, the revolutionary illusion: thanks to 'revolutionary energy', which Barère compared to the sun of Africa that makes plants grow more quickly, any project could be carried out very rapidly, in the space of, if not several months, at least one or two years. Now of course, the 'revolutionary sun' caused the rapid growth of a harvest of projects: but as for their realisation, the sun was not enough: the mass of cultural assets that needed looking after turned out to be too great (more than a million books piled up in improvised depôts, across the whole country), and if the means were lacking, the purposes were imprecise. 1789 claimed to be the continuator of a certain cultural past but above all a *break* which gave a new departure to History. Its ambition was therefore *to regenerate and to purify*, especially when faced with a cultural heritage soiled by centuries of tyranny and prejudice. But to regenerate and to purify are two words of the period which barely conceal an insurmountable contradiction: it was necessary to conserve the past, but not *all* of the past, and only on condition that it had *eliminated* from it what was not worthy of the attention of a people itself regenerated, and what did not deserve to be preserved and integrated into the new civilisation to be created. (The élites were aware that this people was, for the most part, still deep in 'prejudices' and illiteracy, but they would discover the political and cultural effects of this only in the course of the Revolution.) The revolutionary élites had no doubt that they possessed infallible criteria, founded both on the attainments of the Enlightenment and on the progress of the Revolution, for embarking on a selection of their heritage. Now, these criteria will always remain fluid, and will keep coming into question. They will prove to be practically indefinable. The frontiers between destruction and preservation are unstable, elusive. Examples abound. Thus, the famous decree on the suppression of 'emblems of royalty and the feudal system' instructed the temporary Commission of the Arts to 'watch over' the preservation of objects which could be of 'essential interest to the arts'. But were royal statues of 'essential' interest to the arts or were they simply 'emblems of tyranny'? Was the obliteration of the coats-of-arms on a painting destroying it or preserving it? In Year II, Urbain Domergue, head of the Bureau of Bibliography, wanted to speed up the work of establishing a union catalogue of all nationalised books, an immense labour which dragged on despite the efforts of the Commission entrusted with the task. Meanwhile, the books, piled up in improvised stores, were rotting. So to *conserve* what 'genius has fathered for the happiness and glory of the peoples', would it not be necessary to *get rid of* useless and harmful works, like, for example, those which 'are not worth the slip of paper on which the titles have been copied'? So it would be necessary to 'wield the revolutionary scalpel in our vast stores of books and cut away all the gangrenous limbs of the bibliographic body'. Domergue consented to keeping, at the very most, one or two copies 'of all the productions of human foolishness' on the same grounds that a botanist puts poisonous plants in his herbal. The rest, all that theologico-aristocratico-royalist rubbish, could be sold abroad. The Republic could profit from this in two ways: 'it would obtain money for its armies and induce in the minds of its enemies, by means of these books, vertigo and delirium'.[5]

The same contradictions can be found in the educational policy and achievement of the Revolution, as well as the extremist strategies which proposed to cut through them by applying the 'revolutionary scalpel'. An absorbing and passionate debate began at the very heart of political discourse on the choice or choices to be made concerning the guiding models of culture and morality, relations between culture and power, tradition and innovation, liberalism and central planning, religion and secularity in a democratic society which was still to be invented.[6] To these complex problems was added the religious question, which cut across the

---

[5]  'Rapport fait au Comité d'instruction publique', by Urbain Domergue, head of the Bureau of Bibliography, in J. Guillaume, *Procès-verbaux du Comité d'instruction publique de la Convention nationale*, Paris, 1891–1907, vol. 2, p. 798. The remarkable paper of P. Riberette, *Les Bibliothèques françaises pendant la Révolution (1789–1795). Recherches sur un essai de catalogue collectif*, Paris, 1970, brings out all the contradictions and difficulties with which the enterprise of creating a 'union catalogue' struggled. It must be added that the Committee of Public Instruction rejected Domergue's proposals.

[6]  We have discussed these problems more widely in Baczko, ed., *Education pour la démocratie*, pp. 8–58.

entire revolutionary cultural experience (and, quite particularly, educational experience). The Revolution does not have the same universal content in all places and at all times; the same actions do not necessarily possess the same cultural and social significance. This is the case with iconoclastic gestures: in the course of certain revolutionary festivals in Paris, when feudal title-deeds were officially burnt, the organisers took care to preserve the ancient charters, considered to be 'precious monuments'. This was not at all the case with the peasants who lit fires of joy in the country during the 'Great Fear' of 1789 or the festivals of Year II. Dechristianising iconoclasm, inspired and directed from above by revolutionary élites, did not necessarily have the same cultural significance as the devastating actions perpetrated by the revolutionary armies in the little towns and villages. Jacobin power imagined itself to be a centralising force; in reality, France remained much more federalist. A unificatory decree was put into practice in different ways, depending on the *département* or commune, grafted onto the traditional local conflicts and antagonisms. The revolutionary Committee which decided to destroy the busts of the philosophers at Ermenonville, in the park which surrounded the Ile des Peupliers and the tomb of Rousseau, since they represented 'Englishmen', certainly committed a 'vandal' act. It was also a 'vandal' act to destroy, systematically and by engaging a specialist entrepreneur, the royal tombs at Franciade, hitherto Saint-Denis, as likewise it was a 'vandal' act to install a sugar refinery in the Abbey of Saint-Germain which caused an accidental fire in 1794 that destroyed one of the richest libraries; other 'vandal' acts: speculation in national assets and the demolition, as swiftly as possible, of this or that house, this or that cloister. The list would be long. These acts are vandal in their destructive effects and their irreparable damage, but they are, however, different in their socio-cultural and ideological meanings. There existed during the Revolution several *vandalisms*, in the same way that there were several dechristianisations.[7] All too often these different vandalisms are merged together. All the more reason, then, to comprehend as far as possible their different types and forms, the extent and the detail of each wave, according to region, in order to grasp more distinctly a complex cultural and social phenomenon.[8] An analysis of the kinds of discourse held at the period on vandalism already allows an understanding of the symbolic and cultural stakes of the Terror.

---

[7] Cf. R. Cobb, *The people's armies*, London, 1987; B. Plongeron, *Conscience religieuse en révolution*, Paris, 1969.

[8] Cf. D. Hermant, 'Destruction et vandalisme pendant la Révolution française', *Annales E.S.C.*, no. 4, 1978, an innovatory work which explodes the traditional framework and proposes several interesting lines of research, but not all of whose conclusions we share.

### Barbarians amongst us ...

In the language of the Enlightenment, the vandals figure as 'the most barbaric of the barbaric'; they are even referred to as 'barbaric vandals'.[9]

It is a common-place of revolutionary rhetoric to describe as 'barbaric' the past that is to be destroyed: privileges, unjust laws, the fiscal system, corporations and even the old schools. Barbaric signifies both tyrannical and ignorant. Another common-place of a discourse that claims to be both revolutionary and enlightened: every tyranny reposes on ignorance and generates barbarism. The *ancien régime*, barbaric and tyrannical, kept the Nation in ignorance out of necessity; as for freedom, this could be founded only on Enlightenment; it was the natural enemy of 'barbaric ignorance'.[10]

However, the accusation of barbarity was also brought against the Revolution, after 14 July. It was revolutionary violence which was the main target. For a man like Rivarol, the taking of the Bastille was hardly the heroic act which established liberty. He remembered only the image of the 'barbarian town' and its populace who massacred innocents, carried their heads on pikes, with 'hands red with blood'. This same populace, a 'species of savage', 'all that the hovels and sewers of the Rue Saint-Honoré could vomit that was most vile', slaughtered the king's bodyguards at Versailles, on 6 October, then escorted the king and his family to Paris, again carrying, under the eyes of their prisoners, heads stuck on pikes. 'Woe betide those who stir up the dregs of a nation! There is no century of Enlightenment for the populace; it is neither French, nor English, nor Spanish. The populace is always and in every country the same: always cannibal, always man-eating.'[11] The increase in revolutionary violence, notably after the *journée* of 10 August and during the massacres of September, was even more often condemned as 'barbarian' and 'vandal'. In counter-revolutionary discourse it was a case of the expression of indignation and fear, but also of a sort of exorcism of the Revolution which remained, at bottom, incomprehensible. The 'barbaric' Revolution had come from elsewhere, an invasion which belonged outside history, like a natural catastrophe or a monstrosity (the comparison with 'cannibals', human monsters, is revealing).

[9] Cf. P. Michel, *Un mythe romantique. Les barbares, 1789–1848*, Lyon, 1981; Hermant, 'Destruction et vandalisme'.

[10] This *topos* can be found in texts devoted to national education; cf. for example, in Baczko, ed., *Éducation pour la démocratie*, the remarks of Mirabeau (p. 79), of Talleyrand (p. 109), of Romme (p. 269), of Barère (p. 429). We shall find the same common ground, although the political context will be quite different, in Thermidorean discourse against Robespierre's tyranny.

[11] Rivarol, 'Journal politique et national' in Rivarol, *Œuvres complètes*, Paris, 1808, vol. 4, pp. 64 *et seq.*, pp. 286 *et seq.* In the descriptions of the massacres, the terms 'barbarians', 'vandals', and 'cannibals' keep returning; on the other hand, the revolutionary pamphlets vilify the king as a 'blood-drinker' and a 'cannibal'.

Only Mallet du Pan, one of the most perceptive of counter-revolutionary observers and analysts, used the idea-image of the vandal not just to brand the Revolution, but to *understand* it. As early as 1790, he noticed that the analogy between revolutionary events and the barbarian invasions had a limited explanatory power. It was only to the point if it brought out the *novelty*, the unprecedented character of the Revolution. Of course, in its ferocious and hideous aspects, the Revolution recalled the invasion of the barbarians, evoked that 'memorable overthrow'. But, this time, the 'Huns and Herules, the Vandals and the Goths will not come from the North, nor from the Black Sea, *they are amongst us*'. Beyond the 'instability of events' which rushed along at an unprecedented pace, it was necessary to disentangle the 'destructive nature' of the Revolution as well as its overall aim. To bring these out, Mallet du Pan appealed to a very recent neologism, the use of which underlined the unprecedented character of the revolutionary phenomenon. What was at stake in the Revolution was no longer, as was thought at its beginning, the old or the new regime, Republic or monarchy, but civilisation. It followed that the struggle against the Revolution was not an internal French matter; nor was it a war, like so many others, between nations and states. Mallet du Pan launched an appeal for a new crusade in the name of *civilisation*. The whole of 'old Europe' was in danger of death faced with this 'system of invasion' from within and which was like no other. It was the 'last fight of civilisation' in which 'every European is today involved'.[12]

It was only at the end of a long and remarkable detour that the revolutionary élites would come to the strange discovery, following Mallet du Pan, that the 'barbarians' could be found amongst them. Of course, they indignantly rejected the aristocratic accusations: the Revolution was not a purely destructive force. On the contrary, its objectives and its work were essentially constructive. If the regeneration of the Nation passed through destruction, it was precisely because the past was 'barbaric', in the manner of the Bastille, symbol of 'barbarian tyranny'. In the same way the interior and exterior enemies of the Revolution became 'savage and barbarian hordes' launched by a coalition of tyrants against France. But a sort of fixation on 'barbarism', which might become established in the Revolution itself and pervert its cause, worked secretly on people's minds. It appeared openly when faced with an explosion of brutal and blind violence, especially

---

[12] Cf. M. Mallet du Pan, *Considérations sur la nature de la Révolution française et sur les causes qui en prolongent la durée*, London, 1793, pp. v *et seq.*, pp. 27 *et seq.* These 'barbarians amongst us' were so many 'brigands without bread and leaders without property', 'a people freed from fear of heaven and the courts'. With mass conscription, France had been transformed into a 'vast barracks' and 'every militant *sans-culotte* will have the right to the distribution of land and booty': *ibid.*, p. 34.

after the massacres of September which the Girondins denounced as 'barbaric' while the Jacobins called for 'a veil to be thrown' over them. It also appeared in the interminable debates on the new system of public education, when it had to be admitted that the Revolution, by abolishing the old institutions, had created an enormous vacuum which it was unable to fill. Because of this, the Nation risked plunging into ignorance and barbarism. 'Let us not have, as our domestic enemies allege, a revolution of Goths and Vandals', cried Mirabeau in 1791, defending his plan for public education and calling on the members of the Constituent Assembly to maintain the 'talents', arts and letters, in order to avoid the danger that the Revolution, 'an achievement of letters and philosophy, might make genius regret the period of despotism'.[13] In the debates on public education in December 1792 and the spring of 1793, this anxiety became sharper and sharper and employed the same vocabulary. Accordingly, Fouché barely concealed his anxiety in his report of 8 December 1793, presenting to the Convention in the name of the Committee of Public Instruction the plan for a decree on the sale of college assets:

The houses of education in our *départements* are now no more than ruins ... One might say that we are going to fall back into the *barbarism of our first beginnings*; one might say that we desire only the liberty of the savage who sees in the Revolution just the sterile pleasure of overturning the world and not the means of ordering it, of making it perfect, of making it freer and happier; one might say that, just like the tyrants, we deliberately leave man in shadows and brutishness, in order to transform him, at the mercy of our interests and our passions, into a ferocious beast.

Of course, this was only a slander; nevertheless it grasped 'certain features' in order to turn them against the Revolution. This was an anxiety that could be soothed by exalting the people who already felt deeply 'that it can be free only through education, that liberty and education are inseparable and that they need to unite to make human nature perfect, and to fulfil our twin hope of becoming the example and model of all the peoples of the earth'.[14] It was also an anxiety that increased, as the documents of the Commission of Monuments and the renewed decrees of the Convention bear witness, when confronted with the destruction of books, the deterioration of paintings, the mutilation of sculptures, that had, however, become 'assets of the Nation', a condition which should have ensured their protection. The responsibility for this was shifted onto strangers and men of ill-will, onto the 'outrages of aristocrats' (they deliberately destroyed their own property as soon as they were deprived of it ...), onto greedy speculators and onto

[13]  Mirabeau, 'Travail sur l'éducation publique', in Baczko, ed., *Education pour la démocratie*, pp. 79–80.
[14]  Cf. Guillaume, *Procès-verbaux*, vol. 1, p. 340; cf. also *ibid.*, p. 122 (speech by J.-M. Chénier), pp. 276–7 (text of Jeanbon Saint-André).

igorance – all forces hostile to the Revolution and, therefore, *external* to it.[15] Even ignorance was only the heritage of a pernicious and barbaric past. Care was taken, however, to avoid saying clearly who the ignorant were, as this ignorance was an established fact as well as a mark of dishonour. Because in identifying the ignorant, was there not a risk of insulting the key symbol of all revolutionary imagery: the sovereign People? How could it be ignorant? To admit this would be to join the ranks of those counter-revolutionaries who 'paint us in the eyes of the nations as a ferocious and barbarian people, that wants to live in the crassest ignorance, even of the first truths',[16] and running that risk would be dangerous in the period of the law on suspects. What is implicit and unspoken can only be guessed at in the description of the *recipient* of these appeals which sometimes take an emotional turn. The people, 'armed with its club', could, at the beginning of the Revolution, have 'struck everything'; now, in Year II, this people, a new Hercules, should understand that 'these houses, these palaces which they still look at with indignant eyes no longer belong to the enemy; they belong to themselves'. And it is with them, 'the French people, protector of all that is useful and good', that the responsibility lay to declare themselves 'the enemy of all the enemies of letters' as well as to guard against 'misguided hands' destroying what was respected even by the 'conquering barbarians'.[17]

One could add more quotations illustrating the dilemma, if not the impasse of the revolutionary élites: to preserve intact, beyond any suspicion of barbarism, the representations of the Revolution and the sovereign People, and to denounce, in one way or another, the 'barbaric' acts that, from all the evidence, were not the acts of princes or priests but were to be ascribed, well and truly, to the patriotic and civic behaviour of the revolutionary armies, of the surveillance Committees, of agents of the Republic, protected, if not encouraged, by a representative *en mission*. In other words, how to denounce 'barbarism' and 'barbarians' as forces *exterior and hostile* to the Revolution when, from all the evidence, the presence of 'barbarians amongst us' was an established fact? How could anyone do this, especially in the middle of the Terror, when words were

[15]  Cf. Tuetey, *Procès-verbaux de la Commission des monuments*; Rücker, *Origines de la conservation*, pp. 26–9; 76 *et seq.*; 93 *et seq.*

[16]  Order of the district of Jussey (Haute-Saône) on 8 Floréal, Year II, quoted from Riberette, *Bibliothèques françaises*, p. 51.

[17]  *Instruction sur la manière d'inventorier et de conserver, dans toute l'étendue de la République, tous les objets qui peuvent servir aux arts, aux sciences et à l'enseignement*, Paris, Year II. This text, discussed by the temporary Commission of the Arts in November–December 1793, was adopted on 15 Ventôse, Year II (5 March 1794) by the Committee of Public Instruction. Certainly written by Vicq d'Azyr, the instruction was signed by Lindet, in his role as president of the temporary Commission of the Arts, and by Bouquier, president of the Committee of Public Instruction. Cf. Guillaume, *Procès-verbaux*, vol. 3, p. 545.

carefully weighed and fear tormented the intellectual élites who were the product of the *ancien régime* even if they had sincerely joined the revolutionary cause (which is far from being always the case)? Revolutionary discourse got round these obstacles by sliding from the very vague condemnation of 'barbarians' to the invention of the *vandal plot*. Is this just a combination, a faking, a shrewd manipulation of words? Matters are more complex. Even when they admit that this is a matter of manipulation, are not the manipulators themselves manipulated by images that are out of their control? The success, sociologically speaking, of an idea-image – and that of the 'vandal plot' will be a good illustration – is revealing of the collective imagination in which it is set as well as of the discourse which puts it into circulation. The 'vandal plot' combined not only two words but also *two obsessions*. The first was that of the political and intellectual élites confronted with the 'barbarism' which the Revolution had caused to loom up from the ranks of the people and of which the destructions were the most visible sign, the symbol of a danger which threatened a whole culture – the culture in which these same élites recognised themselves and through which they identified themselves. But a second obsession – which is familiar to us from the rumour of Robespierre-the-king – undermined the revolutionary imagination and *mentalités*, with a quite different sociological scope: the fear of the many-faceted plot unceasingly hatched by the enemies of the revolutionary cause.[18]

This second obsession would show, under the Terror, an astonishing manipulative malleability. It was the time for generalised suspicion of those who had not yet been unmasked, who were hiding in the army, in the revolutionary committees and societies, in the Convention itself. A full *technique aiming to exploit* this obsession was being perfected for service in the political struggle. It was largely utilised not only by the political professionals at the national level (and, obviously, by the police) but also to settle accounts on the local level. In the concept of the 'plot', the 'unmasked enemies' are interchangeable. The art and technique of manipulation are brought to bear by a fusion which removes the frontiers between all the possible 'enemies', especially between those which are visible and exterior – tyrants, aristocrats, etc. – and those who 'are hidden' and bury themselves in the ranks of the people. The manipulatory technique is plastic: it proceeds by a kind of moulding of the profile of the new 'enemy', to be unmasked, on the model furnished by the old 'enemy', already 'unveiled'. In tortuous political circumstances, with sharp lurches from side to side, the slide of ideologies and beliefs towards pure manipulation becomes irreversible (inversely, the practice of manipulation nourishes in its turn suspicion,

---

[18]  On the idea of the plot and its central place in the revolutionary imagination, cf. Furet, *Penser la Révolution*, pp. 79 *et seq.*

informing, and ideological exaggeration, until political activity finishes by involving only an ever more restricted number of protagonists, plagued by personal grudges and animosities). The 'discovery' of the 'vandal plot' is only an example of this complex interplay of obsession and ideology, of the social imagination and manipulation where, in a short time and a precise context, the political and cultural fear of the 'barbarian danger' turns into a discourse which is employed in the political struggle and in police repression.

On 21 Nivôse, Year II, Grégoire presented to the Convention, in the name of the Committee of Public Instruction, a report on the inscriptions on public monuments. It was proposed to the legislators, who had already passed 'sensible measures', that others should be added in order to ensure 'the preservation of ancient inscriptions whose existence time has respected'. The report, with a single exception, brought hardly anything new to the discourse on the defacement of monuments. The Convention 'wisely ordered the destruction of all that bore the imprint of royalism and feudalism'. Even the 'fine verses of Borbonius inscribed on the door of the Arsenal' were not saved, and rightly so since 'they were tarnished by flattery of a tyrant'. (He meant Henry IV.) But these sensible decrees were not enough, for also being destroyed were ancient monuments that should be preserved 'in their totality'. These monuments were 'medals in another form, and what reasonable man would not tremble at the very thought of taking a hammer to the antiquities of Orange or of Nîmes'? To destroy them would be a barbaric act. Now, the sole novelty in Grégoire's report is precisely the definition of barbarism: 'One cannot inspire too much horror among the citizens for this *vandalism* which knows only destruction.' The word is underlined in the text to show that it is a neologism. Retrospectively, its introduction has been considered as a sort of turning-point in the history of the discourse on 'vandals'. The text however is not conspicuous for its originality. It takes up the clichés already mentioned and 'vandalism' is swiftly attributed to 'counter-revolutionary' barbarism which seeks to 'impoverish us by dishonouring us'. The agents of 'vandalism' are hardly distinguished from other, always treacherous, counter-revolutionaries. In pleading the cause of ancient inscriptions ('to destroy them would be a loss; to translate them would be a kind of anachronism'), Grégoire praised the superiority of French – destined to become the 'universal idiom' of which Leibniz dreamt – over the ancient languages, in the same way that he exalted the superiority of the French revolutionaries over the 'ancient republicans'. Of course, 'we cherish their memory', but who could prefer 'on any terms to be Greek or Roman, when he is French'? This is either over-excitement or a figure of speech which recalls another: in his report on the project for a decree proposing the suppression of the former academies, Grégoire did not hesitate to declare that 'true genius is nearly always *sans-culotte*'.[19]

Three months later, on the occasion of his report on bibliography, Grégoire returned to the attack of the 'counter-revolutionaries' who destroyed our monuments. If the neologism 'vandalism' was not re-used, the speech innovated on another point. In mentioning 'the conspiracies of our enemies to degrade and impoverish a people who, despite all attempts, will be always rich and always great', these enemies who committed crimes in order to 'blame them on us and call us barbarians', Grégoire was not content to denounce the defacement of monuments. The danger was much more serious and general. So, 'it is suggested, without any distinction between talents that are useful or harmful, that a learned man is a curse in a State'. What was more, 'in Paris, in Marseille and elsewhere it was proposed to burn the libraries' on the pretext that 'theology, it was said, was fanaticism; jurisprudence, chicanery; history, lies; philosophy, dreams; science, not needed'. All culture was therefore threatened and this at the moment when, more than ever, it was necessary to 'revolutionise the arts'. This arduous labour should, however, be carried out according to the lines laid down by the Convention and its Committees and not in a savage and disorderly manner. So it was necessary to put 'absurd books on the Index of reason', but these could be exchanged with other countries. As for the 'enemies', responsible for these 'barbaric acts', Grégoire took up the old clichés: aristocrats, foreign speculators, etc. But he added a new enemy to this list-litany: 'fools have slandered genius to console themselves for not possessing any'; the counter-revolutionaries who destroyed the monuments hid themselves 'under the mask of patriotism'. Vague allusions which the text does not make explicit; moreover, the predominating impression is that the indictment of the 'fools' and the 'false patriots' who threatened the sciences and the talents had been added at the last moment to a report dealing with another subject, the work on bibliography.[20] The context of this report, however, clarifies these allusions. In fact, Grégoire was speaking to the Convention on 22 Germinal, eighteen days after the execution of Hébert and at the very beginning of the trial of Chaumette; in his first report

[19]  *Rapport sur les inscriptions des monuments publics*, by citizen Grégoire, in *Œuvres* of the abbé Grégoire (reprint), Paris, 1977, vol. 2; *Rapport et projet de décret présenté au nom du Comité d'instruction publique, le 8 août 1793, ibid.* On the history of the neologism itself cf. J. Guillaume, 'Grégoire et le vandalisme', *Révolution française*, 1901; F. Brunot, *Histoire de la langue française*, Paris, 1967, vol. 9, pp. 857 *et seq.*; M. Frey, *Les Transformations du vocabulaire français pendant la Révolution (1789–1800)*, Paris, 1925, p. 265.

[20]  Grégoire, *Rapport sur la bibliographie*, presented in the name of the Committee of Public Instruction, on 22 Germinal, Year II, in Grégoire, *Œuvres*, vol. 2, pp. 208–12; cf. Guillaume, 'Grégoire et le vandalisme'.

on vandalism, Grégoire would later set out exactly the same criticisms by denouncing Hébert, this time without ambiguity. Moreover, other documents of the Committee of Public Safety as well as of the Committee of Public Instruction attacked Hébert. Barère, a member of the Committee of Public Safety responsible for the problems of education, in his report on the 'revolutionary manufacture of powder', while praising the 'revolutionary courses of instruction' which involved the greatest experts in the training of the skilled men which the Republic so badly needed, thundered against a 'plot'; a 'faction' was endangering both science and the Revolution:

This revolutionary mode of public courses has become a standard model of education for the Committee which will serve it well for all branches useful to the Republic; and you will soon feel the need for it *in the heart of a vandal or Visigoth faction that still wishes to proclaim ignorance, persecute educated men, banish genius, and paralyse thought.*[21]

This forceful description of the 'vandal faction' came in the context of an entire campaign fought by the Committee of Public Safety. In fact, Payan, recently appointed by the same Committee as commissioner of the executive Commission of Public Instruction, was at the same time writing a report on 'the corrections to the opera *Castor et Pollux*; libretto by Bernard, music by Candeille'. It was an idle excuse: a 'proof-reader' had replaced those words in the libretto, which seemed to him to be contrary to republican morality, with others more suitable. So, instead of 'present from the Gods', he put 'present from the sky'; for 'divine friendship' he substituted 'celestial reason'; 'love leaves you constant' was replaced by 'who follows the laws with constancy', etc. The procedure was common in Year II; in older plays even 'monsieur' was replaced by 'citizen' and the former 'vous' by the republican use of 'tu' ... But, from its first lines, the report forcefully announced the true target of its attacks. 'Ignorance, crudeness, barbarity, in a word *all that can be called Hébertism in the arts*, marching to counter-revolution by the brutalising of thought, like political Hébertism with its plots, disorder and murder.' The report would be sent to all the popular societies of the Republic, to all the small towns and communes where no one had ever dreamt of opera performances. For the libretto of *Castor et Pollux* became an example of a vast plot which extended sinister political aims into the cultural domain.

---

[21] Barère, *Rapport sur l'état de la fabrication du salpêtre et de la poudre*, presented on 26 Messidor, Year II; cf. Guillaume, *Procès-verbaux*, vol. 4, p. 820. On the revolutionary courses which served as an example for the Ecole de Mars as well as the Ecole Normale, cf. Baczko, ed., *Education pour la démocratie*, pp. 38 *et seq.* In Floréal, Year II, the Committee of Public Safety in fact took a series of measures aiming to encourage the arts, the sciences and the fine arts: cf. the long list in Guillaume, *Procès-verbaux*, vol. 4, pp. 248–53.

Never were the attacks on the moral spirit of the nation seen more closely linked to the crimes which attack its government ... The hydra of factions had raised all its heads at once, to clasp all limbs of the political body; one found it in theatres and in public squares, on the rostrums and in journalists' lairs; serpents hissed on all sides; everywhere it exuded its poisons.

'The *vandal scythe*' had thus fallen upon all culture with an unheard-of fury. In order to seize power and blow up revolutionary government the 'factious' were proposing 'to mark everything or rather, brand everything with the seal of that man whose surname alone [le père Duchesne] was a revolting platitude'. Of course, republican virtue and vigilance, embodied by the Committee of Public Safety and by the revolutionary Tribunal, had undone Hébert's plot. The task was not, however, complete. The Commission of Public Instruction had as its duty to 'prosecute the idiocies of literature, just as the government crushed the crimes of Hébert; they were the accessories to his crimes and prepared their power; they dared to reappear; thus the *roots of a tree* are still alive when its top has been thrown down by a thunderbolt.'[22]

The denunciation of 'Hébertism in the arts' does more than point to a scapegoat whom revolutionary power could blame for 'crudeness and barbarism'. A complete paradigm is also invented. In fact, the frontier which separates 'us', the enlightened revolutionaries, from 'the vandal and Visigoth faction', finds itself promptly displaced. The representation of the vandal retains its primary function: to point out *the other*, opposed to civilisation and the Enlightenment, which cannot be dissociated from the revolutionary cause. But this other has since slipped in amongst 'us' and done so in a treacherous and ignoble manner, as is shown by the idea-image of the 'plot'. The men who wielded the 'vandal scythe' were certainly enemies, but *hidden* enemies. This explains how all these evils can arise in

[22] 'Commission d'instruction publique. Rapport sur les corrections de l'opéra de "Castor et Pollux", paroles de Bernard, musique de Candeille', *Moniteur*, 7 Thermidor, Year II. The report is not dated; for the probable date of its drawing up, cf. Guillaume, *Procès-verbaux*, vol. 4, p. 714. The denunciation of 'Hébertism in art' seems otherwise to be inspired by the indictment launched by Camille Desmoulins in *Le Vieux Cordelier* against Hébert and his obscene and barbarous language, which compromised the Republic.

But is there nothing more disgusting, more obscene than most of your newspaper? Do you not know, Hébert, that when the tyrants of Europe wish to disgrace the Republic, when they wish to make their slaves think that France is *covered with the shadows of barbarism*, that Paris, that town so vaunted for its atticism and its taste, is peopled with Vandals; do you not know, unfortunate man, that it is the scraps from your paper that they place in their gazettes ... as if it were the language of the Convention and of the Committee of Public Safety, as if your filth were that of the Nation; as if a sewer were the Seine? (*Le Vieux Cordelier*, no. 5, Nivôse, Year II)

We quote from the excellent edition by Pierre Pachet: Camille Desmoulins, *Le Vieux Cordelier*, Paris, 1987, p. 85. As is well known, Desmoulins was executed on 5 April, 1794, ten days after the execution of Hébert.

the Revolution – the destruction of monuments, the persecution of scientists and artists, etc. – and pervert the noble cause. 'Barbarism' is hardly inherent in it; on the contrary, the fact that the conspirators would like to debase the 'moral spirit of the Nation' is an additional proof of the deep identity between the Revolution and the Enlightenment. At the same time, the cultural and educational vocation of revolutionary power is also confirmed. 'Hébertism in the arts' represents a ramification in the cultural domain of the essentially *political* plot which attacked this power. It is also through political means that the very roots of 'vandalism' have to be dug up, by unmasking trouble-makers and punishing them with full 'revolutionary energy'. The anti-vandal discourse, by embracing the idea of the Hébertist plot, therefore asserts itself as a *terrorist* discourse; it is an appeal for the denunciation and punishment of the guilty, both suspects and plotters.

Who was the target of the Committee of Public Safety in launching this violent campaign against 'Hébertism in the arts', three months after the execution of Hébert himself? No precise name was mentioned but the *-ism* indicates that they were thinking of a complete system with many ramifications. During the trial of Hébert, there was no question of 'vandalism'; the Hébertists were accused of having plotted against the revolutionary government by setting themselves up against the authority of the people whom they were starving, with the support of foreign powers, if not at the very instigation of Pitt. Revolutionary power seemed to open an entire cultural offensive by broadening the political 'plot' into a cultural plot, which was expressed by the 'crudity and barbarism' of the 'vandal and Visigoth faction' who were persecuting scientists and the arts. This 'revolting platitude' of *Père Duchesne*, did it not symbolise social and cultural behaviour, a 'populist' language and style of life, which in Year II the political élites had themselves borrowed?[23]

We shall never know what turn a campaign against 'vandalism' directed by the 'terrorists' and 'Robespierrists' would have taken. The report of Payan announcing it was published in the *Moniteur* only on 7 Thermidor (the very day of the execution of the poet André Chénier ...). It was also in the context of the struggle against the 'vandal and Visigoth faction' that the Committee of Public Instruction, on 27 Messidor, gave Grégoire and Fourcroy responsibility for 'gathering the facts and preparing a report to

[23] In his analysis of Hébertism, which is very questionable as a whole, A. Soboul has pertinently brought out the mistrust of Jacobin power with regard to this infatuation for a certain 'populist' manner. Cf. A. Soboul, *Mouvement populaire et gouvernement révolutionnaire en l'an II, 1793–1794*, Paris, 1973, pp. 372 *et seq.*, p. 391 (trial of Chaumette).

unveil the counter-revolutionary manoeuvres by which the enemies of the Republic attempt to lead the people into ignorance, by destroying monuments of the arts and by persecuting the men who unite patriotism with talent.'[24] So if the Convention could quickly, scarcely a month after 9 Thermidor, work out its anti-vandal discourse, which was the cornerstone of the *anti-terrorist* discourse, this was because a report against 'vandalism' had already been ordered in the middle of the Terror and because the *terrorist* schema of a 'vandal plot' had been invented and set to work in the struggle against 'Hébertism of the arts'.

### Robespierre-the-vandal ...

Out of the three famous reports by Grégoire, which mark a new stage in the development of the discourse on the 'vandals' and consolidate the stereotype of 'vandalism', certain leading themes emerge.[25]

a) Grégoire presented his reports to the Convention *after 9 Thermidor* (14 Fructidor, Year II; 8 Brumaire and 24 Frimaire, year III). The break they mark in the working out of the discourse on vandalism is quite evidently bound up with the 'fall of the tyrant', a break which nevertheless did not remove the continuity of the central concept of the 'vandal plot'. The Convention, which very quickly made the denunciation of 'vandalism' its warhorse in the fight against 'Robespierrism' and 'Robespierre's tail', had not, to tell the truth, given much attention to Grégoire's reports themselves. Grégoire, it is true, was hardly lucky in his choice of the dates for his speeches. So the first report was read before a half-empty chamber. On the same day the explosion at the powder factory of Grenelle had taken place, claiming several victims; its cause was not yet known: accident, sabotage or prelude to a 'Robespierrist' insurrection. The reports did not lead to major debates and aroused no objections. The Convention ordered them to be printed, and the first report was published in an edition of ten thousand copies, distributed throughout the country where it found a wide response (the temporary Commission of the Arts, replying to requests from local administrations, decided to send several hundred extra copies).[26] After the second report, the Convention ordered an enquiry in all districts on the state of libraries and historic buildings of the sciences and the arts; it also promised to make the struggle against vandalism 'the order of the day' and to hear a report on the subject every month. These good intentions lasted

---

[24] J. Guillaume, *Procès-verbaux*, vol. 4, p. 819.

[25] J. Guillaume has provided a critical edition of Grégoire's first report; cf. 'Grégoire et le vandalisme'. His commentary and notes, remarkably exact, are however marked by the historiographical quarrel of the period. The three reports are reprinted in Grégoire, *Œuvres*, vol. 2.

[26] Cf. L. Tuetey, *Procès-verbaux de la Commission temporaire des arts*, vol. 1, p. 515.

only one month. Nevertheless, with the last report the neologism 'vandalism' became part of current speech: swiftly assimilated, it kept returning in the debates of the Assembly, in the press, in official and private correspondence. The 'axe of vandalism', the 'fury of vandalism', so many expressions which from now on went without saying. So, to take a particularly savoury example, the administrators of Jussey (Haute-Saône) announced that 'vandalism has not had the barbarous satisfaction of destroying anything in our administration'. But they announced this with a twin regret. For it was, alas, proof that their *arrondissement* had no monuments and, with that, no possible opportunity of showing their patriotism and of 'fighting [vandalism] in order to save from its fury what should be respected even by the erosion of time ...'[27]

b) Grégoire's reports broke new ground in one important respect. Contrary to previous denunciations of the defacement of monuments, which remained general and woolly, the indictment was now extended by a *long list* (which got larger from one report to another) of monuments, 'objects of the sciences and the arts', which had been destroyed: the works of Bouchardon in Paris; the excellent copies of Diana and of the Medici Venus at Marly; the tomb of Turenne at Franciade (previously Saint-Denis; however, Grégoire does not consider it vandal that 'the national hammer rightly struck the tyrants, even in their graves' in the course of the destruction of the royal tombs); at Nancy, within a few hours, '100,000 *écus*-worth of statues and paintings were burnt'; at Verdun a Virgin by Houdon was destroyed; at Versailles a head of Jupiter was broken which dated from 'four hundred and forty-two years before the vulgar era'; in Chartres 'it was doubtless useful to remove the lead [from the roofs], for the first thing is to crush our enemies', but the building left exposed continued to fall into disrepair; at Nîmes ancient monuments were destroyed which had been spared even by the Vandal invasion of the fifth century; at Carpentras, two fine figures (of Saint Peter and Saint Paul) were reduced to powder; in the *département* of the Indre they wanted to sell magnificent orange trees 'on the pretext that republicans need apples and not orange trees'; whole libraries rotted in damp stores and very recently the library of the Abbey of Saint-Germain-des-Prés was consumed by fire, etc. It was therefore hardly a matter of isolated cases but of a 'destructive passion' which had descended on the whole country, sparing no *département*: 'On every side, pillage and destruction were the order of the day.' The grandiloquent speeches during the period of the Terror on 'virtue as the order of the day', as well as on the Republic as protectress of the arts and sciences, came up against a brutal reality. It is true that, in Grégoire's long

---

[27] Letter to the Commission of Public Instruction, 22 Brumaire, Year III; quoted from P. Riberette, *Bibliothèques françaises*, p. 96.

list, many details were wrong. To the real facts were added rumours: in Paris, there was a proposal to burn the Bibliothèque Nationale; likewise in Marseille, people wanted to burn *all* the libraries; they tried to destroy all the monuments which honoured France ... (We know very well, however, to what extent the information available to Grégoire was partial and incomplete and that his list could have been longer and more sensational.) The reports on vandalism thus follow a more general tendency, characteristic of anti-terrorist discourse: to spread out in full daylight and in the smallest detail the startling realities of the Terror and confront them with the rhetoric of virtue, of justice, of liberty which sought to justify and sublimate the repression at one and the same time.

Grégoire's reports on vandalism are woven from the cloth manufactured by the trial of the revolutionary Committee of Nantes, followed by that of Carrier. A series of horrors is set out (the revolutionary Tribunal had in the same way revealed the premeditated massacres, the mass drownings, the executions without trial). By this means a *counter-imagery* is established that opposes all the heroic and exalting symbolism of a revolutionary power which is without weakness but remains just in its struggle for victory with the enemy and the guilty. The force and aggression of this counter-imagery come, among other things, from the fact that it permitted the fear repressed for months to be released and expressed without constraint.

This is shown by the wider and wider use which Grégoire made of his neologism. From his first report onwards, he mentioned not only the monuments and 'objects of the sciences and arts' over which 'barbarism wielded its axe'. 'Vandalism' was also the paralysis of public education; reasonable and realistic projects were sabotaged, while others that could only plunge France into ignorance were favoured. 'Vandalism' was also 'a real fanaticism' which persisted in the useless changing of the names of communes and for which 'the mania has gone so far that, if all these misplaced wishes were complied with, soon the whole plain of the Beauce would be called *mountain*'. 'Vandalism' was not a succession of individual and episodic actions; in the manner of the Terror, it was an 'organised system' which attacked 'men of talent'. Again, the reports were not content with generalities, but furnished a long list of scientists, artists, men of letters who had been imprisoned: Dessault, one of the leading surgeons of Europe, who, furthermore, 'teaches trainees for our armies'; Bitaube, 'celebrated translator of Homer', groaned for nine months in a prison, although he had shown his patriotism; La Chabeaussière, author of the *Catéchisme révolutionnaire*, François-Neufchâteau, Volney, Chamfort, who committed suicide, Rouget de l'Isle, who 'through his hymn gave perhaps a hundred thousand men to our armies': all imprisoned. The grand-daughter of Corneille, once sheltered by Voltaire, was detained fourteen months 'under the reign of the vandals' and did not even have 'a bed to rest her head on'.[28] And to finish, the most overwhelming example, which must be 'transmitted to history': that of Lavoisier who expressed the desire 'to delay mounting the scaffold by just fifteen days so that he could complete his experiments, which would be useful to the Republic'. Dumas (vice-president of the revolutionary Tribunal) replied, 'We no longer need chemists.' (It is well known that this phrase, destined to have a long future, was never spoken and that the facts reported by Grégoire are not correct.) With this reference to the punishment of Lavoisier – the pride of both French science and science as a whole – the working out of a counter-imagery took an important step. The 'anti-vandal' cause here found its martyr and, at the same time, its symbol. For the names of the most celebrated 'men of talent' were only examples of a 'disorganising system which spurned all talents'. Had not the same Dumas said that it 'was necessary to guillotine all men of learning'? In Strasbourg 'professors were imprisoned'; in Dijon 'teachers and doctors were driven out to be replaced by the ignorant'; everywhere 'in positions where it was necessary to have a brain, were found men who could use only their hands'. In all of France 'it was necessary to paralyse or destroy men of genius ... it was necessary to refuse them, without distinction, certificates of good citizenship, to shout in the *sections: beware of this man, he has written a book.*' So there could be no doubt: if during 'a whole year of terror and crimes barbarism placed mourning crape on the cradle of the Republic [it was because there existed] *a plan to dry up all the springs of enlightenment*', to destroy 'all the monuments which honour French genius ... in a word *to barbarise us*': a vandal strategy, worthy of these 'new iconoclasts', more impetuous than the old; a premeditated strategy that was not explained by ignorance, which, in itself, was not always a crime. Behind it was hidden *a counter-revolutionary spirit*.

c) Grégoire's reports provide in their turn a reply to the troubling question: how could vandalism strike so deep into the very heart of the Revolution, with the result that the Revolution itself bears responsibility? Grégoire took up the old accusations against the 'aristocrats', the 'rogues', the 'speculators'. Their activities did not, however, explain the extent and the systematic character of vandalism, despite the many decrees of revolutionary power. To understand these hidden causes, one must refer to 'a series of facts, the bringing together of which is a mark of understanding'. Then he denounced the 'old conspirators', already unmasked under the Terror, Hébertists and Dantonists confused together, the very same people Grégoire alluded to before Thermidor but without naming. This time, their names were given: Hébert, who 'insulted the national majority by debasing

---

[28] This case was mentioned by J.-M. Chénier, in his report on the protection of men of science, of 14 Nivôse, Year II, which extended the list given by Grégoire.

the language of liberty'; Chaumette, who 'had trees dug up on the pretext of planting potatoes'; Chabot, who 'said that he disliked *men of learning*' and who, with his accomplices, 'had made the word synonymous with *aristocrats*'. Hanriot wished to 'renew the exploits of Omar in Alexandria'; he proposed the burning of the Bibliothèque Nationale, and 'his proposal was repeated in Marseille'. Finally, there came the key name: Robespierre, the 'infamous Robespierre', the 'cruel Robespierre', who 'stirred up vandalism in all of the Republic'. It was still frightening to recall the speed with which the 'conspirators', Robespierre and his acolytes, 'demoralised the Nation and led us through barbarism to slavery. In the space of a year they nearly *destroyed the fruit of several centuries of civilisation* . . . We were on the edge of the abyss.' The subject of a painting by Franck, fortunately saved from the hands of the vandals, had shown itself, alas, prophetic: 'Ignorance can be seen breaking sculptures, while a barbarian armed with torches is busy setting things on fire.' The symbolic figure of 'vandalism' here found a new incarnation: Robespierre exploited ignorance and released the 'iconoclastic fury'. His 'vandal plot' therefore had a double objective: to attack the Revolution and the Enlightenment. Or rather, these were only the two masks of one and the same overall plan since the two causes, that of Revolution and that of Enlightenment, made but a single cause.

By denouncing 'Robespierre-the-vandal', Grégoire followed exactly the same schema that was put in place in the middle of the Terror, in Messidor, Year II, against 'Hébertism of the arts'. If vandals were, well and truly, to be found 'amongst us', this could only be explained by the plot of 'hidden enemies'. The terrorist schema was simply turned against the 'terrorists', which was in itself a remarkable phenomenon and very revealing of the circumstances of the Thermidorean period. To paraphrase the formula of Payan (accused of 'Robespierrism' and of 'vandalism', he had been in hiding since 9 Thermidor to escape the repression), 'vandalism' was 'Robespierrism of the arts', the extension and complement of the Terror in the cultural domain. In the schema of the 'plot' the forms of the 'conspirators' were, as we have seen, interchangeable. But in terms of the concrete incarnations of this form, the fantasy of the 'vandal plot' carried new meanings, in the same way that the political and cultural stakes of its operation and manipulation changed.[29]

Grégoire's reports amplify and erect into a system a theme which became prominent in political discourse following the 'fall of the tyrant'. In fact, in the fantasy of the 'Robespierrist plot' spread by Thermidorean propaganda, the ramifications of the 'plot' in the cultural domain occupied a prominent position. Already, on 11 Thermidor, in his first report on the

---

[29] In the paragraphs devoted to Grégoire's reports, all quotations (except for other references) are taken from the three reports on vandalism; cf. Grégoire, *Œuvres*, vol. 2.

great *journée* which had saved the Republic from the 'atrocious conspiracy', Barère denounced, among other crimes of the 'factious', the one most essential to their treacherous strategy: their plan of 'poisoning the most precious well-spring, that of public education'.[30] On 13 Thermidor, at the Jacobins, in the course of a session which saw the members of the Society unleashed and erupting in mutual denunciations, against a background of generalised distrust and fear, Hassenfratz exclaimed:

Is the shadow of Robespierre at this moment hovering over our chamber? It is exactly by individual denunciations that this tyrant, dividing everyone, making everyone quarrel, wanted to establish his authority and reign despotically over opinion, and keep us under the yoke . . . The Society should now concern itself with an object more worthy of its attention: I mean public education, which the tyrant always pushed to one side, in order more easily to reach his goal by holding sway over the ignorant and the blind.[31]

Certainly we find here an umpteenth variation of a theme already fully embroidered: the 'true' Jacobins were themselves victims of the 'tyrant' and they should now join ranks and affirm their unity; but there is also the accusation which established a link between Robespierre-the-tyrant and Robespierre-the-vandal, between terrorism and vandalism. This in turn permitted the presentation of both phenomena as instruments of the same conspiracy and, consequently, allowed them to be exorcised.

For a better understanding of how this discourse worked, a discourse which both accused and exonerated, it is not without interest to extract, from this flood of Thermidorean speech, the precise facts blamed on Robespierre as proof of his 'vandalism'. This is not easy. In fact, the image of 'Robespierre-the-vandal' became, especially after Grégoire's reports, so stereotyped that very often speakers were content either to repeat it as a kind of evidence, or to enrich it with rhetorical and demagogic flourishes, such as, for example, Fréron denouncing 'this new Omar who wanted to burn the libraries'.[32] Some accusations were more precise. Fourcroy, who was conspicuous for his attacks on the 'vandalism' of the 'last tyrant', declared:

He knew nothing, he was crassly ignorant, he collected evidence against those of his colleagues who were friends of the Enlightenment and the sciences, whom he had led to the scaffold; the last tyrant delivered five or six speeches to you in which, with shocking art, he tore apart, slandered, heaped loathing and bitterness on all those who dedicated themselves to noble studies, on all those who possessed wide knowledge.

---

[30] Cf. *Moniteur*, vol. 21, p. 359.    [31] *Ibid.*, p. 540.
[32] *Ibid.*, p. 645, speech at the meeting of 14 Fructidor, Year II, during the debates on Grégoire's first report.

Lindet, in the report which drew up the balance-sheet for Year II, was not slow to reproach Robespierre with never having dared 'to look a learned or a useful man in the face'; nor was J.-M. Chénier who described him as an 'ambitious ignoramus' who fell 'little by little into shameful barbarism'; nor again Jean Débry who accused the 'tyrant', 'a man whose jealousy could never suffer the idea, I shall not say of superiority, but of equality', of having for these reasons delayed the admission of Rousseau to the Pantheon.[33] These were personal characteristics, to be sure, but typical of the personality of any tyrant. The main proof of Robespierre's 'vandalism', if not the only one that was more or less concrete, and to which speakers returned insistently, was the report of 13 July 1793 on public education. As is well known, Robespierre presented and supported the plan for education found in the papers of Louis-Michel Le Peletier. This plan adopted the principle, in particular, that the child belonged to the *patrie* and that its parents were only its trustees; he therefore proposed an obligatory and common education for all children from five to twelve years, separated from their families and gathered together in municipal buildings, half boarding-school, half barracks. Now, 'what in Le Peletier's case was only an error, in Robespierre's is a crime. On the pretext of turning us into Spartans, he wanted to make helots of us and prepare a military regime, which is nothing else but tyranny.'[34] This plan, 'which could not be carried out in the Republic's current circumstances' was presented only 'so that there should be no education and to destroy all public establishments, without putting anything in their place'.[35] Marked by 'the seal of stupid tyranny', he introduced 'a barbaric arrangement that would snatch the child from the arms of its father, turn the benefit of education into harsh servitude and threaten with prison and death those parents who could and wanted to fulfil the sweet duty of nature'.[36]

Let us go on to examine the obvious distortion: Robespierre did not 'impose' Le Peletier's plan, but the Convention had fairly accepted it after a long debate, while suppressing the clause on obligatory schooling. This plan, never put into practice, was introduced in the middle of the Terror: to accuse Robespierre was, in this case as in several others, a means of discharging the members of the Convention of any responsibility for a terrorist past in which they had been involved, but with which they no longer wished to be identified. The 'affair' of the Le Peletier plan was

[33] Fourcroy, speech at the session of 14 Fructidor, Year II, in *Moniteur*, vol. 21, p. 645; Lindet, report presented to the meeting of the fourth *sans-culottide*, Year II, in *Moniteur*, vol. 22, p. 21; Débry, speech at the meeting of 6 Fructidor, Year II, in *Moniteur*, vol. 21, p. 574.    [34] Grégoire, *Premier rapport sur le vandalisme*, in his *Œuvres*, vol. 2.

[35] Fourcroy, *Rapport sur l'établissement de l'Ecole centrale des travaux publics du 3 vendémiaire, an III*, in Baczko, ed., *Education pour la démocratie*, p. 459.

[36] Daunou, *Rapport sur l'instruction publique du 23 vendémiaire, an IV, ibid.*, p. 509.

supposed to provide evidence, if not *proof*, that Robespierre, marrying ignorance to the Terror, wished to establish *barbarism as a system*. At the same time, it showed up the treachery of this 'conspiracy against the progress of human reason', of the 'system that they [the last conspirators] had adopted to extinguish the flame of education', of 'this horrifying plan, exploding with full force', which would lead to the 'pushing back by several centuries of the march of the human spirit and its incredible progress in France'. In this way everything was connected: the acts of vandalism were presented as manifestations and ramifications of the 'vast conspiracy, planned with the most dangerous and treacherous cunning by the last conspirators', concerning which Fourcroy takes it upon himself to give 'a light sketch':

To convince the people that enlightenment is dangerous and serves only to deceive them; to grasp every occasion to rail, vaguely and in their usual way, against the sciences and the arts; to accuse even gifts of nature and proscribe intelligence; to dry up all sources of public education, so as to destroy in a few months the fruit of more than a century of hard effort; to propose the destruction of books, to debase the productions of genius, to mutilate masterpieces of art on pretexts which cunningly deceive men of good faith; to place the torch of Omar near all the precious stores of arts and letters, so as to burn them at the first signal; to keep preventing, by frivolous objections, the plans of education proposed by this chamber . . . in a word reduce to nothing all things and all men useful for education.[37]

Such relentlessness and treachery could be explained only by the objective pursued by the 'tyrant': 'He wanted to make France barbaric in order to enslave it more securely.'[38] In this way Thermidorean discourse took over and exploited, to the point of wearing it out, the governing idea of 'every enlightened mind': tyranny naturally rested on ignorance and so felt an immeasurable hatred for the Enlightenment and its dissemination. But education, on the other hand, the 'progress of the human spirit', the acquisitions of 'civilisation', were indissociable from liberty and, consequently, from the Republic. Robespierre-the-tyrant and Robespierre-the-vandal were one person: the 'vandal plot' was the most treacherous and most certain means of providing the firmest foundation to tyranny. Did not the existence of this plot, its breadth and its destructive effects prove, in their turn, that the 'cruel Robespierre' aspired to absolute tyranny, worse even than that abolished by the Revolution? And this would explain, by tautology, how the 'vandal phenomenon', foreign to the *revolutionary cause*, to the Revolution in capital letters, was inherent in the course of *revolutionary events*.

[37] Fourcroy, *Rapport du 3 vendémiaire, an III, ibid.*, pp. 458–9.
[38] Lindet, report presented to the meeting of the fourth *sans-culottide*, Year II, in *Moniteur*, vol. 22.

It is not part of our task to analyse here the many ramifications of the anti-vandal discourse which, throughout the Thermidorean period and then under the Directory, became protean in form, to the point of losing its shape. Two aspects of this discourse allowed it to take on specific functions in the system of Thermidorean imagery. The anti-vandal discourse adopted the logic of anti-terrorist discourse as a whole. As we have observed, this latter grew rapidly from the denunciation of Robespierre-the-tyrant to accusations, more and more violent and frequent, of 'Robespierre's tail', of 'blood-drinkers', of 'wicked Jacobins', etc. In the same way, the anti-vandal discourse, having attacked Robespierre-the-vandal, took violently against the 'vandals' (the word 'vandalists' was also used), wicked agents of the Terror and of vandalism. In other words, the anti-vandal discourse was integrated, as a part, into the *discourse of revenge* against the 'terrorists'. To the desire for vengeance it brought a matching justification: the 'blood-drinkers' and the 'cannibals' were so many enemies of the Enlightenment. It was precisely these *others* who were designated by the term 'vandal'. Pushed to its conclusion, the anti-vandal discourse insisted on their *radical otherness*, to the point of becoming a violent call for the *exclusion* of the vandals. But to oppose 'vandalism' was also, and contradictorily, to orientate oneself in a completely different direction as implied by the notorious ambiguity, inherited from the Enlightenment, from which were minted the words 'barbarian' and 'vandal'. If the 'barbarians' were *other* in certain circumstances *their otherness was not insurmountable*. 'Barbarians', so to speak, called down upon themselves measures which would make them evolve, 'soften' their manners, enlighten them – in short, measures to civilise them. Pushed to its limits, this orientation of the anti-vandal discourse therefore tended to *justify the inclusion of 'barbarians'* and their progressive accession–ascension to civilisation, through protective and educational action, which implied benevolent supervision by revolutionary authority and, consequently, by its enlightened élites.

This is certainly an over-simplification, since in reality these two tendencies were quite rarely pushed to extremes, and were opposed to each other. But precisely because they became entangled with each other to the point of merging together, it seemed to be useful to point up the – at first sight – paradoxical character of their complicity.

### Vandals and cannibals

In most communes there still remains a little Robespierre; and while the modern Catiline has atoned for his ferocity on the scaffold, his lieutenants are undisturbed. In the different places where the arts have suffered so many outrages, the authors, for the most part, are known, and national agents become their accomplices in not denouncing them to public prosecutors.[39]

By becoming more general, by calling for the hunting down of the 'little Robespierres', the anti-vandal discourse (whatever Grégoire's intentions were otherwise) did not aim solely at those who had directly contributed to the destruction of monuments and works of art. It attacked all those who during the Terror exercised power at the local level, all members of the revolutionary committees and militant *sans-culottes*, perpetrators of repression inspired from 'above' by central power, but also the organisers and agents of the Terror carried out on the spot. In passing from the denunciation of the 'plot' of Robespierre and his acolytes, a small group, to the pursuit of 'little Robespierres' scattered through the country, Grégoire adopted the logic of all anti-terrorist discourse, which from the denunciation of the 'tyrant' progressed with large strides towards attacks on 'Robespierrism' as a 'system of terror'.

This development of the discourse marks a remarkable change in the representation of the 'vandals'. The 'little Robespierres' were not considered as blind instruments in the hand of the 'tyrant'. They were not mystified by the Machiavellian plot, which would have, in a way, exonerated them; they recognised themselves in him. Increasingly in Thermidorean discourse, within the space of a few months, the feeling of hatred and vengeance was established against all those who, emerging from 'below', took over power and tyrannised, imprisoned, humiliated the 'good citizens'. 'Executioners reigned, fools got rich, the ignorant filled important offices', Tallien kept repeating in his newspaper.[40] The 'tyrant' wished to debase the Nation by exacerbating the most pernicious and cruel characteristics of human nature. As a result, criminals, slaughterers, thieves, moved spontaneously towards him, as was shown by the trial of the revolutionary Committee of Nantes. During the winter of 1794–1795, Thermidorean discourse employed a particularly aggressive vocabulary for designating these 'little Robespierres': former terrorists, personnel of the revolutionary committees, they were anthropophagi, cannibals, drinkers of human blood. Insult and invective, to be sure, but they revealed phantoms whose power was very real. In the course of the trial of the revolutionary Committee of Nantes, was there not evidence that during their meetings, the members of the popular society indulged in a cruel rite, a sort of counter-mass: as a sign of solidarity, each man drank from a cup filled with blood? 'Cannibals', those who were *outside civilisation*, 'monsters' those

---

[39] Grégoire, *Troisième rapport*, in *Œuvres*, vol. 2.
[40] *L'Ami des citoyens. Journal du commerce et des arts*, no. 5, 5 Brumaire, Year III.

who, by their cruel and savage nature, had condemned themselves to exclusion from society, if not to extermination pure and simple. This is what was proclaimed by *Le Réveil du peuple*, that 'counter-Marseillaise' of the *jeunesse dorée*, a real call to murderous vengeance, sung in the theatres, in the cafés, under the arcades of the Palais National (previously the Palais-Royal):

People of France, people of brothers
Can you see without shivering with horror
Crime raise the banners
Of carnage and of terror?

You endure the vile horde
Of assassins and brigands
Soiling with its fierce breath
The land of the living.

What! This cannibal horde
Which hell vomits from its womb,
Preaches murder and carnage!
It is covered with your blood!

What is this barbarian slowness?
Hurry, sovereign people,
To return to the monsters of Tenaerus
All these blood-drinkers.

Sad shades of innocence
Lie quiet in your tombs
The belated day of vengeance
At last makes your executioners turn pale.

Yes, we swear on your tomb
By our unhappy country
To make but a hecatomb
Of these frightful cannibals.[41]

Cannibals, but also barbarians and vandals. In Thermidorean imagery and language, the two concepts complemented each other to the point of becoming merged together. Babeuf, therefore, used the two terms as synonyms when he denounced the crimes of the Terror ('horrors which astonish the centuries and the nations') as both 'frightful cannibalism' and

---

[41] *Couplets chantés à la réunion des citoyens de la section de Guillaume Tell*, words by citizen Souriguère, music by citizen Gaveaux; *Le Réveil du peuple* was performed in public for the first time on 2 Pluviôse, Year III and published the following day by *Le Courrier républicain*. Cf. Aulard, *Paris pendant la réaction*, vol. 1, pp. 408–11.

'the fruits of barbarism'.[42] The two terms had in common a similar function of defamatory exclusion, of banishment from civilisation; they branded the 'enemies of humankind' emerging from the universe of shadows, of crime and murder – except for one nuance, however, insofar as it is possible to grasp nuances in this convulsive verbal violence, which, let us not forget, justified, excited and orchestrated physical violence, the hunt of 'Jacobins' and of 'terrorists': the 'cannibal', the 'blood-drinker', symbolised the bloody terror, the terror of proscriptions, of the guillotine, of prison; the 'vandal' personified the tyranny of ignorance, of anti-culture. The 'vandal' was, so to speak, the other face of the 'cannibal', the man-eater of culture. The reign of the Terror had not only brought on the massacres and death of the innocent (there was no miserliness about the figures: tens of thousands, hundreds of thousands, some even spoke of millions . . . ). The Terror was also triumphant vandalism and, at the same time, the desolate image of the nation plunged into the shadows of ignorance.

Tyranny found in ignorance an almost unconquerable support; and *barbaric vandalism*, itself a child of tyranny, came to aid it with new forces. While the scaffolds were soaked with the blood of victims, all the monuments of the fine arts, all the repositories of science, all the sanctuaries of letters were prey to the burning and devastation of the tyrants. Doubtless these wild enemies of humanity only consented to their crimes being lit up for a moment by the light of burning libraries, because they hoped that the shadows of ignorance would only become thicker. The barbarians! they have made the human spirit regress by several centuries; they wanted to snatch from France its finest titles to glory; they seemed in essence to conspire to deprive it of the dictatorship it has always exercised over the nations, the dictatorship that comes from the education of genius.[43]

In this tirade the essential themes of Grégoire's reports can be easily recognised, but they are amplified, exaggerated, turned into hyperbole by a rhetoric well-rehearsed throughout the Revolution (Grégoire spoke only of intentions to burn the libraries; if one is to believe Boissy d'Anglas, they were in fact all burnt). However, the denunciation of vandalism went beyond its initial sphere: vandalism was no longer uniquely the destruction of monuments, books, works of art; it was from now on an entire way of life, a model of behaviour and language, which the Terror imposed on the country and, in particular, on cultivated people. Or rather, it was the opposite of a way of life, the very negation of culture. The 'cannibals', those who directed the Terror, were ignorant and vile, the dirty and the brutish who did not even speak a civilised language. This is how La Harpe, who had just been released from prison, denounced vandalism, 'this war declared by

---

[42] Babeuf, *On veut sauver Carrier!*, p. 12.
[43] Boissy d'Anglas, *Discours préliminaire au projet de Constitution de la République française du 5 messidor an III*, Paris, Year III.

our last tyrants on reason, on morality, on the letters and the arts', and drew the frightful picture:

I seem to see these brigands still, under the names of patriots, these oppressors of the nation, under the name of magistrates of the people, spread in a crowd among us with their grotesque clothing which they called exclusively patriotic, as if patriotism must necessarily be ridiculous and filthy; with their crude tone and brutal language which they called republican, as if crudeness and indecency were essentially republican.[44]

Just as much as the destroyed monuments, it was the obscene language used by civil servants and representatives *en mission* and considered to be truly 'popular' and 'patriotic' that Cambry was denouncing. He saw in this language an overall symbol of vandalism, the 'characteristic which best reveals the degradation of the constituted bodies in this period ... days of fury, ignorance, imbecility, brutality'.[45]

This is how, by the description of 'vandals–cannibals', the discourse on vandalism was extended. The destruction of books and works of art, its departure point, is only a particular epiphenomenon in a more universal drama, the *mixing with the rabble* of both France and the Republic. For these 'little Robespierres', of which Grégoire spoke, were quite simply the *rabble in power*. Disguised as patriots and revolutionaries, this rabble was not content to slaughter honest people, to sow terror, to pillage and rob. It degraded all of public life by plunging it into barbarism. This rabble, the lower depths of society, was the spontaneous enemy of educated and cultured people, who shrank from it. What better image of the rabble vandalising France than the one given in the play of Ducancel, *L'Intérieur des Comités révolutionnaires ou les Aristides modernes*, which had an immense success in the spring of year III?[46] The play presents a revolutionary committee where the dregs of the people are installed, crooks, former lackeys or house porters, adventurers, etc. No one goes under the name of Jeannot or Pierrot anymore, but each person now has himself called Torquatus, Brutus or Cato. Instead of speaking French, they express themselves in a grotesque patois.

[44] J.-F. La Harpe, *De la guerre déclarée par nos derniers tyrans à la raison, à la morale, aux lettres et aux arts*, speech delivered at the opening of the Lycée Républicain on 31 December 1794, Paris, Year IV, p. 4.

[45] Cambry, *Voyage dans le Finistère ou état de ce département en 1794 et 1795*, Paris, Year VIII, vol. 3, pp. 93–4.

[46] *L'Intérieur des Comités révolutionnaires ou les Aristides modernes*, play in three acts in prose by citizen Ducancel (C.-P.), Paris, n.d. The action takes place at the revolutionary Committee of Dijon (in Fructidor, Year II, the popular society had sent to the Convention and the Jacobins an address condemning *modérantisme* and the release of detainees; cf. above). On the triumphant reception of the play, cf. E. and J. Goncourt, *Histoire de la société française pendant le Directoire*, Paris, 1864, pp. 122 *et seq.*; L. Moland, *Théâtre de la Révolution*, Paris, 1877, pp. xxvi–xxvii.

ROGUE, WITH A LETTER IN HIS HAND, RECOGNISING TORQUATUS: Look, it's
Fétu, the chair-mender; good day, my friend Fétu.
TORQUATUS: Who are you calling Fétu; I are Torquatu.
VILLAIN: Right, Torquatu it is. It's worse than madness, you don't know the men or
the streets these days.
TORQUATUS: All us patriots has Roman names. I wants to unbaptise you and call
you Caesar, damn! Wasn't it him as was a proud republican?

[The letter addressed to the Committee causes panic: all its members are illiterate.]

TORQUATUS, ASIDE TO BRUTUS: Brutus, can you read, my friend?
BRUTUS, ASIDE TO TORQUATUS: Alas, I'm still on the alphabet; if you knew how
difficult it is to read.

Wearing their red bonnets, dressed in carmagnoles as dirty as the
bonnets, these members of the revolutionary Committee are all ardent
partisans of the Terror and their idol Robespierre. Illiterate, they still
decide on the provision of certificates of good citizenship; ignorant, they
carry out interrogations and suspect agents from abroad everywhere,
although Barcelona is, for them, only a distant chief town of a district
somewhere in France, in a department called Catalonia. But all show
themselves prodigiously adept in manipulating the popular society by
revolutionary slogans expressed in their ridiculous and effective language.
They handle the weapon of denunciation superbly. They imprison honest
people in order to take over their property, but also because they hate their
education, their culture, the knowledge they possess and the books they
know how to read. They especially hound the single member of the
Committee, 'merchant, persecuted honest man, municipal agent', who
opposes their pernicious activities at the risk of his life and whose son is
fighting at the frontiers to defend his country. They bring against him false
and absurd accusations in order to have him arrested and then share his
fortune. They would have succeeded (passing over the details of the
intrigue) but for the famous letter, finally opened and read, which brought
the happy news that the 'infamous triumvirs are finally defeated' ('Oh! the
virtuous, incorruptible Robespierre', cries Cato, former lackey and crook,
completely crushed) and that 'the partisans of the Terror and the blood-
drinkers will be prosecuted'. So virtue and justice triumph over the rabble
and, with them, reason and enlightenment triumph over ignorance and
barbarism. The moral of the play is expressed by its hero, the young officer,
son of the 'persecuted honest man and merchant':

As long as education has not brought enlightenment and reason to all classes of
society, the people will always need educated and innocent men to direct its energy
and plan its activity.

Ducancel's play (he was a royalist) was finally banned, after about a hundred performances in Paris (it was also performed with the greatest success in several provincial towns). It caused a scandal, for beyond the 'vandal–cannibals' it denounced and ridiculed revolutionary power as such. The Brutuses, the Tarquini and the Catos are, of course, the rabble and there did appear in the play vaguely, as if in the wings, a good people (in fact symbolised by the faithful young servant of the persecuted honest man) who rejoice at the triumph of reason and virtue. But this people who let themselves be manipulated by the big and the little Robespierres, by all these Cato-crooks, were they really blameless? The vulgar and ridiculous patois, the obscene language, the use of 'tu', symbols of triumphant vandalism and which perverted the public spirit, did these not make up its day-to-day language? In full expansion, widening out, the discourse on vandalism slid towards putting back into question the key concept of the revolutionary symbolic system, the sovereign people.

### A people to be civilised, a civilising government

On 1 Ventôse, Year III, delegations from the *section* of the Halle-au-Blé and the *section* of the Bonnet-Rouge (which was quickly to drop this name) were admitted to the bar of the Convention. In their addresses, they congratulated the Convention for having initiated the inquiry into the members of the former Committee of Public Safety, this government which 'burdened our fatherland with more evils, in fifteen months, than all the tyrants of the human race made it suffer in fifteen centuries'. They also congratulated the legislators for having decreed the expulsion of Marat's ashes from the Pantheon and for having thus called 'a shameful enthusiasm' to order. The Halle-au-Blé *section* violently denounced the members of the revolutionary committees, these 'wild men who have done so much damage'; it should be made impossible for them, 'whether they are vile or idiotic', 'to cause harm'. The *section* called on the legislators to be even more energetic and to go forward courageously: in order to remove the memory of these horrifying fifteen months and to re-establish the unity of the French people,

make all these monuments which recall your former divisions disappear; that Mountain, raised up in front of the Invalides, which has brought forth so many Mountains; those awful events recalled on its base, the reptiles that are also to be seen upon it and which recall hateful names; that figure crushed by the giant, an allegoric and chimerical figure, like the phantom of which it is the emblem, let them all disappear and recall only sad memories.

These proposals were welcomed by the applause of members of the Convention who all knew this monument very well. In fact, they themselves had ordered, in August 1793, the erection of this statue, whose symbolism, designed by David, had at that time seduced their imaginations:

On the summit of the mountain will be represented in sculpture, by a colossal figure, the French People, raising with vigorous arm the fasces of the *départements*; ambitious federalism emerging from its muddy bog, with one hand pushing back the reeds, attempts with the other to detach a portion of it; the French People notices this, takes its club, strikes it and makes it withdraw into the stagnant water, never to emerge again.

Seven months after Thermidor, there were few members of the Convention who saw themselves in this People-Hercules rising on the mountain; they now considered the statue 'terrorist and vandal'. The monument bears a giant; now, 'this giant is Robespierre'. It was armed with a club; 'they made a mistake, it's a guillotine that it should be carrying'. A single voice was raised to defend the monument:

Out of respect for the French people, do not grant the spectacle of its destruction to the aristocrats. You will insult your constituents, you will insult *the people every time that you destroy images that represent it*.

The assembly became indignant, several voices were raised: 'It is not the image of the people, it is that of the tyrant who mutilated the Convention'; destruction was voted on.[47]

But was it possible not to touch 'images which represent the people'? The debate on the statue of the People-Hercules itself carried a symbolic sense. The free and sovereign People, one and indivisible, marching ever forward, this key representation of the revolutionary imagination, could it emerge intact from the complications in which this same *imagination* found itself involved as a result of the prosecution of those 'truly responsible' for the Terror and for vandalism? The whole Thermidorean discourse was to undermine this representation by an underhand action. Let us recall how the members of the former Committees, denounced by Lecointre, defended themselves; if they carried responsibility for having tolerated the 'tyrant', then they shared this error with the Convention and also with the whole people.

Was the Convention itself sheltered from the tyrannical influence of Robespierre or from the illusions that he produced through his patriotic speeches? Was not the

[47] Cf. *Moniteur*, vol. 23, pp. 516–18. The description of the statue is taken from the programme of the festival of 10 August 1793, written by David; cf. B. Baczko, *Lumières de l'utopie*, Paris, 1978, pp. 377 *et seq.* Let us recall that in Year II, this image of the People-Hercules had been mentioned by the temporary Commission of the Arts in its guidance on the conservation of monuments. The club then came to symbolise the protection of works of art against the 'vandals' . . . On the history and symbolism of this statue, cf. the sensible observations in L. Hunt, *Politics, culture and class in the French Revolution*, Berkeley, Calif., 1984, pp. 98 *et seq.*

People itself, by its own error or by blind confidence, the most active agent of the despotism exercised by this man ... who was in that period a popular power?[48]

For political reasons that we know are quite different, the counter-revolutionary publicists also sought to avoid limiting reponsibility for the Terror and vandalism to 'Robespierre's conspiracy' alone, and to extend the accusation as far as possible: against the Revolution and the people itself. Robespierre was directly supported by the revolutionary committees, most of whose members 'were men without education, drawn from the lowest classes of society, with savage manners, with a brute ignorance'. If he had succeeded, this was not only because he had drawn to his side 'all the bandits, all the assassins to be found in France' but above all – an unheard of fact which made his tyranny unprecedented in history – because 'the bulk of the nation more than once plunged into the mire which Robespierre and his accomplices had stirred up ... We descended to this degree of degradation, of adopting the most shameful follies of the least orderly peoples.'[49]

In Thermidor, everything was in conflict and increasing: political and rational strategies, the specific logic of the development of a system of representations, and the dynamic of social conflicts. In the starving Paris of that particularly harsh winter of 1794–5, where social contrasts broke out in the full light of day, the arrogant luxury of the *nouveaux riches*, speculators and purchasers of nationalised assets, and the poverty of those who, at night, formed queues outside the breadshops; where the ostentatious elegance of the *jeunesse dorée* was a sign of scorn for the carmagnoles and red bonnets; where those who came out of the prisons passed those who were condemned, while only yesterday the latter were handing out certificates of good citizenship – in this Paris haunted by the tales of the recent horrors of the Terror, the sovereign people no longer really appeared as 'one and indivisible'. Certainly, Thermidorean political discourse could not accept or legitimise the shattering of this essential concept by taking responsibility for doing so; it attempted therefore to preserve the concept and to do this it would tolerate only one distinction in civil society, that between 'good' and 'bad' citizens. However, under the pressure of social conflicts, this Thermidorean discourse split up into a language which spoke brutally of the division of the 'people' if not into classes, at least into the rich and the poor. So while Dubois-Crancé proclaimed that the Convention, representing the People, should remain united, in order to remove the ultimate consequences of the Terror, he also called on the legislators never

---

[48] *Réponse de Barère, Billaud-Varenne, Collot d'Herbois et Vadier aux imputations de Laurent Lecointre et déclarées calomnieuses par décret du 13 fructidor*, reprinted in *La Révolution française*, 1898, vol. 34, pp. 71–8.

[49] Montjoie, *Histoire de la conjuration de Robespierre*; Montjoie denounced also the deleterious effects of classical studies in the *lycées* and their hold on the imagination.

to lose sight of this 'simple consideration': 'The fortune of a million men in France maintains the industry of twenty-five million others; destroy the resources of these million men and the counter-revolution is accomplished.' (These remarks were often attacked by the Jacobins.) The people, to be sure, was neither 'cannibalistic' nor 'vandal'; it 'has never been misled', but often it had been 'cruelly deceived'. Otherwise, how would it have had confidence in those who no longer pursued the aristocrats, 'but all the rich, all those whose fortune activated the talents and industry of the people, whom they pillaged, whom they slaughtered, under the name of aristo-crats'?[50] Bourdon (from the Oise) denounced the demagogic illusions and promises employed by the 'terrorists' in order to delude the people: because, in the Terror, 'they flattered the people with foolish hope', 'owners of property are everywhere insulted, accused, condemned; their domestics are corrupted into denouncing them; the vilest treason is elevated into public virtue; the monuments of the arts are mutilated; everything that recalls the opulence of the nation is destroyed'. It was because a 'horde of cannibals' had criminally promised 'the properties of the rich to the poor' that the 'vandalism of our dictators' could triumph. The only ones to profit from this 'infernal system' were that 'host of barbarians [who], to the sound of the assassins' swords, gorged themselves with gold and blood, and insulted modesty, outraged virtue, massacred innocence and ate up [sic] our monuments into ruin, our cities into tombs, our fields into desert'.[51] So it is necessary

courageously to recall the first truths: the mass of all men born on the soil of France, this is the people. A portion of this people has obtained property by inheritance, by acquisition or by its industry; a second portion of this same people works to acquire property or add to it. Imperceptible gradations of ease or poverty exist between these two portions of the people, under the names of poor and rich; they are both indispensably necessary.

Of course, the 'virtuous and able legislator' should stifle the vices of both, the rich and the poor, and thus ensure their union. But the essential lesson to be drawn from the Terror, 'from the system of crime masked as patriotism', was vigilance against

these men with fierce eyes, with pale complexions, with angry voices, who excite the resentment of the people against a part of itself whom they call, treacherously, the gilded million.[52]

---

[50] Speech given at the session of the second *sans-culottide* of Year II, 'frequently interrupted by loud applause': *Moniteur*, vol. 22, pp. 6–7.

[51] Speech given on 10 Ventôse, Year III, *Moniteur*, vol. 23, p. 578.

[52] Boissy d'Anglas, speech given at the session of 21 Ventôse, Year III, *Moniteur*, vol. 23, pp. 660–3.

A childish people, a people misled, a people which had become involved in vandalism and terror – the frontier which separated it from the rabble was increasingly obliterated. The Thermidorean discourse risked becoming confused in the future with the attacks of enemies of every stamp against the Revolution and the Republic, denounced as the tyranny of the populace. The regicide Convention – the Thermidorean change of direction mattered little – would be no more than a wretched band of criminals and assassins. A problem of discourse, a problem of the portrayal of the people, but also, if not especially, a problem that was above all *political*, to do with *power* and its legitimacy. Also, at the same time that Thermidorean discourse removed the frontiers between the 'vandals' and the 'people', it attempted, by a strange exercise, to re-establish them; if it insisted on the division of the 'people' into rich and poor, into one million and twenty-five million, it was to more strongly reaffirm the solidarity between the two which ought to be ensured by the 'virtuous legislator'. All the legitimacy of Thermidorean power rested on the will – one and indivisible, like the Republic – of the people, 'free and sovereign'. The reference to the people, to the 'twenty-six million French who have sent us here', is ever present in Thermidorean discourse. The people are seen less and less as a stirring and heroic figure, more and more as emblematic and problematic, undermined from within by accusations against the 'vandals and cannibals', and yet indispensable. All the contradictions of the Thermidorean system of power are found in the double desire – if not the necessity – of preserving in its discourse this basic political concept which legitimises it, and of forestalling a revival of the terrorist effects of this unitary concept in the revolutionary imagination. The *people* were therefore increasingly reduced to a single function: to legitimising the Republic and, consequently, its authority. At the same time, the reality granted to this people was simply that of the institutions supposed to embody it. So the people were embodied in the army which fought victoriously, beyond the frontiers, in the name of the Republic; it was embodied also and above all by authority: the members of the Convention increasingly identified the *people* with themselves, with a political personnel on whom the continuation of the Republic depended. The People, in Thermidor, is a figure of speech whose use has been perfected throughout revolutionary experience; it becomes the symbolic support of skill in exercising power, a skill acquired in the course of this same experience.

In this system of political concepts, the people could not then be completely 'vandal' nor completely 'civilised'; it had to occupy a median position, half-way between civilisation and barbarism. The discourse against vandalism was the vehicle for the concept of a *civilising power*.

Thermidor marks, in effect, that 'happy period of the Revolution when ignorance and the vices it engendered are banished from the places surrendered to them like prey by the conspirators', that moment when

the legislators of France, witnesses of the evils with which barbarism and vandalism had threatened it, came out strongly against these enemies of humankind, and destroyed, through institutions established to increase human knowledge, the guilty hopes of tyranny.[53]

All the great cultural and educational creations of the Thermidorean period – the Ecole Polytechnique, the Ecole Normale, the Institute, the Museum of French Monuments, etc. – took their impetus from the discourse against 'vandalism and its damage'. The arts had followed, for three years, the destiny of the National Convention.

They have groaned with you under the tyranny of Robespierre, they mounted the scaffolds with your colleagues and, in this time of calamity, patriotism and the sciences, mingling their regrets and their tears, called back from the same tombs victims who were just as dear. After 9 Thermidor, by regaining authority and liberty, you have dedicated their first use to the consolation and encouragement of the arts. The Convention did not wish, like the kings, to degrade men of talent, by requiring them to beg for gifts; it hurried to offer honourable help to men whose poverty would have accused the nation they had made illustrious by enlightening it.[54]

The Thermidorean Convention offered help to men of learning and artists: it rendered homage to the 'martyrs of the vandal Terror', to Lavoisier and Condorcet; it brought iconoclastic acts to a permanent end. Of course, it did not halt the destruction of all monuments: mansions, cloisters, châteaux, so many national assets, were still sold at low prices and were the object of unrestrained speculation. It also destroyed, as is too often forgotten, a large part of what was outlined in Year II as the draft of a culture that was, if not specifically revolutionary, at least 'sans-culotte'. If the statues raised in Year II have not come down to us, it is not only because they were made of plaster, but because they were destroyed, like the People-Hercules, and the Lenoir Museum hardly welcomed them. The *sans-culotte* costume, the obligatory use of 'tu', the revolutionary christian names, the pikes, the politicisation of militant minorities, all this was abolished because the Thermidoreans saw in it the signs of vandalism and the Terror. What was to survive from the revolutionary symbolic repertoire would be, by contrast, the elements which authority considered as educational tools

[53] Fourcroy, *Rapport sur les arts qui ont servi à la défense de la République et sur le nouveau procédé de tannage* ..., presented on 14 Nivôse, Year III, in *Moniteur*, vol. 23, p. 139.
[54] Daunou, *Rapport sur l'instruction publique*, p. 504.

intended to consolidate republican mores: among others, the Republican calendar and the decadal feasts, which were increasingly neglected; the trees of liberty, increasingly withered and which the administration's circulars called to be replanted and maintained; the republican system of weights and measures, the republican catechisms.[55]

Denouncing vandalism and terrorist tyranny, Thermidorean power identified itself, and so asserted itself, as the single legitimate heir of the Enlightenment. The anti-vandal discourse combined with the educational discourse to legitimise a clear-cut allotment of symbolic roles to a power that civilised and a people to be civilised. Government had to make this people emerge from ignorance, but also had to watch over it so that it did not succumb once more to the temptation of anarchy and vandalism. So, in the drawing up of the Constitution of Year III, which should have marked the completion of the Revolution, the two tendencies of the anti-vandal discourse overlapped: the desire to *exclude* the 'vandals' from the political arena and the wish to *include* the people in a Republic that embodied progress and civilisation. This union of the *cultural* and the *political*, concerning which we have already drawn out some general features and

[55] Once the emergence from the Terror had been completed and a relative stabilisation of post-Thermidorean power ensured, the spectre of 'vandalism' and its possible return seemed to be exorcised. It was, in fact, spoken of less and less, except to evoke the dark past to which enlightened power had put a definitive end. However, the mention of its destructions could still serve other purposes. Saved from vandalism, France, where Liberty and Enlightenment triumphed over 'barbarian' despotism, was, because of this triumph, called to be the very centre of culture and civilisation, to a universal and conquering vocation. A centre of influence, but also, so to speak, a land of welcome. Between two sessions devoted to the reports of Grégoire on vandalism, the Convention loudly applauded Luc Barnier, lieutenant of the 5th regiment of Hussars, who brought it good news from the army of the North.

The immortal works which have been left to us by the brushes of Rubens, Van Dyck and other founders of the Flemish school are no longer in a foreign land. Carefully brought together under the orders of representatives of the people, they are today lodged safely in the *patrie* of art and genius, in the *patrie* of liberty and holy equality, in the French Republic. It is there, in the National Museum, that henceforth the foreigner will come for instruction. (Session of the 4th *sans-culottide*, Year II, in *Moniteur*, vol. 22, p. 27)

With remarkable continuity, dropping any mention of 'holy Equality', but adding a reminder of the destructions of vandalism, the executive Directory gave, on 7 May 1796, the following order to General Bonaparte:

The executive Directory is persuaded, citizen general, that you regard the glory of the fine arts as bound up with that of the army which you command. Italy owes [its glory] in a large part to its riches and its celebrity; but the time has come for their reign to pass to France in order to strengthen and embellish the reign of liberty. The National Museum should contain the most celebrated monuments of all the arts, and you will not neglect to enrich it with those which it expects from your present conquests with the army of Italy, and from the conquests which are yet to come. This glorious campaign, while putting the Republic in a position to grant peace to its enemies, should also repair the destructions of vandalism at its heart and join to the glory of military trophies the charm of the bountiful and consoling arts. (*Actes du Directoire exécutif*, published and annotated by A. Debidour, Paris, 1911, vol. 2, p. 333)

which in reality experienced many incarnations, defines one of the characteristics of the *Thermidorean moment*. By protecting the people against its
own ignorance and against any return of the 'vandal Terror', the clear-cut
allotment of the social and cultural roles should have simultaneously
completed the emergence from the Terror, brought the Revolution to a
close and established solid foundations for the Republic.

# 5     The Thermidorean moment

How could the 'present circumstances bring an end to the Revolution' and on what principles 'should the Republic be founded'? This concern, expressed by Mme de Staël in 1797,[1] was deeply felt in the winter and spring of Year III. The political and social crisis which marked this period made it all the more urgent. The policy of revenge carried out by representative government power responded to the passionate demands of the moment (yet it still did not satisfy the unchained and vengeful passions; on the contrary, it stirred them up, thus setting in motion new cycles of violent and arbitrary action). But it brought no response to the cardinal problem raised by the condemnation of the 'system of Terror': what was the political and institutional arena that needed to be created for *after the Terror*? *To emerge from the Terror* was, of course, first of all to dismantle all its institutions and personnel. But the further this dismantling went, the more it became confused with the anti-terrorist and anti-Jacobin repression whose forms and extent became less and less easily controlled by central authority.

For the 'Thermidoreans', as we have seen, did not possess a *political strategy*, neither on 9 Thermidor, nor in the first months that would follow this 'memorable revolution'. The series of problems which they had to face imposed on them a certain logic of political action. Each provisional solution raised new problems for which they had to find resources. In the final reckoning, the desire to prevent any return of the Terror demanded that from now on the political problems should be expressed in *terms that were positive, institutional and constitutional*. The question slid from *how to finish with the Terror* to *how to terminate the Revolution?* The 'Thermidoreans' then had to express their answers to all these preoccupations both in terms of a *reaction* to the Terror and in terms of a *promise for the future*. It was necessary for them to invent a new utopia that responded to the new departure of the Republic, connecting up again with its origins and founding principles, its expectations and promises, all compromised by the

[1] Mme de Staël, *Des circonstances actuelles qui peuvent terminer la Révolution et des principes qui doivent fonder la République en France*, critical edition by Lucia Omacini, Paris and Geneva, 1979.

Terror. To consider together the *reaction* and the *utopia* is also the challenge
that has to be met by any historian who means to understand how the
Thermidorean period came to an end and what perspectives it offers.


## Ending the Revolution

Theoretically, the Republic had a constitution. It had been drawn up in
June 1793, after the fall of the Girondins, and had never been applied. It had
been written very quickly, in the space of a week, by Hérault de Séchelles,
and as quickly adopted, almost without debate, by the Convention. This
hurried procedure expressed a political will; Jacobin and Montagnard
authority sought to show that it was qualified to resolve 'energetically' the
problems which the Girondins had left to drag on (the plan for a
Constitution drawn up by Condorcet was the particular target; it was
criticised for being too complex and too liberal). Those in power wished
especially to transform the referendum on the adoption of his plan into a
plebiscite in favour of the Montagnard dictatorship and against the
Girondins, thus sanctioning the show of force on 31 May. The vote (public
and oral, subject to numerous irregularities) took place under the pressure
of the revolutionary authorities and committees. Its results were no
surprise: 1,801,918 for; 11,600 electors dared to vote against; at least
4,300,000 citizens did not take part in the vote. The adoption of the
Constitution was solemnly celebrated during the festival of 10 August 1793.
On the evening of the festival, the text was, just as solemnly, enclosed in an
'ark of cedar wood' and placed in the hall of the Convention. The
application of the Constitution was postponed until France should be at
peace.

Revolutionary historiography has liked to insist on the democratic
character of this Constitution (particularly in view of its introduction of
universal suffrage) and the proclamation of 'social rights' in the Declaration of the Rights of Man; there has also been discussion of the difficulties
that would have been raised by its eventual application 'in time of peace'
(very frequent referenda and elections; very extended powers of the
Assembly, etc.). Whatever the case, the text was botched; the off-handed-
ness with which it had been prepared contrasted singularly with the
seriousness of the debate on the Constitution of 1791. One can even
question the actual intentions of its authors: from the first steps in drawing
it up, were they thinking of anything besides a propaganda operation? Did
they sincerely think of one day applying this text, for which an 'ark' was
being made in advance? Did they rather hope to re-examine it before
eventually applying it in a time of peace? The Montagnard Convention
never set to work on the fundamental laws; the Jacobins were the first to

denounce as a counter-revolutionary idea any allusion to the application of the Constitution and, especially, to the convening of primary assemblies. (As we have noticed, this was also the case after 9 Thermidor, in view of the initiatives of the electoral Club, which brought together opponents of the anti-terrorist repression; on this point, in Fructidor of Year II, the Convention, although already split, easily rediscovered its unanimity.) The Constitution of 1793 was particularly badly adapted to the problems of the redefinition of the political arena imposed by the dismantling of the Terror. It is enough, in fact, to recall the uncertainties that it left hovering over the relationships between two sources of authority – authority that was the product of the representative system and authority that would devolve on a rival power, appealing to the right of 'each *section* of the people' to resist, claiming to be the 'risen people' and to exercise its un-limited sovereignty directly, by violence in the course of *journées*. (Thus, for example, article 23 of the Declaration of the Rights of Man and the Citizen which stipulated that 'resistance to oppression follows from the other Rights of Man' or article 35, of the same Declaration: 'When the govern-ment violates the rights of the people, insurrection is, for the people and each portion of the people, the most sacred and most indispensable of duties.')[2]

Although the Constitution of 1793 could be challenged on two grounds, on the conditions of its drawing up and its adoption, its actual content was not, however, a problem in the first days that followed 9 Thermidor: no one thought of taking it out of its 'ark'. It was only in the winter and the spring of Year III that it became an obstacle to the dismantling of the Terror and to the redefinition of the political machinery.

The initiative for making the Constitution of 1793 a current problem came, paradoxically, from the Jacobin deputies; they saw it as the pretext for a political manoeuvre. On 24 Brumaire, Year III, they surprised the Convention by suddenly manifesting an interest in the application of the Constitution. They proposed to begin work on the fundamental laws and, consequently, to prepare the suppression of revolutionary government and the re-establishment of constitutional government. With a period of peace coming, it was necessary to end the Revolution by applying the Constitu-tion of 1793: 'Let the National Convention invite each of its members to turn their attention to the fundamental laws of the Constitution, which the French people will embrace with rapture, now that they have crossed the

---

[2] Cf. *Les Constitutions de la France depuis 1789*, ed. Godechot, p. 83. On the drawing up of the Constitution of 1793, its voting through and the problem of its possible application, cf. Godechot, *Les Institutions de la France sous la Révolution et l'Empire*, Paris, 1968. Concerning article 35 the pamphlet *Insurrection du peuple . . .* will argue for the legitimacy of the *journée* of 1 Prairial, Year III.

revolutionary torrent and have dictated, from a position of independence, an honourable peace to their enemies.' Barère, seconding Audoin, gave to this proposal, which was complicated by a rhetoric on the principles of the Republic and its radiant future, its immediate political significance: it ought to reassure the people on the subject of the 'real meaning of the revolution of 9 Thermidor' and halt the activities of the 'secret committee of the foreign party' which, without any doubt, was hiding itself behind the 'latest events' and, by a crafty arrangement of roles, was 'plaguing public opinion', corrupting public feeling, slandering energetic patriots and accusing liberty of 'all the abuses which belong only to the circumstances of war'. These all too transparent allusions to very recent events explain the abrupt awakening of Jacobin interest in the Constitution. In fact, the proposal for its application was advanced two days after the closing of the Jacobin Club. To demand at this precise moment that the Constitution should be taken out of its ark came down to indirectly contesting the legality of that decision (did not the Constitution guarantee the rights of popular societies?) and to put into question, as improper and arbitrary, the whole anti-Jacobin policy of the Committees, who exercised their power by virtue of the laws on revolutionary government.

The manoeuvre was, however, crude. Several deputies, Tallien in the lead, had a good time recalling that the very same people who had most opposed the idea of constitutional government and who had denounced as criminals those of their colleagues who had dared to refer to it, today 'throw themselves into the arena and call for it [the Constitution] with loud cries'. They turned against the Jacobins their own argument, which had often been employed: they were proposing to make fundamental laws at the very moment that the armies were struggling against the enemy, when all consideration should be given to the measures to be taken to ensure victory; their manoeuvre recalled too well that of the 'Hébert faction'. To the struggle on the frontiers was added the one that the Committees and 'twenty-five million Frenchmen' carried out in the interior. 'The men who defeated the tyrant on 9 Thermidor, the men who destroyed an authority that competed with national representation, form, as a matter of fact, a redoubtable faction, it is a faction of twenty-five million Frenchmen against the rogues and scoundrels.' On 9 Thermidor, a 'beneficial revolution defeated the *tyrant*'; on 22 Brumaire, with the decision to close the Jacobin Club, the 'same thunderbolt struck *tyranny*'. This struggle should be pursued, but in order to weaken it those who had demanded the Terror yesterday, today preached leniency and demanded the application of the Constitution. It was therefore against the *leniency* of the Jacobins that, without throwing doubt on the legality of the Constitution itself, the 'men of 9 Thermidor' opposed from the first the drawing up of fundamental laws.[3]

This political imbroglio could not last, however. In the course of the debate on the recall of the Girondins (18 Ventôse, 8 March 1795), Sieyès warned the Convention that it would no longer be possible to evade constitutional problems and remain content with extending the provisional regime of 'revolutionary government' indefinitely. To recall the Girondin deputies was for Sieyès both an act of justice and a logical consequence of the policy initiated on 9 Thermidor. In fact, it was with the insurrection of 31 May, the 'work of tyranny', that this 'fatal period began ... *when there was no longer a Convention*; the minority ruled, and this overturning of all social order was the result of the appearance of a portion of the people who were said to be in insurrection'; after 10 Thermidor the majority had 'returned to carrying out its legislative function'. These two dates therefore marked off a period to which applied

principles which are everybody's: a deliberative assembly where violence keeps away a party of those who have the right to vote is wounded in its very existence, it *ceases to deliberate according to its function* ... a law which issues from a legislative body ceases to have this true character if one of its members, whose opinion and vote could have changed the result of its deliberations, cannot have his voice heard when he considers it necessary.[4]

Sieyès was not explicitly referring to the Constitution of 1793; no one doubted, however, that he was thinking of it. A recognised authority in constitutional matters, he advanced a legal argument that demonstrated the invalidity of the Constitution by reason of its terrorist origins. The Jacobin and Montagnard deputies, along with the *sans-culottes* militants, in brief the former political personnel of the Terror, kept brandishing as a political slogan the necessary application of the Constitution, and using it as a means of pressure on the Committees and the majority of the Convention. To apply the Constitution thus became an overall political

---

[3] *Moniteur*, vol. 22, session of 24 Brumaire, Year III. On this debate and the 'impossible constitutional republic', cf. F. Diaz, *Dal movimento dei lumi al movimento dei popoli*, Bologna, 1986, pp. 618 *et seq.*

[4] Cf. the speech of Sieyès, in the course of the meeting of 18 Ventôse, Year III, *Moniteur*, vol. 23, p. 640. Boissy d'Anglas, in his *Discours préliminaire au projet de Constitution*, to which we shall return, took up the argument of Sieyès to show the invalidity of the Constitution of 1793

thought up by intriguers, dictated by tyranny and accepted by Terror ... Let us throw this work of our oppressors into eternal forgetfulness, so that it can no longer serve as a pretext for the factious. All of France, in admitting it has been tyrannised, has sufficiently shown the invalidity of this pretended acceptance that is alleged today, and the adherence of all Frenchmen to the proscription of our tyrants condemns to shame their system, their plans and their odious laws.

To the invalidity of the deliberations of the Convention was added the invalidity of the referendum itself.

symbol, a roundabout way of contesting the anti-terrorist policy, of demanding the liberation of 'persecuted patriots' and the re-establishment of the activities of the Jacobin societies, of condemning the purges as well as the denigration of the symbolic heritage of Year II. This fixation on the Constitution revealed, moreover, the political weakness of the whole campaign. The Jacobin discourse is, we have said, trapped by its reference to the founding event of the whole period, the 'revolution of 9 Thermidor'. Its authors and partisans could not and, perhaps, did not even want to put back into question this symbolic date without, at the same time, proclaiming the return, pure and simple, of the Terror and rehabilitating the 'tyrant'. Paradoxically, it was in the name of the 'true meaning of 9 Thermidor' that they denied the consequences of this event and demanded the 'democratic constitution of '93'.

Everything took place, then, as if the Jacobin and Montagnard members of the Convention accepted the principles of 9 Thermidor, summed up in the slogan *Down with the tyrant!*, but denied the consequences, the political dynamic which it produced. This was to demand, so to speak, a return to the starting point, to renounce the route taken towards dismantling the Terror. In this context, Barère's allusions to 'the secret committee of the foreign party' were too much of a reminder of the most sinister periods of the recent past.

This campaign encouraged, in consequence, attacks against the Constitution of 1793. It was denounced not only because of its 'suspect' origins, but above all because of its content: any attempt to apply it could only mean the return of the Terror. On 1 Germinal there took place a particularly stormy debate, revealing the increasing importance taken by the Constitution in the political and symbolic stakes. On this day the petition of the deputation from the Quinze-vingts *section* provoked a storm: in scarcely veiled terms it demanded, as a remedy for all evils, 'the organisation as of today of the popular constitution of 1793' which 'is the palladium of the people and the dread of its enemies'. On the 'left', the petition found the warmest support; Chasles proposed the immediate ordering, as a first symbolic act, of the exhibition of the Declaration of the Rights of Man and the Citizen in 'all public places', and the care of executing this measure should be 'entrusted to the public itself'. Tallien replied, thanks to his already well polished anti-terrorist arguments, that the men who now called so strongly for the Constitution were 'the same as those who enclosed it in a box' (it was no longer the 'solemn ark' ...); they followed it not with fundamental laws but with revolutionary government. Tallien, however, did not dare challenge the Constitution itself; in order to take the initiative, he proposed, carried away by his usual rabble-rousing, the drawing up of fundamental laws within two weeks. That bridge would be crossed by

Thibaudeau, president of the session: the majority of those who today called for the exhibition of the Constitution, for 'publicising' it, did not even know it. Now, the Constitution was not 'democratic', as was claimed, but terrorist, and hidden behind the demand for bringing it into force were terrorist manoeuvres.

I know only one democratic constitution, which is the one that will offer to the people liberty, equality and the enjoyment of its rights. In this sense the Constitution at present existing is not at all democratic, for national representation would still be in the power of a conspiring commune, which several times has tried to destroy it and to kill liberty.

Thibaudeau brandished the spectre of the return of the Terror; to put the Constitution back into action was to provide Paris with a council and to restore the Commune; it was to see, within three months, the Jacobins re-established and representation dissolved; it was to leave factions with the right of 'partial insurrection'; it was to concede the initiative for insurrection to the 'scoundrels'; it was to annul the 'revolution of 9 Thermidor'. In conclusion, the Convention disregarded the demand to have the 'table of the laws' exhibited and appointed a commission responsible for working out the fundamental laws, without, however, fixing a deadline.[5]

## Archaic violence and representative government

The day after Saladin's report concerning the denunciation of former members of the Committees, presented in the name of the Commission of Twenty-one (21 Ventôse, Year III, 2 March 1795), the Convention became bogged down in a procedure which risked becoming interminable, to judge by the time the indictment of Carrier had taken. Still, his case, directly implicated in the horrors of the Terror of Nantes, was relatively easy to deal with quickly and his responsibility much more evident than in the case of Barère, Billaud-Varenne, Collot d'Herbois and Vadier. For this was no longer a matter of flagrant excess, but of the whole policy of the Terror, and even of the evaluation of Year II. The political struggle became more and more poisonous as it obeyed the political logic of revenge and the will to exorcise the memories of the Terror by exemplary punishment of the 'guilty'. This struggle was to experience a brutal acceleration as a result of the intervention from the street, on 12 Germinal and, especially, on 1 Prairial. In the political confrontation between the 'Thermidoreans' there

[5] *Moniteur*, vol. 24, pp. 31–2. At the same time, in order to confront the growing agitation in the *sections*, the Convention voted through, following Sieyès's report, *La Loi de grande police pour assurer la garantie de la sûreté générale, du gouvernement républicain et de la représentation nationale*, granting increased powers to the Convention against 'seditious assembly'.

suddenly stepped forward an unexpected protagonist who seemed to belong to the past: the *popular crowd* with its primitive and archaic violence.

The *journées* of Germinal and Prairial have been the subject of many works.[6] Let us recall only that on 12 Germinal and 1 Prairial the Convention was attacked by a crowd of demonstrators to the cries of 'Bread and the Constitution of 1793!' These attacks, which had been preceded by particularly stormy assemblies, were all repulsed. On 12 Germinal, the crowd, led by the women, occupied the hall of the Convention for several hours, and dispersed after the intervention of the National Guard, without shots or casualties. The events of 1 Prairial took a more bloody turn; a young member of the Convention, Féraud, was killed, in the very hall of the Assembly, during the fight which broke out when the crowd forced the door of entry. He had his head cut off, which was then carried, stuck on a pike, into the hall of the Convention and then to the Place du Carrousel. The crowd remained in the hall for about nine hours (from 3 o'clock in the afternoon to midnight); during this time, under the pressure of a party of the invaders, there was a pretence at discussion in which some Montagnard deputies took part. On their initiative, a handful of the deputies present voted through a series of measures demanded by the demonstrators, conforming, in large part, to the pamphlet-manifesto *Insurrection du peuple pour obtenir du pain et reconquérir ses droits*, peddled in the street the day before. Towards midnight, the Convention was liberated by battalions from moderate *sections* and by the armed force that its commissioners had succeeded in bringing together. Heavy rain dispersed the people assembled in the Place du Carrousel. The disturbance continued the following day; it began once more with a gathering of women at the Tuileries; in one of the *sections* (Arcis) the Assembly moved to the Maison Commune (Hôtel de Ville) and even proclaimed itself the *National Convention*. The crowd of demonstrators arrived at the Convention and the gunners aimed their cannons at them. To prevent a repetition of the scenario of the day before, the Convention sent a delegation which 'fraternised' with the crowd. A deputation of the latter was received at the bar of the Convention, after which the 'reunited people' withdrew. The last act was played out on 4 Prairial, when the Committees decided to attack the faubourg Saint-Antoine, with a double objective: to arrest the presumed assassin of Féraud (a certain Jean Tinel, apprentice lockmaker, who, the evening before, had been snatched from the cart which was taking him to

6  On the *journées* of spring, Year III, cf. R. Cobb and G. Rudé, 'Le Dernier Mouvement populaire de la Révolution française. Les *journées* de germinal et prairial an III', *Revue historique*, 1955, pp. 250–88; K. D. Tönnesson, *La Défaite des sans-culottes. Mouvement populaire et réaction bourgeoise de l'an III*, Paris and Oslo, 1959; E. Tarlé, *Germinal et prairial* (French trans.), Moscow, 1959; G. Rudé, *La Foule dans la Révolution française*, Paris, 1989. On the political consequences of the crisis, cf. Diaz, Movimento, pp. 626 *et seq.*

the scaffold by his comrades of the Popincourt *section*) as well as to seize the representatives Cambon and Thuriot (they had been proclaimed, on 2 Prairial, respectively mayor and public prosecutor of the Commune, according to a rumour which has since been shown to be false). The first 'expedition' against the faubourg Saint-Antoine, undertaken by the *jeunesse dorée*, having failed (the 'young people' came up against barricades and had been attacked by women and children who, from roofs and windows, threw tiles and stones upon them), the Convention, which from now on had a regular armed force, issued a decree calling on the faubourg to give up the assassins of Féraud as well as the cannons of its three *sections*. Threatened with being declared to be in a state of rebellion, with being deprived of bread and bombarded by the artillery, the faubourg gave itself up on the same day by surrendering its cannons and gunners to the army commanded by General Ménou (Tinel was to commit suicide).

The repression that followed these *journées* took place on two fronts. In town, about three thousand people were arrested (the gazettes speak of eight to ten thousand), the *sections* severely purged, the National Guard was reorganised and the citizens were ordered to give up their pikes, that symbol of the 'risen people'. At the Convention, the victorious majority turned all the experience of Jacobin-style purges to its account. Already on 12 Germinal, in flagrant violation of its own decrees guaranteeing denounced deputies the possibility of presenting their defence, the Assembly ordered, without any other procedure, the immediate deportation of Barère, Billaud-Varenne, Collot d'Herbois and Vadier. On the same day, and on those that followed, more than fifteen other representatives were arrested. On 2 Prairial, it decided to bring before a military Commission the deputies judged guilty of complicity with the crowd of insurgents (six deputies, tried on 27 Prairial and condemned to death, would try to kill themselves: Romme, Goujon and Duquesnoy would succeed; Soubrany, Duroy and Bourbotte, severely wounded, would be dragged to the guillotine; the condemned were to come down to posterity under the name of the 'last Montagnards' or the 'martyrs of Prairial'). The Convention would not cease, during the sessions of collective exorcism where passions and resentments were to be unchained, to surrender to the mania for denunciation, as if it wished to efface, once and for all, its terrorist past. To do this, however, it had recourse to the means it had already used and polished during the Terror: exclusion and arrest would be aimed at all members of the former Committees (with the exception of Carnot) as well as several former representatives *en mission*.

This brief summary will make it easier to place in the sequence of events the phenomenon with which we are concerned: the crowd and its violence, and their role during the *journées* of the spring of Year III. These *journées* are, without doubt, an integral part of the *experience* and *dynamic* of the Thermidorean period, but they are not to be confined to their strictly political consequences. In fact, they present a remarkable example of the *inextricable tangle of the archaic and the modern*, a more general phenomenon which we have already mentioned many times and which is peculiar to the *mentalités* and political culture of the Revolution. The same is true of the sociocultural context in which the *journées* of the spring of Year III are set and over which we should like to pause. We shall emphasize in particular the *journée* of 1 Prairial, in the course of which the role of the crowd and its violence in the confrontation between the 'risen people' and the representative government comes out very clearly, as in a laboratory experiment.

The *journées* of Germinal and Prairial originated in an economic crisis: a, so to speak, classical subsistence crisis, peculiar to the economy of the *ancien régime* (despite a harvest which looked promising, famine fastened on the population because of a very harsh winter; the Seine was frozen, transportation of corn and wood was severely disrupted); a 'new' financial crisis, peculiar to the economy of the Revolution. (The famine was set off by the depreciation of *assignats* and the suppression of the *maximum*. The authorities, counting on a good harvest, considered the application of a doctrinaire liberalism the only adequate means of reviving the economy. The sudden rise in prices and scarcities, especially of bread, thus came from the combined action of these two factors.) The crisis flagrantly brought out the social divisions and contrasts: on one side, the interminable queues, where women predominated, in front of the bakeries; on the other, the taverns, the restaurants, the markets and *pâtisseries* abundantly provisioned and displaying luxury products, but at prohibitive prices for the 'poorer classes'. These social divisions could also be seen in their very different preoccupations: while the assemblies of the well-to-do *sections*, from the west and the centre, were enthusiastic about the 'great political affair', that is the putting on trial of the four members of the former committees, the assemblies of the *sections* in the poor quarters, particularly the faubourgs Saint-Antoine and Saint-Marcel, were especially preoccupied by the scarcities and demanded that the Convention ensured the people had a bread ration, which in fact kept diminishing. But it was not only, not even principally, in the assemblies of the *sections* that popular opinion was expressed. Its place of expression moved towards the queues in front of the bakeries which formed in the night, where during the long hours of waiting gossip and rumour kept circulating. At least a part of this gossip has come down to us thanks to the daily reports of the agents of the Committee of General Security, who slipped in among the queues and 'groups' and then informed their superiors of the 'state of the public mind'.

What did they speak of in the queues? First and especially of the scarcities and their disastrous consequences. There are comments on the cases of people dead of hunger and cold whose bodies were found in the street, in the early morning; the cases of suicide, among others that of a mother who took her life after killing her own children. The discontent swiftly became politicised. People were heard to say that under the king they did not go without bread and that a new king was needed if they were not to starve. A campaign of royalist inscriptions and circulars developed. But also heard were comments that under Robespierre the people had, at least, some bread and the hoarders did not dare starve the poor people. To call this 'public mind', which appeared in the queues, 'royalist' or 'Robespierrist' would be hasty and mistaken. Rumour became politicised and violently attacked those in power when, in order to explain the famine, the people came to draw on their own sociocultural past and again reactivated the spectre of the 'famine plot'. Except that this was a new version: it was today no longer the monarchy, but the Convention and its Committees who were accused of *organising the famine*, of hiding the corn, in order to starve the people and thus strike at its vital substance, but also its most vulnerable, the women and children. This rumour had several versions: famine was established artificially in order to drive the people to extremes or even, according to another version, so that it demanded, in its despair, the return of the king, which the Committees were dreaming of, while not daring to admit it. At the same time there circulated rumours according to which the Convention was preparing to quit Paris, so as to abandon the people and leave it to die more quickly of hunger. The rumour even found an echo at the Convention where the Montagnard deputies accused the Committees of 'organising the famine'.

In these different variations, rumour pointed to authority as the sworn and treacherous enemy of the people; rumour was an accusing and mobilising force, which justified in advance all popular action against the Convention by putting forward the necessity of self-defence: the people had not only the right but the duty to *protect itself* against this 'wicked plot'. The anti-Jacobin majority of the Convention in fact took the spread of these rumours very seriously and did not underestimate their impact on people's minds; it tried to counter them by attributing their propagation to another plot, hatched by the 'blood-drinkers' or again by 'terrorism and royalism joined together'. It threw responsibility for the famine back onto the terrorists who assassinated thousands of farmers and on Robespierre himself, whose 'tyranny' was the origin of all evils, including the famine.[7]

---

[7] Cf. the proclamations of the Convention of 12 Germinal and 2 Prairial, *Moniteur*, vol. 24, pp. 122–3, 518. On the rumours reported by the agents of the Committee of General Security, cf. Aulard, *Paris pendant la réaction*, vol. 1, pp. 361, 370, 545, 546, 584, 663, 684,

Women, often with their children, were very numerous in the crowds which invaded the Convention on 12 Germinal and 1 Prairial; the queues in front of the bakeries were often the departure points for the gatherings. Now, the massive presence of women, surrounded with their children, is a characteristic of traditional revolts, especially those provoked by the scarcity of wheat. Marching in the leading ranks, crying 'Bread!', the women formed the avant-garde, both real and symbolic, of a spontaneous movement demanding the satisfaction of the most basic needs; the presence of the children underlined the *defensive* character of the movement as well as its legitimacy, beyond any political catchword. It was for the men to link the political claims to the simple demand: 'Bread!' Among these claims, two are the most frequent: immediate application of the Constitution of 1793 and liberation of the 'patriots' oppressed after 9 Thermidor.[8]

During the *journée* of 12 Germinal, it was the women who firstly, if not entirely, occupied the chamber of the Convention. To the eloquence of the representatives, to their appeals for calm, to the long explanations of the situation on food and the efforts of the Committees, they had one and the same response, the collective cry: 'Bread! Bread!' The crowd was not satisfied with merely listening to this strange dialogue between the women and the orators of the Convention; it occupied the seats of the deputies, jostled them and broke out in shouts. 'Instead of an ordered and under-standing group we had under our eyes the deplorable picture of a true popular orgy', declared, not without regret, Levasseur (from the Sarthe) in his *Mémoires* (he was in fact to be arrested the same day, as an accomplice of the rioters, as soon as the Committees succeeded in taking the situation in hand and evacuating the chamber).[9]

The *journée* of 1 Prairial had been much better prepared, and a political plan worked out in advance was to guide the crowd. Of course, at the origin

686. Michelet emphasised the rumours and their impact; in them he found both the resurgence of the 'legend of the famine pact' and the distant echo of the 'system of depopulation', which was Babeuf's fantasy.

It is certain that two legends dominated the situation, both on the whole absurd, although there was a little reality involved. On one side the working masses, the people in general, were saying: 'They want us to die of hunger'. On the other, the merchant classes, the numberless small investors were saying and thinking: 'There is a plot among the Jacobins to restart the Terror, massacre the Convention and half of Paris.' The terrible legend of the famine pact returns to people's minds in a different form. Listen to the long queue that forms in the night for bread. You would hear this: 'There are too many people in France. The government is putting that in order. We must die, we must die ... ' It is the sentiment which in Babeuf, Vilatte, etc. takes the horrifying formula of the system of depopulation. Everyone speaks of it, and the worst is that they believe it. (Michelet, *Histoire du dix-neuvième siècle*, vol. 21, p. 158.)

[8] On the subject of crowds during the Revolution and, especially, the presence of women and children, and the modes of action, cf. the stimulating study which I have found very useful: C. Lucas, 'Crowds and politics', in Baker (ed.), *The French Revolution and the creation of modern political culture*, vol. 2: Lucas (ed.), *The political culture of the Revolution*, Oxford, 1988.      [9] R. Levasseur, *Mémoires*, vol. 4, Paris, 1831, p. 210.

of the *journée* the same factors as in Germinal were to be found: throughout the seven weeks which separated the two *journées*, the famine had become still worse (and that despite the real efforts of those in authority to have corn brought to Paris). In the queues there circulated the same rumours and, after the repression that followed 12 Germinal, new ones were added: the Convention wanted to put Paris 'to fire and sword'; troops, even some of foreign origin, were concentrated in the Bois de Boulogne, in order to attack the people; on 12 Germinal, the women who called for bread had been ill-treated and savagely beaten on the orders of the Convention. The great difference consisted, however, in the attempt to channel and direct the spontaneous movement, to provide it with political objectives that could be carried out through a precise plan of action.

In fact, in an already overheated atmosphere, at the end of Floréal, a pamphlet entitled *Insurrection du peuple pour obtenir du pain et reconquérir ses droits* began to circulate in Paris. The text had been read in the *sections* and had a quite large circulation. On 1 Prairial in the morning, Isabeau even read it at the tribune of the Convention, presenting it in the name of the Committee of General Security, as flagrant proof 'of the revolt in preparation'.[10] The text is anonymous, but according to what Buonarotti says in his *Conspiration pour l'égalité*, it had been written by *sans-culotte* militants detained on charges of terrorism in the prison of Plessis. The text, which opened with a preamble, presented itself overall as a sort of proclamation made by the sovereign people. It took over and repeated, as a kind of evidence, the rumour denouncing 'the government that makes the people cruelly die of hunger'; all its promises to improve the supply of food were only 'deceitful and lying'. The authors stated that the government possessed stores where it had 'supplies locked up' kept in reserve in order to carry out its 'infamous plans', while the people died of hunger (we find here another archaic rumour). The sufferings of the people were such that the living envied 'the unfortunate fate of those whom famine piles daily into the tombs'. Because of this, the people would stand guilty towards itself and 'the future generation' if it did not ensure its own subsistence and recapture its rights. For a government which brought famine was also a usurping and oppressive government. What better proof of its tyranny than to have 'arrested arbitrarily, transferred from cell to cell, from commune to commune, and massacred in the prisons those who have enough courage and virtue to call for bread and common rights' ? Now, such a power could establish its strength only on the 'weakness, ignorance and wretchedness of

---

[10]  Cf. *Moniteur*, vol. 24, pp. 497–8. The text presented to the Convention corresponds, apart from a few minor details, to the original in four sheets, which is frequently mentioned in the records of the repression. Cf. Tönesson, *La Défaite des sans-culottes*, pp. 250 *et seq*. In what follows we quote the version in the *Moniteur*.

the people'. The 'risen people' had a single means of action to maintain its survival and reconquer its rights; its insurrection was perfectly legitimate and, as was stated in the Constitution, it represented 'for the people and each *section* of the oppressed people *the most sacred of rights, the most necessary of duties'*. Hence the objectives of insurrection. Firstly: 'Bread'; the pamphlet was content to take up this rallying slogan without, however, being more precise as to how this 'bread' would be provided. It was, on the other hand, much more precise in fixing specifically political objectives: abolition of revolutionary government, which 'each faction abuses in turn, in order to ruin, starve and enslave the people'; immediate proclamation and establishment of the 'democratic Constitution of 1793'; removal of the present government, arrest of all its members and their replacement by other representatives; 'immediate release of citizens detained for having called for bread and expressing their opinions with frankness'; finally, the summoning on 25 Prairial of the primary assemblies and the summoning, for 25 Messidor, of a legislative Assembly, which would replace the Convention. The *Insurrection du peuple* also defined the means of action: an appeal to 'citizens and citizenesses' to appear, *en masse*, on 1 Prairial at the Convention and this to be carried out 'in *fraternal disorder* and without awaiting action from neighbouring *sections'*. It was therefore an appeal to form a crowd which would avoid, precisely because of its 'fraternal disorder', government tricks and 'leaders who have sold themselves'. This crowd would have a rough model of structure and organisation, thanks to a sign of recognition: each person would carry on his hat the rallying cry, written in chalk, 'Bread and the democratic constitution of 1793'. The other points indicated other measures to be taken: the closing of the gates of the town; the seizing of the alarm cannon and the bells meant to sound the tocsin; the rallying of the body of the people.

The language as well as the minutiae of the arrangements reveal a full fund of political and technical experience, accumulated by a personnel trained and practised as a result of its participation in previous *journées*, particularly that of 31 May 1793; this experience was put at the service of a political strategy which appealed to the 'risen people', taking back its sovereignty. The measures proposed constituted, in reality, a call for the return of the Terror which would find its personnel, the 'oppressed patriots', freed from the prisons, and would be set in train by a new Montagnard government. It is in fact striking that neither the word 'Terror' nor the name 'Robespierre' are mentioned; from all the evidence the authors wish to be likened neither to the 'terrorists' nor the 'Robespierrists', terms generally considered to be compromising. It is even more striking that the plan sought to circumvent the structures of the *sections*; it counted on the spontaneity of the crowd and, possibly, on its leadership by 'patriots', the terrorist personnel liberated from the prisons. (It is not, moreover, out of the question that the authors also counted on a group of their accomplices whose number is difficult to evaluate; among the leaders of the crowd, tried after the failure of the revolt, were found militants from the *sections* who, following 9 Thermidor, had seen their revolutionary careers, their vocations almost, ruined.) [11] This political plan, uniting 'bread', the release of terrorist personnel and the immediate application of the Constitution of 1793, was perfectly in keeping with the *political logic* of the confrontation around the dismantling of the Terror. The *Insurrection du peuple* reveals the bitterness and the rage of despairing and persecuted men who no longer hesitated to push Jacobin and Montagnard ideas to their furthest and extreme consequences.

Once the chamber of the Convention was attacked and invaded, the crowd, however, shunned logic and the political plan it should pursue. It was a politicised crowd, certainly, at least in the sense that it attacked the Convention and that some of them shouted the 'rallying slogan': 'Bread and the constitution of 1793!' In its behaviour, however, the crowd found and followed another logic, which called for the secular rites of popular revolt. The premeditated revolutionary *journée* was therefore both extended and, to a large extent, emptied of its political substance. The crowd incorporated the plan into its own ritual of violence and reduced it to a simple fragment of a 'world upside down' which its own behaviour acted out. Let us take up just two examples of these quite complex phenomena: the assassination of Féraud and the behaviour of the rioters.

Colin Lucas stresses that the popular crowd adopts for preference an open space, a street or square, as its scene of action. Now, in attacking the Convention, it found itself necessarily in an enclosed space, in a hall. A large part of the crowd remained outside, in the Place du Carrousel, and between these two spaces, 'inside' and 'outside', was established a network of quite complex relations, a sort of double exchange of men and symbols. The most macabre symbol was Féraud's head. As we know, this young member of the Convention had been wounded by a shot, fired, according to the most plausible hypothesis, accidentally during the fight which broke out when the crowd was trying to force the door of entry and invade the chamber. This shot and its blood-covered victim triggered off the explosion of collective and gratuitous violence. Wounded, but still alive, Féraud was finished off by several assailants who, in a sort of collective rage, fell upon him with their knives. The accounts vary on the manner in which the symbolic act was accomplished: cutting off the head and impaling it on a pike. According to some, this took place in the chamber itself; using knives

[11] Tönnesson, *La Défaite des sans-culottes*, pp. 358 *et seq.*

they separated the head from the body with difficulty, under the very eyes of the deputies and among laughter and cries of encouragement from the rioters. According to another version, the corpse had been thrown outside, offered, so to speak, as a gift to the crowd which occupied the square, and it was there that the cries resounded: 'Cut off his head.' One of the rioters did it with a single blow of a sabre, cutting it 'like a radish', arousing the admiration of those around him. Whatever the truth of the matter, the head, skewered on a pike, was carried from hand to hand by men in relays, under the laughs and insults of the crowd massed in the square. (As for the body, this was dragged about somewhere else.) This unchaining of violence was all the more gratuitous in that some of the crowd was unsure of the exact identity of the victim, while others were completely ignorant of whose head it was that they insulted. This spectacle of horror lasted about two hours; it was only when the pike returned with the head to the chamber, where it was again received with laughter and applause, that it was finally planted in front of Boissy d'Anglas, the president of the meeting. All of these are so many familiar images and actions which evoke and revive an entire traditional ritual of collective violence.

In the chamber itself, the crowd seemed to behave in an almost carnival manner. It ejected the deputies, insulted them, took their places, surrounded the rostrum, was not sparing with blows of the fist, without in fact knowing too much about the political opinions of the deputies they struck. So Bourbotte, who was to be executed as an accomplice of the insurgents, a declared Montagnard, bore witness that a man 'with haggard eyes, a black face, armed with a long pike, stayed close to him, and in these moments of passion . . . repeatedly punched him in the head'.[12] The crowd parodied the behaviour of the deputies during debates and held it up to ridicule. Accordingly, the military Commission condemned one of the assailants, a journeyman locksmith, 'for having gone up to the desk of the President and behaved in an indecent manner' (sic).[13] A large number of the occupiers, whose number is difficult to estimate, was drunk. The incessant to-ing and fro-ing between the chamber and the square is explained above all by the presence of barrels of wine in the square, brought it is not known from where or by whom. The assailants drank a lot and on empty stomachs. In this atmosphere, some militants read the list of demands taken from the Insurrection du peuple and some Montagnard deputies, who would pay for it with their heads and their lives, attempted to channel the passions and the violence, by proposing to adopt measures which would calm the crowd (at least, this was the explanation of their behaviour before the military Commission which condemned them to death).

---

[12] Evidence quoted by Tönnesson, ibid., p. 271.    [13] Ibid.

The actions of the crowd have left a painful and lasting trace in collective memory. 'The people', writes Quinet, 'appeared more frightening than at any other period of the Revolution. They frightened their own friends. This moment was the worst.' Michelet speaks 'of a terrible drunkenness, a strange thirst for blood' and quotes, with approval, the words of Carnot: 'It is the only day that the people appeared to me to be ferocious.'[14] It is in fact striking that the neo-Jacobins and the Babouvistes who were going to glorify the 'last Montagnards' and their heroic suicide, by presenting them as so many martyrs of the people's cause, would pass over, in an embarrassed silence, the raging violence of this same 'people' during the *journée* of 1 Prairial.

The failed revolt would have many immediate and serious consequences for what was to follow in Thermidorean political experience.

The disordered, brutal and ineffective action of the crowd showed up the fragility of the *sans-culotte* phenomenon as well as its sporadic nature. This phenomenon became increasingly reduced to the former political personnel of the Terror, hunted down everywhere, trying to escape the massacres and the 'legal revenge', as pitiless as it was systematic. The failure of the revolt completed 9 Thermidor; it was a victory, without any possible ambiguity, for the Convention over the street, for the 'representative system' over the methods of direct democracy, now reduced to the 'anarchy' of a violent crowd. Germinal and Prairial present, in a way, the reverse of the 'revolutionary *journées*'. They show the decline, even the end, of the heroic and militant imagery of Year II, that of the 'risen people' ready to recover its sovereignty.

The twenty-five million men who sent us here did not place us under the control of the markets of Paris nor under the assassins' axe. It is not to the faubourg Saint-Antoine that they delegated legislative power; it is to us ... And you, citizens of Paris, who keep being called *the people* by all the sedition-mongers who have wished to raise themselves upon the debris of national authority, who have long flattered you like a king but to whom the truth must at last be told, great and glorious things have brought you honour during the course of the Revolution; but the Republic would nevertheless have serious criticisms to make to you if the *journée* of 4 Prairial [capitulation of the faubourg Saint-Antoine] had not made amends for the appalling days which preceded it.[15]

And how significant is the counter-imagery that was forcefully asserted in the funeral eulogies to the memory of Féraud which consecrated him as a martyr to liberty and the anti-terrorist cause.

Let us do our duty as he did, by imitating his heroism, by celebrating his memory. The honours bestowed on the dead render the living more virtuous. Never forget,

[14] Quinet, *La Révolution*, pp. 613–15; Michelet, *Histoire du dix-neuvième siècle*, vol. 21, pp. 170–1.    [15] M.-J. Chénier, speech of 6 Prairial, Year III, in *Moniteur*, vol. 24, p. 548.

representatives, this horribly memorable day, when the National Convention, outraged by the factious, beleaguered, forced open, invaded by a bloodthirsty horde, saw the majesty of the people trampled under foot, and the will to crime insolently called *law*, in the sanctuary of the law itself. Never forget these seditious cries, these horrifying shouts, this delirious and homicidal drunkenness, this deplorable spectacle of representatives of the people seated on the very benches that their executioners usurped.[16]

This imagery linked up with the portrayal of the 'vandal people' by reanimating it. The 'people', to be sure, was not guilty as a whole; it let itself, however, be too easily led astray and it therefore required permanent surveillance and education. The 'childish people' was separated from the 'vandal people' only by a single step that transformed error into crime. And so Louvet recalls this 'horrible day' when the 'scoundrels' brought to the president different writings 'which they called motions; they said to him: "We do not need your assembly; the people is here, you are the president of the people; sign and the decree will be good, sign or I kill you."' Féraud wished to save the Convention from this 'people', by sacrificing his own life:

This is unreason, imposture, anger, impudence; this is vengeance, hatred, vile oaths, ferocious curses, all the hideous passions, all the fury, all the furies. Everywhere hunger acts and cries; and on all the faces red with drunkenness one sees only debauchery gorged with meat and wine. And yet it is still passed off in the name of women! and all that calls itself the people!

Certainly, the day would come when the 'true people' would recover its 'so unworthily prostituted' title, but, for the moment, even to 'brothers gone astray . . . you [members of the Convention] will not return their arms! They were deceived, they can be deceived again. *One does not give back to a child the instrument he has hurt himself with.*'[17]

The revolts of Germinal and Prairial and their brutal repression did not fundamentally modify the major *political problem* of the closing of the Revolution; on the contrary, they aggravated it even more and made a solution yet more urgent. The *journées* of Germinal and Prairial provoked new surges of anxiety about the possible return of the Terror, including a dramatic intensification in the revenge taken on 'terrorists', which went into paroxysms during the massacres of prisoners at Lyon and in the Midi. These lynchings sometimes took place with the tacit support of the population, but more and more often they became the work of specialised bands of killers recruited from the 'young people'. The limits between 'justice as the order of the day' and the massacres, whose royalist inspiration was scarcely veiled, tended to be erased. In the same way, the frontiers became fluid between a *reaction* to the Terror which appealed to

[16] *Ibid.*
[17] J.-B. Louvet, speech at the official session of 14 Prairial, *Moniteur*, vol. 24, pp. 608 *et seq.*

legality and a reaction which itself had recourse to arbitrary action and established a sort of counter-Terror. On the other hand, the crowd offering violence to the Convention, to the cries of 'Bread and the Constitution of 1793!', brought to the Assembly, if it were needed, the proof that the dismantling of the Terror and the abolition of the Constitution of 1793 were only two aspects of the same problem. To defeat the Parisian revolts was to condemn in fact, *en bloc* and without appeal, the illegal and terrorist Constitution. The Republic should therefore cease to be provisional and provide itself with the foundation of a new Constitution.

### Reaction and utopia

The day after 9 Thermidor, there was no hesitation as to the term to be applied to the event which had just been carried out: the *fall of the tyrant* and the *triumph of liberty* were, necessarily, a *revolution*. 'On 31 May the people carried out its revolution, on 9 Thermidor the national Convention carried out its own: liberty applauded both equally', declared the Convention in its official proclamation addressed to the French people on 10 Thermidor. The countless addresses which reached the Convention employed the same terminology. The word *reaction* did not begin its true political career until the end of the Thermidorean period – as if, only at that moment, was the need felt to find a specific term that would allow the identification of the events which followed one another and would make sense of them.

Like the word *Thermidorean*, the term *reaction* (and its derivatives: *reactionaries, reactionary*) is still waiting for someone to describe its history and vicissitudes.[18] Some texts testify to the need and, consequently, the feeling held by contemporaries of having lived through unprecedented experiences in the Revolution and that it was necessary first to *name* them in order to then *recognise* them. In the same way as *revolution* or *progress*, the term *reaction* was borrowed by politics from the science of mechanics. It was then broadened into the moral domain. It had the sense of an opposite movement caused by a preceding movement, a simple recoil. Rousseau, for example, used it in this sense: 'No human art can prevent sudden action by the strong against the weak, but it can prepare the springs for the *reaction*.'[19] Before the Thermidorean period it was, however, a rare word and one which in fact attributed no specific characteristic nor political 'colour' to *action* or *reaction*. This latter word, a 'contrary' movement of

---

[18] Jean Starobinski has shown the way in his stimulating study: 'Réaction. Le mot et ses usages', *Confrontations psychiatriques*, no. 12, 1974.

[19] J.-J. Rousseau, *Considérations sur le gouvernement de Pologne*, in *Œuvres complètes*, Pléiade, Paris, 1964, vol. 3, p. 1018.

ideas and feelings, was only the repercussion of the first shock. In this sense, *reaction* is not in fact opposed to *revolution*; rather, the two terms are complementary. This is how the term *reaction* had been for the first time, it seems, associated with the consequences of 9 Thermidor. In so far as this *journée* was precisely a *revolution*, a powerful liberating action, it caused a *recoil*, a *release* of feelings of justice and sympathy, repressed during the Terror, towards innocent victims. 'Great events took place in Paris a few days ago; a great revolution has occurred; the tyrant exists no longer, the *patrie* breathes, liberty triumphs . . . After such a long repression, one must expect a *powerful and proportionate* reaction to the evils that we have had to deplore; one must grant to sensitivity all that humanity requires.'[20]

Rare at the end of Year II, the word *reaction* was quite current after the crushing of the royalist revolt of 13 Vendémiaire, Year IV (5 October 1795). It then became firmly established in political discourse, especially in official vocabulary, all the while growing richer with more meanings. So Joseph-Marie Chénier, whose reports on the massacres of prisoners at Lyon and in the Midi played an important role in the spread of the word, did not mean to confuse the *Thermidorean* political strategy with *reaction*; to speak of *Thermidorean reaction* would have been a misconception. In his report of 29 Vendémiaire, Year IV (therefore two weeks after the crushing of the revolt of 13 Vendémiaire), Chénier insisted on the opposition between the Thermidorean *period* and the *reaction* which followed it in time but which perverted it and represented a movement contrary to its work and spirit. Chénier even proposed a sort of periodisation of the Republic since 9 Thermidor. This memorable date announced the end of the Terror, with its cortège of tribunals and revolutionary committees, of scaffolds and prisons, of ruins and highway robbery held 'in high honour'. This bloody period was followed by the *Thermidorean period*, 'memorable, immortal period, when the National Convention alone, recovering the force that people thought it no longer possessed, reconquered public liberty; then

---

[20] *La Société des amis de la Liberté et de l'Egalité séante aux Jacobins de Paris à toutes les Sociétés populaires de la République, le 18 thermidor, an II*, in Aulard, *Société des Jacobins*, vol. 6, pp. 323–5. In what followed, however, the address insisted on the risks of this *reaction*, 'noble and natural' as it was: 'it is necessary to stop this sensitivity at the point where ill will would like to grasp it as a weapon against public liberty . . . It is not for them [the enemies of liberty] that the Convention has carried out this *astonishing revolution*.' Six weeks later, the term *reaction* returns, but this time it calls to mind a disquieting context and is bracketed with the adjective *cruel*. The Jacobins were drawing up a positive evaluation of the revival of their activities after the 'fall of the tyrant', of the purging of their members, of the reparation of abuses which 'had slipped in among the efforts of patriotism on its revolutionary march'; but they recorded that 'nevertheless, *a cruel reaction has made itself felt*: from all points of the Republic the affiliated societies report: aristocracy and federalism raising their heads, the freeing of men regarded until now as suspect, their movement to avenge themselves on the patriots': *Rapport fait à la Société des Jacobins par son Comité de correspondance, 5 vendémiaire an III, ibid.*, pp. 517–18.

both the dictatorship and the decemvirate were thrown down, then tears were dried, the cells opened, the scaffolds overturned'. The Convention was generous enough to 'forget wrongs, even crimes'; it believed in the repentance of those who had been enemies of liberty and the Revolution for a long time. Yet,

these *new republicans* entered the enlightened ranks of the old patriots, but it was to slaughter them; they declared their praise of representation, but it was to destroy it. The system of *indulgence and generosity*, followed so courageously by the Convention . . . only sharpened their resentment and encouraged them to crime. Scarcely set free, the faithful friends of slavery covered their freedmen's robes with blood; it is always by abusing principles that they have led the Republic to the edge of the abyss.

Thus was born the *reaction* whose treachery, misdeeds and crimes were denounced by Chénier. He even drew up a sort of inventory of acts and phenomena peculiar to the *reaction*: persecution of patriots on the pretext that they were terrorists; bands of arrogant and provocative 'young people' invading public places, even banning the 'Marseillaise'; the mysterious 'companies of Jesus' and 'companies of the Sun' who had carried out real massacres, notably in the Midi. Now, it was 'in the name of humanity, of justice, of the national Convention itself', that these 'scoundrels', calling themselves the 'avengers of their fathers and sacrificed patriots', attacked the Republic and even found accomplices among the constituted authorities. These were all so many political phenomena which resembled and complemented each other to the point that Chénier dedicated the single word 'reaction' to them. Still shocked by the riot of 13 Vendémiaire against the Convention, he had no doubt about the political colouring of this reaction: it was royalist. On the other hand, he seemed to hesitate between two interpretations of its origins: sometimes he was content to re-employ the, so to speak, classical format of the 'plot' hatched abroad, the émigrés, refractory priests, etc.; at other times it occurred to him to explain the *reaction* by a sort of turning of the 'system of generosity', created by 9 Thermidor, into a 'machine' of vengeance and proscription. These two versions do not in fact exclude each other and Chénier did not push too far his questioning of the reasons for this 'perversion': faced with *reaction*, he expressed above all his surprise and indignation.[21]

[21] Chénier even suggested a date after which the *reaction* perverted the 'memorable Thermidorean epoch': six months after 9 Thermidor, that is, during the winter of Year III. Chénier's speech deserves a fuller commentary, in particular for its demagogic ingredients as well as its apologetic character. The exposure of the horrors carried out by 'reactionaries' in the Midi, notably during the massacre of Fort Saint-Jean, at Marseille, aimed at compromising the riot of 13 Vendémiaire and its authors; Chénier breathed not a word of the responsibilities of the Convention itself, which had nevertheless *tolerated* the massacres (by reacting, at the very most, quite weakly, as had Chénier himself, in his report of 6 Messidor on the massacres at Lyon, in which he in fact did not use the word *reaction*). Chénier became quite emotional when he exalted the work of the Convention and the

Some months later, Mailhe varied both the sense of the term *reaction* and the phenomena in question. '9 Thermidor, which should have simply done for the throne of anarchy what 10 August had done for the throne of royalty, was imperceptibly diverted from its aim of making peace and presented as the principle of a bloody and arbitrary *reaction*.' This was not simply a recoil; the political phenomenon was more complex. It was necessary to distinguish it from attacks and intrigues that were simply counter-revolutionary, launched by sworn and old enemies of the Revolution, in the name of values and principles which were always hostile to it. The *reaction* and, therefore, the *reactionaries* took over principles inherent to the Revolution and perverted them; they reversed its march and its progress. From this point of view, the reactionaries curiously resembled the terrorists against whom they nevertheless cried for revenge: the latter had established the Terror 'in the name of liberty'; the former perverted justice, a sacred principle of 9 Thermidor, and employed it as a pretext for their violence and their arbitrary revenge. Both parties (and there is nothing surprising in that they are sometimes the same men ...) followed 'the same plan of disorganisation, of invasion of legitimate authority, of discord, of civil war'.[22]

The pamphlet by Benjamin Constant, *Des réactions politiques*, constitutes both the culminating point of Thermidorean discourse on the *reaction* and the breaking-point. Constant, at the beginning of his political career and thought, accepted the republican order defined by the Constitution of Year III, but he refused to share with the Thermidoreans their past and their responsibilities for the *political reactions*. (*Reaction* became, for the first time, the subject of systematic discussion, a proof of the success of the term in political discourse and of the importance attached to the problems it pointed to in discussion of revolutionary experience.) For Constant, *political reactions* are explained by revolutionary phenomena; they are the result of revolutions which have not succeeded at the first blow and which, consequently, go on for too long.

When the agreement between the institutions and the ideas [of a people] finds itself destroyed, revolutions are inevitable. They aim to re-establish this agreement ... When a revolution carries out this purpose at the first blow and stops at this limit, without going beyond, it does not produce a reaction because it is only a crossing over and because the moment of arrival is also that of rest.

destiny of its members: 'One day, when the years will have ripened the Republic, the members of this Convention, slandered, attacked, assassinated by all factions, will remain standing like scattered oaks in a forest ravaged by fire.' This description would have been even more eloquent if it had not been in justification of the decree imposing the re-election of two-thirds of the Convention's members to the new Assemblies.

[22] Cf. Mailhe, *Rapport du 8 germinal an IV, au Conseil des Cinq-Cents, sur les sociétés populaires*, in *Moniteur*, vol. 28, p. 89.

When a revolution goes beyond these limits, it is transformed, in some way, into a mad balance-wheel, oscillating with an uncontrolled and uncontrollable movement:

When a revolution, carried beyond its limits, ceases, it is first put back within its limits. The further one has moved forward, the further one goes back. Moderation ends and reactions begin . . . There are two sorts of reaction: those which hold sway over men, and those which have ideas as their object. I do not call the just punishment of the guilty reaction, nor the return to sound ideas. These things belong, one to the law, the other to reason. But what, on the contrary, essentially distinguishes reactions, is arbitrary power in place of the law, passion in place of reason: instead of judging men, people proscribe men; instead of examining ideas, people reject them.

It is not our place to follow the developments of these definitions which are extended by a quite original political discussion. Let us discuss only one point. Constant is particularly sensitive to the phenomenon of *political defectors*, which is inseparable from reaction. He denounces 'these atrocious and cowardly men, keen to buy with blood pardon for the blood they have shed, who put no limit to their excesses', the 'converted assassins, repentant proconsuls' – a transparent allusion to the former terrorists who 'giving way to the force of the reaction, let [the Convention] replace the evils it had carried out by evils it should have prevented', especially during the 'reaction which followed 1 Prairial'. *Reactions*, then, only change what is arbitrary, 'the great enemy of all liberty, the corrupting vice of all institutions'. They have recourse to arbitrary power to re-establish justice and liberty, but this same recourse to arbitrary power has the effect that 'redressing wrongs becomes reaction, that is to say, vengeance and fury'. On the other hand Constant attacks the 'defectors from philosophy' who, like La Harpe, were converted into bigots and wanted to re-establish 'prejudices and fanaticism'. Abruptly changing sides, all these political and ideological defectors risked dragging the country into a violent *reaction* which, of necessity, would cause in its turn another reaction, in the opposite direction, and thus perpetuate the Revolution. Now, the essential thing was to terminate it, to bring it within limits and so return to its principles. The Constitution of Year III offered, for the first time, the opportunity to halt the pendulum movement that replaced one kind of arbitrary power with another, to put an end to 'political reactions', to substitute law for arbitrary power. So Constant partly shared the Thermidorean discourse on the reaction, while keeping his distance. One might say that he wants to detach the Constitution of Year III, the work crowning the Thermidorean period, from its evil antecedents, to save it from the disquieting inheritance of extremisms on all sides, bequeathed by this same period in which the Constitution was worked out. 'If reactions are something terrible and disastrous, avoid arbitrary power, for it necessarily drags reaction in its train; if arbitrary power is a destructive scourge, avoid reactions, for they ensure the domination of arbitrary power ... Only a system of principles offers a lasting peace. It alone provides an impregnable bulwark against political agitation.' For Constant, there exist then reactions of 'left' and 'right', if one maintains the metaphor of the movement of a pendulum, the one causing the other. It is only a return to the *centre*, to the principles of 1789, of liberty and law, that can ensure political stability.[23]

These are all illustrations of the omnipresence, so to speak, of a word which is, however, in search of its meaning. This presence demonstrates, as we have said, the need, keenly felt by those involved in politics, for the invention of a term to identify the political facts, events and tendencies which formed an unprecedented phenomenon, with fluid contours and uncertain frontiers. This indecision over the sense to be given to this term shows an unease and a situation that is itself confused. Official discourse reserved the term *reaction* only for the *going out of control* of the initial Thermidorean political project, for its perversion, its diversion, even, by forces hostile to the Republic. The apologetic character of this discourse is evident: it aimed to clear the Convention of its responsibility in the rise of the 'reaction'. It was easy to accuse it of having for too long tolerated, even encouraged, all these phenomena for which Chénier had drawn up an inventory after 13 Vendémiaire: arbitrary and savage persecution of the political personnel of Year II, lumped together as 'terrorists'; tolerance, even goodwill, towards the *jeunesse dorée*, who were taking over the public space, the street, the squares, the theatres; systematic denigration of the symbolism and ritual of Year II, etc. To adopt *legal revenge* as a political response to the problems posed by the dismantling of the Terror was a booby-trapped choice that implied a risk of escalation in the repression. Certainly, the Convention and its government committees did not themselves organise any massacres; the excesses of legal and systematic repression against the 'blood-drinkers' were however foreseeable and inevitable; furthermore, in certain cases, especially at Marseille, the representatives *en mission* became open accomplices of those carrying out the massacres. After the revolt of 1 and 2 Prairial, the Convention surrendered to a sort of collective exorcism of its own terrorist past during its meetings, where dozens of denunciations against the deputies flowed in, offering to the country a spectacle that shamelessly reduced politics to a simple settling of scores. To move from this to accusing the 'Thermidoreans' of being 'reactionaries', even scarcely disguised counter-revolutionaries, was but a step. The former Jacobin and *sans-culottes* militants, persecuted, charged,

---

[23] Benjamin Constant, *Des réactions politiques* (Year V), in his *Ecrits et discours politiques*, edited by O. Pozzo di Borgo, Paris, 1964, vol. 1.

placed under house-arrest, would not hesitate to take it. The reaction ceased to be an episode and became an *overall system of power*, summing up in itself alone all the political developments since 9 Thermidor.[24]

There were, then, *several reactions* in what people were now sometimes beginning to call the *Thermidorean reaction*. There was an anti-Jacobin and anti-terrorist *reaction*, a recoil of public opinion which demanded reparation for the evils and sufferings undergone during the Terror and which appealed to 'justice as the order of the day'. There was a *reaction* which, often driven by the will to revenge, identified the Revolution with the Terror and its consequences and so put back into question the Revolution's principles themselves. The *reaction* then took the form of a denial of the principles of 1789, or, in another variation, of again discussing whether a Republic was inappropriate, as a form of government, in a large country (a classic problem of political thought inherited from the Enlightenment). There was also a *reaction* in the domain of ideas when the 'publicists', freshly converted to Catholicism, denied and condemned with the zeal of the neophyte the enlightened mind which they had favoured just the day before. The contours and limits of each of these *reactions* are difficult to trace and so make the use of this term in Thermidorean *discourse* fundamentally ambiguous. In practice, and especially in the behaviour of the political protagonists, these rather too subtle differences had a tendency to be overlooked and the *reaction* finished by covering a range of positions passing from republican liberalism to intransigent royalism.

But the *reaction*, in the sense of a movement of rejection of the founding principles of the Revolution, constitutes only a secondary aspect of the Thermidorean moment. The paroxysms of violence, the horrors of the massacres remained episodic and did not find any continuation in a *system of power*, contrary to the violence that was elevated into a system during the Terror. The crisis of the spring of Year III was to bring, as its immediate result, the rise of the 'reaction' but it would also accelerate the search for *positive and institutional responses* to the problems which the first months of the Thermidorean political experience had already brought into view. The strength and the weakness of Thermidorean politics came from the fact that it was defined, first and foremost, in negative terms with respect to the two

---

[24] Concerning the repression of the political personnel of the Terror by the Thermidorean authorities, cf. the fundamental work of R. Cobb, *The police and the people*, Oxford, 1970. Cobb observes, moreover, that the repression of the 'terrorists' enjoyed the support of quite a large part of the population who were taking their revenge on those who had dominated their towns during the Terror. Elsewhere, in Lyon where the massacres were the work of small bands organised into commandos, the lynchings sometimes enjoyed real popular approval: there were as many as 40,000 people present and showing their approval of the 'punishment' of the former terrorists; cf. Fuoc, *Reáction*.

political extremes: neither Terror nor monarchy – a sufficiently vague formula, on 9 Thermidor, to rally all those who wanted the 'fall of the tyrant' without, however, compromising the Republic, but a formula too vague to define a more lasting and coherent political strategy. At the beginning of Year III, such a strategy was becoming urgent. *A new Constitution* would respond to this twin need: *to draw the lessons of the past and establish a strategy for the future*. It would crown not only the political experience of the Thermidorean period but, more broadly, the complex and painful history of six years of revolution.

The Thermidorean experience, like all political experience, carried with it memories and expectations, fears and hopes. The constitutional debate of Year III as well as the Constitution itself offer to the historian the possibility of scrutinising the political consciousness of the Convention as it comes to an end, the complex movement established between memory and the hopes of the political protagonists.[25]

The authors of the Constitution were aware of the novelty and originality of the undertaking that had befallen them. The new Constitution should define the principles and institutions of a *constitutional Republic* and, at the same time, *end the Revolution*. It could re-use neither the foundations nor the institutions of the Constitution of 1791: firstly, the latter was monarchical and, next, it had made the country ungovernable. Nor could it draw inspiration from the Constitution of 1793 (for reasons we have already mentioned: it was a botched and impracticable Constitution, confusing direct democracy and representative system, the bitter fruit of the Terror and demagogy). Of course, there existed the plan bequeathed by Condorcet, abandoned under the pressure of the Mountain and the street before even being discussed. This suffered, however, from a capital fault: for obvious reasons it could not take into account the experience of the Terror. Now, the new Constitution had to respond to the twin expectations of the Thermidorean Convention: *preserve the Republic* and *protect it effectively* against any risk of the re-establishment of the Terror; it was only in this way that it could bring the Revolution to a close and maintain the Republic, by detaching its *principles* from the *first two years* of its actual history. It therefore had to take its inspiration from the founding principles of 1789 but by drawing the lessons imposed by the experience of the Terror; in this way it could give 9 Thermidor its true sense. *End the Revolution*: neither the project nor the slogan were new. The promise of bringing the Revolution to its close had served, we know, many times as the occasion, even the pretext, for the will to radicalise it. In 1795 it was the opposite that was wanted: the Revolution could not end with the realisation of all the hopes and all the

---

[25] Cf. B. Baczko, *Les Imaginaires sociaux. Mémoires et espoirs collectifs*, Paris, 1984, pp. 34 *et seq*.

promises, as vague as they were demagogic, which it had engendered. Disillusion or, if the term is preferred, realism presided over the drawing up of the Constitution. *To end the Revolution* was to establish the Republic as a State of law on solid and enduring foundations and so protect it against the return of its own past, appealing to the indefinite revolutionary promise and the unlimited sovereignty of the people.

In 1795, the awareness of being faced with an unprecedented task curiously recalled the spirit which animated, in the summer–autumn of 1789, the first great constitutional debate, in the course of which the 'patriotic party' split into a 'left' and 'right'. But in six years the terms in which the drawing up of a Constitution for France were posed had radically changed and this change could, to a certain extent, serve as a yardstick with which to measure the development of the political culture and *mentalités*. Let us examine, very briefly, just a few details.

In 1789, emphasis was placed on the radical refusal of the past: to draw up a Constitution was to redefine the social contract of the French and this could only be a founding contract. The French were, certainly, an ancient nation; the Revolution had, however, regenerated it and so it could act as if History had just begun with it. The regenerated Nation, from now on taking full responsibility for its sovereignty, fully turned towards the future, based its identity not on its past, marked by tyranny and prejudice, but on *the political and moral programme to be carried out*. In Year III, the new Constitution proposed to cement the Nation by turning towards the future and by formulating a programme for society, but the collective identity was conceived *with respect to the past for which the Nation and, consequently, the Republic, should take responsibility*. The Revolution had behind it a past which it could not be relieved of; its present followed the immediate past of the Terror.

Ah! It is a great enterprise to obtain through wisdom what often is obtained only by time; but since we wish to out-distance the future, let us enrich ourselves with the past. We have before us the history of several peoples; we have our own: let us go over the vast field of our revolution, already covered with so many ruins that everywhere it seems to offer us the remains and ravages of time; this field of glory and grief, where death has harvested so many victims, where liberty has gained so many victories. *We have gone through six centuries in six years. Let this costly experience not be lost for you.*[26]

Contrary to its symbols and images, the Revolution is not a fountain of eternal youth. It grows old and makes people old. The feeling of living in a time that wears out and devastates people and things provided the refrain of the constitutional debates.

[26]  Boissy d'Anglas, *Discours préliminaire au projet de Constitution*, *Moniteur*, vol. 25, pp. 81 *et seq*.

The desire to take into account the experiences of other nations, as much as France's own, is just as clear. In 1789, they had especially insisted in their debates on the *absolute originality* of the plan for a society to be invented for France: a regenerated nation, starting from nothing, has everything to imagine and nothing to imitate. It would not imitate England, a corrupt people, whose institutions were marked by prejudices and the aristocratic spirit; no more would it imitate the States of America, certainly a new and free country, but which lived in a savage environment and not in the centre of old Europe. But in the debates of Year III, the example of the United States was often referred to; their experience was, in particular, the major argument in favour of a bicameral system. A positive experience, all the more appreciated in that it tallied with the lessons to be drawn from the errors committed during the Revolution: a single Assembly, endowed with exorbitant powers, lets itself be too easily dominated by demagogues and apprentice tyrants. To study the Revolution's past came down to seeing it as relative to time and history. Thus a debate began on the question of whether the vicissitudes of the Republic had not come from the fact that the French were too corrupt a Nation and not civilised enough to be able to live in democracy.[27] In 1789, the description of the radical break with the past and the will to produce something entirely new and original went hand in hand with the assertion of the unlimited sovereignty of the Nation. *The Nation's* will being unlimited when it dealt with itself, the Nation could and should exercise its *power to frame a constitution* in complete fullness, without any hindrance. In Year III the sovereignty of the Nation did not cease to be recognised as the very foundation of the Republic; it was, however, admitted that it should be necessarily limited. The dogma of the unlimited sovereignty of the people served to justify the Terror, its destructions, and the tyranny exercised in the name of the 'risen people' by an ignorant rabble appealing to direct democracy. Wisdom and the lessons drawn from the past demanded, therefore, the imposition of legal, moral and institutional limits to the sovereignty of the people. Sieyès provides a very revealing example of this development of ideas. The author of *Qu'est-ce que le tiers état?* who, in 1789, established the unlimited character of the power which had the authority to frame a Constitution, and which embodied the general will of the sovereign nation, did not hesitate, in Year III, to combat this 'dogma' so abused by the 'fanatics' and the 'demagogues'. 'Unlimited powers are a monster in politics, and a great error of the

[27] The polemic on the Terror between Lezay-Marnesia (*Des causes de la Révolution et de ses résultats*) and Benjamin Constant (*Des effets de la Terreur*) is particularly revealing of Thermidorean thought on the history of the Revolution. Cf. the study of F. Furet, 'Une polémique thermidorienne sur la Terreur: autour de Benjamin Constant', *Passé-présent*, no. 2, 1983.

French people ... When a political association is formed, not all the rights which each individual bears in society, nor all the power of the entire mass of individuals are held in common.' The allusion to the *Contrat social*, from which this formula is borrowed almost word for word, is evident. Now, continued Sieyès,

what is held in common in the name of public or political power is only the least possible power, and only what is necessary to maintain each person in his rights and in his duties. This amount of power falls far short of approaching the exaggerated ideas with which people have been pleased to dress up what is called sovereignty – and note that it is certainly the *sovereignty* of the people of which I speak, for if there is one, that is it.[28]

The representative system necessarily limited popular sovereignty. This word 'sovereignty' appeared 'so colossal in the imagination' only because of 'royal superstitions, which impregnate the minds of the French; with despot-kings attributing to themselves an unlimited and terrible power, the sovereignty of the people should be even greater'. It was therefore necessary that sovereignty should return within just limits, if one did not want to fall back into the errors of the Constitution of 1793. The disastrous error came from the Rousseauist concept of the general will, single, indivisible and inalienable, which could not be mistaken. Now, this voluntarism was itself pernicious, as the Terror had shown. 'Woe to the peoples who believe they know what they want when they merely want.' 'To want' was the easiest thing, and so it was all the more necessary to know how to organise the body politic.

The authors of the Constitution of Year III shared the preoccupations of Sieyès and accepted some of the solutions that he put forward: the representative system should necessarily limit popular sovereignty; it protected individual inalienable liberties against the risks and dangers of their being set aside by what was claimed to be the general will, therefore against an unlimited power which could appeal to it; it reposed on the rational principle of division of labour which, applied to politics, demanded the consideration of the latter as a specialised activity, confined to educated and competent persons, with the time and means to devote themselves to it.

This was the only way that the common interest could be elucidated and it was with the representatives alone, and not the represented, that responsibility lay for expressing the general will. The specific version of French liberalism which seeks to reconcile inequality in fact with equality before the law, the sovereignty of the people with the power exercised by

---

[28] Sieyès, *Discours du 2 thermidor an III*, in P. Bastid, *Les Discours de Sieyès dans les débats constitutionnels de l'an III*, Paris, 1939, pp. 17–18, 32 *et seq*. I have discussed at greater length Sieyès's ideas on unlimited sovereignty and the power to draw up a constitution in my study: 'Le Contrat social des Français: Sieyès et Rousseau'.

educated élites, was thus drawn up in reaction to the Terror. The establishing of a *democracy of capacities* would respond, in constitutional terms, to a twin preoccupation: locking up the political system by an institutional arrangement which would prevent the Revolution from starting again; and formulating a programme for the future which would gather together all citizens by recognising their civil equality but which, at the same time, would guarantee 'the government of the nation by the best'. In other words, how to bring the Revolution to an end and offer a hope, even a utopia, for the period after the Revolution?

From our perspective, two promises of the Constitution of 1795, which was the result of the creation of a new political and institutional arena, take on a particular importance: order in stability and progress by education. After the years in which regular upheaval had become the rule, the dream of *another reality*, breaking with recent experiences, aimed to ensure stable and enduring frameworks for collective life. The Convention that was coming to an end produced a *republican utopia* which would resist disruption thanks to its mechanisms of self-preservation. Sieyès, in this plan from Year III to which we have just referred, proposed therefore the creation of a *'constitutional* jury', a representative authority with responsibility for looking after the continuation of the institutions and preventing any precipitate change. The Constitution of Year III did not retain Sieyès's proposal but it did have the same preoccupation with maintaining institutions. The procedure set out for any eventual revision of the Constitution bears witness to this: it was particularly unwieldy, imposing as a prerequisite condition for any change a proposal from the Conseil des Anciens, repeated three times, 'passed on three different occasions, each to be not less than three years from the next', ratified by the Council of Five Hundred, etc. Any recourse to any form of direct democracy was rigorously dismissed; countless precautions were taken to protect an Assembly to revise the Constitution from pressures coming from the street or from executive authority.[29] Retrospectively it is, of course, very easy, and even too easy, to show to what extent the hopes of stabilisation were illusory and to what extent the Thermidorean Convention was deceived in its institutional plans. The two boundaries that it sought to establish, 'neither tyranny nor anarchy', seemed to the Convention to mark out a broad highway for the progress of the Republic. In reality, they defined only a very narrow margin for political manoeuvre. The Constitution erected institutions

---

[29] Cf. Titre II, in Godechot, *Les Constitutions*, pp. 138–9. This makes a striking contrast with the plan of Condorcet, who wished to ensure periodic revision of the Constitution by means of referendum, so that the 'general will' of one generation did not hinder in any way the general will of a following generation: a striking example, which deserves a long commentary, of the impact of the experience of the Terror on the development of French liberalism.

which were meant to maintain themselves in equilibrium by the complex play of their reciprocal powers. Historians have often criticised these institutional mechanisms for excessive complexity, which provoked their paralysis and precipitated 18 Brumaire. The fundamental political pheno-menon, however, lies elsewhere: despite this ample institutional and legal sophistication, it was a matter, in a word, of a *democracy at a quite rudimentary stage of its historical development*. On this point, the Constitu-tion of Year III is particularly significant concerning the limits of the political and social imagination of the revolutionary period, precisely because of all the accumulated precautions.

This Constitution interpreted the political arena, at the very most, in terms of the separation and equilibrium of powers, of the exercise of sovereignty by a representative government and of the frequent change of deputies (this in order to prevent the retention of the same personnel in public affairs, so as to give better access to the 'best'). But it shared the *monistic and unitary* representation of the political domain, common to the Jacobins and the liberals. The representative institutions, the free press, etc., had to manage, organise and educate the *general will* and, conse-quently, contribute to the unity of the Nation. Any *division* could only benefit particular and partisan interests, and so generate disorders and factional struggles. In other words, the Thermidoreans were unable to consider or imagine the political arena *as necessarily divided into opposing tendencies, therefore as necessarily contradictory and causing conflict*. In this, the Constitution of Year III remained a prisoner of the revolutionary mythology of the *one Nation* and of political life perceived as the expression of this unity. The Thermidorean Convention did not admit political pluralism, not even as a necessary evil; so it did not invent any mechanisms for it to function. Adjustments between public opinion, which necessarily varied from one election to another, and the group in power would be from now on the result of *coups d'état*.

As for the dream of progress as a civilising force through education, nothing illustrates this better, paradoxically, than the setting up of a cultural qualification for the franchise. The Constitution laid down that 'young people can be entered on the civic register, if they can show that *they know how to read and write*, and that *they have a trade* ... This article will come into force only from Year XII of the Republic.'[30] This article, establishing an educational qualification, has too often been interpreted as simply a corollary of the abandonment of universal suffrage. In effect, the only people who are citizens are those who pay a direct contribution. Also seen in this is the intention of eliminating the most disadvantaged social

---

[30] *Ibid.*, Titre II, art. 16, p. 105.

groups from the 'sovereign People' and, consequently, the confirmation of the 'bourgeois' character of the Constitution. The problems raised by this article are however infinitely more complex than these clichés. This series of measures is revealing both of the fears and the hopes of the republican élites of the period. Certainly, the will to emerge from the Terror as well as the new political choices necessarily imposed a redefinition of social alliances. In this sense, the 'Thermidoreans' turned, quite naturally, towards the 'proprietors', the most well-off social groups, the buyers of national assets (their acquisition was in fact guaranteed by the Constitution) and, especially, towards people of standing, a social strategy which went hand in hand with the desire to revive manufacturing and commerce, ruined by the Terror. But it is a matter, here also, of a return to the origins, ideas and principles of the Enlightenment, rethought and adjusted in the light of revolutionary experiences. Hence the model of a 'democracy of capacities', of a Republic governed by the most enlightened.

We should be governed by the best; the best are the best educated and those most interested in maintaining the laws; now, apart from a few exceptions, you will not find such men except among those who, possessing an estate, are attached to the region which contains it, to the laws which protect it, to the tranquillity that preserves it, and who owe to this estate and the ease it brings the education which has made them able to discuss, sensibly and accurately, the advantages and inconveniences of the laws which determine the fate of their country. The man without property, on the contrary, needs a constant effort of virtue to feel an interest in an order which maintains nothing for him, and to oppose movements which give him some hope. One has to suppose such a man's ideas to be fully worked out and quite profound for him to prefer the real good to the apparent good, the interest of the future to that of the present.[31]

This undeniable social choice is revealed above all by the conditions to be filled for appointment as an 'elector' (each primary assembly appointing one elector for every two hundred citizens). Now, these electors, brought together in electoral assemblies, elected in their turn the members of the legislative body, the members of the Tribunal of appeal, the judges of civil tribunals, etc. (The Constitution introduced a secret ballot in all elections.) For these electors the requirements were placed very high: in particular they had to possess considerable revenues, which limited their number, in the whole of France, to about 30,000 people. But the introduction of a financial and educational qualification had in itself limited political consequences. The re-establishment of a system with electors qualified by property raised, in fact, scarcely any notable opposition; it was accepted with quasi-unanimity by the Convention as well as by the primary assemblies, despite the fact that, according to this system, there would be only six million active

[31] Boissy d'Anglas, *Discours préliminaire au projet de Constitution*, p. 92.

citizens out of seven and a half million Frenchmen authorised to vote. This absence of interest in the re-establishment of a qualification for the franchise is explained by an essential fact: throughout the Revolution, whatever the electoral system, whether it was universal or required a property qualification, abstentions continued, and they could rise to as much as 90 per cent. This mass abstention confirms the general characteristic of the revolutionary political culture we have already mentioned: the apprenticeship of democracy is slow and difficult; it is carried out in the specific situation of a *modern political arena created in a largely traditional cultural and mental environment*.

The establishment of a franchise requiring an educational qualification justified, indirectly and furtively, those who claimed that the Republic had come too soon, before the Enlightenment had educated the whole population and not just the élites alone. Political upheaval had slowed down progress towards civilisation. But it was also a clear refutation of an axiom of the political philosophy of the period, according to which the republican system was adapted only to small countries and not to great modern nations. On this point, the Constitution left no doubt. If the people had been more enlightened, they would certainly have avoided the evils of the first two years of the Republic. But these dark hours should not compromise either the principles or the evaluation of the Republic. The latter should not 'take place on the scaffolds'. 9 Thermidor showed that the republican Nation was capable of overcoming the dangers which lay in wait for it; the new Constitution manifested the will to overcome the cultural backwardness of the country and see to it that the people, once civilised, could never turn back on the route traced by progress. The setting up of an educational qualification, therefore, like so many other Thermidorean measures, showed the ambiguity in aiming to do two opposing things at once: it meant both to ward off the return to public affairs of the 'rabble' and the 'vandals', ignorant people who thought they could govern without knowing how to govern themselves, since they were unable to read nor write, and also to establish the conviction that by education, by the acquisition of a minimum of culture, the prerequisite condition for the enjoyment of civic rights would be ensured. In this way the Republic would be protected from the vandal people by protecting the people against itself. This constitutional programme goes back, when all is said and done, to another hope and fleshes it out: the Enlightenment and the Revolution were necessarily linked; the ordeals through which the Nation had passed would not have been in vain. At the end of its journey France would be a country of educated men and citizens, or, if it were preferred, of citizens *because* they were educated. The Enlightenment was at the origin of the Revolution, and it was for the Enlightenment to bring it to an end. So revolutionary power gave itself an educational mission to carry out: it was necessary to give effective aid to the arts, to education and, quite particularly, to the creation of new élites. The Constitution of Year III was completed by the decree on the organisation of public education, one of the last acts of the Convention. Daunou, in his report, sums up better than anyone else the educational dreams and symbols of Thermidor: Thermidor or an enlightened Republic which would return to the very sources of the Revolution, Thermidor or the victorious Enlightenment which would put a full stop to the revolutionary ordeal.

The arts have followed, for three years, the destiny of the National Convention. They have groaned with you under the tyranny of Robespierre; they mounted the scaffolds with your colleagues; and, in that time of calamity, patriotism and the sciences, mingling their regrets and their tears, called back from the same tombs victims who were just as dear. Having recovered power and liberty after 9 Thermidor, you have dedicated their first use to the consolation and encouragement of the arts ... Representatives of the people, after so many violent shocks, so much anxious suspicion, so many necessary wars, so much virtuous distrust; after five years so full of torments, exertions and sacrifices, [the hour has come] for good-will, for reconciliation, for reunion, for rest in the bosom of gentler passions and peaceful feelings. Now, what better than public education to perform this ministry of general reconciliation? Yes, it is reserved for the arts to finish the revolution that they began, to remove all dissension, to reconcile all those who cultivate them; and no one can pretend that in France, in the eighteenth century, and under the rule of enlightenment, peace among enlightened men is the sign of the peace of the world.[32]

Thermidor lastingly entrusted the republican State with a mission to educate which reproduced and embodied the opposition between *a civilising government and a people to be civilised*: an opposition inherited from the Enlightenment, but reanimated and adjusted in order to draw the necessary conclusions about power and the people from the Revolution, and in particular from the Terror. No legitimate power without the sovereignty which resides in the universality of citizens, but no citizens without a State that provides access for them to knowledge, therefore to politics and which, if necessary, can protect the people against the awakening of its own demons.

[32] Daunou, *Rapport sur l'instruction publique*, in Baczko, *Education pour la démocratie*, pp. 504 *et seq*. The young Constant concluded his reflections on 'political reactions' by a profession of faith in the progress which would ensure the triumph of the 'system of principles' over the 'upheavals of the moment':

Overall harmony, firmness in the details, enlightened theory, practical action which preserves, these are the characteristics of the system of principles. It is the bringing together of public and individual happiness ... It belongs to the centuries, and the upheavals of the present can do nothing against it. In resisting it one can still, without doubt, cause disastrous shocks. But ever since the spirit of man has started marching forwards and the art of printing has recorded his progress, there is no invasion of barbarians, no coalition of oppressors, no appeal to prejudices, that can make it retreat. (Constant, *Des réactions politiques*, pp. 84–5)

The Convention granted itself the last word in the Thermidorean debate on
the Terror, during the last day of its labours, on 4 Brumaire, Year IV. In the
course of this last session, it discussed the project of an amnesty, presented
by Baudin in the name of the Commission of Eleven. The plan had been
drafted in the feverish hours of the crushing of the royalist agitation and the
insurrection of 13 Vendémiaire. The anti-terrorist discourse wished to be
moderate: from then on, it was a question of bringing the Revolution to a
close by conciliatory measures. 'Has not experience taught us the danger of
vicissitudes, do we not know that it is only after having gone through
extremes that one reaches a happy medium?'[33] In retrospect, was not the
Terror one of these 'vicissitudes'?

There are evils inseparable from a great revolution, and among these evils there are
some which, by their nature, can no longer be remedied.

No one could ask the victims of the Terror or their family to forgive, but
one had the right to ask them to forget. To require an abstract justice leads
only to a renewal of evil: 'If it is necessary to establish as many juries as there
were revolutionary committees, then it would become necessary to cover
the Republic with prisons and scaffolds so as to console it for so many
prisons and scaffolds.'[34] The plan even proposed to abolish capital
punishment, thus demonstrating the desire to finish the Revolution once
and for all by having the Terror forgotten. This abolition should have been
consecrated by a symbolic act: the Convention would pronounce its decree
on the Place de la Révolution; the president 'would trample under foot the
scythe of death' which would be solemnly broken and the remains of the
blade placed in the archives. The scaffold would be burnt, and the square
change its name: it would henceforth be called the Place de la Concorde.

After an animated debate, when once again political passions, which
should have been condemned to oblivion, were unchained, the Thermidorean Convention decreed in its usual way, with one of those acts of
ambiguous compromise in which it had always shown great skill. The
amnesty was proclaimed for 'deeds relating purely to the Revolution'
(except for those against which there existed charges relating to the
'conspiracy of 13 Vendémiaire'). Capital punishment was not abolished, or
to be more exact, its aboliton was postponed 'until the day of declaration of
general peace'. So the symbolic ceremony of the destruction of the
guillotine became pointless.

It was decreed, on the other hand, that the Place de la Révolution would
henceforth bear the name of the Place de la Concorde.

As for the Revolution, its name was given to a street leading from the
Boulevard to the Place de la Concorde.

[33] Report of Baudin, in the name of the Commission of Eleven, in *Moniteur*, vol. 26, p. 303.
[34] *Ibid.*

# By way of a conclusion: Thermidor in history

Perhaps we can now reply to the question raised at the threshold of this essay: was Thermidor a 'paradigm' in History, repeated in the course of revolutions which came after the French one?

In the course of the Thermidorean period and under the Directory, the anniversary of 9 Thermidor was officially celebrated as that of the 'happy revolution'. After that there was never any further question of commemorating this event. However, Thermidor became memorable. Like certain other phenomena of the revolutionary period such as *Jacobinism* or *Bonapartism*, it was elevated into a paradigm of the course of history by all the ideologies which made the French Revolution their reference or source as an explicatory model of historical deviation from the correct path.

On the death of Lenin, did not Trotsky and then the Trotskyists employ Thermidor to understand Stalin's ascent to power? According to this view, the October Revolution had experienced *its* Thermidor, and the Stalinists, the new Thermidoreans, were former revolutionaries who had 'degenerated' into profiteers and grave-diggers of the Revolution. This falling away from the people's side distinguished them from the counter-revolutionaries, 'class enemies' from the very first and even for all eternity. In reaction, Trotsky and his partisans were accused by the Stalinists of Bonapartism, then they were reviled, even liquidated, as agents in the service of, among others, Japan, Poland, the Gestapo and the British Intelligence Service . . . The Trotskyist metaphor of Thermidor is, by a long way, the best known, to the point of being the trade-mark of Trotsky's supporters. But every revolution of the nineteenth and twentieth centuries was haunted by the spectre of *its own* Thermidor, of that moment when the spirit of the revolution would be defeated by the revolutionaries themselves, who would waver, betray the historic movement and turn against it.

If, for the revolutionary mythologies of the nineteenth and twentieth centuries, Thermidor became such a 'paradigm', this was not because the French Revolution had really been betrayed or diverted on 9 Thermidor, Year II. The debate aiming to establish the identity of the 'true' grave-diggers of the Revolution – the Girondins or the Dantonists, the Jacobins or the Thermidoreans, the Directors or the First Consul – is never-ending and sterile; it itself has some characteristics of the revolutionary myth and only reproduces it. Like every myth, that of the assassinated Revolution hides the reality but reveals its own truth. This truth lies in the very metaphor that the myth provides for the event: the Revolution had been strangled, frozen, killed – it does not matter which – the essential thing is that it happened when it was *still young*, before being able to fulfil its promises. The myth of Thermidor is only a variation of the myth of *the eternal youth of the Revolution*. Now, the Thermidorean moment first compromised this myth and its imagery, and then finished by destroying them. The Thermidorean discourse overflowed, so to speak, with metaphors which all revealed the tiredness, the wearing out of revolutionary mythology by time. Listen to Boissy d'Anglas: the field of the Revolution seemed 'to offer us everywhere *the traces and ravages of time*'; the revolutionaries had consumed 'six centuries in six years'. Does each year of the Revolution count for a century? Then what has made it age the most? Sixteen months of Terror or fifteen months of Thermidor? The mass-drownings of Nantes or the truth about the massacres on public display in the course of the trial of the revolutionary Committee of Nantes and of Carrier? The indictments of Fouquier-Tinville to the revolutionary Tribunal under the Terror or his defence statements, throwing all responsibility onto the Convention?

The Terror produced a heroic imagery at the same time as it held back reality and generated a black legend. In Thermidor, everything rises abruptly to the surface. The Thermidorean moment is the explosion of a clear fact: the Revolution is tired, the Revolution is old.

Thermidor is the key moment when the Revolution must carry the weight of its past and admit that it will not keep all its initial promises. It is above all the moment when the protagonists proclaim that they wish neither to recommence its history nor remake its experience.

Thermidor is the moment when the revolutionaries retain only one desire, are motivated by only one wish: to end, finally, the Revolution.

Revolutions grow old quite quickly.

They age badly, with their symbolic obstinacy in always wanting to mark a new start in History, to be a radical break in time, to remain a work always at its beginning, to embody the youth of a world which will last for ever. The Revolution sings of tomorrows, but never wishes to leave the inaugural today of its coming into the world.

The French Revolution did not age any worse than all the other revolutions which followed it and were inspired by it. Not one of its younger sisters wanted, however, to recognise itself in the Thermidor of its elder. Quite rightly: the Revolution, even when grasped through its myths, is not a fairy-tale. And Thermidor is that mirror without magic which shows to each dawning revolution the only image that it would not like to see: that of the wearing down and decay which kills dreams.

# Chronology of events mentioned in the text

This is not intended to provide an exhaustive chronology of the Revolution, but to list the main events mentioned in the text.

**1789**
*14 July*                        Storming of the Bastille.

**1791**
*14 June*                        Le Chapelier's law, prohibiting workers'
                                 associations and strikes.
*3 Sept.*                        Proclamation of the first Constitution.
*29–30 Sept.*                    Le Chapelier's report on popular societies.

**1792**
*10 Aug.*                        Insurrection and taking of the Tuileries. Overthrow
                                 of the monarchy.
*14 Aug.*                        Decree on the 'suppression of signs of feudalism'.
*2 Sept.*                        Parisian crowd massacres over 1,000 inmates of the
                                 prisons.
*21–22 Sept.*                    Abolition of the monarchy. Year I of the Republic
                                 proclaimed.

**1793**
*21 Jan.*                        Execution of Louis XVI.
*9 Mar.*                         The Convention passes a law requiring journalist-
                                 deputies to choose between their work in the
                                 Convention and their profession. Representatives *en
                                 mission* sent into the *départements*.
*29 Mar.*                        The Convention decrees the death-penalty for
                                 anyone calling for the re-establishment of the
                                 monarchy.
*31 May*                         Insurrection against the Girondins, led by the
                                 Jacobins and the Paris Commune.
*2 June*                         Insurrection continues. The Convention agrees to
                                 the arrest of twenty-nine Girondin deputies.
*24 June*                        The Convention adopts the Constitution of Year I.
*13 July*                        Robespierre puts forward the plan for national
                                 education drawn up by Louis-Michel Le Peletier.

| | |
|---|---|
| *10 Aug.* | Results of the plebiscite ratifying the Constitution of Year I. |
| *5 Sept.* | Terror the 'order of the day'. |
| *17 Sept.* | The Convention passes the law of suspects. |
| *17 Oct./26 Vendémiaire, Year II* | Law on the personal responsibility of publishers for any writings containing criticism of the Convention or the Committees. |
| *21 Oct./1 Brumaire* | Carrier in Nantes as representative *en mission* with the army of the West. |
| *14 Nov./24 Brumaire* | The revolutionary Committee of Nantes draws up a list of 132 'conspirators' to be arrested. |
| *27 Nov./7 Frimaire* | The convoy of 132 leading citizens of Nantes sets off for Paris. They will arrive forty days later, reduced in number to ninety-seven. |
| *4 Dec./14 Frimaire* | The law of revolutionary government passed. |
| *23 Dec./3 Nivôse* | Decisive Vendéan defeat at Savenay. |

**1794**

| | |
|---|---|
| *3 Jan./14 Nivôse* | Chénier's report on the protection of scientists. |
| *10 Jan./21 Nivôse* | Grégoire presents a report to the Convention on the use of French in inscriptions on public monuments. |
| *8 Feb./19 Pluviôse* | The Committee of Public Safety revokes Carrier's mandate in Nantes. |
| *5 Mar./15 Ventôse* | The Committee of Public Instruction adopts the text of the *Instruction* on the preservation of cultural goods outlined by Lindet and Bouquier. |
| *13 Mar./23 Ventôse* | Arrest of Hébert. |
| *24 Mar./4 Germinal* | Execution of Hébert. |
| *5 Apr./15 Germinal* | Execution of Danton and the Dantonists. |
| *11 Apr./22 Germinal* | Grégoire's report on libraries. |
| *13 Apr./24 Germinal* | Chaumette condemned to death. |
| *22 Apr./3 Floréal* | Execution of Le Chapelier. |
| *20 May/1 Prairial* | Ladmiral attempts to assassinate Collot d'Herbois. |
| *23 May/4 Prairial* | Cécile Renault, would-be assassin of Robespierre, arrested. |
| *10 June/22 Prairial* | Law of 22 Prairial: reform of the revolutionary Tribunal to make it provide more convictions. The Great Terror begins. |
| *12 June/24 Prairial* | Arrest of members of the revolutionary Committee of Nantes. |
| *27 July/9 Thermidor* | Fall and arrest of Robespierre. Couthon, Lebas and Saint-Just also arrested. |
| *28 July/10 Thermidor* | Robespierre guillotined. |
| *29 July/11 Thermidor* | Sixty-six Robespierrists executed. The Convention decrees that a quarter of the personnel of the committees are to be renewed each month, with re-eligibility after a month's absence. |
| *1 Aug./14 Thermidor* | Repeal of the law of 22 Prairial. Fouquier-Tinville arrested. |

| | |
|---|---|
| *5 Aug./18 Thermidor* | The Convention entrusts the Committee of General Security with the mass release of prisoners. |
| *10 Aug./23 Thermidor* | Reorganisation of the revolutionary Tribunal. |
| *24 Aug./7 Fructidor* | Suppression of revolutionary committees in communes with a population of less than 8,000 inhabitants. |
| *25 Aug./8 Fructidor* | The Jacobins warn the Convention against *modérantisme*. |
| *26 Aug./9 Fructidor* | *La Queue de Robespierre* appears. Fréron's speech on freedom of the press. |
| *28 Aug./11 Fructidor* | Tallien's speech on the Terror and justice as the order of the day. |
| *29–30 Aug./12–13 Fructidor* | Great debate in the Convention on responsibility for the Terror. Lecointre attacks seven members of the Committees. |
| *31 Aug./14 Fructidor* | Accidental explosion at the powder-factory of Grenelle. Grégoire's first report on vandalism. |
| *1 Sept./15 Fructidor* | First renewal of the personnel of the Committee of Public Safety. |
| *3 Sept./17 Fructidor* | Tallien, Fréron and Lecointre expelled from the Jacobin Club. First issue of Babeuf's *Journal de la liberté de la presse*. |
| *6 Sept./20 Fructidor* | Auguis and Serres appointed representatives *en mission* in the Midi. |
| *7 Sept./21 Fructidor* | Attempted 'assassination' of Tallien. |
| *8 Sept./22 Fructidor* | Trial of the ninety-four leading citizens of Nantes opens. |
| *9 Sept./23 Fructidor* | Tallien's *L'Ami des citoyens* reappears. |
| *10 Sept./24 Fructidor* | Durand-Maillane attacks the Jacobins. Merlin formulates the three essential problems of the Republic. 'Where have we come from? Where are we? Where are we going?' |
| *11 Sept./25 Fructidor* | Fréron beings a new series of his *Orateur du peuple*. |
| *12 Sept./26 Fructidor* | Arrest in Marseille of Reynier, leader of the local Jacobins. |
| *14 Sept./28 Fructidor* | Reynier freed by a group of Jacobins. Edme Petit's speech in the Convention on Robespierre and the Terror. Verdict in the trial of the citizens of Nantes. |
| *15 Sept./29 Fructidor* | Chasles and Lebois launch *L'Ami du peuple*. |
| *19 Sept./3rd sans-culottide* | The Convention decides on the expulsion from Paris of all those who were not residing there before 1 Messidor. |
| *20 Sept./4th sans-culottide* | Lindet presents his report to the Convention in the name of the Committee of Public Safety. |
| *21 Sept./5th sans-culottide* | Marat's body placed in the Pantheon. The Convention outlaws Reynier and orders a purge of the Jacobins of Marseille. |
| *26 Sept./5 Vendémiaire, Year III* | First arrests in Marseille. |

| | |
|---|---|
| *29 Sept./8 Vendémiaire* | For the first time, Carrier's name is linked in the Convention with the massacres of Nantes. |
| *8 Oct./17 Vendémiaire* | Leblois draws up the indictment against Carrier. |
| *9 Oct./18 Vendémiaire* | Address of the Convention to the French people. |
| *11 Oct./20 Vendémiaire* | Rousseau's ashes transferred to the Pantheon. |
| *14 Oct./23 Vendémiaire* | The trial of the revolutionary Committee of Nantes opens. |
| *16 Oct./25 Vendémiaire* | Decree of the Convention prohibiting affiliation between societies. |
| *29 Oct./8 Brumaire* | Grégoire's second report presented to the Convention. |
| *9 Nov./19 Brumaire* | The *jeunesse dorée* attack the Jacobin Club. |
| *11 Nov./21 Brumaire* | In the Convention, Romme sums up the prosecution case against Carrier. |
| *12 Nov./22 Brumaire* | Jacobin Club closed. |
| *14 Nov./24 Brumaire* | Some Montagnard deputies call for the application of the Constitution of '93. |
| *24 Nov./4 Frimaire* | Decision to send Carrier before the revolutionary Tribunal. |
| *8 Dec./18 Frimaire* | Recall to the Convention of the Girondin deputies. |
| *14 Dec./24 Frimaire* | Grégoire's third report. |
| *16 Dec./26 Frimaire* | Carrier condemned to death and executed. |
| *27 Dec./7 Nivôse* | Commission established to examine the past conduct of Billaud-Varenne, Collot d'Herbois, Vadier and Barère. |
| *31 Dec./11 Nivôse* | La Harpe's speech on vandalism. |

## 1795

| | |
|---|---|
| *3 Jan./14 Nivôse* | Fourcroy's report on civilisation and terror. |
| *8 Jan./19 Nivôse* | Marat's bust damaged in the Convention. |
| *8 Feb./20 Pluviôse* | Marat's remains removed from the Pantheon. |
| *28 Feb./10 Ventôse* | Bourdon's speech against terrorism. |
| *2 Mar./12 Ventôse* | Saladin's report condemning the ex-members of the Committees. |
| *11 Mar./21 Ventôse* | Speech by Boissy d'Anglas on criminal 'patriotism'. |
| *21 Mar./1 Germinal* | Law of 'grande police'. |
| *1 April/12 Germinal* | Uprising of *sans-culottes* against the Convention. |
| *20 May/1 Prairial* | Another uprising. The crowd invades the Convention and kills Féraud, a deputy. |
| *23 May/4 Prairial* | The Convention overcomes the resistance of the faubourg Saint-Antoine. |
| *31 May/12 Prairial* | The Convention suppresses the revolutionary Tribunal. |
| *23 June/5 Messidor* | Speech by Boissy d'Anglas on a new constitution. |
| *24 June/6 Messidor* | Chénier's report on the massacres in Lyon. |
| *20 July/2 Thermidor* | Sieyès's speech on a new constitution. |

| | |
|---|---|
| *21 Oct./29 Vendémiaire, Year IV* | Chénier, in a report to the Convention, contrasts the Thermidorean period and the reaction which follows it. |
| *26 Oct./4 Brumaire* | Last session of the Convention. |

# Index